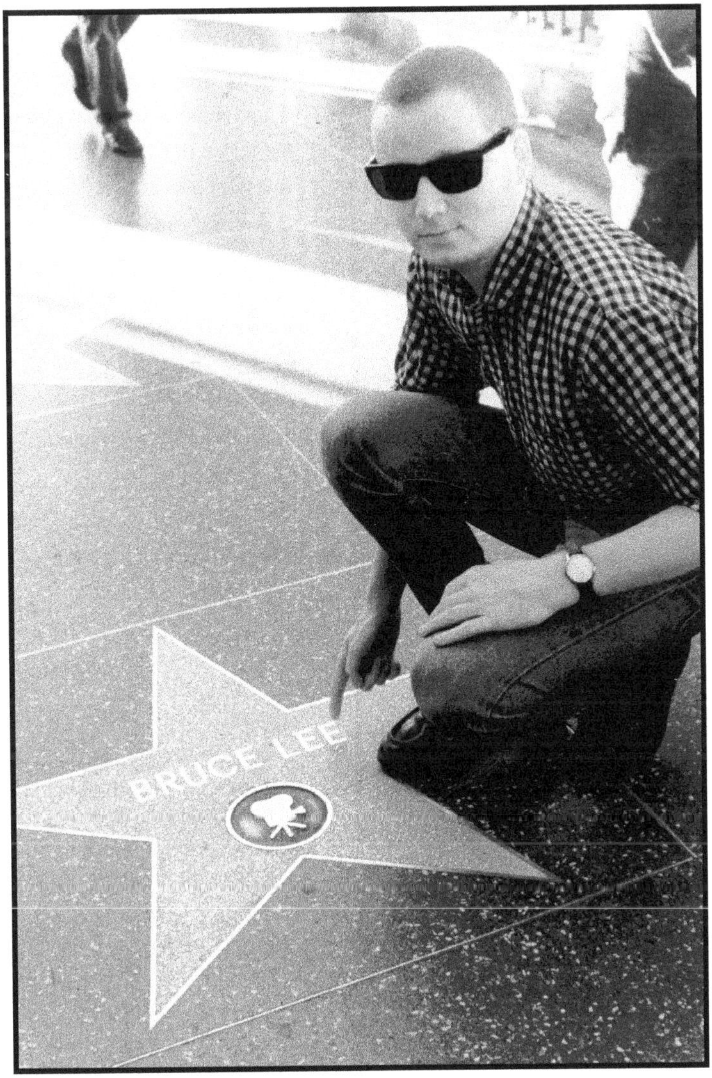
BRUCE LEE

STOP PRESS

As final proofing was being done on this book *Bruce Lee: A Life* by Matthew Polly was published (Simon & Schuster, New York, 2018). This confirms once again that Bruce and Betty Ting Pei were lovers and provides accounts of Lee having many other extra-marital affairs, as well as further commentary on his recreational drug use. It also gives additional detail on Lee's establishment family background on his mother's side and provides a new albeit unproven theory on his death — viz that he died of heatstroke rather than an allergic reaction. While we haven't had the opportunity to read the entire book yet, it doesn't look like there is anything in it that would necessitate revisions of the text of *Re-Enter the Dragon*. Polly's book doesn't contain much about Brucesploitation but will doubtlessly provide a great deal of fascinating background material for those interested in the subject.

ISBN 9780994411280 (hardback)
ISBN 9780994411273 (paperback)

© 2018 Stewart Home

Produced by The LedaTape Organisation
on behalf of the author
Book designed and indexed by Simon Strong
Back cover author photo by Chris Dorley Brown

September 2018

Thanks to The AFI Research Collection, Mara Coson, 5 Years (London), Michael Helms, Leanne Hopper, Patrick Jameson, Vivien Leung, Esther Planas, Queens Park Railway Club (Glasgow), Liz Rever, Samuel Wong.

BOOK PRODUCTION WAR ECONOMY STANDARD

This book has been produced in complete conformity with the authorised economy standards

Also by Stewart Home

Novels
The Nine Lives of Ray The Cat Jones
Mandy, Charlie and Mary-Jane
Blood Rites of the Bourgeoisie
Memphis Underground
Tainted Love
Down and Out in Shoreditch and Hoxton
69 Things To Do With a Dead Princess
Whips and Furs: My Life as a Bon Vivant,
　Gambler and Love Rat 'by' Jesus H. Christ
Cunt
Blow Job
Come Before Christ and Murder Love
Slow Death
Red London
Defiant Pose
Pure Mania

Short Stories
No Pity

Poetry
SEND CA$H: Collected Poems

Non-Fiction
Confusion Incorporated:
　A Collection of Lies, Hoaxes and Hidden Truths
The House of Nine Squares:
　Letters on Neoism, Psychogeography
　and Epistemological Trepidation
Cranked Up Really High:
　Genre Theory and Punk Rock
Neoism Plagiarism and Praxis
Neoist Manifestos
The Assault on Culture:
　Utopian Currents from Lettrisme to Class War

RE-ENTER THE DRAGON

Genre Theory, Brucesploitation and the Sleazy Joys of Lowbrow Cinema

By

STEWART HOME

SERAFIM KARALEXIS presents

ENTER THREE DRAGONS

Starring DRAGON LEE

with BRUCE LEA, YANG TSZE, SAMUEL WALLS, BRUCE LI AND JACKIE CHIN Produced by JOSPEH LAI Directed by JOSEPH KONG & GODFREY HO Action Director LEUNG-SIU-CHUNG

R RESTRICTED

MADISON WORLD FILM CO.

distributed by CINEMATIC RELEASING · IN COLOR

CONTENTS

Mapping Brucesploitation	7
Brucesploitation Rankings	19
■ **CORE**	25
■ **SEMI-PERIPHERY**	87
■ **PERIPHERY**	113
■ **OUTER LIMITS**	137
Bruce Lee, Brucesploitation and Joseph Velasco but no full-blown theoretical summing up!	199
A Note on the Title of this Book	205
10 Brucesploitation flicks to check out if you're new to the genre and want an overview	206
Anti-acknowledgements and further sources of confusion	207
Index	216

NOW THE KING OF KUNG-FU COMES BACK TO LIFE!

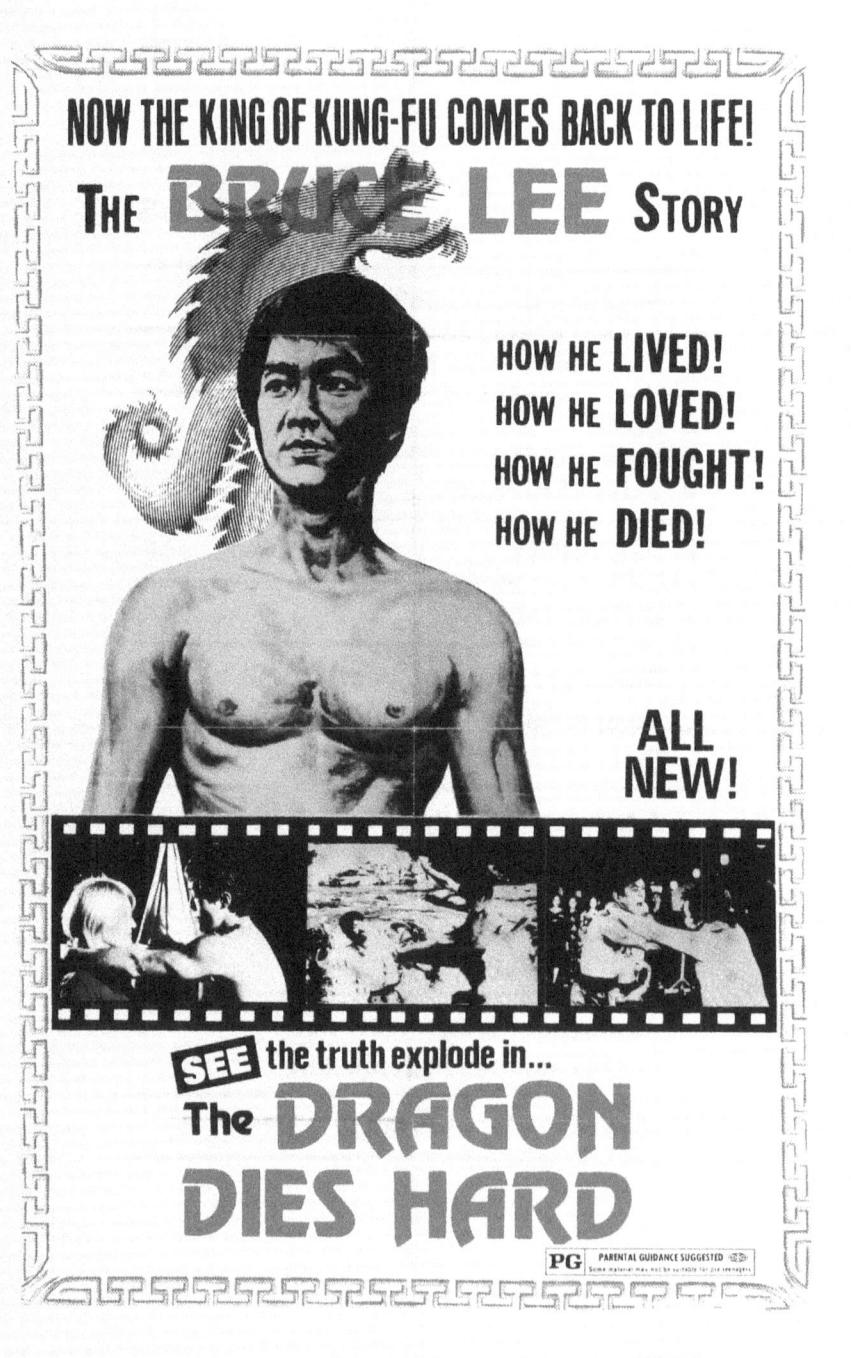

The BRUCE LEE Story

HOW HE LIVED!
HOW HE LOVED!
HOW HE FOUGHT!
HOW HE DIED!

ALL NEW!

SEE the truth explode in...

The DRAGON DIES HARD

PG PARENTAL GUIDANCE SUGGESTED
Some material may not be suitable for pre-teenagers

An **ALLIED ARTISTS** Release

MAPPING BRUCESPLOITATION

If you're reading this then you're probably interested in action movies or genre theory—or both! While it was a liking for old school kung fu films that led me into the labyrinth of Brucesploitation, I soon came to realise that although they overlap in places, the two genres are distinct. Given that Filipino, Korean, Indonesian, Japanese and even American movies belong to the Brucesploitation genre, as well as flicks from Hong Kong and Taiwan, it is evident that the martial arts on display are not restricted to kung fu, or indeed unarmed combat, since even some Chinese entries into the category cross-over into wuxia swordplay.

When it comes to genre what makes a film a good example of a particular category is its lack of uniqueness. To state the obvious genre films are meant to be generic, this is not an area in which so-called originality is particularly valued or appreciated. Brucesploitation, of course, doesn't just draw on the films of Bruce Lee; it has a wider take on the history of martial arts films to which the Little Dragon made an important contribution. For me, like many others born in the overdeveloped world in the early 1960s, Bruce Lee served to draw my attention to kung fu but once that happened I quickly saw there was so much more to martial arts flicks than both this one actor and films from Hong Kong and Taiwan.

There is no simple explanation as to why I enjoy old school kung fu movies and the related but distinct Brucesploitation genre, that does justice to my multiple and overlapping reasons for diggin' this trash. The fact that I am a man of a certain age makes me a more likely candidate to exhibit these tastes than if I was younger or had different gender identifications. That said, one of the things I've always liked about South East Asian cinema is that historically it has been far better at putting women in the lead roles of action films than Hollywood. Nonetheless, a martial arts movie genre populated in part by a troop of Bruce Lee clones is not as good at putting women in control as regular kung fu and wuxia flicks. But since Brucesploitation is particularly prone to hypermasculine posturing, it also provides a perfect subject for demonstrating how an exaggerated embrace of one stereotypical gender role can easily collapse into its 'other'. Moving on, my interest in identity and loss of identity, and in avant-garde attempts to subvert the bourgeois subject, also predispose me—if not many others—to take an interest in something like Brucesploitation.

Before diving more deeply into the genre, I will briefly wind back to a time when my comprehension of the issues touched on above was less theoretically developed than it is today. Indeed to a time before I'd heard the phrase 'so bad it's good', and I felt little need to think about why I liked kung fu movies. In the mid-seventies my taste for eastern action flicks was a matter of gut instinct, not something I'd conceptualised. My memories of how I was first exposed to martial arts are somewhat hazy. Initially it was through television and feature films shown on TV, which even in the sixties when I first found my eyes glued to the gogglebox sometimes depicted judo, jiu jitsu, karate, and other even more exotic—to me as a small child born in London—fighting styles. An example of this is episode 7 of the first series of *The Atom Ant Show* where *Atom Ant Meets Karate Ant,* this cartoon was first broadcast on 13 November 1965, although I doubt I caught this first airing of it. When I was 5 years-old my favourite TV show was *The Man from UNCLE* and episodes such as The *Five Daughters Affair* (first broadcast in two parts on 31 March 1967, and 7 April 1967) featured some Japanese martial arts; these instalments were later re-cut into a movie *The Karate Killers* (1967). My exposure to misrepresentations of oriental martial arts via TV in the sixties was far greater than this, but these examples give a flavour of it. It piqued my interest enough for me to join a judo club in the early seventies, and I was also fascinated by the ads I saw for mail order martial arts courses in imported American comics. Boxing and wrestling were of interest too.

Apart from soccer players, the two biggest sports stars for kids like me in the UK in the early seventies were the boxing heavyweights Muhammad Ali and Henry Cooper—even if they were eclipsed in my schoolboy milieu by the likes of footballer Bobby Moore. I also used to see a teacher at school who was a black belt in karate practice his katas; unfortunately our Christian fundamentalist headmaster who had been in a Japanese prisoner of war camp—and as a result had an aversion to anything from the east—wouldn't let Mr Beach teach us how to break bricks with our bare hands!

As a kid I watched the *Batman* TV series so it is probable I was exposed to Bruce Lee's guest appearances as Kato before I learnt he was the 'king of kung fu'. There were many things to prep my interest in Lee but probably just feeling angry and disempowered was the most important factor. Constantly having teachers tell me and all the other kids at school that we were stupid and would never do anything with our lives—other than work in a factory—was more than enough to make me want to breakout from such drab surroundings. Music was one way to escape this sham reality, but by the time I was twelve years-old glam rock was on its last legs, so martial arts flicks filled a void by providing a better form of contemporary escapism—at least until punk rock came along.

I first took a conscious interest in Bruce Lee when the London based *Kung Fu Monthly* began publication in 1974. This was a fan magazine that turned into a giant fold-out poster. After seeing early issues I was desperate to catch the Little Dragon's flicks. More than anything else in *Kung Fu Monthly* I found a picture of Bruce in his coffin morbidly fascinating since it was in such contrast to the other images of him as a seemingly super-fit movie star. Since I wasn't old enough to see X-rated films, I had to lie about my age to gain admittance to *Enter the Dragon* (1973) and innumerable other martial arts movies. When I first saw Lee's flicks, I was less sceptical about the fighting skills on display than I am now; of course there is nothing wrong with movie kung fu, it just isn't real world fighting. Nonetheless, from the get-go one of the things I liked about these films was how ridiculous they were; they definitely made me laugh.

By the time I was eighteen, I was still going to see a wide variety of movies around London, but somehow the Brucesploitation flicks that got released onto UK cinema screens at that time passed me by. I was probably too busy catching up on old films by the likes of John Waters and Alain Robbe-Grillet at repertory cinemas, and watching horror movies on first run screens. In the mid-eighties I bought myself a multi-region video player—so that I could watch American NTSC art films as well European PAL VHS—and this is when I began to catch up with the Brucesploitation genre. Most Sundays I would go to Brick Lane market—then still quite ungentrified—in east London. There was a video stall there connected to a shop on Whitecross Street, and I started to pick up films like *Bruce Lee: The Man, the Myth* (1976) and *True Game of Death* (1979) at 50p a pop. These were ex-rental tapes and some of them may have pre-dated UK certification of videos. I still liked kung fu films but I was more focussed on other genres and didn't pay a whole lot of attention to the Brucesplotation releases I was viewing on tape back then. Certainly my passion for old school kung fu was for a time overtaken by a liking for Hong Kong's new wave film-makers like John Woo.

My interest in Brucesploitation was rekindled about twelve years ago when various movies featuring the likes of Bruce Li, Dragon Lee and Bruce Le, began turning up in the UK discount chain Poundland. While the picture quality of the Brucesploitation on many of these DVDs was poor, contemporary online versions are often even worse! However, that hasn't stopped many of the Brucesploitation films posted on YouTube racking up hundreds of thousands of hits—so the genre seems to retain some popularity today; although without access to the relevant data it is impossible to know how many of these views represent people watching the films from beginning to end, rather than just dipping into them.

There are various perils associated with these changing formats. Digging back into my memories of watching Brucesploitation on VHS in the eighties, I recalled my disbelief the first time I saw a softcore sex scene in which the Bruce Lee character jammed his fingers into the butt of a Linda Lee knock-off. I was sure this occurred in *The True Game of Death* (1979) but when I checked the movie out again on YouTube—about twenty-five years after I'd last seen it—it seemed I was mistaken. I then thought the scene must have been in a Bruce Li flick because my first experiences of Brucesploitation had been with vehicles for this anti-star, and I knew I'd encountered the wacked out softcore I wanted to revisit early on in my exposure to the genre. However after watching through some Bruce Li movies I still couldn't find what I was pursuing. Finally I scored two different DVD reissues of *The True Game of Death* and discovered I'd been right all along, since the episode in question is on every English language edit I've viewed of the film apart from the version I found on YouTube.

As the formats on which Brucesploitation was viewed changed, my critical understanding of it mutated too. The more I watched Brucesploitation, the more I saw it as deconstructing the myth of Bruce Lee—even if most of those involved in making these movies were looking to the bottom line and didn't care whether they were celebrating or denigrating the Little Dragon. The isolation and repetition of gestures and tropes from Lee movies within Brucesploitation serve to undercut fan discourse about the uniqueness of this star and sharpen our grasp of the semiotics of his celebrity. This is how I understand Brucesploitation; not everyone sees it this way. Audience reaction to any film or genre is more likely to be split than unified, what some view as ideological contestation or deconstruction—accidental or otherwise—others see as celebration or travesty.

For me *The True Game of Death,* is as an outstanding example of the best of the Brucesploitation genre. But from reading the handful of reviews I was able to find online I could have easily concluded it wasn't worth watching had I not already seen it. A squib on the *City on Fire* website claims it: "...is not one of the worst Bruceploitation movies ever made, it IS the worst." These divergent receptions emerge from opposing understandings and perspectives. I view this flick as a parody of the official *Game of Death* (1978); while those who denigrate it insist it is a cheap rip-off of the Robert Clouse movie.

The more deeply I looked into Bruceploitation, the clearer it became that those who have written about the genre to date have done so inadequately. Although it is easy enough to find at least sparse coverage of much of what I deal with here online, I approach this material from a different perspective to the instantly available (dis)information. I'm also super-aware of the need to theorise exploitation flicks in ways that break with ideology of 'quality cinema'; something many of those writing about Brucesploitation don't do. By 'quality cinema' I mean the pseudo-realist standards of Hollywood film, with generic plot points and an emphasis on the craft of acting and the cult of the auteur.

I've no time for those who want to bog cinema down with outmoded ideas from nineteenth-century literature and literary theory, 'coherent' plots, and stagey theatrical traditions all of which are completely moribund. Cinema should relate to dreams and allow us to escape the ideology of realism! Bruce's Lee's rhetoric about realism—which bore little relation to what he actually did on film—emerged at least in part from his immersion in Cantonese cinema as a child actor. Please note that being aware of the influence of melodramatic Chinese opera traditions on kung fu films is not the same as unreservedly endorsing this connection.

I have looked for and failed to find a convincing critical overview of Brucesploitation. In the English-speaking world the focus of interest seems to be the very bland 'actor' Bruce Li. A 2010 fan publication by Carl Jones, *Here Come the Kung Fu Clones* (Woowums Books), showed little interest in anyone beyond Li, and became really confused when trying to disentangle the film appearances of Bruce Le. Not that Jones was the only bewildered fan; many online reviewers leave opinions about one Brucesploitation movie on pages dedicated to a completely different flick.

Somewhat more sophisticated in its understanding of film as a medium than *Here Come the Kung Fu Clones* was Leon Hunt's *Kung Fu Masters: From Bruce Lee to Crouching Tiger* (Wallflower Press, London 2003) but here Brucesploitation is only really touched on in passing and again the focus is very much on Bruce Li and the Hollywood bio-pic *Dragon: The Bruce Lee Story* (1993, directed by Rob Cohen). Even when Hunt writes briefly about *The Clones of Bruce Lee* (1980) his focus is on Dragon Lee at the expense of Bruce Le, Bruce Lai and Bruce Thai; he has nothing to say about putative director Joseph Velasco, who might be viewed as 'the king of Brucesploitation'. Contra Hunt, Cohen's *Dragon* is a Hollywood drama and is not even an exploitation film let alone Brucesploitation.

The period with the greatest cluster of Bruc-esploitaton productions covers less than a decade from the mid-seventies to the early-eighties, but the genre spluttered on into the twenty-first century. Although it didn't exist as a recognised category before Bruce Lee's death, there are several films that pre-date the Little Dragon's demise that belong to it. While death added another dimension to Bruce Lee's celebrity status, he was already a huge star in South East Asia before he passed away so cynical movie producers did not need to wait for this event to exploit popular interest in Lee—even if the term Brucesploitation had yet to be coined. Early entries in film genres inevitably have to be made before the category to which they belong comes into being. Likewise the links between the films that make up any given genre are relational and not rational, and ultimately what belongs to any given cinematic category must be argued on a case-by-case—that is a movie-by-movie—basis.

I have seen it falsely asserted in a number of places—including Wikipedia—that Brucesploitation movies attempted to exploit interest in Bruce Lee after his death. *Fist of Unicorn* (1973) can and should be treated as a part of the genre, and it was made and released before Lee died on 20 July 1973. Brucesploitation dates back to at least 1972 and includes the Ramon Zamora comedy kung fu vehicle *The Pig Boss* (1972) that riffs on Bruce Lee's first adult star vehicle; it may also encompass Zamora's *Fish and Fury*—although whether this second item is actually a stand alone feature or just segment of *King Plaster* (1972) is currently unclear to me. These Zamora flicks belong to a Filipino tradition of parody films that include *Iking Boxer* (1973, a slapstick version of *King Boxer*) and *Lasing Master* (1980, a spoof of *Drunken Master)*, but which also encompassed off-the-wall remakes of both local and international hits that had no martial arts content whatsoever. Despite being aware of Zamora's early involvement in the Brucesploitation genre, I haven't actually seen the titles I've just mentioned because they've never been available in English;

indeed these movies are assumed to be completely lost, with no prints in Tagalog having surfaced in the last thirty-five years. Below I do deal with Zamora's later dubbed into English Bruce Lee related output.

Within both Brucesploitation and the related Chansploitation phenomena, actors who copy and clone Bruce Lee or Jackie Chan make up one strand of these subgenres, but their importance can and has been over-stated. This is evident not just from the title of the book *Here Come the Kung Fu Clones* by Carl Jones, but also the UK fan site *Clones of Bruce Lee* run by Lee Holmes. Both Jones and Holmes treat Bruce Liang as a clone. My own view is that when Liang appears as Bruce Lee in *The Dragon Lives Again* (1977) he is there as an actor playing the Little Dragon in the underworld after death rather than a clone; this is emphasised by dialogue in the English dub addressing head on the fact that Liang doesn't look like Bruce Lee. Liang also played Lee's Chen Zhen character in two Hong Kong TV series; 1981's *The Legendary Fok* and 1982's *The Fist*. I do not address these TV shows because I approach Brucesploitation as a film genre.

Movies such as *The Black Dragon's Revenge* (1975), with a narrative that revolves around a fictional investigation into the death of Bruce Lee, belong to the Brucesploitation genre without even featuring a clone so copyists are not essential to this film category. Lee Holmes on his *Clones* website at one time listed *Black Dragon's Revenge* supporting actor Charles Bonet as a Bruce Lee clone, but given this martial artist's karate leanings and rejection of kung fu, this is not a claim I take at all seriously. I would further argue that those who see figures like Bonet as clones do so because they approach Brucesploitation in thrall to the misleading idea that copyists define it. Tadashi Yamashita, sometimes called Bronson Lee after a character he played, is another example of a karateka I do not accept as a Bruce Lee clone; despite both Jones and Holmes—among others—mistakenly asserting he is one.

While I am in agreement with those critics who say the official *Game of Death* (1978) is Brucesploitation because among other things it uses doubles for the dead star, it seems to me that the two films edited into movie features from Lee's 1960s TV appearances as Kato—*The Green Hornet* (1974) and *Fury of the Dragon* (1976)—should also be treated as a part of the genre. All three of these films deploy the cut-and-paste technique. There is a long history in exploitation film of multiple edited versions of individual movies being made to appeal to different markets—and address the varying types of censorship encountered around the world at different historical periods. Sometimes new material was filmed by distributors in a specific region or at a later date, at others variant scenes were shot as the flick was made, particularly if it had been pre-sold internationally. Old sexploitation features were often spiced up with distributors adding racier scenes as censorship rules relaxed in the post-World War II period, and films were also given new titles to tie-in with contemporary trends.

The two features in which Bruce Lee posthumously 'stars' as Kato are simply episodes in a much older and longer history of cut-and-paste films. That said, *The Green Hornet* is definitely one of the earlier (if not the earliest) Brucesploitation cut-and-paste movies—taking material from different sources (in this case various episodes of a TV series) and then cobbling them together to make what more or less looks like a full-length film. While the use of funeral footage in early Bruce Lee biopics might also be described as cut-and-paste, this functioned more to lend a little documentary-style credibility to what were highly mythologised storylines. The cutting-and-pasting of fictional footage generally has a more surreal collage feel than the addition of pseudo-realist elements; for example the meta-fictional effect achieved by (or at least credited to) Joseph Velasco in movies such as *Treasure of Bruce Lee* (1979)—and later by Godfrey Ho with his notorious ninja productions.

Cut-and-paste movies serve to destabalise conventional notions about authorship, and raise many curious questions about who should really be credited with directing all sorts of martial arts and other pictures. Both Velasco and Ho have had their names attached as directors to films with which their real involvement was actually production and/or distribution; in at least some instances other people can be identified as being the 'real' directors. Leaving aside possible vanity motives, the main purpose of director misattributions to both Ho and Velasco seems to have been an attempt to fool at least sections of international audiences that films originating from places like Korea and Indonesia are 'authentic' Chinese kung fu films made in Hong Kong. Often cast and crew names were also altered to make them appear Chinese—and Velasco is generally credited under his Chinese monikers —variations on Joseph Kong Hung. It seems Velasco came from a Filipino family but was born in Taiwan.

There has also been the deliberate miscrediting of lesser known Bruce Lee copyists as more 'famous' clones, since fans of Brucesploitation are perceived by distributors as more likely to purchase product featuring Bruce Li, Bruce Le or Dragon Lee, than actors even lower down the rungs of martial arts movie stardom. That said, not all mangled credits are the result of deliberate chicanery, DVD and video companies sourcing public domain films from dodgy VHS tapes sometimes didn't know— and didn't care about—the difference between say Bruce Le and Bruce Li.

Returning to the matter of cut-and-paste movies, one I won't be investigating here is *Fist of Legend 2: Iron Bodyguard* (1996). This is actually a re-edited version of *The Bodyguard* (1974) designed to cash in on the success of the *Fist of Fury* (1972) remake staring Jet Li that is known in English as *Legend of the Fist* (1994). As my overview of it below makes clear, *Legend of the Fist* adheres more to notions of 'quality cinema' than exploitation. Films like *Fist of Legend* and *Dragon: The Bruce Lee Story* (1993) may have 'Bruce Lee' content but since they are not exploitation films, they cannot be Brucesploitation. *Fist of Legend 2* is exploitation and it exploits public interest in Jet Li, it was packaged as a vehicle for 'Jet Le'. While this prime example of Jetsploitaion angered his fans and amused me, it isn't Brucesploitation because it's riffing on an actor who'd reprised Bruce Lee's Chen Zhen role.

Another flick I won't be covering is *The Bruce Lee Connection,* one of many old school kung fu bashers released in North America in the aftermath of Bruce Lee's death with a title designed to exploit public interest in the Little Dragon. I've found newspaper ads for this 'Johnny Chang' ('star of *Snake Fist Vs the Dragon')* vehicle online but haven't figured out what the film was originally called, so was unable to source it. I don't deal with *Rebellious Reign* (1980) either; it is sometimes claimed this was a film intended for Bruce Lee. It would be more accurate to say the Little Dragon had plans to play the historical figure featured in this flick, but with a different director, scriptwriters, co-stars and producers. The connections to Lee's unrealised plans are so tenuous that it just isn't worth considering *Rebellious Reign* as an example of Brucesploitation.

I'm skipping *Big Boss Part II* (1976) directed by Chan Chue and starring Lo Lieh, Wang Ping, Michael Chan Wai-Man and Bruce Le amongst others, because it is essentially lost. Like everyone else with a deep interest in Brucesploitation, I've seen the trailer for this movie and the opening nine plus minutes, both of which are—or were—uploaded to YouTube. Allegedly the one known existing print of the whole movie was repeatedly screened at a cinema in Zimbabwe a few years ago; nonetheless like most people who'd like to see this flick, I'm unable to view it since the former and current owners supposedly refuse to make it publicly available other than by showings at one venue in Africa. Since I haven't seen the entire film, I won't cover it here.

This 'lost' film should not be confused with two others sometimes known as *Big Boss II,* but at other times billed as *Dragon Lee Fights Again* (1978) and *Lone Shaolin Avenger* AKA *Bruce Against the Odds*

(1977). Likewise, given that the original Bruce Lee movie title *The Big Boss* (1971) is fairly generic, I'm not going to cover *The Big Boss of Shanghai* (1979), which in terms of content has little to do with the Little Dragon but does resemble the earlier kung fu movie *Boxer from Shantung* (1972). Even Fernando di Leo's poliziottesco *The Boss* (1973) came out after Bruce Lee's first adult star vehicle, and although it is a prime slice of Eurosleaze, I can see no justification for covering it here simply because the title is similar to that of a Bruce Lee flick.

I also ignore films that don't actually exist. A notorious example is *Ilsa Meets Bruce Lee In the Devils Triangle.* This was a mooted flick staring Dyanne Thorne (of the *Ilsa* series of sado-masochistic sex movies) and a Bruce Lee clone. The planned release date according to pre-shooting promotional posters—which may or may not be genuine—was late 1976. Thorne when interviewed about this mythical title stated she started martial arts training for it but since the money needed wasn't raised, it didn't even get as far as having a written script. This was a pre-sell that didn't sell, but that hasn't stopped someone placing a long review online claiming they have seen it and that the movie is circulating as a bootleg (it isn't) from Death's Door Video.

Much of the writing about Brucesploitation is fan and internet based, and many of those producing this discourse make little attempt to explain why they insist certain films belong to the genre. Too many fans write as if genre is somehow natural rather than created and shaped both through bald assertion and by more critical discussion and thinking. It is all too common to find any martial arts film featuring certain actors and themes, or with Bruce in the title, being accepted as Brucesploitation without any debate around the issue. That isn't to say one can't find online reviewers questioning whether a movie is or isn't Brucesploitation; it's just that an unthinking attitude of acceptance of the genre label dominates online talk about the films I'm discussing—alongside a strong desire on the part of some of those involved in such debate to 'empire build' by finding more films to add to this category.

One of the aims of this text is to stimulate debate about what should and should not constitute the genre of Brucesploitation. While genres (filmic or otherwise) are subject to ongoing change and mutation, this does not mean it is pointless to define them; while simultaneously understanding that such categories are evolving rather than static and therefore no definition can be fixed for all time. Attempting to map genres is a part of the process of their social negotiation.

I'm going to divide a number of the films that have been described online and/or in print as Brucesploition into the categories of core, semi-periphery, periphery and outer limits. I will then organise these categories by year of release and alphabetically by title. That said, year of release is sometimes hard to determine, so at times I am guessing. Likewise cinema, video and DVD releases of these films can—and often do—misattribute credits.

I decided not to organise my overview of 'Brucesploitation' films by actor since this places too great a stress on their clone aspect, and leads to the inclusion of titles that don't merit a place in the genre. Likewise classifying by director removes our focus from the content of the movies and thus whether they really belong to the genre. Nonetheless, it is clearly useful to talk about actors and directors in relation to Brucesploitation once we have a broad understanding of it, and can sensibly judge which works by specific individuals might be included (and which should be excluded).

I have no understanding of most of the languages spoken in the areas in which the films under review were made. I can't speak Cantonese, Mandarin, Hokkien, Hakka, Korean, Japanese, Tagalog or Indonesian. Although these languages would have been used on set when many of the movies I'm dealing with were shot, so was English; just as importantly the films tended to be lensed silently and dubbed in post-production. Therefore despite some differences in the telling of the stories—and sometimes visual edits—in the various language versions of these movies, there is generally no original to watch. Given it's my native tongue and the language in which the reception of these films is being addressed, whenever possible I've viewed them in English dubs. In a few instances I was only able to source subtitled versions, for example *Ghost of the Fox* (1990).

There is a rich hybridity to the English dubbing that emerges from the complex—and obviously problematic—colonial history of Hong Kong. The mix of accents used on English language versions of films dubbed in Hong Kong are more often commented upon by North Americans than viewers from the British Isles. In part this is due to the worldwide dominance of Hollywood movies and American TV. United States residents tend to view a Cockney or Glaswegian accent as quirkier than a UK or Eire based individual will find a Texan or Brooklyn twang. I am aware of the wide variety of accents used—including north American and Australian ones—on the English language soundtracks to Brucesploitation and other martial arts movies, but since I was born in London, I am less inclined to comment on them than if I'd grown up in Pittsburgh.

Returning briefly to my inability to speak any South East Asian language, this means that I do not list the films I'm reviewing under the titles given to them in that region. If I was able to understand the languages in question, then using Cantonese, Mandarin, Korean, Japanese, Tagalog and Indonesian (as appropriate) titles might help dispel the confusion that surrounds the identity of some of these flicks. However, since I can't speak any South East Asian language and I don't trust the accuracy of sites such as the *Internet Movie Database* on matters relating to Brucesploitation, it would be foolish of me to try to crib this information from what are clearly unreliable sources. Instead I have little choice but to leave this work—which I'd very much like to see properly accomplished—to those both interested in exploitation film and fluent in English and one or more of these other languages.

With specific regard to Hong Kong and Taiwan, actors and directors often have different English, Cantonese and Mandarin names. I simply use the name that I like the best; for example, Joseph Velasco over Joseph Kong Hung, Kong Hung, Joseph Hung and Chiang Sung (all of which I might use to refer to the same person). Likewise I prefer Bruce Le to Huang Kin-Lung, Wong Kum-Hung, Lui Siu-Lung, Huang Chien-Lung, Jacky Lui, Wong Kei-Lung, Wong Kin-Lung, Yeo So-Ryong, or Wang Chien-Lung—all of which might be used to invoke the same Bruce Lee clone cum film director.

I have excluded all films that were unavailable to me in an English dub or at the very least with English subtitles. This means that I do not cover flicks such as *Bruce Lee Vs Gay Power* (1975), which is only available in Portuguese under the title *Kung Fu Contra as Bonecas*. According to the online translator I used the original title means 'Kung Fu Against Dolls' not *Bruce Lee Vs Gay Power*—but given that online translators are notoriously bad at dealing with slang, it might be better rendered as 'Kung Fu Against Gays' or 'Kung Fu Against Transvestites'. This film doesn't appear to have been released under the English title that made it notorious. Rumours about this movie spread by word of mouth and in print for more than a dozen years, until the entire flick—or at least a Brazilian TV edit of it—finally appeared on YouTube in 2011 (which is where I saw it). Once the film could be viewed it was obvious—even to those like me who don't speak Portuguese—that this was a Brazilian comedy that parodied firstly the local Cangaco (bandit) genre, and secondly the TV series *Kung Fu* starring David Carradine. As far as I can tell it has nothing to do with Bruce Lee.

Likewise I am not going to address *Cameroon Connection* (1985) either because I can only source it in French and Spanish dubs. I regret skipping over this title a little more than I do *Bruce Lee Vs Gay Power*, since Bruce Le and Paco Rabanne appearing in the same movie is something that grooves me.

But since my rule is that I will only deal with what is available to me in English, I will stick with it. *Cameroon Connection* isn't actually Brucesploitation, even if some online sources treat is as such because Bruce Le appears in it. Other movies I knowingly skip over are those that have no Brucesploitation content but were marketed in languages other than English with Bruce or Bruce Lee in the title. An example of this would be the movie which I know as *Chiu Chow Kung Fu* (1973) but that was released in Italy under the title *La sorella di Bruce Lee (The Sister of Bruce Lee)*. Although I have a copy of *Chiu Chow Kung Fu* in English dub, I don't cover it here because only Italian speakers are at all likely to associate it with Brucesploitation; my focus is on the English language reception of these movies.

I have also excluded animations—for example *Chinese Gods* (1976)—and documentaries about Bruce Lee from my consideration of Brucesploitation. Thus while a documentary like *Bruce Lee, the Man and the Legend* (1973) is extremely exploitative, I do not view it as part of the genre, but the mockumentary *Fist of Fear, Touch of Death* (1980) is Brucesploitation because it clearly assumes reasonably intelligent viewers will understand it as comedy fiction. Likewise because to me genre classification means dealing with a movie in its entirety, I am not going to address films that have scenes within them that invoke Bruce Lee without him being a selling point for the entire flick. So although some Brucesploitation fans place the likes of *Kentucky Fried Movie* (1977), *Raw Force* (1982) and *Shaolin Soccer* (2001) within the genre, I will ignore these flicks. And again, unless material from a TV series has been edited into something approaching a standard exploitation film format for cinema then I skip over it. Thus while I cover *The Green Hornet* (1974) and *Fury of the Dragon* (1976), I will not address *Legend of Bruce Lee* (2010), since even the 'film' edit of this 2008 TV series is twice as long as a normal exploitation feature and therefore excludes itself structurally from my understanding of Brucesploitation.

I treat Brucesploitation as a subgenre of a broader martial arts film category. I do not automatically accept Little Dragon bio-pics as belonging within it. The term Brucesploitation implies we are dealing with exploitation films and straight-ahead drama doesn't fit this category and nor do high budget Hollywood movies. Therefore films like *Young Bruce Lee* (2010) AKA *Bruce Lee, My Brother* are not Brucesploitation. Since earlier bio-pics such as *Bruce Lee: The Man, the Myth* (1976) function as kung fu flicks even if they can also be 'read' as dramas, they are Brucesploitation. For a film to make the Brucesploitation category it needs to be a low-budget martial arts movie, and it should go without saying these are also a subgenre of the action film.

The length of my plot summaries varies greatly. There are a variety of reasons for this, some of which are subjective and simply reflect my tastes and interests. However, where there was little information on a film in English—or the reviews and plot synopses I could find in my native tongue seemed wildly inaccurate—I sometimes felt a title merited extended exploration. One of the flicks I give a lengthier treatment is *Muscle of the Dragon* (1981, AKA *Dragon Lee Fights Back)*, in part because at the time I wrote about it I could not find a single plot synopsis for it—let alone a review—in English online; that isn't to say there weren't any but if synopses or reviews did exist they were hard to find. The situation may have changed by the time you read this, but right now—as I write—what I could find were the English language entries for *Muscle* on the Hong Kong Movie Database, Hong Kong Cinemagic and possibly the Internet Movie Database; although whether the last of these actually had an entry for the flick in question is an issue in itself—it had a page with a French language poster for the film, but lists a different title and crew to the movie I'm interested in. These entries are (currently) all bare bones partial and skimpy cast and crew listings that don't even mention that the film was padded out with cut-and-paste scenes from *The Clones of Bruce Lee* (1980), and all fail to provide a plot outline.

Likewise, I have *Muscle* on DVD as part of the *Grindhouse Experience Presents Ultimate Dragon Collection 10 Film Set* from VideoAsia. There is no information about *Muscle* on the packaging to this collection, although the back cover of the DVD does contain the dubious claim that Bruce Lee's: "*Fist of Fury* has been re-worked and remade more times than any other film in history..." (really, more times than say *Dracula?*). VideoAsia have also released *Muscle* as a two film set with *Kung Fu Superman* (the disk, transfers and lack of extras are identical to what's included in the *Ultimate Dragon Collection*), and the full back sleeve blurb on that DVD edition of the film reads: "For the first time ever, this 'long lost' Dragon Lee classic has been found and available on DVD! (sic) Dragon pits hit (sic) muscular skills against an army of lethal mobsters."

Sale page reviews of both these VideoAsia releases tend to focus on the other films and skip over *Muscle*. On an Amazon.com page for the two disk set this is the nearest thing there is to anyone passing an opinion on *Muscle* (there is a lot more about *Kung Fu Superman*): "There is another movie on this disc called *Muscle of the Dragon* and it is completely unwatchable. Don't waste your time on it. Just watch *Kung Fu Superman*, better known as *Little Superman*." Contra this Amazon reviewer, I'd say the DVD transfer of *Muscle* is very poor but it isn't unwatchable and the film itself is something of a cut-and-paste anti-classic. When I last looked at it, a YouTube posting of *Muscle* had nearly 27,000 hits in just under two years but no useful information about the film other than a throwaway comment saying the beginning of the movie came from *Clones of Bruce Lee* and seemingly blaming Godfrey Ho for this, who as far as I know wasn't involved with *Clones* or *Muscle* but who is notorious for taking credit for pieces of film-making that are nothing to do with him.

Returning to the varying length of plot exposition provided here, since I assume readers are either familiar with Bruce Lee's biography, or will look it up, I do not feel bio-pics require detailed summary; although all of them tend to play fast and loose with the actual facts of the Little Dragon's life. Likewise, since I presuppose either an acquaintance with Bruce Lee's adult films—*The Big Boss* (1971), *Fist of Fury* (1972), *Way of the Dragon* (1972) and *Enter the Dragon* (1973)—or an ability to check them out, I do not feel in-depth synopses of the many remakes and sequels to *Fist of Fury* are necessary. And again, I won't repeatedly justify providing sometimes relatively long assessments of flicks that are at best only peripheral to Brucesploitation, since I am dealing with movies that other people have claimed belong to the genre, and if I wish to dismiss their assertions then it is sometimes necessary to examine the films in question in detail in order to do so.

Since I don't view the flicks I'm writing about as having characters in a classical literary sense, and because a number of their directors take a cut-and-paste approach to film-making, I often refer to actors by their stage names rather than their 'fictional' identity in a particular movie. I find it productive to view the entire Brucesploitation genre as one massively long dream-like avant-garde film with deliberately repetitive scenes that can be endlessly re-edited, re-ordered and re-looped. It is a huge mistake to judge these films mainly on the supposed fighting skills of their actors—although some fans do just this. The martial arts they feature are mugged up for the camera, and while one might find much of interest in the fighting styles they draw on, they should ultimately be assessed on how entertaining they are on film—and not for how effective or believable they might be. Others with different views will just have to argue their own corner. "Your kung fu, sorry I mean bullshit theory, is pretty good—but it can't beat my trash cinema dialectics!"

Some might find elements of Orientalism at work in the subject matter I've been drawn to here, but if that proves to be the case then my strong attraction to Filipino entries and elements in the Brucesploitation genre still needs to be unpacked. I'd say it's the ultra-hybrity of Filipino culture that pulls me towards it. The fact that Spanish and American influences are an important part of this super-phat amalgam—alongside equally significant Chinese and Polynesian elements—results in films made in and around Manila being far more immediately accessible to me than say the very curious Korean entries into the Brucesploitation genre. Of course this situation is further complicated by the fact that many of the Korean flicks that pique my interest with regard to this subgenre were re-edited in Hong Kong for international audiences; where they were faked up to be passed off as Chinese. With regard to Korea, I love the kicking techniques that often make martial arts from that peninsula seem more like dance than fighting. I am less keen on the historical obsessions evident within many strands of Korean popular culture, which result in films from this location being far more likely to have period settings than flicks from The Philippines.

Both Korean and Filipino Brucesploitation entries problematise dualist notions some critics have put forward about there being a local and international Bruce Lee. Local more often than not means Hong Kong, since both Xianggang pride and a largely unconscious neo-colonial mindset among 'British' 'critics' contributes to the bias. In Manila and Seoul, Bruce Lee could be viewed as both a 'local' South East Asian star and an international celebrity. That said, I'm not convinced that in Hong Kong—or indeed California—Bruce Lee was universally treated as a local boy. Discourse about a local and an international Bruce Lee too often turns out to be a faux-'sophisticated' academic argument that obscures the real diversity in the reception and understanding of the Little Dragon's films and celebrity both in South East Asia, the West Coast of the USA, and elsewhere.

While researching Brucesploitation I came across many factual errors when reading what others had written about it in English. By sitting down and watching these movies, and then writing about them, I hoped to clarify my own and some other people's understanding of this genre. However, I am certain that I too will have made some factual errors and I would welcome their correction. Before I finish this introduction I should mention there are at least two ways to spell Brucesploitation with an 's' at the start of the second syllable, or 'Bruceploitation' without that 's'. I've even seen the term rendered 'Brucexploitation'! I favour the first spelling because I tend to pronounce that 's' but obviously the other renderings are not necessarily incorrect.

Given my understanding of genre as shifting and mutating, I make no apologies for the fact that my 'overview' of Brucesploitation is incomplete. Any discussion of a genre is necessarily partial since its shifting boundaries make it impossible to definitively pin down and of course new films are always being released and lost ones rediscovered!

To conclude this preamble, what I label core below definitely constitutes Brucesploitation, what I call semi-periphery still more or less works as Brucesploitation, the periphery can be argued over and what I describe as outer limits definitely isn't worth treating as part of the genre. Although I will make judgements of films in my overviews, my categorisation of them between core and outer limits simply indicates what I think of them in relation to Brucesploitation—and some of those I place in the periphery and outer limits, I still view as classics of trash cinema. So while I might see a film as peripheral to Brucesploitation that doesn't mean I dislike it or think it's not worth viewing. Likewise, movies like *Goodbye Bruce Lee, His Last Game of Death* (1975) clearly belong to the core of the genre but are nevertheless complete turkeys and aren't really worth watching unless you want to discuss Brucesploitation.

You Can't Keep a Good Man Down!
BRUCE LEE 1940-1973
BRUCE LEE FIGHTS BACK FROM THE GRAVE
R RESTRICTED
Under 17 requires accompanying Parent or Adult Guardian
also starring DEBORAH CHAPLIN ANTHONY BRONSON STEVE MACK
directed by BERT LENZI music by MAURICE SARLI HEAD GORILLA RELEASING, INC.
1978 HEAD GORILLA INC.

BRUCESPLOITATION RANKINGS

CORE

1 *Bruce Lee: A Dragon Story* (1974) — 27
AKA *Super Dragon: The Bruce Lee Story*
AKA *The Bruce Lee Story*
Directed by Shut Dik

2 *Black Dragon Vs the Yellow Tiger* (1974) — 27
AKA *The Growling Tiger*
AKA *Tiger from China*
Directed by Yang Yang

3 *Chaku Master* (1974) — 28
Directed by Luis San Juan

4 *The Game of Death* (1974) — 30
Directed by Jun Gallardo

5 *The Black Dragon's Revenge* (1975) — 31
AKA *Death of Bruce Lee*
Directed by Tony Liu Chun-Ku

6 *Bruce Lee Against Supermen* (1975) — 35
AKA *Bruce Lee Vs the Supermen*
AKA *Superdragon Vs Superman*
Directed by Wu Chia-Chun

7 *The Dragon Dies Hard* (1975) — 36
AKA *Bruce Lee We Miss You*
Directed by Li Kuan-Chang

8 *Goodbye Bruce Lee, His Last Game of Death* (1975) — 37
AKA *The New Game of Death*
Directors Lin Bing and Harold B Swartz

9 *Bruce Lee: His Last Days, His Last Nights* (1976) — 38
AKA *Bruce Lee and I*
AKA *I Love You, Bruce Lee*
Directed by John Law Ma

10 *Bruce Lee: The Man, the Myth* (1976) — 40
AKA *Bruce Lee True Story*
Directed by Ng Sze-Yuen

11 *Bruce's Deadly Fingers* (1976) — 41
AKA *Bruce's Fingers*
Directed by Joseph Velasco

12 *Exit the Dragon, Enter the Tiger* (1976) — 41
AKA *Star of Stars*
Directed by Lee Tso-Nam

13 *Cobra* (1977) — 42
Directed by Rempo Urip (sometimes attributed to Joseph Velasco)

14 *The Dragon Lives Again* (1977) — 45
AKA *Deadly Hands of Kung Fu*
Directed by Law Kei

15 *The Real Bruce Lee* (1977) — 47
Directed by Jim Markovic and Shi Hyeon Kim

16 *Return of Bruce* (1977) — 48
AKA *Bruce's Return*
AKA *The Dragon Returns*
Directed by Joseph Velasco

17 *Story of the Dragon* (1977) — 49
AKA *Bruce Lee's Deadly Kung Fu*
AKA *Bruce Lee's Secret*
AKA *Bruce Li's Jeet Kune Do*
Directors Chan Wa and William Cheung Kei

18 *Big Boss 2* (1978) — 49
AKA *Dragon Lee Fights Again*
AKA *Dragon Bruce Lee 2*
Directed by To Man-Bo and Lee Eun

19 *Dynamo* (1978) — 51
Directed by Hua Shan

20 *Enter the Game of Death* (1978) — 54
AKA *King of Kung Fu*
Directed by Joseph Velasco and/or Lam Kwok-Cheung and/or Choe U-Hyeong

21 *Game of Death* (1978) — 55
Directed by Robert Clouse

22 *Bruce the Super Hero* (1979) — 56
Directed by Bruce Le

23 *Kung Fu Fever* (1979) — 57
AKA *Black Dragon Fever*
AKA *Bruce Lee Strikes Back*
Directed by Kim Si-Hyeon and/or David Poon

24 *They Call Him Bruce Lee* (1979) — 57
Directed by Jun Posadas

25 *The True Game of Death* (1979) — 59
Directed by Chan San-Yat and/or Steve Harries

26 *Bruce King of Kung Fu* (1980) — 61
AKA *Legend of Bruce Lee*
Directed by Bruce Le

27. *Bruce's Fists of Vengeance* (1980) — 62
Directed by Bill James

28. *The Clones of Bruce Lee* (1980) — 64
Directed by Joseph Velasco and/or Nam Gi-Nam and Pracha Poonvivat

29. *Fist of Fear, Touch of Death* (1980) — 65
AKA *The Dragon and the Cobra*
Directed by Matthew Mallinson

30. *Golden Dragon Silver Snake* (1980) — 68
AKA *Dragoneer 5: The Indomitable*
AKA *A Fight At Hong Kong Ranch*
Directed by Godfrey Ho and/or Kim Si-Hyeon

31. *Muscle of the Dragon* (1981) — 69
AKA *Dragon Lee Fights Back*
Directed by To Man-Bo

32. *Tower of Death* (1981) — 72
AKA *Game of Death II*
Directed by Ng See-Yuen

33. *The Chinese Stuntman* (1982) — 74
AKA *Counter Attack*
Directed by Bruce Li

34. *Jackie and Bruce to the Rescue* (1982) — 76
AKA *Jackie Vs Bruce to the Rescue*
AKA *Fist of Death*
Directed by Ng Ka-Chun and/or Choe Dong-Joon

35. *Ninja Strikes Back* (1982) — 78
AKA *Bruce Strikes Back*
AKA *Bruce Fights Back*
AKA *Eye of the Dragon*
Directed by Joseph Velasco and Bruce Le plus allegedly André Koob (uncredited) and Jean-Marie Pallardy (uncredited)

36. *Ninja Vs Bruce Lee* (1982) — 80
AKA *Concord of Bruce*
Directed by Joseph Velasco

37. *The Young Bruce Lee* (1987) — 81
Directed by Larry Dolgin

38. *Bruce Lee in G.O.D.* (2000) — 81
Directed by Toshi Ohgushi, Toshikazu Ôgushi and Bruce Lee (uncredited)

39. *Dragon the Master* (2001) — 82
Directed by Ray Wu Wai-Shing

40. *Hero Youngster* (2004) — 83
AKA *Juvenile Chen Zhen*
Directed by Law Kei and Hung Kong

41. *The Real Bruce Lee 2* (2004) — 85
Directed by L Dolgen and Kant Leung Wang-Fat

SEMI-PERIPHERY

42. *Fist of Unicorn* (1973) — 89
AKA *Unicorn Palm*
AKA *Bruce Lee and I*
Directed by Tang Ti

43. *The Chinese Godfather* (1974) — 89
AKA *Chivalrous Knight*
Directed by Lui Gin

44. *The Green Hornet* (1974) — 92
Directed by William Beaudine, Darrell Hallenbeck and Norman Foster

45. *They Call Him Chop Suey* (1975) — 93
Directed by Jun Gallardo

46. *Fury of the Dragon* (1976) — 94
Directed by William Beaudine, Robert L Friend (uncredited) and Seymour Robbie (uncredited)

47. *Bruce and Shaolin Kung Fu* (1977) — 95
AKA *Ching Wu and Shaolin Kung Fu*
Directed by James Nam

48. *Bruce and the Golden Chaku* (1977) — 96
AKA *Golden Chaku*
Directed by Ronaldo San Juan

49. *Fist of Fury II* (1977) — 97
Directed by Iksan Lahardi, Lee Tso Nam and Jimmy Shaw

The Last Fist of Fury (1977) — 97
AKA *The Ultimate Lee*
AKA *Dragon Lee Does Dallas*
AKA *The Last of the Ching Wu School: Righteous Martial Party*
Directed by Kim Si-Hyeon
See the entry for *The Real Bruce Lee* in the core section, since this film is incorporated into that movie

50. *Soul Brothers of King Fu* (1977) — 97
AKA *The Tiger Strikes Again*
AKA *The Last Strike*
AKA *Kung Fu Avengers*
Directed by Hua Shan

51. *Soul of Bruce Lee* (1977) — 98
AKA *Soul of Chiba*
Directed by Chan Tung-Man and Noda Yukio

52. *Steel Fisted Dragon* (1977) — 98
AKA *Fistful of Dragons*
AKA *Duel Maut (Deadly Duel)*
Directed by Iksan Lahardi and Lee Tso Nam

BRUCESPLOITATION RANKINGS

| 53 | *Bruce Lee's Greatest Revenge* (1978) | 100 |

AKA *Bruce Le's Greatest Revenge*
AKA *Way of the Dragon 2*
Directed by To Man-Bo

| 54 | *Dragon Lee Vs the 5 Brothers* (1978) | 101 |

AKA *The Five Brothers*
AKA *The Angry Dragon*
Directed by Kim Si-Hyeon

| 55 | *Enter the Fat Dragon* (1978) | 102 |

Directed by Sammo Hung Kam-Bo

| 56 | *Enter Three Dragons* (1978) | 103 |

AKA *Dragon on Fire*
Directed by Joseph Velasco

| 57 | *Image of Bruce Lee* (1978) | 103 |

AKA *Storming Attacks*
Directed by Richard Yeung Kuen

| 58 | *Bruce Against Iron Hand* (1979) | 104 |

AKA *Bruce Against Iron Finger*
AKA *Iron Finger*
Directed by To Man-Bo

| 59 | *The Dragon's Snake Fist* (1979) | 105 |

Directed by Godfrey Ho and/or Kim Si-Hyeon

| 60 | *Fist of Fury III* (1979) | 105 |

AKA *Fist of Fury 3*
AKA *Chinese Connection III*
AKA *Avenging Fury*
AKA *Fist of Fury II*
AKA *Fist of Fury*
Directed by To Man-Bo

| 61 | *Three Avengers* (1979) | 106 |

AKA *The Lama Avenger*
Directed by Wong Wa-Kei

| 62 | *Challenge of the Tiger* (1980) | 107 |

AKA *Gymkata Killer*
AKA *Seize the Formula*
Directed by Bruce Le and Luigi Batzella (uncredited)

| 63 | *Skinny Tiger and Fatty Dragon* (1990) | 110 |

Directed Lau Kar-Wing

| 64 | *Legend of the Fist:*
The Return of Chen Zhen (2010) | 110 |

AKA *Fist of Fury: The Legend of Chen Zhen*
AKA *The Legend of Chen Zhen*
Directed by Andrew Lau Wai-Keung

PERIPHERY

| 65 | *On the Verge of Death* (1973) | 115 |

AKA *Line of Death*
AKA *Bruce Lee Vs Chinese Frankenstein*
Directed by Li Fai-Mon

| 66 | *Martial Arts* (1974) | 117 |

AKA *The Chinese Mack*
Directed by Chui Dai-Chuen

| 67 | *The Dragon Lives* (1976) | 117 |

AKA *He's a Legend, He's a Hero*
Directed by Wong Sing-Loy

| 68 | *Super Dragon* (1976) | 117 |

AKA *The Young Bruce Lee*
Directed by Lin Bing

| 69 | *Return of the Tiger* (1977) | 118 |

AKA *Silent Killer from Eternity*
Directed by Jimmy Shaw

| 70 | *Bruce and Shaolin Kung Fu 2* (1978) | 119 |

AKA *Ching Wu and Shaolin Kung Fu 2*
Directed by James Nam

| 71 | *Bruce Lee in New Guinea* (1978) | 120 |

AKA *Bruce Li In New Guinea*
AKA *Bruce Li in Snake Island*
Directed Yeung Gat-Aau and/or Joseph Velasco

| 72 | *Deadly Strike* (1978) | 121 |

AKA *Wanted! Bruce Li, Dead or Alive*
AKA *Bruce Has Risen*
Directed by Wong Fei-Lung

| 73 | *My Name Called Bruce* (1978) | 122 |

Directed by Joseph Velasco

| 74 | *Return of Fist of Fury* (1978) | 122 |

Directed by Joseph Velasco and/or James Nam

| 75 | *Bruce Against Snake*
in the Eagle's Shadow (1979) | 124 |

AKA *Bruce Vs Snake in the Eagle's Shadow*
Directed by Wu Chia-Chun

| 76 | *The Dragon, the Hero* (1979) | 125 |

AKA *Dragon on Fire*
Directed by Godfrey Ho

| 77 | *Fists of Bruce Lee* (1979) | 126 |

AKA *Interpol*
Directed by Ho Tsung-Tao (AKA Bruce Li)

| 78 | *The Treasure of Bruce Lee* (1979) | 127 |

Directed by Joseph Velasco

RE-ENTER THE DRAGON

79 *The Dragon's Infernal Showdown* (1980)   128
AKA *Dragon's Showdown*
Directed by Kim Si-Hyeon and/or Godfrey Ho

80 *Mission for the Dragon* (1980)   129
AKA *Rage of the Dragon*
Directed by Kim Si-Hyeon and/or Godfrey Ho

81 *Bruce and the Shaolin Bronzemen* (1982)   130
AKA *Enter the Game of Shaolin Bronzemen*
AKA *King Boxer II*
Directed by Joseph Velasco

82 *The Supergang* (1984)   131
AKA *The Super Gang*
Directed by Wong Siu-Jun

83 *Bruce's Ninja Secret* (1988)   133
AKA *Bruce's Secret Kung Fu*
AKA *Bruce's Last Battle*
AKA *Bruce the Top Master*
Directed by Joseph Velasco

84 *Ninja Over the Great Wall* (1990)   133
AKA *Shaolin Fist of Fury*
Directed by Bruce Le and Yim Leung

85 *Black Spot* (1991)   134
AKA *Earth and Fire*
AKA *Vicious Passageway*
Directed by Bruce Le

86 *Fist of Fury 1991* (1991)   135
Directed by Rico Chu Tak-On

Big Boss Untouchable (2002)   136
AKA *Dragon the Master 2*
Directed by Kant Leung Wang-Fat
See *The Real Bruce Lee 2* in the core section since this film is incorporated in its entirety into that movie

OUTER LIMITS

87 *Kung Fu Master—Bruce Lee Style* (1972)   139
AKA *Tough Guy*
AKA *Kung Fu the Head Crusher*
AKA *Revenge of the Dragon*
Directed by Joseph Velasco

88 *Queen Boxer* (1972)   139
AKA *Kung Fu Queen*
AKA *The Avenger*
Directed by Florence Yu Fung-Chi

89 *Lightning of Bruce Lee* (1973)   140
Directed by Chung Gwok-Hang

90 *Spirits of Bruce Lee* (1973)   141
AKA *Spirit of Bruce Lee*
AKA *Angry Tiger*
Directed by Heung Ling

91 *Bruce Takes Dragon Town* (1974)   142
AKA *Bruce Takes the Dragon*
AKA *Dare You Touch Me?*
Directed by Liu Hung-Sheng

92 *Chinese Iron Man* (1974)   143
AKA *Iron Man*
AKA *Young Hero of Shaolin II*
Directed by Joseph Kuo Nam Hung

93 *The Fierce One* (1974)   144
AKA *Jaws of the Dragon*
Directed by James Nam

94 *Bronson Lee, Champion* (1975)   145
Directed by Noda Yukio

95 *Bruce, D-Day at Macao* (1975)   147
AKA *Little Superman*
AKA *Little Hero*
AKA *Fist of Vengeance*
AKA *Kung Fu Superman*
Directed by Ng See-Yuen

96 *Bruce Hong Kong Master* (1975)   147
AKA *Hong Kong Superman*
Directed by Ting Shan-Hsi

97 *Bruce, Kung Fu Girls* (1975)   147
AKA *Five Pretty Young Ladies*
Directed by Shut Dik

98 *Enter the Panther* (1975)   149
AKA *Conspiracy*
Directed by Hon Bo-Cheung

99 *Bruce Lee Fights Back from the Grave* (1976)   150
AKA *Visitors In America*
Directed by Lee Doo-Yong

100 *New Fist of Fury* (1976)   151
AKA *Fists to Fight*
Directed by Lo Wei

101 *Revenge of the Ming Patriots* (1976)   152
AKA *The Ming Patriots*
Directed by Ulysses Au-Yeung Jun

102 *Bruce Against the Odds* (1977)   153
AKA *Big Boss 2*
AKA *The Mighty Four*
AKA *Four Brave Dragons*
AKA *Lone Shaolin Avenger*
Directed by Kim Jung-Yong

103 *Bruce and the Dragon Fist* (1977)   153
AKA *Furious Dragon's Rage*
Directed by Shim Wu-Seob and Zackey Chan Ngai-Wai

104 *Bruce and the Shaolin Poles* (1977)   154
AKA *Secret of the Shaolin Poles*
Directed by Ulysses Au-Yeung Jun

105 *Bruce Is Loose* (1977)   155
AKA *The Green Dragon Inn*
Directed by Wu Min-Hsiung

106 *Bruce Lee's Ways of Kung Fu* (1977)   156
AKA *Dragon Lee's Ways of Kung Fu*
AKA *Ways of Kung Fu*
Directed by Kim Jung-Yong

107 *The Dragon, the Lizard, the Boxer* (1977)   158
Directed by Ngai Lai and/or Law Kei

108 *The Fierce Boxer and Bruce* (1977)   159
AKA *The Fierce Boxer*
Directed by S. A. Karim and/or Joseph Velasco

109 *Return of Red Tiger* (1977)   160
Directed by Nam Gi-Nam and/or James Nam

110 *Return of the Dragon* (1977)   162
Directed by Celso Ad. Castillo

111 *10 Commandments of Lee* (1978)   162
AKA *Master and the Kid*
AKA *Shaolin Master and the Kid*
AKA *Fury of the Shaolin Master*
AKA *One Man Army*
Directed by Lin Fu-Ti

112 *Bruce Lee's Dual Flying Kicks* (1978)   163
AKA *Dual Flying Kicks*
Directed by Lin Bing

113 *Bruce Lee the Invincible* (1978)   163
AKA *The Invincible*
AKA *Bruce Li the Invincible Chinatown Connection*
Directed by Law Kei

114 *Bruce Lee Vs the Chinese Frankenstein* (1978)   164
Directed by Kwok Shek Ske

115 *Bruce Li's Magnum Fist* (1978)   164
AKA *Magnum Fist*
AKA *Great Hero*
Directed by Hon Bo-Cheung

116 *Death Dimension* (1978)   165
Directed by Al Adamson

117 *Edge of Fury* (1978)   166
Directed by Lee Tso Nam

118 *The Dragon, the Young Master* (1978)   167
AKA *Dragon the Master*
AKA *Dragoneer 8—The Unbeatable*
AKA *The Deadly Silver Ninja*
Directed by Godfrey Ho and/or Kim Si-Hyeon

119 *Blind Fists of Bruce Lee* (1979)   168
AKA *Blind Fist of Bruce*
Directed by Kam Bo

120 *The Gold Connection* (1979)   168
AKA *Iron Dragon Strikes Back*
Directed by Kuei Chih Hung

121 *Champ Against Champ* (1980)   169
AKA *Champ Vs Champ*
AKA *Twelve Gates of Hell*
Directed by Godfrey Ho and/or Lee Hyeok-Su

122 *Bruce Vs Bill* (1981)   171
Directed by Lam Kwok-Cheung

123 *Cold Blooded Murder* (1981)   172
Directed by Albert Law Do-Bong

124 *Enter the Invincible Hero* (1981)   173
AKA *Dragoneer 13—The Significant*
Directed by Godfrey Ho and/or Kim Si-Hyeon

125 *Enter the King of Kung Fu* (1981)   175
AKA *Zen Kwan Do Strikes Paris*
AKA *Kung Fu Leung Strikes Emmanuelle*
AKA *Kung Fu Emmanuelle*
Directed by John Liu

126 *The Furious* (1981)   175
AKA *The Furious Killer*
Directed by Joseph Velasco

127 *Dragon Force* (1982)   177
AKA *Power Force*
Directed by Michael Mak

128 *Secret Ninja, Roaring Tiger* (1982)   178
AKA *Secret Ninja*
Directed by Godfrey Ho and/or Kim Si-Hyeon

129 *They Call Me Bruce* (1982) — 180
Directed by Elliott Hong

130 *5 Pattern Dragon Claws* (1983) — 180
AKA *Fists of Lightning*
AKA *Thunderfist*
AKA *Thundering Fist*
Directed by Godfrey Ho and/or Kim Si-Hyeon

131 *Lee the Angry Man* (1983) — 181
AKA *Angry Young Man*
Directed by Wong Sing-Loy

132 *Martial Monks of Shaolin Temple* (1983) — 182
Directed by Godfrey Ho and/or an unidentified South Korean film-maker

133 *The Last Dragon* (1985) — 183
Directed by Michael Schultz

134 *Future Hunters* (1986) — 184
AKA *Spear of Destiny*
Directed by Cirio H. Santiago

135 *Ninja Champion* (1986) — 185
Directed by Godfrey Ho and/or Kim Si-Hyeon

136 *No Retreat, No Surrender* (1986) — 188
AKA *Karate Tiger*
Directed by Corey Yuen

137 *Mission Terminate* (1987) — 188
AKA *Return of the Kickfighter*
Directed by Anthony Maharaj

138 *They Still Call Me Bruce* (1987) — 189
Directed by James Orr and Johnny Yune

139 *Chinatown Connection* (1990) — 191
Directed by Jean-Paul Ouellette

140 *Ghost of the Fox* (1990) — 192
AKA *Way of Fox*
Directed by Bruce Le

141 *Comfort Women* (1992) — 192
Directed by Bruce Le

142 *Fist of Fury 1991 II* (1992) — 193
Directed by Rico Chu Tak-On

143 *Return of the Fat Dragon* (1993) — 194
AKA *King Swindler*
Directed Kevin Chu Yen-Ping

144 *Fist of Legend* (1994) — 194
Directed by Gordon Chan Ka-Seung

145 *Dragon in Fury* (2004) — 195
Directed by Mau Kin-Tak

146 *Finishing the Game:*
The Search for a New Bruce Lee (2007) — 196
Directed by Justin Lin

CORE

Goodbye, BRUCE LEE
HIS LAST GAME OF DEATH

Atlas International and Robert Chow present a Yu - Yun Production »Goodbye Bruce Lee - his last Game of Death«
Directed by: Lin Pin and Harold B. Swartz
Music: Arpad Bondy

with: Lee Roy Lung, Ronald Brown, »Big« Jonny Floyd, Mun Ping
Produced by: R. Chow and Chang Lung
World distribution Atlas International, Munich
Technicolor/Scope

1 BRUCE LEE: A DRAGON STORY   1974

AKA *SUPER DRAGON: THE BRUCE LEE STORY*
AKA *THE BRUCE LEE STORY*

DIRECTED BY SHUT DIK

It has been claimed this is the first Brucesploitation film ever made (not true because flicks like *The Pig Boss* and *Fist of Unicorn* pre-date it) and it is the first time Bruce Li played Bruce Lee. Many Little Dragon fans hate this movie but its sleaziness will keep trash hounds amused. It focuses on Bruce's love affair with fellow actor Betty Ting Pei. Like all bio-pics, the whole film plays fast and loose with the actual facts of Bruce Lee's life, serving to transform an ordinary human being into something mythological. Ting Pei's suicide attempt in the movie and loss of a love child with Lee appear to be entirely fictional. The first time Bruce and Betty have sex the lighting around the bed is red and there is a jazzy version of *I Heard It Through the Grapevine* playing on the soundtrack. Aside from the lascivious element of the affair with Ting Pei, it is the portrayal of various backstabbing Hong Kong movie moguls that really makes this film worth watching. There seems to be a settling of scores going on. Now that's what I call Brucesploitation! Director Shut Dik was not exactly prolific –*The Guy! The Guy!* AKA *Kung Fu Revenger* (1974) and *Bruce, Kung Fu Girls* (1975) are apparently the only other films he helmed; although he has at least seven assistant director credits between 1968 to 1973, and did scriptwriting, props and even make-up as well.

2 BLACK DRAGON VS THE YELLOW TIGER   1974

AKA *THE GROWLING TIGER*
AKA *TIGER FROM CHINA*

DIRECTED BY YANG YANG

This is an unofficial sequel to Bruce Lee's *Way of the Dragon* (1972) AKA *Return of the Dragon*. In *Black Dragon Vs Yellow Tiger*, Tang Lung plays the cousin of Bruce Lee's character of that name in *Way of the Dragon* and is called Tong Fu (or Tang Fu). I will refer to him by his stage name. There are some groovy animated credits before we get into the story.

The mob are incensed that Bruce Lee (referred to as Tang Lung in the story) has taken out their number nine man in Rome, presumably Chuck Norris. In revenge they want to kill Bruce Lee, but they don't know where he is. In order to track Lee down they send representatives of their Hong Kong branch to the house of Bruce Lee's uncle in Kowloon. Lee's uncle is away in Taiwan recovering from an injury with a friend who is a martial arts master, so in a bid to discover where the Little Dragon is, the hoods menace his daughter. Lung who has been messing about with his little brother turns up and beats up the gangbangers. The girl he's saved appears to be Lung's cousin but she refers to him as brother; likewise her father seems to be an uncle but as he is Tang's kung fu sifu, throughout the English dub the star refers to him as master. This master gets a message from his daughter telling him to return home since there is trouble. Upon arriving back from Taiwan he finds mobsters at his house demanding to know where Bruce Lee is, but the old kung fu fighter batters them. After this, Lung spots the hoods while he's on his bicycle and follows them to their HQ, where he beats them up after telling them he's Bruce Lee and they better leave his family alone. The mobster's bring in a couple of foreign fighters to kill Lung and his sifu, but Lung kills them. The uncle's martial arts friend is visiting from Taiwan when the hoods next show up at the family home, and so now it is the turn of this master to thrash them. The gangbangers decide they need to get even better fighters to kill this troublesome family and bring more in from abroad. They've also kidnapped Lung's little brother, who they eventually murder. When Lung and his cousin find the little boy's dead body, the star of the show goes nutzoid and sets out to kill the entire Hong Kong branch of the mob. With revenge as his motivation, Lung easily beats the hoods and most of the extra fighters they've brought in. Finally Lung has his climatic fight in what I assume is an iconic building (although I don't recognise it) that in some way makes it as good a venue for a final showdown as The Colosseum was for the battle between Bruce Lee and Chuck Norris in *Way of the Dragon*. Lung's opponent is Clint Robinson, an American taekwondo practitioner who served in the U.S. Air Force in Taiwan among other places. Robinson may have been chosen because he was available locally and therefore much cheaper than flying someone in; while the bulk of the action is set in Hong Kong, it seems much of it was actually shot in Taiwan. There are shots in the battle between Lung and Robinson that make it clear it is meant to invoke the climatic combat between Lee and Norris in *Way of the Dragon.* Lung, of course, wins. Afterwards the cops turn up saying they've had an eye on the mob he's almost wiped out for a long time, and more or less thank Lung for his good work.

At various points the *Enter the Dragon* theme is used to play up the connection between Lung and Lee, and of course there are the usual Lee-alike come on gestures. The film is absolutely hilarious despite not being an overt comedy like *Way of the Dragon*. Lung looks nothing like Bruce Lee and I wouldn't see him as a clone, more like a pretender to the 'king of kung fu's' throne. Lung is way more muscular than Lee, and not nearly as graceful when he moves. His earlier film *On the Verge of Death* (1973) concludes with some *Enter the Dragon* rip-off moments, and I deal with that below as part of the Brucesploitation periphery. Other films Lung stars in—such as *Way of the Tiger* (1973) AKA *Challenge the Dragon*—are standard kung fu fare, and despite a tiger theme in various titles (also a feature of some later Bruce Li Brucesploitation flicks) they do not fit the genre I'm addressing here. The fact lead actor Tang Lung has the same name as Bruce Lee's character in *Way of the Dragon* may have helped him land the role. Depending on which sources you believe (if any) this actor first appeared on screen as Tang Lung in 1970 or 1972; if the second date is correct he may have adopted the name (or had it foisted on him by producers) to cash in on Bruce Lee's first wave of success. However since this is a fairly common name, it almost seems plausible it is coincidence he shares his moniker with a character played by the Little Dragon. However, since the Taiwanese actor/choreographer/director Alexander Lo Rei (AKA Law Yui, Lo Yiu, Law Cheung-On, Alexander Lou) is Lung's brother, it seems unlikely his family name is Tang! Likewise, the star of *Black Dragon Vs the Yellow Tiger* should not be confused with the Korean actor Kim Tai-Jong who also used Tang Lung as a screen name, and who was one of Bruce Lee's doubles for the Billy Lo character in the official *Game of Death* (1978) and played Billy's brother Bobby Lo in *Game of Death II* (1981). Note also that Tang Lung in all these instances might also be rendered as Tong Lung in English transliteration.

3 CHAKU MASTER   1974
DIRECTED BY LUIS SAN JUAN

'Somewhere In China' is the title over the first pre-credits scene which features outdoor kung fu fighting with cars going by and a pagoda in the background; there follows a cut to 'Somewhere In Thailand' with sparring in a Thai boxing in a gym, next comes karateka action at a dojo 'Somewhere In Japan'. This is to establish that Bruce Ly/Rey Malonzo has been travelling throughout South East Asia to perfect his martial arts skills. Finally Bruce arrives at Manila airport before making his way home through the countryside. Since this is a martial arts film, he is randomly attacked along the way, first by a car full of jive talking guys with Afros, then by more extras on foot who look like regular Filipinos. This is followed by a woman in a sports car nearly running Bruce down and caking his nice white suit with mud; after his clothes had miraculously stayed clean throughout his previous fights. Back home Bruce's family and friends are having problems with hoods running a protection racket. They think Bruce could sort it out if he was around, which may or may not be the reason for him being attacked on the way back from Manila (although he hadn't told anyone he was heading home). Shortly afterwards Bruce's bag is found at the scene of a murder, but as Ly explains to the cops, obviously someone stole it and planted it there to implicate him in the crime. The dead man owned land the gangbangers who killed him want to take over, but his daughter Connie won't let them have it. Bruce gets in another fight then jumps into an open top car being driven by a chubby girl in shorts and a crop top. Bruce is skinny but muscled and often takes his shirt off; he makes all the women who show their bellies in this movie look out of condition.

Out in the country the chubby girl gives Bruce a blowjob; rather than showing anything explicit the director and editor cut between shots of Ly's ecstatic facial expressions and stock footage of a rooster. Given the kind of metaphors used for sexy and seductive women in the Filipino culture, we can safely conclude this scene doesn't represent a desire on Ly's part to indulge in animal abuse; one example of the rooster being used as a symbol of feminine wiles in Tagalog is found in the folk song *Sitsiritsit Alibangbang*, which describes a flirtatious woman with the words 'kung gumiri'y parang tandang' ('gyrates like a rooster' or 'sways her hips like a rooster'). The head shots of Bruce in ecstasy reminded me of Andy Warhol's famous short film *Blow Job* (1964), but with the stock footage cut into it, this becomes a parody of that art piece if we chose to ignore it's Filipino cultural context.

Ly leaves the girl asleep and takes her car so that he can drive back to his family. He finds they've all been slaughtered by unknown killers. Meanwhile, Andy the young son of the murdered man has been kidnapped and Bruce is accused of this crime. Out in the swamp that night the kidnapped boy stumbles towards the campfire Ly is chilling beside. Before Bruce can get the boy to safety someone shoots the kid. Bruce picks the boy up so he can get him medical attention but the police arrive before he can leave. When the boy dies without being able to verify Ly's story, our hero is arrested. Once he is banged up, Bruce fakes an injury and when the cop guarding him opens the cell to see what's up, Ly locks him in and escapes. Because Bruce wants to clear his name he goes to the plantation now owned by the dead boy's sister to investigate, and when he gets there pretends to be looking for work. Connie, the owner now that her father and brother have been murdered, thinks Bruce has been sent by Fidel and Linus to spy on her. That is until Fidel and Linus show up. The top man decides he can handle Bruce solo, however when Ly kicks him there is a shot of his lieutenant falling backwards before the fight with the boss continues to its inevitable conclusion with Ly's victory. After this Bruce battles and takes out the other man. Seeing Ly kick her enemies' butts, Connie is happy to employ him, but before long the cops turn up to arrest our hero so he has to trash them in another fight. Bizarrely the police wear cowboy hats and casual clothes, so they don't look anything like the filth.

Having escaped the long arm of the law, Ly moves along a beach fighting a succession of martial artists, including a fat sumo wrestler and a swordsman. Although nothing is made of it in terms of plot exposition, most of the fighters appear to be using Japanese martial arts, so this may remind some viewers that The Philippines was occupied by the Japanese military in World War II. During the Battle of Manila the city suffered some of the worst devastation seen anywhere during this inter-imperialist conflict, with much of it razed to the ground—alongside the massacre of between one hundred and five hundred thousand civilians by the Imperial Japanese Army, as well as the systematic gang rape of children by these fascist troops, war crimes for which commanding general Tomoyuki Yamashita and his chief of staff Akira Mutō were subsequently tried and executed. That said, Filipino martial arts films don't obsess on Japanese cruelty in the way that Korean and Hong Kong ones do—in part because The Philippines just doesn't have the long history of Japanese incursion and occupation that Korea and parts of China suffered; nonetheless there are plenty of Filipino World War II films featuring Japanese atrocities and brutality such as Eddie Romero's *Manila Open City* (1968).

Returning to the narrative of *Chaku Master*, the fights with the bad guys—Japanese or otherwise—are interrupted by a face-off between Bruce and one of the cops who wants to arrest him. During this martial encounter, Ly talks to the rozzer and convinces him that he saw the man who killed Andy, and that he is escaping. The cop stops fighting Bruce and together they go chasing after Fidel and Linus. The bad guys have hired a motorised bangka taxi boat to make their getaway, so Ly and the cop jump into a double outrigger taxi canoe with an outboard motor too. When the good guys' boat catches up with the bad guys' canoe, Bruce leaps from his bangka to the other one, and soon he's taking on one villain, while the cop is fighting the other. The movie ends when Ly kicks his foe into the water. The climatic fight taking place on two bangka taxi boats nicely signifies the hybridity of Filipino culture—representing as it does the Polynesian heritage of The Philippines, which is of course mixed with many other influences, but predominantly Chinese (represented by Bruce Lee and kung fu here), Spanish (most obvious in cast and crew names) and American (most glaringly represented in the Jeepnees seen in passing in this and so many other Filipino films).

The UK release of this flick removes all the nunchaku footage because the British censor at the time always cut such material. You'd have thought that a 'chuka master' movie with all the nunchuka scenes removed would transform this flick into an avant-garde classic; instead all the censor has done is mildly improve the film because the fights are so frequent and repetitive that trimming one and removing another improves the overall flow and experience. That said, there is nothing wrong with the five minutes or so removed from the UK cut, and in fact seeing Bruce throw his nunchucks up into the air so that they land in the twin chaku holsters on his back when he's finished using them looks seriously groovy.

Like *The Game of Death* (1974) with Ramon Zamora (not to mention Zamora's even earlier Bruce Lee parodies which date from 1972), this flick shows how the Filipino industry was quick off the mark when it came to the amplic phase of Brucesploitation and played a key role in shaping the genre and moving it away from bio-pics. Ly does the requisite come on gestures and stomping on opponents; not to mention playing a lead character called Bruce who is given to using nunchucks as his weapon of choice. Hong Kong and Korean film-makers took a year or two longer than those in Manila to understand what international audiences required in terms of fictional and fake Bruce Lee fodder.

While *Chaku Master* seems to be from 1974, some sources suggest 1976. It should also be noted that while Rey Malonzo seems to have been the first actor to be billed as Bruce Ly, he is not the only one. Malonzo (now a politician in The Philippines) should not be confused with Hong Kong based Henry Yu Yung who was billed as Bruce Ly in the American 'action' movie *Chinatown Connection* (1990). They don't look at all alike, and neither of them looks like Bruce Lee either!

4 THE GAME OF DEATH 1974
DIRECTED BY JUN GALLARDO

The flick uses the title of Bruce Lee's uncompleted final movie and is basically an ultra-low budget rip-off of *Enter the Dragon* (1973). It stars Ramon Zamora ('the Bruce Lee of the Philippines'), Evangeline Pascual (Miss Philippines 1973 and 1st runner up in Miss World 1973) and Eddie Garcia (who has appeared in more than 300 movies, as well as being a film director).

Zamora plays Charlie, a skilled martial artist and government agent, investigating the disappearance of various Filipino socialites. He participates in a karate competition in order to get invited to a more exclusive martial arts tournament on a private island owned by Colonel Von Stouffer (Eddie Garcia). Garcia has guards dressed in yellow suits a bit like those worn in *Enter the Dragon* (and which resemble karateka clothing but in an unusual colour), and acts out like Han in that Bruce Lee vehicle. Zamora eventually discovers that Garcia is holding various socialites and models hostage, and that all those who participate in his martial arts contest are killed (with the winner being stuffed and kept in a special cellar trophy room). Zamora persuades his fellow martial artists to fight back against Von Stouffer and his guards. The film ends by cloning *The Most Dangerous Game* (1932) as Von Stouffer armed with a crossbow hunts down Zamora, Pascual and some other 'hot chicks'; while the other fighters and another government agent battle it out with the rest of the guards. Good triumphs over evil in the end. Some of the martial arts on display are a little lacklustre, but Zamora is charismatic and does a good Bruce Lee impersonation in terms of hand gestures and facial ticks.

5 THE BLACK DRAGON'S REVENGE 1975

AKA *DEATH OF BRUCE LEE*

DIRECTED BY TONY LIU CHUN-KU

A rich Chinese man played by Phillip Ko wants to know who killed Bruce Lee. He pays Ron Van Clief AKA The Black Dragon $100,000 to go to Hong Kong and find the killer. Despite being given an air ticket, Van Clief decides to save on expenses in Hong Kong by staying with his buddy Charles Bonet AKA The Latin Panther. They are both Americans (albeit one is Afro-American and the other Latino) and know each other from Nam. Bonet has an antique shop and an assistant in the form of Addy Sung Gam-Loi. The Panther tells his friend he isn't interested in antiques and the shop is only a front; towards the end of the film one of the villains reveals in a throwaway remark that Bonet is actually an undercover agent. Meanwhile a group of martial arts students including Thompson Kao Kang and Yuen Qiu also view Lee's death as suspicious and are making their own enquiries into it.

Possibly because Bruce Lee's name has been rendered inaudible in many places on the soundtrack—apparently due to legal threats from his estate—it isn't until towards the end of the English dub that we discover these students belong to The Bruce Lee School in a throwaway remark from the top Hong Kong bad guy. The master at the Bruce Lee School is Chan Lau and, while he trains the students and offers wisdom, he never gets directly involved in their quest for the truth about Bruce Lee's death. Instead the sifu imparts wisdom such as: "The summer insect will never see the winter snow. The frog in the well will never know the vastness of the sky. He who has seen little admires much."

While shooting the shit about Lee's death, The Black Dragon and The Latin Panther flip through press coverage of Bruce with a bundle of publications covering The Little Dragon spread out on the table between them. Bonet: "There seems to be a lot of talk about his death and everyone seems to have his own story." Van Clief holding up a photograph of Lee in his coffin: "Man look at his face it doesn't even seem like the same person." Bonet: "Yeah it looks like he went through some changes." Van Clief: "He sure did. I think we better go to the house where he died." Bruce Lee passed away in Betty Ting Pei's bed, but here she is called Miss Tang and is played by another actress. I will refer to this character as Betty Ting Pei because that is who she is intended to represent—despite the disclaimer at the beginning of the flick about all the characters in it being fictional, including presumably both Bruce Lee and Ron Van Clief who plays himself.

After going to Betty's house and introducing themselves as 'friends of Bruce Lee'—on his DVD commentary for this movie, Van Clief says he'd known Lee in real life and it was Lee who gave him the name The Black Dragon—Ron and Charles are told she isn't in. The man looking after the house then makes a phone call which results in The Black Dragon and The Latin Panther being attacked in the street by three guys armed with blades and wooden poles. Bonet steps aside and lets Van Clief take them out bare handed. Some of Chan's students also go to Ting Pei's house but scarper when the cops show up. After a few more scenes we are introduced to the local big boss Lau Hok-Nin and he is mad at his goons for getting beaten by The Black Dragon. Chinese American actress Linda Ho gets a kick for not being present to sort things out; she's the gang's secret weapon, a seductress with poisonous serpents hidden in her handbag. One of the beaten hoodlums tries to explain the situation to Hok-Nin: "The black man he was good! In the cat stance he managed to hit me with the monkey fist boss!" A second defeated fighter backs this up: "He's good boss!" Hok-Nin spits back fake wisdom: 'One man, how good can he be? Beyond the high mountains there are even higher mountains yet!" Hok-Nin is placated when one of his goons says they've traced 'Bruce Lee's friends' back to Bonet's antique shop. And this is a typical Hollywood style action point —yes we're one-third into the movie when the Hok-Nin and Ho are introduced, and we discover the gangbangers have inside information on their foes. Immediately after this our two sets of heroes are introduced to each other.

All the main hero characters return to Ting Pei's house at night in an attempt to discover who killed Bruce Lee. Not knowing they are all on the same side, The Panther and The Dragon battle it out with Chan's students. The next day our American heroes go to the Chinese opera to talk to Miss Lee Kam because she knows Betty Ting Pei. While waiting, The Dragon gets into conversation with another Chinese actress who is blacked-up for a performance. Van Clief after running his finger over the woman's cheek: "Shoe polish?" Actress: "No, special Chinese make-up!" Then she touches The Black Dragon on the cheek and asks: "This make-up?" Van Clief shaking his head and smiling replies: "No baby it's the real shit."

When Miss Kam turns up, The Black Dragon says he's trying to find out who killed Bruce Lee, and the woman he presents flowers to tells him she's sorry but she can't help. Cut to Chan discussing Bruce Lee with his students: "Battle wounds can be cured, fate (is) incurable. The man has already died, to investigate his death you must first check the motive." Thompson: "But master, (inaudible—one of many places in which the word 'Lee' seems to have been removed after legal threats from the Little Dragon's estate) was a great kung fu man. Why should he take drugs to keep physically fit?" Chan: "That is not fact, only rumour." Second student: "People say he died of over-sex." Chan laughs: "Only a fool can make such a statement! Eating and mating are man's nature!" Thompson: "So I must find out the truth about his death." Cut back to the Chinese opera and Bonet speaking: "Miss Kam, do you know of any organisations who wanted him dead?" Kam: "No. I don't know." Van Clief: "I'd like to talk to Miss Tang. Can you tell me where I can find her?" Kam: "No, I don't know where she is… I think you might as well see my cousin. He's a reporter has written long stories about (the words here—Bruce Lee's—are deliberately rendered inaudible on the English dub) death but the newspapers refuse to print it…" Kam provides The Black Dragon with her cousin Wong Ping's telephone number before departing. However, Thompson and another of Chan's pupils get to a reporter who appears to be Kam's cousin before the Americans, and this man spins a wild yarn about Bruce Lee. Before doing so Wong Ping explains he will be killed if he reveals anything about the king of kung fu's demise, but still lets slip the following: "Drug dealers in order to expand their business have been trying to incorporate Bruce in the syndicate but he repeatedly turned them down. The Hong Kong drug king tried every method to get Bruce to work with them, they offered him everything money could buy, when he refused they threatened to kill him… when they could not buy him they used a expert way to kill him. Then they left traces of drugs to be found in his body. They did it in order to convince young people that their idol was a drug user and that's how he maintained his superb form…. I've told you enough, after all silence or six feet under leaves me with no choice." When Van Clief and Bonet go to meet Wong Ping, they are actually met by a gangbanger posing as the reporter and led into a trap, which they have to fight their way out of.

Next Chan and his students hear a rumour a martial artist accidentally killed Bruce with his iron fist, however they soon disprove this theory by beating him up. The logic here seems to be if they can easily defeat him, then he's obviously bullshitting when he claims he killed Bruce Lee. Van Clief and Bonet meet up with The Latin Panther's assistant, and Gam-Loi tells them Wong Ping was killed that morning. Next the gangbangers attack one of Chan's students and murder him. After this Chan's students discover The Black Dragon is on their side. When they consult their master, Chan tells them: "To find out the cause of Bruce Lee's death, this is the duty of all kung fu people. Now the Black Dragon is here. He is a mythical man. His martial art is great. Top man from the west. And of course four times world champion. He's the head instructor of twenty Black Dragon schools. An honourable young master. Now that he's here (words—Bruce Lee's deliberately rendered inaudible on soundtrack) death will receive much attention…. With his status The Black Dragon will probably work alone. Let's see how things develop before we get involved in it…"

Just in case we'd believed the disclaimer at the beginning of the film that all characters were fictional, here we get a more or less accurate run down of Van Clief's real world status in American martial arts, and this is one of the ways the film-makers let us know The Black Dragon is actually playing himself. Another way this is signified is by Van Clief spending much of the movie sporting a tight T-shirt with the words 'Ronnie Van Clief, Chief Instructor, Chinese Goju' circled around the logo of his martial arts school. The logo is a radiant red sun (reminiscent of the Japanese Rising Sun flag) against a black sky and with the green earth beneath, because Van Clief has combined Chinese and Japanese fighting systems with the fact he's saying it loud, he's black and proud and wants the colour scheme of the Pan-African flag on his school insignia. To clarify further I'm deliberately invoking a James Brown song in what I just said precisely because on his commentary for the DVD reissue of this film The Black Dragon claims to have done bodyguard work for this singer, as well as acting as his martial arts instructor. Winding back, there was an error in the editing out of Bruce Lee's name in the last speech I quoted and it was left in at one point but removed at another. Not that we need to hear the name, the visuals in the film make it obvious whose death is being investigated and talked about; not to mention the titles the flick sometimes went out under.

When The Black Dragon and The Latin Panther finally catch up with Miss Lena Tang AKA Betty Ting Pei and ask her about Bruce Lee's death, she tells them: "The truth is he died of an allergy as the doctor reported." This is what the real life coroner concluded about Lee's death, but Van Clief doesn't buy it from Betty, asking her: "Do you know why it was reported he died in a hospital instead of a house?" Of course, to protect Lee's image in Hong Kong there was an attempt to cover up the fact he'd died in Ting Pei's bed but this doesn't necessarily have to be turned into a conspiracy theory about how he died. The Black Dragon brings up fight and drug addiction rumours but gets nothing out of Betty. He concludes she'll talk later.

On the DVD commentary Van Clief says Bruce Lee was a heavy recreational drug user (mentioning pot and cocaine), and makes it clear that his view is the Little Dragon's death was brought about by a combination of high living and tough training, which proved too much for his body and killed him. Cutting back to the flick, the gangbangers murder The Latin Panther's assistant Gam-Loi, and as he isn't a kung fu fighter in this film, he's easy meat. The hoods' next victim is another of Chan's students, but he's a good martial artist, so Linda Ho has to help out by pulling a snake from her handbag and throwing it at him; the reptile kills him. Linda Ho laughs like a maniac as she watches her victim die. Then she changes from a brightly coloured ankle length dress to thigh high boots, skimpy white shorts and a blouse tied at the front to expose her midriff. Of course, Ho isn't the only character here who digs the hipster looks of the mid-seventies. The Black Dragon sports mutton-chop sideburns, tight tops, bellbottoms and sunglasses, all of which would look cool on a movie pimp. That said, it's Ho's attire and the body it is used to frame that attracts Bonet's attention as he returns home alone after helping the police over his assistant's death. Before The Latin Panther can say 'hola guapa como estas', Linda's gangbanging friends appear from nowhere to confront him. However not even weapon wielding kung fu hoods can beat the unarmed Bonet. This time Ho doesn't have her handbag full of serpents with her, so she pulls a blowpipe from her shorts and fires a poisoned dart into The Panther's neck. Bonet does some deep breathing and is able to fight on a bit longer before dropping dead. This is a two-thirds into the movie plot transition point, and with his best-friend/sidekick murdered, The Black Dragon now has the motivation to go nutzoid and kill the leaders of the gang in typical martial arts revenge-cum-vigilante style. The gangbangers with Linda Ho directing them attack Thompson and Qiu, just as The Black Dragon is coming home from identifying The Latin Panther's body. Chan's students are getting the better of the hoods until Ho deploys a snake and Thompson is bitten by it. Fortunately just after the tables have been turned on Chan's students, Van Clief jumps in.

In the melee, The Black Dragon is bitten by one of Ho's serpents, and this enables her and the other gangbangers to get away. Later Chan tends to Van Clief's wounds. There's some throwaway dialogue to show that the Betty Ting Pei character is under heavy manners from the gangbangers and to reintroduce earlier speculation about the causes of Bruce Lee's death. After this Hok-Nin makes it clear he wants top kung fu men hired to take out The Black Dragon and Chan's best students. Having hooked up with The Bruce Lee School, Van Clief trains alongside Thompson, Qiu and their friends. This trio go off to see Betty Ting Pei who has agreed to meet them but they find her drugged on the sofa in her home; this is not the house they were all trying to break into early on in the movie—maybe Betty moved. Moments later, Hok-Nin enters with a couple of thugs and The Black Dragon finally gets to call the gangbangers' Hong Kong boss a 'jive turkey'. After the obligatory insult, a fight breaks out with more and more goons appearing to battle our 'heroic trio'. When Linda Ho turns up, The Black Dragon gets to call her a 'fucking bitch' before giving her a smack in the mouth, this is after the snake she threw at him missed its target. After quite a bit more fighting with a slew of gangbangers, Van Clief takes out Hok-Nin. The Black Dragon goes back into the house and finds Phillip Ko who hired him to investigate Bruce Lee's death sitting inside with The Latin Panther's most valuable jade statue. Ko asks Van Clief if he can tell him who killed Bruce Lee, and The Black Dragon replies: "I don't think it's necessary."

After this The Black Dragon and Phillip Ko's climatic fight kicks off. Linda Ho regains consciousness, misses when she aims a blow dart at Van Clief, who pulls it from the wall beside him and throws it into the hand of a gunman who appears from nowhere; it's actually producer Serafim Karalexis, who has a small cameo as Ko's assistant. Taking time out from Ko, The Black Dragon knocks Ho to the ground and then stamps on her. She's presumably killed this time although the delivery of the final blow is out of shot. Returning to the big boss, the fight between The Black Dragon and Ko tumbles out of the house, around a swimming pool and along the beach. It also switches from unarmed combat, to weapons, and back to fists and feet. At one point Ko tries to run away but Van Clief magically appears in front of him. Having finally got the better of Ko, The Black Dragon grabs his head and twists it around on his shoulders so that he dies looking backwards—presumably something that many viewers at the time equated with Linda Blair's ability to twist her head when possessed in *The Exorcist* (1973). The sound effects that accompany this visual indicate the filmmakers want viewers to make this connection—in other words, Ko was 'a human devil'.

Finally the film is wrapped up with a scene featuring Van Clief, Chan, Thompson and Qui, which serves to underline Hollywood style that our trio of young heroes survived the final fight. Since the action during the climatic showdown focussed on The Black Dragon, inattentive viewers may not have noticed the other two battling alongside him were still alive. Van Clief addresses Chan: "Master all that I've told you and all that you know, what is the real reason for Bruce Lee's death?" Chan replies: "You asked a difficult question my son. That I can only answer you the words of my teacher and his teacher teacher (sic). In my search for the truth I was told that the sky has unexpected clouds and storms, and man has sudden fortune and misfortune. Nothing depends on man's own dream. His whole life is arranged by fate. Nature needs no weapon to kill a man, as you know there is only one way to be born but a hundred ways to die, and a path of death walks men of all ages, and you find out the universe is ruled by letting things alone."

This speech in faulty English is the perfect get-out clause. Those that don't believe Phillip Ko killed Bruce Lee can believe whatever else they want, he was killed by gangsters, he faked his own death, or even as the coroner found he had a fatal allergic reaction to a pain killer! My own view is despite all the flaws in the British legal system—no longer an issue in Hong Kong since it ceased to be a British colony twenty-four years after Bruce Lee died—in this instance the coroner probably got it right. Despite holes in the plot (the Betty Ting Pei character for instance is left comatose—maybe even dead—on her sofa, and we never find out whether or not she recovers), the narrative is over linear and too close to Hollywood conventions for my taste. The wisdom dished out by Chan seems closer to the philosophy imparted to David Carradine by his Shaolin masters in the American TV series *Kung Fu* (popular at the time this film was made) than anything in those Hong Kong action films which were happily bereft of occidental producers and/or scriptwriters. I wish to underline that similar criticisms might be made about the 'reflective' dialogue in *Enter the Dragon.* Nonetheless this is a relatively early film exploiting the rumours that circulated about Bruce Lee's death and Van Clief is charismatic in a calmer and much less cocky way than say Jim Kelly or indeed his apparent acquaintance whose death warrants the ninety minutes of celluloid under review here.

Despite the fact that the investigation into Lee's death is mostly an excuse for a series of enjoyable set-piece action sequences, and there are no obvious Bruce Lee clones or imitators (some see The Latin Panther as such, but I don't), *The Black Dragon's Revenge* nevertheless belongs to the core of the Brucesploitation genre because of its relentless and very sleazy desire to run with the scummiest rumours about the Little Dragon's death, while attempting to placate his more conservative fans by explaining away Lee's apparent use of cannabis.

6 *BRUCE LEE AGAINST SUPERMEN* 1975

AKA *BRUCE LEE VS THE SUPERMEN*
AKA *SUPERDRAGON VS SUPERMAN*

DIRECTED BY WU CHIA-CHUN

Riffing on Bruce Lee's role as Kato in *The Green Hornet* television series, what we have here is Bruce Li starring as 'Carter'. This seems to be both a homage to and a burlesque of 1960s American TV, mid-century superhero movie serials and early silent cinema along the lines of Louis Feuillade's *Les Vampires.*

Pre-credits Bruce Li appears in a reasonable approximation of Bruce Lee's Kato uniform from *The Green Hornet* TV show. This is followed by a credit sequence that also immitates the original show. Post-credits 'Carter' and The Green Hornet (when he appears which isn't much) wear either groovy seventies menswear or a red superhero costume that bears no relationship to the uniforms sported by Britt Reid/Van Williams and Kato/Bruce Lee in the 1960s TV series (and this gear has nothing to do with the 1940s *Green Hornet* movie serials released by Universal Pictures either).

The plot revolves around the attempts of a criminal gang to kidnap Dr. Ting who has come up with a formula for producing cheap food from petroleum. Since this is an exploitation movie, the villains are obliged to spy on Dr Ting's daughter Alice skinny-dipping before attempting to kidnap her father. Fortunately when the kidnap attempt is made, Carter and one of his kung fu buddies are coming home in a taxi just as the villains are making their getaway. There follows a really slow car chase in which not even the speed limit is broken. Finally the cabbie is directed to take a short cut. Carter and his buddy lie in the road and the gangsters stop to help them. Carter and his mate beat up the bad guys and rescue Dr Ting and his daughter Alice. This is followed by a romantic interlude between Carter and Alice. The chief gangster is really mad about Carter meddling in his affairs so he hires a hitman to knock him off. The sniper misses and Carter goes after him on a really long foot chase, until the gunman falls to his death from the top of an under construction building. The crime boss then hires superman (no not the caped crusader but a kung fu calligraphist in a black suit and with a white towel functioning as a cape over his shoulders) and his students for "$100,000 cash, ten nice girls, and a truck full of booze!" However before superman can challenge the superdragon, the bad guys send a girl to seduce Carter. While Bruce Li is doing the shag nasty with this sexual wonder woman, they kidnap Dr. Ting. Realising her father is missing, Alice goes searching for Carter and finds him in bed with another woman. Jealousy overcomes her and temporarily forgetting about her father, Alice indulges in a catfight with her love rival; they rip each other's outer clothes so that we can see their underwear and inevitably end up in a shower. Meanwhile Dr Ting is tortured—this consists of stage lights being directed at him while his hair is pulled. To show how painful this is his face is stretched and distorted in a cheap and cheesy special effect. Chastised by Alice, Carter takes her in a rickshaw to a rendezvous with the bad guys who need her father's medicine to prevent him dying. After Alice is picked up by a car at the meet, Carter follows all the while dragging his rickshaw behind him. Alice is used as bait to get her father to agree to give the villains his formula, then kept prisoner and sexually assaulted. Carter uses his rickshaw to rescue doctor Ting, and then has to fight superman and his students.

After some typical kung fu movie tricks involving speeded up and reversed film, Carter cuts off superman's manhood. Superman's students no longer want to fight because they've discovered their teacher is being paid but he isn't giving them any of the dosh. The Green Hornet who has been largely absent appears to make a final mop up of the bad guys.

Although the early parts of *Bruce Lee Against Superman* are plodding, it is still one of Bruce Li's better efforts since it isn't hampered by the realist tropes that result in so many of his later movies coming across as dull and conventional.

7 THE DRAGON DIES HARD — 1975

AKA *BRUCE LEE WE MISS YOU*

DIRECTOR LI KUAN-CHANG

This movie tells the story of Stone (Bruce Li), who is devastated when he learns Bruce Lee has died. He drowns his sorrys in drink, until Bruce Lee appears to him either in visions or as a ghost. Stone then decides he has to investigate Lee's death.

First port of call is Betty Ting Pei who seems to be called Betty Ching in the dubbed dialogue. Betty clearly wants to seduce Stone and freaks out at one point about how much he looks like Bruce Lee. Before Betty has the opportunity to screw Stone, she gets a phone call from a gangster telling her to dump the boy. Stone pursues the truth, which results in the gangsters attacking his kung fu school.

He eventually gets Betty to describe Bruce's death in her apartment. It seems Lee was a victim of the touch of death or dim mak or quivering palm technique. A martial master gave him a special strike that killed him later. This isn't explained in words in the English dub, the film-makers presumably assumed the audience were sophisticated enough work this out from a combination of the visuals and prior knowledge There were rumours at the time of Lee's death he'd been a victim of dim mak. Like other mythical martial arts techniques, dim mak doesn't actually work and in this instance the term originated in wuxia fiction.

Returning to *The Dragon Dies Hard,* in the shots of Bruce Lee jumping around Betty's bed before he dies, a dark bruise is shown on his body, and that alongside his bizarre expiration antics are best explained by the touch of death. Having discovered the truth about who killed Bruce Lee, Stone then battles the gangsters who mistake the clone for his idol. They think the Little Dragon must have survived their attempt to murder him because he'd refused to participate in their fixed martial arts matches. Since Lee never participated in matches and only did demonstrations this isn't exactly convincing as an explanation for his attempted 'murder'. But then neither is his death scene or his cause of death in this movie.

The best things about *The Dragon Dies Hard* are the sleazy portrayal of Betty Ting Pei, alongside Bruce Lee having the most insane demise in movie history! Bruce appearing in visions and showing Stone how to fight may have inspired the ghost training scenes in *No Retreat, No Surrender* (1986). On the Asia Video DVD I have of this under the title *Bruce Lee We Miss You* there are long sections of silence and black between some scenes bringing to mind Guy Debord's *Screams In Favour of De Sade* (1952).

8 GOODBYE BRUCE LEE, HIS LAST GAME OF DEATH — 1975

AKA *THE NEW GAME OF DEATH*

DIRECTORS LIN BING AND HAROLD B. SWARTZ

This was one of a number of films that attempted to pass themselves off as Bruce Lee's unfinished final film *Game of Death* before the official version was released in 1978.

Goodbye Bruce Lee was co-produced between Taiwan and the German company Atlas Films. It stars Bruce Li and starts with this clone being recruited to finish Lee's *Game of Death.* It then runs through a fictional version of this final and unfinished Little Dragon film with Li acting as stand in. The fights are tedious and the film lacks any sleaze factor. When Li fights his way up the Pagoda of Death at the end of the film, encountering a different fighter on each floor, he sports a baggy version of the yellow and black one-piece tracksuit Bruce Lee had been seen wearing in publicity stills for *Game of Death.*

In combat with a swordsman, camera edits are used to give the illusion that Li jumps from one side of the room to the other in the blink of an eye. This fakery so incenses the swordsman he starts slashing at himself because he can't make contact with Li's body. The painted backdrop showing the sky 'outside' on the different levels of the pagoda is so patently fake it will make your jaw drop.

This is a really mediocre flick, which might have been more entertaining if it had been made on an even lower budget. In the English dubs there are two quite different openings. The beginning used on the Region 1 US DVD issued by Legacy makes use of a filmed interview with Kareem Abdul-Jabbar but lacks the fight footage he shot with Bruce Lee for *Game of Death.* Further celebrity elements are provided by quotes from actor Steve McQueen about Bruce Lee. Unfortunately despite using Abdul-Jabbar and Lee to make anti-racism points, this intro still stinks of cultural imperialism.

Screenwriter, producer and Bruce Lee's pre-fame friend/collaborator Stirling Silliphant is quoted as saying: "Bruce was more than just a single success story. He represents a whole race finally being accepted in films." Of course this is only true from a Hollywood perspective. In places like Shanghai and Hong Kong there had been no parallel history of Chinese actors encountering racist blockages to cinematic success. Silliphant's refusal to acknowledge that non-Hollywood cinema exists is worse than stupid.

The slightly shorter opening used on the British Region 2 DVD issued by Arrow simply shows Bruce Li being recruited to play the Little Dragon and has a better edit of him performing gymnastics to demonstrate his athletic skills. This is one of the most boring Brucesploitation flicks ever made—although the official *Game of Death* does give it a run for its money on this score!

9 Bruce Lee: His Last Days, His Last Nights 1976

AKA *Bruce Lee and I*
AKA *I Love You, Bruce Lee*

Directed by John Law Ma

This is a beautifully surreal film, even if commercial considerations resulted in too great an emphasis on Bruce Lee and the inclusion of too many fight scenes. Danny Lee gives a good performance as the Little Dragon, but there is too much of him. Betty Ting Pei appears as both herself and her fictional double. Ting Pei's life is rewritten as if she really were one of the characters she'd previously played in a string of mildly risqué melodramas. The obvious clue about what's going on in this flick are the divergent depictions of the death of Bruce Lee at the beginning and end.

First time around Betty and Bruce make love on Ting Pei's bed, although whenever there is female nudity we can't see the female star's face so it is safe to assume a body double was used. After sex Betty emerges from the shower and finds Bruce dead on the bed. When Bruce dies at the end of the film, Betty is dressed up to go out to a party where she'll sign a big film contract. This time Betty and Bruce haven't made love. Instead the Little Dragon suddenly goes into an epileptic fit and dies. These two versions of the death of Betty's lover make her an unreliable postmodern narrator in a film whose pure surface is used as a mirror to reflect the delusions of fanboys back at them.

Clearly nothing in the movie is to be taken at face value. A further framing device is Ting Pei drowning her sorrows in a bar, when a gang of Bruce Lee fans come in to beat her up but fortunately the barman is able to throw them out and lock Betty in with him. Betty spends the night telling the bartender a tale of woe. Rather than relating the actual story of Ting Pei's life, she provides her onscreen confidant with a fictional version. In this flick she grew up with no one to help or support her, whereas in real life she came from a wealthy and well connected family. Instead of the true story of Betty having made six movies in Taiwan and then being spotted by Shaw Brothers who signed the actress up and brought her to Hong Kong, here she pretends that as a naïve teenage girl she was drugged and stripped naked by an exploitative film producer, who took compromising photos of her that were subsequently used to try and blackmail her into doing sex scenes on camera. Since in this fictional story Betty doesn't want to go nude on set, she fails to complete her first film in Taiwan, fleeing instead to Hong Kong where the abusive film producer catches up with her; he has his thugs smack Betty around in the street until the then unknown Bruce Lee intervenes and beats up the hoods. It seems that Betty and Bruce were actually introduced to each other by Raymond Chow. Rather than being portrayed as the successful Shaw Brothers star she actually was, in the film Betty becomes a high-class prostitute catering to the needs of rich men. For this fiction once Bruce Lee has become a famous movie idol, Ting Pei sees him in a restaurant and approaches him, but he thinks she's just a fan so she runs away. Realising that Ting Pei is the girl he helped out before he made it, Lee goes chasing after her. Gradually an affair develops between them, but when the course of true love fails to run smoothly, Betty becomes addicted to gambling. Betty's casino debts cause her more problems with thugs, but Bruce is able to sort them out with his kung fu heroics.

However, it isn't just Betty who is wilfully fictionalised here into a Bruce Lee fanboy's fantasy of who and what she is or was, the Little Dragon is given a mythological make-over too. This flick self-consciously sends up fan stereotypes about Betty and Bruce and shows that the world they found themselves living in as a consequence of senseless adulation was a very empty gilded cage. Bruce's wife and kids are mentioned but never shown. They don't seem to be in Hong Kong during the days and nights Bruce and Betty spend together in the movie, but they were there with Bruce in real life. As a part of this make-believe world, Bruce's apartment is filled with huge pop art style images of himself, mirrors and gym equipment. It is way more stylish and less cluttered than his actual Hong Kong home as seen in various documentaries. Likewise comparing Betty's movie set flat with footage of her actual pad at 67 Beacon Hill Road, we can once again see that the fictionalised setting is considerably more glamorous than the real one. That said, Ting Pei's Beverley Heights apartment was part of a relatively exclusive complex, and Lee really was living a highly privileged suburban life in his gated mansion at 41 Cumberland Road in Kowloon Tong. Nonetheless, these real life movie star residences look squalid when compared to the colourful and beautifully filmed interiors of their fantasy doubles as depicted in this film.

When Betty finishes telling her story, the gang of Bruce Lee fans are still waiting to beat her up, but when they attempt to do so the barman takes them all out in yet another kung fu fight. The point here is, of course, that Bruce Lee as we know him is simply the creation of fan fantasies, and these could be projected onto anyone, including the bartender who saves Betty. What this film allows Ting Pei to do is tell the world in fictional form that she was indeed Bruce Lee's lover, something others pressurised her into denying when she was interviewed about it at the time; since many believed she had been Bruce Lee's girlfriend, this just led to her being seen as a liar.

While Ting Pei's portrayal of herself is on one level tongue in cheek, in other ways it is tragic. By the time this was made Betty had been horrifically vilified by both Bruce Lee fanboys and the media, something that continues to this day, at least among the fanboys; she must have known that many would claim the obviously fictional version of Bruce Lee in this movie was disrespectful, while taking the fantasy version of the female lead as being a factual representation of who she was. While one might see elements of masochism or even self-aggrandisement at work here, for me Ting Pei's decision to do the movie is an expression of her grief; it provided her with a rare opportunity to express in public what she really felt about a man she deeply loved. When we lose someone extremely close, we often blame ourselves and obsess on what we might have done differently that would have avoided the death.

Needless self-blame in these situations is common, and it was surely almost impossible for Ting Pei to resist the urge to behave in this way when she was being endlessly trolled and turned into a scapegoat by both rabid fanboys and the press. Likewise Ting Pei was bullied by powerful Hong Kong film industry figures into not revealing publicly the real nature of her relationship with Lee, and indeed immediately after this death even that he'd actually died at her home. She was browbeaten to the extent that aside from her involvement in this obviously fictional film, she remained silent on the matter for forty years. While I understand how it is possible to watch this movie and find Ting Pei amusingly sleazy, I don't think that's the best reading of what's going on. When you think about the fact that Ting Pei's relationship with Lee got virtually no sympathetic public acknowledgement after his death, then it becomes clear she isn't demeaning herself here at all, she is using the film as an outlet for her love and grief.

Bruce Lee: His Last Days, His Last Nights is simultaneously a postmodern parody of fan fantasies and an extremely moving expression of loyalty and love on Ting Pei's part. In order to fully appreciate this it is better to watch the Hong Kong edit of the film and skip the butchered American re-cut. Looking at what the press and Bruce Lee fanboys have to say about this movie is to expose yourself to a tidal wave of misogyny. Ron Van Clief, for example, has not been subjected to anything like the same level of abuse for taking the lead role in the movie that is best known as *The Black Dragon's Revenge* (1975), a celluloid outing that is extremely cynical as regards its exploitation of Bruce Lee's death. The contempt and hatred the fanboys have for a woman who loved their idol as whole heartedly as Ting Pei obviously did, says a lot about the twisted nature of the relationship between celebrities their 'admirers' from afar. Even if you don't accept that Ting Pei was Lee's lover, which I do, it is clear she was very close to him and the way in which both she and this movie have been treated is disgraceful.

While Bruce Lee isn't responsible for his fans, and would doubtlessly be mortified by the way they've treated Ting Pei, as someone who obsessively pursued fame, he may have deserved the fanboys he got but his lover did not. Of course, Ting Pei did not need to be Lee's real life lover for this film to work as a parody of fan fantasies. *Bruce Lee: His Last Days, His Last Nights* clearly belongs to the core of the Brucesploitation genre, although at the same time it is not really an exploitation film at all but (among other things) an attack on the delusional beliefs fans hold about their idols. It is the reception of this film as much as anything else that makes it Brucesploitation.

10 BRUCE LEE: THE MAN, THE MYTH 1976
AKA *BRUCE LEE TRUE STORY*
DIRECTOR NG SZE-YUEN

This Bruce Li vehicle had a bigger budget than most other Brucesploitation movies, and the money spent on it helps lift it above the bland as a slice of processed cheese rut the lead actor Bruce Li fell into for much of his short film career, and this despite the flick suffering from a lack of sleaze.

One of the things that keeps this bio-pic surreal is the fact that despite spending money location shooting in American, Rome and Thailand, everyone is geared up in groovy mid-seventies threads. Since the film starts with Bruce Lee in Hong Kong in the fifties and moves on to the Seattle and San Francisco in the early sixties, we are obviously living in an eternal and very funky seventies 'present', where 'real' as opposed to 'reel' history counts for nothing. The mythological aspects of the film are continued in the endless street fights and other entirely fictional battles the Little Dragon engages in. Bruce Li's exercise regime is nonetheless problematic, he has expensive weight training machines so he can't really compromise on movement, but the constant fast paced repetitions seem a bit silly. The real Bruce Lee would have varied the speeds and used more muscular control. Li also subjects himself to severe electric shocks as part of his training, which is a nice touch in an exploitation movie, especially as the real life Little Dragon was a sucker for this muscle development gimmick. A Betty Ting Pei character only appears in the looped opening and closing 'medical emergency' scene, which shows Bruce innocently going through the script of *Game of Death*, rather than engaging in some sexual freakery at the starlet's apartment.

Tacked on at the end is brief footage that suggests Bruce faked his death and will reappear as a public figure in 1983 (he didn't). Bruce Li's acting is a better in this than most of his movies, so maybe he had a coach. His fights are reasonably choreographed too.

All the UK Region 2 releases I've seen of *The Man, the Myth* cut out the nunchacku fights in Rome, which makes for a surreal win for Bruce who beats his opponents with no more than a very sudden jump cut. Of course, for English language speakers, it's easy enough to get hold of American Region 1 versions of the movie that include this action.

11 BRUCE'S DEADLY FINGERS 1976

AKA *BRUCE'S FINGERS*

DIRECTED BY JOSEPH VELASCO

In this movie Bruce Wong (Bruce Le) arrives in Hong Kong from the USA to track down the Little Dragon's *Kung Fu Finger Book;* he wants to prevent this secret and deadly fighting style from being appropriated by bad guys. There are subplots involving the sale of Wong's sister into prostitution and later her kidnap—but these are really just an excuse to include various unpleasant but nonetheless fairly common seventies sexploitation elements such as a nude woman being tortured with a lizard which is dropped between her legs, and gang rapes taking place within a circle of fire. However, what really matters is the *Kung Fu Finger Book!*

A crime boss and his gangbangers are after Bruce Lee's *Kung Fu Finger Book,* which is why Le must rescue it. Le's Wing Chun sifu in the film is played by Wong Shum Leung, who taught Wing Chun and it is said gave Bruce Lee more kung fu instruction than their joint master Ip Man. A whole scene is built around Le breaking a teacup that allegedly belonged to Ip Man. There are also the usual sleazy nightclub and Hong Kong poverty row locations. Bolo Yeung (who appeared with Bruce Lee in *Enter the Dragon*) and Nora Miao (who gave Lee his only screen kiss and appeared in *The Big Boss, Fist of Fury* and *Way of the Dragon*) have supporting roles; as do Brucesploitation regulars Michael Chan Wai-Man and Chiang Tao. We even have Lo Lieh from *King Boxer* (1972) as the boss villain. Bruce Le sports oversized shades and a mop top hairstyle and wears tight wife-beater vests and tracksuit bottoms in almost the same colours as Bruce Lee's iconic *Game of Death* (1978) jumpsuit. Le also indulges in lots of iconic Bruce Lee gestures like nose thumbing. When he recovers the *Kung Fu Finger Book* he even gets to learn the iron finger technique and using a tip from Wong Shum Leung finally defeats Lo Lieh.

The point of this movie seems to be to get the actors in the dubbed version to say the word 'finger' as many times as possible—presumably because it works as a double entendre by referring to both a kung fu technique and a sexual act. In short, *Bruce's Deadly Fingers* is a sleaze classic!

12 EXIT THE DRAGON, ENTER THE TIGER 1976

AKA *STAR OF STARS*

DIRECTOR LEE TSO-NAM

Bruce Li stars as the Little Dragon's friend/disciple investigating the martial artist's death. There is some tastelessly used stock footage of Bruce Lee's funeral and a great scene of a go-go dancer in a night club which brings to my mind the similar (but superior) footage of Barbara Bouchet in Fernando di Leo's *Milano Calibro 9* (1972). The go-go dancer, like Bouchet in Di Leo's Italian gangster movie, is scantily dressed in a gold bikini! More sleaze comes in the form of having film star Suzy Yung (the Betty Ting Pei character) and her actress friends used as drug mules by the mob. This is achieved in part by addicting some of them to heroin. There is a hilarious scene of a one of Suzy's friends going through an enforced cold turkey treatment as a form of torture, which is ridiculously over-acted.

Unfortunately as the film progresses the sleaze elements start to be eclipsed by fight scenes rather than balanced against them. The idea that Bruce Lee was murdered by gangsters because he refused to be their drug mule is patently absurd but sadly that and the far-out seventies décor aren't enough to prevent the blandest clone of all time turning this into a snooze fest. The tape Suzy Yung has recorded to expose the truth about Bruce Lee's death is the

MacGuffin around which much of the plot swirls and while ridiculous, this might have made for an entertaining flick had the woman whose bed Bruce Lee died in been portrayed as less prim and proper.

13 COBRA   1977
Directed by Joseph Velasco and/or Rempo Urip

This opens with Bruce Lei/Steve Lee (his character name here is Indra) practicing martial arts on the beach; his master throws rocks at him and he has to defend himself while *Magic Fly* by Space plays on the soundtrack. The sifu goes home to his daughter Yanti but this quiet domestic scene is interrupted by the arrival of Wong Kwok-Leung (Tobias in the movie) who is armed with a trident that has three cobra heads. The master hasn't seen Wong in twenty years and he makes it clear they didn't part on the best of terms. Wong demands that Lee's master agrees to be his friend but since this isn't about to happen, the intruder attacks the man he wants to chum up to. Before departing, Wong easily defeats some of the old man's martial arts students. The mortally wounded master calls his daughter who has been pushed to the ground, she is told to go and get Lee. The old man tells his daughter and surviving pupil to go away together. Lee is not to try and get revenge because he isn't a good enough fighter to defeat Wong. Yanti and Lee move to Jakarta and start a family. However Lee is unable to get work because he's an uneducated country boy who never went to school. Walking the streets looking for a job, Lee sees several carfuls of Scorpion gangbangers attacking two Cobra men. Lee jumps in because the chauffeur is being beaten up and the hoods look like they're about to get his boss too. It is Wong who is sitting on the back seat of the car failing to deploy any of the fearsome kung fu he displayed when he murdered Lee's master. Wong thanks Lee and gives him an address where he can get work.

However, the second-in-command requires Lee to prove himself, so he has to fight and defeat a bunch of gangbangers. One called Dira cuts Lee deeply in the leg but still loses and finds himself hanging off a cliff. When Lee helps him to safety they become firm friends. A woman called Linda tends to Lee's wounds and asks him about his wife. Like Dira she's a stray sympathetic character among the mob, most of whom are psychopaths. Lee is given money and is left wondering what he has to do. It turns out to be smuggling, but there are also scores to be settled which involve murder. Lee doesn't see a hood who objected to the killing of women and children being chastised, this man runs out of the gang's HQ but is killed by the second-in-command's main enforcer Chan Lau (Sugara in the movie). This sequence is really bizarrely shot and edited; it starts with the camera showing a carved wooden figure but side on and then the picture tilts around to upright and we see Lau emerging from behind it. There is a cut to Lau inflicting mortal wounds on the renegade gang-banger with high kicks—the edits switch between the foot hitting the victim in the face and Lau without the victim in frame, with no long shot to clarify what's happening. The action may or may not be more easily decipherable on versions of *Cobra* that haven't been panned and scanned, but the way it is cut together on the full screen Kung Fu Theatre DVD makes it look like Lau was filmed in Hong Kong and the other actor in Jakarta, with a body double for Lau's foot. That said, when Lau's victim stumbles mortally wounded back into the gang HQ we get the two of them in the same shot, even if Lau is now wearing tinted glasses that were absent from his immediately preceding sequence. Regardless of what extra information there is, this must look odd in widescreen too. I'd guess some longer shots were taken but as there are focus issues elsewhere in the film, these may have been too poor to use. This is one of the most bizarre edits I've seen of a kung fu murder when cut-and-paste from disparate sources was apparently not required.

Moving on, Linda forgets to turn the hot tap on when she runs the second-in-command a bath, so when he gets in—wearing his swimming trunks, doh!—the cold water gives him rheumatic pain. To punish Linda, the second-in-command shoves her onto her knees and plunges her head repeatedly into the cold bath water. It's at this point that the gang have a party with lots of girls present. One couple head into a bedroom decorated with what look like posters of seventies pop or film stars, these aren't too clear on the Kung Fu Theatre DVD but some might be glam rockers, while others are less flamboyant. The guy gets the girl's top off and there is a softcore scene on the bed. The camera grabs a very short and presumably unagreed shot of one of the actress's nipples. There are the usual cut-aways to naked calves and female hands clutching the bedsheets—but to spice this up the film also flips back and forth between two nude female pin-ups, one of a Caucasian and one of an Oriental model. The best thing about the interior of the gang's HQ is that here their three headed cobra symbol is prominently displayed, and it looks like a simplified and much improved version of the Symbionese Liberation Army logo; it may just be my ignorance that prevents me from identifying this as an ancient design from Indonesia or elsewhere that pre-dates the SLA logo by hundreds—or even thousands—of years.

Although Lee and his family are moving up in the world and now live in style rather than poverty, both he and Dira are having doubts about their life in the gang and both want to leave it. As Dira has no wife or family of his own, he spends a lot of time with Lee's, but the two men have to be on call to do the second-in-command's bidding whenever he needs them. Lee feels bad he isn't around much for his daughter Fifi, especially when he's called away from her birthday party. Eventually he is tricked into killing one of the gang's targets, which he essentially does in self-defence. After this our hero is shown sleeping in bed with an image of his boss crudely superimposed on him to illustrate the nightmares he's suffering. There is another attempt at faking a nude scene, this time it's Lee talking to Yenti through the frosted class door of a shower, she has her back to us and the image isn't all that clear but we can still see she is wearing panties. A couple of Cobra hoods watch Lee leave the house, then try to kidnap his daughter but she runs upstairs to her mommy. Since Lee's family aren't co-operative, one of the thugs holds the girl out of the window and threatens to drop her. Fifi bites his hand and so he lets go and she falls to her death. As the kidnap attempt—part of a plot to get Lee to do the gang's bidding—has gone wrong, the hoods decide they'd better kill Yenti too, so they smoother her. One hood hangs back. He's looking at Yenti's corpse. There are a series of cuts between the gangbanger's eyes and the dead woman's exposed cleavage—which is visible in the gap between the sides of her dressing gown.

Finally the man's shadow falls over this part of the body. The implication is he rapes the dead woman's corpse although this isn't explicitly shown. This is accompanied by some whacked out music cues that are more typical of horror than martial arts films. When Lee gets home he finds Yenti and his daughter dead, and a Scorpion gang jacket lying beside his wife—left by the Cobra thugs to implicate the target they want Lee to take out. The Cobra second-in-command and his men turn up for Yenti and Fifi's funeral, happy to see Lee blaming the Scorpion gang and wanting revenge. Fifi's grave gives us the time frame for the movie, since it bears the dates 21 May 1974 to 9 February 1978—since the start of the film is about a year before her birth, this would be 1973.

Dira has been beaten up by the gang, and he has concealed himself near Yenti and Fifi's graves, once Lee is alone he approaches him and explains that the Cobra gang are responsible for the murder of our anti-hero's wife and daughter. Lee and Dira go after their own gang, and the first to cop it are the two who carried out the murder of Yenti and Fifi. Linda emerges from the gang HQ as Lee and Dira arrive. She tells Lee that the second-in-command's weakness is cold water because he has rheumatism, then she walks the injured Dira away to tend his wounds.

There are three climatic fights but the first is presented as two encounters involving first Lau and then his twin brother. Having a character seemingly rise from the dead is more of a horror than a martial arts film trope and this is effectively what happens with Lau. If the scriptwriter and director really intended us to accept the non-horror rationalisation that Lau's identical twin appears to avenge him immediately after his death, they would have made it clear Lau had a gangbanging twin before he copped it. Instead both the actors imported from the world of Hong Kong films—Lau and Wong—are treated as bogeyman figures who can't be killed; they are used to introduce elements of the macabre and fantastic, and turn this into a martial arts/horror crossover. The first time Lau dies he is impaled on a ship's anchor used as decoration in the gang house; this is his horror film despatch. Bogeyman Lau then resurrects and posing as his twin battles Lee using a triple staff, or three poles joined together by chains.

Eventually our anti-hero succeeds in strangling Lau with the coiling dragon staff that was being deployed against him, and this looks and feels rather like a riff on Bruce Lee defeating Dan Inosanto in the official *Game of Death* (1978) by strangling him with nunchaku (two short sticks joined by a chain). This is Lau's martial arts death. Since the Inosanto footage was shot in 1972 and descriptions of what happened in this and the other scenes made at the same time circulated for several years before the film was commercially released, this is definitely a case of Steve Lee copying Bruce Lee, and not the other way around.

What happens next in *Cobra* resembles something that Robert Clouse shot to 'complete' Bruce Lee's *Game of Death;* the second-in-command momentarily fools Steve Lee into thinking a dummy is his corpse. Since *Cobra* seems to have been made and released before the additional *Game of Death* material was all in the can, and Clouse's official version appears to plunder a number of Brucesploitation movies for ideas, this may be a film that manages to rip-off *Game of Death,* while simultaneously being a source plagiarised by it.

While most English language sources give the release date for *Cobra* as 1981, that seems to be the year in which the English dub was made. The Film Indonesia website, which is probably a more reliable guide in this instance, says it was released in 1977. One assumes that Fifi's grave would provide a death date shortly after the film was completed so that it didn't appear to be yesterday's news; since she dies in February 1978, to me this indicates the movie probably reached Indonesian cinemas in 1977. If the original Indonesian release uses the same music cues as the English dub, then the film couldn't have appeared before 1977 because *Magic Fly* by Space was first issued and became a massive international hit that year. Returning to the second-in-command, he attacks Lee with an orange suitcase that turns into a deadly weapon when blades emerge from it. Lee leads the second-in-command to the sea and by throwing the suitcase (that contains crucial documents) towards the water, tricks him into the cold swell where his rheumatism weakens him and he can be defeated. However, things are not wrapped up yet because Wong appears and reveals he knew all along whose pupil Lee was.

The final battle apparently concludes with Wong disappearing under the water, so Lee starts wading towards the shore. But before our anti-hero can reach dry land, Wong leaps out of the sea from behind him, and we are left with a freeze frame of this bogeyman pouncing at Lee's back. This ending seems more like something out of the *Friday the 13th* horror franchise than a martial arts epic, which isn't so surprising since the flick belongs to both these genres. Given that Steve Lee mugs Bruce Lee in many fight scenes, and that elements from various Bruce Lee films are worked into the fight with Lau—including a brief part of it being shown in a mirror, invoking the climatic fight in *Enter the Dragon*—I'd place *Cobra* at the core of the Brucesploitation genre.

This is another film with misleading opening credits, the director is not Joseph Velasco as is stated on the English language version (which also wrongly gives 1981 as the year of production/release); this is the final film of about thirty made by Rempo Urip over the course of a forty-year career. I don't know much about the star Steven Lee, but P. T. Insantra Film who produced the English language version of *Cobra* chose to credit him as Bruce Lei, and just possibly when they list Bruce Lei as martial arts director on *The Fierce Boxer* (1977), they are invoking the same actor/fighter. Steve Lee also starred in *The Steel Fisted Dragon* (1977), and according to the Film Indonesia website had a supporting role in *Sex dan Kriminal* (1996, *Sex and Criminals*). To further compound the confusion surrounding this film and its false credits, Best Film and Video (VHS 1998) and Kung Fu Theatre (DVD 2006) both released Region 1 English language versions of it with covers falsely marketing it as a Bruce Le vehicle. That particular clone does not appear in this movie, despite having his picture on the front of both these releases, the star here as should already be clear is Bruce Lei/Steve Lee.

14 THE DRAGON LIVES AGAIN   1977
AKA *DEADLY HANDS OF KUNG FU*
DIRECTED BY LAW KEI

After his death, Bruce Lee (Bruce Liang) lies unconscious in purgatory and the King of the Underworld, his queens and various flunkies, are fixated on the fact the kung fu movie star apparently has an enormous hard-on. What the onlookers believe is Bruce's extra-large pork sword, presumably still stiff for Betty Ting Pei, turns out to be his nunchucks. Bruce wakes up to his afterlife and immediately learns of the King's ability to create earthquakes in the Underworld by shaking a pillar, then heads off to the Cool Inn to eat. Here he has a confrontation with The Blind Swordsman. The Japanese fighter leaves and returns with James Bond (Alexander Grand), Clint Eastwood (Bobby Canavarro AKA Ka Wa) and some of Dracula's zombie skeletons. Bruce is surprised to find himself disorientated and defeated by his foes. The injured Lee is nursed back to health by Wa To (Simon Yuen) and his granddaughter; they restore his powers so that he can fight successfully in the underworld. His saviour warns him: "Young fellow I think you've been overdoing it. I cannot say I blame you. But you should just look at yourself. You're wasting away from too much of it."

The granddaughter interjects: "Grandpa don't be so unfair. When a man's endowed like Bruce the girls are bound to want him. He's got to have his fun! Eh Bruce-y!"

Bruce replies: "That's enough. It seemed like I had everything licked, except for just one thing. My Achilles heel. Right! I used to play around just too much. I, I'm sorry Linda."

Granddaughter: "Uh Linda? Whose this Linda?"

Bruce: "Linda was my wife."

By the time this was made there'd been a lot of rumours about the cause of Bruce Lee's death, and one that proved popular was that he killed himself by having too much sex. The movie rolls on with Bruce going gambling, before deciding to close down the casino because it is patronised by those who lost all their money in games of chance on earth and then committed suicide. Lee shares all the money he's won with everyone present except the one-armed swordsman (Cheung Lik), giving the cash to Lik's sister instead because the one-armed swordsman lost the loot he'd borrowed from her at the casino and can't be trusted to repay it. After this good deed, Bruce sets up a gym to teach his new friends including Popeye (Eric Tsang Chi-Wai) and Kwai Chang Caine (from the *Kung Fu* TV series with David Carradine) martial arts. Lee wants them to be able to defend themselves against the gang run by The Godfather and his enforcers including Clint Eastwood, James Bond, Emmanuelle, Dracula with his army of zombies and secretly The Exorcist (who is in charge of the King's bodyguard). Before long Bruce is battling the blind swordsman. Bruce uses this scrap to demonstrate various fighting moves named after his flicks, starting with *The Big Boss*, then moving through *Enter the Dragon, Way of the Dragon, Fist of Fury* and *Game of Death;* finally his nunchucks come out and prove superior to the sword, so the Zatoichi-like figure he's defeated has to leave for elsewhere. Both James Bond and Clint Eastwood think they'll easily take out Bruce Lee, but the Godfather decides to send in Emmanuelle to seduce and then shag the Little Dragon to death (despite the fact he's already dead).

This is the nearest the Brucesploitation genre gets to reinterpreting the death of Bruce Lee through the prism of the Abe Sada saga; a Japanese true crime legend about a woman who strangled her lover after excessive sex and then cut off his penis and carried it with her until she was arrested—an infamous sex murder that inspired the movies *A Woman Called Sada Abe* (1975) directed by Noboru Tanaka, and *In the Realm of the Senses* (1976) directed by Nagisa Oshima. Sadly, Emmanuelle doesn't fuck Lee to death and then carry his manhood around in her purse. Just as she's about to go down on him, Bruce spots The Godfather, Clint Eastwood and James Bond watching, and so pushing his grinding partner aside he gets up. The Godfather then makes Lee an offer only the Little Dragon can refuse, joining his gang.

Next the King of the Underworld's concubines slide into Bruce's pad and try to slip him an aphrodisiac but their plan for sexual satisfaction with the Little Dragon goes wrong, they end up cat fighting and force each other to drink their concoction, which is harmless to men but makes women ugly. When they return to the King of the Underworld, he doesn't want anything to do with them after Emmanuelle turns up to seduce him. Meanwhile, Bruce's gym has been smashed up by the Godfather's gang, so he dons his Kato uniform and goes to the quarry where he'd previously fought the blind swordsman to take on Dracula and his army of zombies. Bruce looks like he's done for as the zombies hold him down and Dracula's fangs descend towards his crotch; however, Bruce briefly acquires a middle leg and kicks Dracula out of touch. This is yet another reference to Bruce's allegedly huge schlong, although it is depicted as just an ordinary trouser clad leg with a shoe and sock on the foot. Bruce recovers a secret document from Dracula and interrupts Emmanuelle attempting to bonk the King of the Underworld to death. After speaking to Bruce and reading the papers, the King exclaims with regard to Emmanuelle: "Her pussy's in this plot too. She was using it to murder me!" The King dismisses the Exorcist as the captain of his bodyguard and replaces him with Bruce Lee. Soon Bruce is beating up James Bond who he's discovered with a suitcase full of stolen money. Clint Eastwood decides to challenge Lee, so it's back to the stone quarry for the showdown. Bruce dodges the bullets from Clint's pistol and soon kills Eastwood.

The ordinary residents of the underworld immediately celebrate the fact that Bruce has taken out the Godfather's three main enforcers. While everyone is distracted, The Exorcist and The Godfather set out to kill the king. The king's only means of defence is to shake his column and cause an earthquake. By this means the monarch saves his own skin but kills many of his subjects. Then it's back to the quarry where Bruce confronts The Exorcist and The Godfather and blames the deaths in the earthquake on their stupidity. He takes out The Exorcist with a flurry of kicks and further blows to the body. With one opponent dead, Lee then kills The Godfather with his 'fingers of fury'. The king still believes the Godfather and The Exorcist are after him, but he's even more worried that Bruce Lee is angry about him killing so many of the undead, so he asks Zhong Kui to help him. In Chinese mythology Zhong Kui is king of ghosts. He agrees to help the King of the Underworld in return for complete obedience. Zhong calls up some demons—they look like mummies with loose bandages—and with the King and his evil spirits heads to the quarry where Bruce is looking for the monarch. After telling Bruce he's an 'ignorant heap of buffalo dung' for demanding 'justice' and insulting the king, Kui tells his demon dozen to kick Lee's ass. Comedy mayhem ensures and part way through the combat Popeye, Kwai Chang Caine and the one-armed swordsman appear to back Bruce up. Popeye's fight game doesn't really take off until he eats some spinach. Lee is freed up to deal with Zhong who he defeats with nunchucks. After this the King of the Underworld has no choice but to agree to Bruce's demands. These are for Lee to be sent back to earth and for the king to treat his subjects well.

Clearly this belongs to the core of the Brucesploitation genre and like *Bruce Against Supermen* (1975) and *Fist of Fear, Touch of Death* (1980) it is a wacky comedy. The fable of there being universal grief around Bruce Lee's death is greatly exaggerated, and this flick is just one example of the man and his passing not being taken too seriously. When anyone dies it is always a tragedy for their immediate family and friends, but media reports of celebrity deaths touching entire populations are always misleading, as this entry in the Brucesploitation genre so ably demonstrates.

The Dragon Lives Again is a hilarious example of cynicism about the spectacle of mass grieving; not to mention a highly effective satire addressing the ways in which pop culture invades and takes over peoples minds. While the film-makers are deploying slapstick and other forms of zany humour, ultimately what *The Dragon Lives Again* gives us is a suprarationalist attack on the stupidity of religious and superstitious beliefs in both their traditional and postmodern forms. Director Law Kei would go on to make *The Dragon, the Lizard, the Boxer* (1977) and *Bruce Lee the Invincible* (1978), which are both addressed below.

15 THE REAL BRUCE LEE   1977
DIRECTED BY JIM MARKOVIC AND KIM SI-HYEON
(LAST FIST OF FURY SEGMENT)

The first thirty or so minutes of this flick consists of footage from films Bruce Lee made as a child actor in Hong Kong, the press conference for *Fist of the Unicorn* with the focus on Bruce Lee (whose contribution was to choreograph some fight scenes as a favour for his friend Unicorn Chan), shots of Bruce Lee's funeral and some edited scenes of Bruce Li (Ho Chung Tao) doing action sequences more or less in the style of The Little Dragon. A voice-over gives this material the feel of a pseudo-documentary. The main part of this movie is an edited version of what is allegedly Dragon Lee's first Brucesploitation film: *The Last Fist of Fury* AKA *The Ultimate Lee* AKA *Dragon Lee Does Dallas*. The Dragon Lee vehicle is directed by Kim Si-Hyeon who isn't credited in the English language edit of *The Real Bruce Lee*; the original full-length Korean version is believed to be lost. The *Last Fist of Fury* is basically a cheap imitation of Bruce Lee's already low-budget *Fist of Fury* (1972).

Members of a Japanese karate school murder one of the leading students of the Ching Wu kung fu school, so Dragon Lee (Shou Lung in the movie) seeks revenge. This entails the defeat of a Japanese villain with a Hitler-style moustache, who is presented with a coffin before the fight to anger him. There is a climatic battle with a half-German/half Japanese villain aided by another samurai fascist with a Hitler tash. Shou Lung's white whiskered master secretly aids his students after dressing up in a ninja suit to fight the bad guys when necessary. The truly ridiculous weapons include an extending sword, metal Frisbee-like objects with sharp edges that are thrown at opponents, and extending metallic tape measures used as blades. The wire work is just as insane.

Moving on, Dragon Lee is a pumped up Bruce Lee, going over-the-top with Lee-alike facial expressions and gestures. The film opens with the clone practicing 'kung fu' by kicking huge rocks against a metal target (to toughen his feet) and stays as crazy. The martial arts are mostly taekwondo with some kung fu animal styles and gymnastics thrown in for good measure, they bear little resemblance to what Bruce Lee did onscreen. Many scenes contain elements lifted from *Fist of Fury* but there are more slapstick elements than in the original. A Ching Wu messenger is debagged, so Dragon Lee returns the insult by getting his side to carry a Japanese fighter stripped to his underpants through the streets. That said, the Japanese don't look convincingly Japanese and the Chinese don't look Chinese either.

The super cheap sets and costumes, alongside bad to non-existent acting, make *The Last Fist of Fury* a comic masterpiece. Everything is completely hammed up and it is this Dragon Lee vehicle that makes *The Real Bruce Lee* worth watching, the documentary section at the beginning is tedious. However without the faux-documentary at the start, the Dragon Lee film on its own would only make the semi-periphery rather than at the core of the Brucesploitation genre. Sequels and remakes aren't riffing on Bruce in the same way as bio-pics or films that incorporate him as a character—albeit one who is present through his absence, that is to say his death is being 'investigated'. This flick was re-edited/remade as *The Young Bruce Lee* (1987), loosing all the Dragon Lee material and greatly expanding the child actor material in the faux-documentary.

16 RETURN OF BRUCE   1977

AKA *BRUCE'S RETURN*
AKA *THE DRAGON RETURNS*
DIRECTED BY JOSEPH VELASCO

Bruce Le arrives in Manila to see his uncle, a plot device also used in Velasco/Le's ultimate anti-classic *Bruce and the Shaolin Bronzemen*. Le's uncle has disappeared and so he has nowhere to stay. He befriends a chubby and homeless orphan kid called Piggy. They go to a restaurant where Le wins a chicken eating competition against another guy, so the loser has to pay the bill. A girl threatened by thugs runs in and Le saves her. He finds out later she's his cousin. Piggy shows Le around Manila. Le's cousin goes looking for him, and when she finds him takes him to her brother's kung fu school. It is at the kung fu school that they work out they're cousins and it turns out the uncle Le couldn't find had been killed by gangsters and the mob now want his children to close down his martial arts school, but his son Cheung Lik (Le's male cousin) won't throw in the towel. The mob think it is unsafe to send the women they've kidnapped and are selling into prostitution abroad until the kung fu school is shut. Le's uncle had stood up to the gang but why they view the dead man's school as a threat isn't elaborated. The caged women are vaguely reminiscent of the prisoners on Han's island in *Enter the Dragon* (1973).

A couple of undercover cops are investigating the hoods and one of them has managed to become the girlfriend of the leader of the gang. The fights between Le's family and the gang escalate to the point where Le accidentally kills the fattest (and hardest) member in a graveyard confrontation. Le feels bad about this and Lik wants him to go back to Hong Kong so that the cops can't get hold of him. Instead, Le makes a deal with the gang. If they leave his cousins alone, he'll give himself up to the cops. The gang agree but they're lying. They've hired a top Japanese fighter who kills Lik using his special 'red palm' technique. When Le finds his cousin's dead body he goes to the gang HQ and takes the hoods on. There are a couple of karate-trained bodyguards to invoke Bruce Lee's climatic fight with Chuck Norris in *Way of the Dragon* (1972). Le pulls chest hair from these Caucasian dudes and blows it off his palm, just like the 'real' Bruce Lee does to Chuckles in their 1972 outing. Le takes out the gang leaders, then he comes across the Japanese warrior who killed Lik, and when this dude attempts to use the red palm on him, he realises this is the guy who murdered his cousin so he wipes him out. Le's female cousin turns up at the gang's mansion for no good reason, as does Lo Lieh who announces he is the brother of the warrior Le just killed. Le doesn't want to fight the 'king boxer', but when Lieh attempts to use the red palm on him, he decides this anti-hero must die too. Lieh has a samurai sword but in one of the most unbelievable movie fight tactics of all time, Le wraps a piece of cloth around one hand, catches the blade using this 'protective' material and breaks the weapon in two. Lo Lieh winds up dead like Le's female cousin who was killed within moments of him finding her in the gangbanger's mansion. Le has been so busy taking out all the bad guys that he fails to turn up at the appointed place to meet the orphan boy Piggy, who wanders off whimpering that once again he is all alone in the world.

Earlier on in the movie Le does some monkey kung fu, but for the climatic scenes it is all Bruce Lee imitations, and there are also music cues stolen from *Enter the Dragon*. There is some female nudity, and an effeminate character who represents what the producers think a lot of the audience either are or would like to be—a sissy! At one point Le kicks dog shit into the sissy's face. In the English dub Le's character is called Wong and despite the title there isn't anyone called Bruce. Nonetheless, this piece of brilliant and blatant stupidity still makes the core of the Brucesploitation genre because of the Lee homages and invocations. This isn't Joseph Velasco at his most insane but there are still lots of groovy shots of both Manila and far out seventies fashions.

17 STORY OF THE DRAGON   1977

AKA *BRUCE LEE'S DEADLY KUNG FU*
AKA *BRUCE LEE'S SECRET*
AKA *BRUCE LI'S JEET KUNE DO*
DIRECTORS CHAN WA AND WILLIAM CHEUNG KEI

Another Bruce Lee bio-pic starring Bruce Li. This movie has little to recommend it beyond the flaws introduced when it was 're-mastered' multiple times. The flick is generally understood as portraying Bruce Lee's first years in America, starting in 1959 when he worked as a waiter for Ruby Chow and began teaching kung fu in the USA. However, Bruce Lee's late-teenage life is then crossed with elements from his first three films for Golden Harvest—creating a hybrid mythological Bruce Lee.

While Bruce Lee first lived in Seattle after moving to the USA, the film is set in San Francisco, but aside from a few establishing shots (all stock footage), it is very obviously filmed in Taiwan. To show Bruce training hard there is an insane sequence of him throwing himself around as he does bicep curls with a pair of dumbbells. He exhibits zero muscular control in these exercises and others with a set of chest expanders. Bruce Li who plays Lee in the film was a gymnast and physical education teacher and should have known how to train correctly. Presumably the incorrect exercise technique in *Story of the Dragon* is there to add excitement and even more unreality. Of course the same could be said of the fighting in nearly all martial arts movies, since anyone attempting to use high kicks in street fights is likely to suffer an ignominious defeat. Likewise, rather than matching the late fifties and early sixties American setting of this film, the characters are all pimped out in funky 1970s hipster gear.

The quality of various English language DVDs is poor and this gives the flick an avant-garde feel. For example the Beverly Wiltshire Filmworks/Telefilms International/Saturn Productions Inc version has a huge split slide down Lee's face when he first appears onscreen in Ruby Chow's kitchen. There are many other flaws recalling lettrist notions of chiselling in film, and despite claiming to be a widescreen edition on the cover, the Beverly Wiltshire release is actually panned and scanned, providing it with even more of a neo-surrealist feel. Despite these flaws adding much to the film this is still one of the more inane entries in the Brucesploitation genre.

18 BIG BOSS 2   1978

AKA *DRAGON LEE FIGHTS AGAIN*
AKA *DRAGON BRUCE LEE 2*
DIRECTED BY TO MAN-BO AND LEE EUN

Dragon Lee is an anti-colonial fighter entrusted with an important list of names that he must take from the south to the north. Just as he is about to leave, the bad guys headed by Bolo Yeung (with Hitler-style moustache so that we know he's a Japanese fascist) turn up. Dragon takes out many fighters but is shot in the leg by Bolo. With help from other members of the resistance he gets away and goes by boat to the north. Dragon has a contact but he gets turned away when he goes to the address he's been given (we find out later the Japanese had visited and the contact has fled). Then because of his bullet wound Dragon collapses in the street, but is picked up and nursed to health by the Cho family who are with the resistance. Cho is a Korean surname and provides an indication of the location, which is never clarified in the English dub. Phillip Ko heads the Cho family and was a friend of Dragon's father. The mother suffers nervous fits that can only be cured with music, and the family's lute-playing daughter takes a shine to Dragon. Bolo and his flunkies turn up in town having followed Lee there. The Japanese come to the house where Dragon is recuperating and after a fight the family escape in one direction, Lee in another. Ko, his wife and daughter go to the house of a relative to hide out. What they don't know is that To Wai Wo is collaborating with the Japanese in return for money. Dragon is helped out by resistance fighter Cheung Lik who is credited as Jacky Chang on the versions I have of this film because he's being used here as a Jackie Chan clone.

The Japanese go around being brutal and there are a bunch of flashbacks to them killing the relatives of various characters and cutting the legs off Cheung Lik's sister Lau Ying-Hung—who is now a crippled lute-player. These fascists also randomly stop people in the street, ask them about Dragon Lee, and then beat them up for not knowing where he is or even who he is. Wo has betrayed his relatives to the Japanese but they've left them alone in his house so that they can act as bait to catch bigger resistance fish. Dragon Lee literally bumps into Wo in the street, the turncoat figures out who he is and tells him to come with him to hook up with the Chos. They enjoy a meal together but Ko's wife has one of her fits and their daughter can't play the lute to calm her because she doesn't have an instrument to hand. Dragon says he'll fetch a lute player and runs off to get Lau Ying-Hung. Wo alerts the Japanese and with them follows Dragon to Cheung Lik's sister. Lau tells Dragon he's to meet a resistance agent, and says she'll go to help Mrs Cho. Dragon leaves before the Japanese burst in and demand to know where Lau's brother is; you'd have thought they'd have asked about Dragon too seeing as they found Lau by following him, but they don't. Lau's lute doubles as a dart firing weapon, and she kills a samurai with this before being mortally wounded. The Japanese get one of their female agents to pretend to be Lau's sister and she takes the lute to where it is needed. The agent plays the instrument for a while and then uses the dart firing mechanism to kill Mrs Cho. She fires darts at Ko but he catches them in his hand and throws them back at her. When Ko advances on her, she throws a powder in his face that blinds him. Moments later more Japanese burst in and Miss Cho gives them better than she gets back. Ko, who is having trouble seeing, is killed. When Dragon comes back and finds Uncle and Auntie Cho dead, he is so angry he smashes a ceiling light with a Bruce Lee style kick (seen in both *Marlowe* and *Way of the Dragon*). Dragon then races to Lau, who he revives briefly. She says he must go to the temple before she finally dies. As a result Dragon finds Cheung Lik, who is overcome with grief and desperate for revenge after hearing of his sister's death. Dragon tells Cheung to wait for him to come back with some men, but once Dragon has gone our Chan clone attacks the Japanese on his own and is killed by Bolo. Deciding he has no more use for the traitor Wo, Bolo then kills him too. In addition to his absurd fascist moustache, by this point in the movie Bolo is also sporting a ridiculous red jacket and bowtie. Dragon eventually finds Miss Cho who is hiding out with the resistance and they decide they will drive the Japanese out. The resistance then go around shouting 'kill the Japs' and 'revenge' as they kill actors portraying Japanese fighters. Since Japanese reinforcements are coming in a few days, Bolo and his men decide to go into the country and confiscate every last piece of ginseng that has been harvested by the farmers. This gives Dragon the excuse to do a flying kick demolition of the ginseng requisitioning sign to parody Bruce Lee's destruction of the 'no dogs or Chinese' sign in *Fist of Fury* (1972). Despite having decided to lie low, Bolo has the inevitable climatic battle with Dragon. Once Bolo is losing he goes to grab his pistol but Dragon is prepared this time and throws a dart in Yeung's right (firing) arm. Miss Cho looks on nervously but inevitably, Dragon beats Bolo.

In *Big Boss 2*, our anti-star really goes over-the-top with his Bruce Lee gestures and screams on the soundtrack, to the extent that once seen they have a viral effect on how anyone with a critical orientation towards cinematic spectacle views Bruce Lee flicks. Dragon Lee's overblown reinterpretation of Bruce Lee comes across more as critique than homage, and for those who were not already able to understand film as film, makes it hard to avoid confronting the fact that under the guise of naturalism and realism what we see in movies like *Enter the Dragon* (1973) and *The Big Boss* (1971) is simply showbiz fakery—and thus something we really can celebrate Bruce Lee for. For those able to move beyond star worship it is liberating to understand that Bruce Lee—like all celebrities—is great because of the aura projected upon him by his fans; in creating Lee the celebrity (I'm not talking about the man) fans show that they are in fact superior to their idol since they brought his myth into being. In this film—and others such as *Dragon Lee Vs the Five Brothers*—where Dragon Lee's Bruce Lee mannerism are really allowed to break free from their moorings, calling the result Brucesploitation seems a little like describing *The Communist Manifesto* as a burlesque. While Marx and Engels were very funny, they had a serious intent. Likewise, regardless of whether it is consciously thought through on the part of those responsible, the way in which *Big Boss 2* serves to smash the (cinematic) spectacle requires acknowledgement. Clearly this places the film at the core of Brucesploitation, but at the same time it should lead us to question the name this genre has acquired; while less catchy, Bruce-deconstruction might be more appropriate. That said, this won't prevent the stereotypical portrayal of the Japanese—about a dozen of them are able to occupy a town—feeding into the bigotry of those already inclined toward nationalist reaction.

19 DYNAMO 1978
DIRECTED BY HUA SHAN

Mary Hon Ma Lee has been sent to Hong Kong to sort out the local branch of an advertising agency that is underperforming. Bruce Li is working as a cabbie when Mary spots him beating up some hoods who'd stolen one his firm's cars.

How quickly Mary discovers Li doing cabbie kung fu depends on whether you watch the US or UK English dub of the flick; events move faster in the North American version and make less sense. In the UK version, Mary explains at an agency board meeting that she's been sent to Hong Kong as: "A sort of laxative. To get rid of the old crap." She is tasked with turning around the Pacific Agency, who have been losing clients to rival firm Cosmo. Her plan is to go on the attack and destroy the competition.

On arrival in the British colony she learned of the death of Bruce Lee and his star pulling power, which 'justifies' the obligatory exploitative documentary footage of his Hong Kong funeral cut into the movie near the start. In the UK English dub Mary is built up as a more or less rounded and ruthless business executive. She headhunts the greatest salesman at the Cosmo Agency by seducing him and blackmailing him. Having spent a wild night with Mary, he's not too bothered about the coercion or having cheated on his wife, and signs her contract. Hoods are then deployed to make the head of Cosmo sign a letter accepting his best worker's resignation. Once Mary has removed the rival company's greatest asset she gives the headhunted executive the cold shoulder. She is a corporate robot who simply wanted to neutralise the guy she blackmailed, she has no use for his talents. Much of this is more akin to drama than action cinema, but it does make a self-serving attempt at exposing what goes on in the advertising and movie business slightly more convincing than the North American English dub that cuts a lot of it.

Having recruited Danny Lau from the local branch of Pacific to act as her assistant, Mary gets him to track down Bruce Li, who she thinks will fill the shoes of the Little Dragon and help place her Hong Kong operation back in the black. Bruce is signed up and Mary instructs a flunky to ensure that Li is seen in all the right places. She outlines plans to teach him French and German since he'll travel internationally; she puts together a committee to dream up publicity stunts to keep her hot new talent in the media spotlight. According to Mary: "The main thing is to make him larger than life. We want a superman." She entrusts Danny Lau with the task of transforming Li into a comic book hero. Lau recruits his old kung fu teacher Ku Feng as a trainer for Bruce. In the US edit Li proceeds to make films at incredible rate; in this version we also see Danny Lee making films for Bruce, and appearing in what are apparently our hero's dreams.

Material from *Bruce Lee, His Last Days, His Last Nights* (1976) is cut in to up the fight content, since US distributors apparently thought there was too much sex, nudity and story exposition in the original edit; they dropped it for cut-and-paste combat from another flick. The US version is thus more surreal but ultimately less satisfactory than the UK edit because it is so repetitive and over focused on 'Bruce', never a good idea when Li is the main clone.

Li's talent agency aren't satisfied with him doing movie kung fu, they want him to be the best fighter in the world, so character actor Feng trains him up to championship standard—while the star they are manufacturing wears clothes that resemble those worn by the 'reel' Bruce Lee in both the official *Game of Death* (1978) and the *Longstreet* TV series. Feng is a drunken and gambling addicted martial arts master and he's the best thing in the movie. At first Bruce doesn't get on with Feng but eventually they become buddies. Nonetheless, Feng subjects Bruce to brutal shocks as part of an electronic muscle stimulation programme. Bruce Lee used a similar machine, and in this movie Li seems to be not just a successor to the Little Dragon, but in many ways also a representation of him. Li is locked up under contract and missing his girlfriend, so Feng tells him to take a day off and visit her. This doesn't go well because LI's girlfriend is angry after reading false stories planted in the press by Bruce's talent agency about his many liaisons with glamorous women. Thus in the English dub Li gets to confront Mary and deliver the hilariously ironic lines: "Because I'm on contract doesn't mean you own me. I'm not a puppet! I'm a man!" If he was even half-a-man surely Li would have made more entertaining Brucesploitation features than this one!

Mary kicks sand in Li's face by arranging for Bruce to be seduced by French actress Angie, who she thinks would make a more appropriate lover for him than his local girl. The talent agency orchestrates a huge traffic jam so that Angie can get out of her car and into Bruce's, with Li taking her to her hotel; which psychologically pulls him down from his celebrity pedestal and back to his old life as a cabbie—the old play mean and beat 'em down in order to seduce 'em ploy. Obviously, if there had been a real traffic jam, Bruce would have been no more able to reach Angie's destination than her driver. Onscreen we see a few vehicles but the dialogue unconvincingly attempts to pretend the producers could afford to hire far more drivers than are shown: "One hundred light trucks, fifty heavy trucks plus one hundred and fifty private cars, and we had to get them all together. It was just like a movie!" If only, coz the flick we're watching ain't showing us that, it's only telling us this is there when it ain't! Before this choice piece of bullshit we get Bruce's big sex scene, there are full nude body shots of Angie in the shower cut into footage of Bruce working out. Then in an excruciatingly French accented English, Angie suggests Bruce gets it on with her. Li complies.

The US edit is far coyer about this than the British one, repeating calf close-ups from the shower in order to cut the breast and bush shots that are seen in the UK version, and slashing most of the bed scene too. Likewise, in the US edit Bruce doesn't seem to canoodle with his local girlfriend as much as he does in the UK version; which means viewers in North America might miss the fact that all this love action invokes the Little Dragon's complicated sex life revolving around his American wife and Taiwanese mistress.

Returning to the flick, Mr. George (James Griffith) the head of the Cosmo Company is angry about Bruce's success and his inability to sign him, and decides Li must be removed from the entertainment industry if his business is to survive. So Cosmo send kung fu killer after kung fu killer to murder or seriously injure Bruce. However, Feng is such a good teacher no one can beat Li. Soon this rising star is sent on a world tour—or rather to a Hong Kong film studio being passed off as elsewhere through the deployment of odd bits stock footage and other cheap tricks. Tokyo consists of a nightclub and a dojo, stock footage, and Li outside what seems to be Hong Kong International Airport—although in the movie it's an airport in Tokyo. Chiang Tao is wasted challenging Li to a fight, since he and his 'Japanese' karatekas are easily defeated. In 'Seoul', Bruce demonstrates his inability to ski and has a fight in the snow. The ski scene was presumably shot on location, and we are even shown a sign for the Dragon Valley Ski Resort. This tourist attraction is owned by the Unification Church (or Moonies) and located in Daegwallyeong-myeon so if this was the actual filming location it is 150km away from Seoul (which is where the screen title places it). In the USA there is a fight in a hotel room that spills into an underground car park; this features American karate champion Steve Sanders and is one of the better battles in the movie. Clearly Li didn't leave Hong Kong for this 'international' incident; the American car park has at least three paper signs saying 'drive slowly' and 'exit' taped over what is presumably Chinese writing —the sloppy signage has definitely been put in place to obscure something that would give the game away that we're not in the USA.

By sending postcards 'home' and other means, Bruce patches things up with his girlfriend. Realising that Li and his teacher Feng are undefeatable, the Cosmo agency eventually kidnap Bruce's true love but say she will come to no harm if he throws a big fight with their fighter Jim Clark in Chicago. This is the climatic battle of the movie and it is one of the most pathetic examples of final combat in the entire history of martial arts flicks. Li goes eight or so rounds without making any effort to win, he simple allows himself to be beaten up in front of the film crew. There is no audience around the ring as Li fails to slug it out with Clark, although every now and then a crowd of American fight fans is cut in from stock footage in a futile attempt to get viewers not to notice the utter lack of action onscreen is taking place in a film studio. Perhaps to make up for the fact he's a crap movie martial artist, Jim Clark with his bad seventies facial hair and curly moptop looks vaguely like Count Dante. What Li doesn't know as he's throwing the fight is that by hiring expert kung fu hoods, the Pacific Agency have freed his girlfriend. To motivate Bruce to win, they tell him the love of his life has been killed. Mad as hell and wanting revenge, Li kicks Clark around the ring and achieves the easy knockout he could have had in round one if he'd not been throwing the match. After this, Bruce is so fed up with the fakeness of showbiz that he turns his back on films and returns to his ordinary life with his everyday girlfriend.

If watching an English dub then the US cut should be avoided, as the UK edit is far better– but it still ain't a great movie. As an allegory about the fakeness of the careers of both Bruce Li and the Little Dragon, *Dynamo* would be groovier if it focussed more on cynicism and less on martial arts. Its most laugh out loud lines are on the subject of exploiting Bruce Lee's success: "A lot of people are cashing in on his death. His magazines that cost fifty cents are selling for three bucks! Quite a mark up! And all the television stations are screening memorial specials. The advertisers love it!"

20 ENTER THE GAME OF DEATH 1978
AKA *KING OF KUNG FU*

DIRECTED BY JOSEPH VELASCO AND/OR LAM KWOK-CHEUNG AND/OR CHOE U-HYEONG

This mashes up elements of three different Bruce Lee movies—*Fist of* Fury (1972), *Enter the Dragon* (1973) and *Game of Death* (1978). *Fist of Fury* gives us the setting, which is apparently China—although the film looks like it was shot in Korea—before World War II. Patriots in a secret organisation called The Blue Robe are trying to recover stolen documents which if they ended up in the wrong hands would threaten national security. Representatives of the German and Japanese governments are trying to obtain these papers too. A Chinese entrepreneur is planning to sell the documents to whoever will pay three million dollars for them.

Bruce Le is the best fighter around and all sides wanting the papers try to recruit him, but he doesn't want to work for anyone. He gets in fights while he's out jogging in his yellow jump suit—that looks like the one Bruce Lee wore in *Game of Death*—and wins a martial arts tournament. One of Le's street fights involves Bolo Yeung, who he then defeats in the ring. At first Bolo seems to be working for the Chinese villain, then he appears to become Japanese, indicated by different clothes.

At night while Bruce Le is lying on his bed he remembers that his cousin was raped by the Japanese and then killed herself; this resembles the opening to *Enter the Dragon* where Bruce Lee's sister—played by Angela Mao—commits suicide to avoid being raped by the villains. The memory leads Le to join up with the Blue Robe after he also discovers the girl who'd tried to get him to work for the Germans—and who looks like his cousin—is actually a double agent and Chinese patriot. The stolen documents are kept at the top of a pagoda defended on each floor by a fighters highly trained in different martial arts. Le has to fight his way up to the top to get the papers. This is the element of the film borrowed from Bruce Lee's *Game of Death* but it dumps the fight philosophy didacticism of the official version and replaces it with a far more enthralling comic book surrealism.

The tower sequence is the best part of the movie, and the finest of the pagoda combat scenes is Le against a snake style kung fu master who holds serpents in his hands as he fights; there are also quite a number of snakes slithering around on the floor, as well as turtles! Once the snake fighter is losing, he bites the head off one of his pets and aims the spurting blood at Bruce Le, who looks like he can't quite believe what's happening—was it in the script? Regardless, Le regains the upper hand and eventually strangles the snake fighter with one of the dude's own slithering ophidians. After this Cheung Lik is seen unconvincingly made up as an old man. Lik shows his martial expertise by putting out candle flames with his nunchaku. This sequence is fun, but like the rest of the pagoda fights comes across as a slight let down after the snake fu. When Le gets to the top of the tower he's still fighting the last 'highly trained' comic book martial artist defending the pagoda, as the Chinese villain makes off with the documents. In the course of battling his way up the tower, Le has acquired slash marks across his face so that he looks like Bruce Lee at the end of *Enter the Dragon*. Returning to *Enter the Game of Death*, the Japanese kill the Chinese villain rather than paying him three million dollars for the papers. Le's Blue Robe associates are chasing after the documents.

In a twist, after the papers are recovered by the Blue Robe, the Germans grab the girl with the documents, necessitating even more martial arts action from Bruce Le—who because no one else is any good at kung fu has to fight pretty much everyone including a tall black guy who acts as a stand-in for Kareem Abdul-Jabbar. In the end Chinese patriotism wins out but rather than getting the girl who looks like his cousin, Bruce Le parts company with her... Doh!

While incoherent, *Enter the Game of Death* is more linear and not as insanely surreal as Joseph Velasco's greatest trash classics. In fact, *Enter the Game of Death* may be one of several instances of Velasco taking credit for a film he didn't direct—which would explain why it is subpar compared to his usual lunacy. That said, it is still worth seeing because Le's Little Dragon muggings become hyperreal and thus completely unbelievable. What clones as groovy as Bruce Le do is undermine Lee's uniqueness by demonstrating the 'king of kung fu's' martial arts 'greatness' was a theatrical simulacrum. Although Le is skinnier and shorter than Bruce Lee, he is just as well cut. What they both have is the look of contemporary female bodybuilders. There is an even more obvious androgyny in their grace than Bolo Yeung and Dragon Lee's hulking 'hypermasculinity'.

21 GAME OF DEATH 1978
DIRECTED BY ROBERT CLOUSE

This is a cut-and-paste movie made using footage of Bruce Lee from completed Hong Kong flicks and the film the Little Dragon left unfinished at the time of his death—from which this takes its title. Rather than attempt to realise Lee's original vision—difficult to accomplish because there was no finished script and Lee's ideas would have evolved if he'd been able to continue working on the project—Clouse decided to rip-off plot elements from Brucesploitation movies such as *The Dragon Dies Hard* (1975), *Goodbye Bruce Lee, His Last Game of Death* (1975), and *Bruce Lee: The Man, the Myth* (1976). In their turn these recycled absurd conspiracy theories that had circulated among fans to 'explain' Lee's death.

Here the mob are getting heavy about wanting to manage the careers of kung fu film star Billy Lo—depicted via archive footage of Bruce Lee and enough unconvincing doubles to make up the fingers on one of Mickey Mouse's hands—and his singer girlfriend Ann Morris, played by dull US actress Colleen Camp who singularly fails to live up to her groovy surname. Rather than cave in to the demands of a bunch of B-list refuges from sub-prime time US TV and movies (i.e. the racketeers), and counselled by journalist Jim Marshal (bland US actor Gig Young in his last film role), Billy decides to fight back. Feeling that rebellion is contagious, and wanting to protect the celebrity assets already under their collective thumb, the mobsters shoot Lo on set as he's filming the final scene of *Fist of Fury* (1972).

Billy recovers but uses this as an opportunity to fake his own death, cue tasteless footage of Bruce Lee's Hong Kong funeral. Using disguises that bring to mind some of those deployed by Bruce Lee in *Fist of Fury*, Billy hits back at the gangbangers and single-handedly takes them out, saving the top men for last. The constant and very obvious shifts between archive footage of Bruce Lee and his various doubles in the Billy Lo role do serve to deconstruct the Little Dragon as a movie icon.

After the spectacle of Bruce Lee (as Billy Lo) fighting Kareem Abdul-Jabbar, we have Billy Lo (as Bruce Lee and his doubles) battling it out with Stick (Mel Novak). As the film editor cuts between Bruce Lee and Kim Tai-Jong (and possibly Yuen Biao too), anyone who isn't a deluded fanboy ought to come to the conclusion that it doesn't really matter whether we're looking at Bruce Lee or one of his stand-ins, thanks to cinematic tricks they all perform the role of Billy Lo equally badly. This serves to underscore that the pagoda fight with Abdul-Jabbar more than almost any other seen on celluloid, has stuck in the minds of international audiences not because Bruce Lee was a great martial artist but rather due to his understanding of showmanship. It's the discrepancy in height between Lee (shortish) and Abdul-Jabbar (ridiculously tall) that viewers respond to; not the supposedly free flowing combat techniques used by the two actors in this staged scene. The image of these two men battling it out became world famous on the basis of still photographs that circulated for five years before anyone was able to watch the footage in a cinema. As part of his expert shilling, Lee had a great line in didactic claims about how *Game of Death* would showcase his martial arts philosophy, but it is impossible to extrapolate this 'wisdom' from the stills that—alongside Lee's untimely death etc.—cemented his international status. Assuming they know who he is, when a member of the general public thinks of Bruce Lee they are quite likely to conjure up an image of him in his yellow jumpsuit because of those stills in which Abdul-Jabbar towers over the Little Dragon in a fictional fight to the death.

Despite its unintentional deconstruction of Bruce Lee, the official *Game of Death* is ultimately a bore—in part because the international edit is way too long. The story also suffers greatly from its indulgence in Hollywood-style plot points and tedious melodrama. Despite some sterling work done on *Game of Death* by the likes of Sammo Hung, ultimately watching it doesn't feel much different to being forced to endure Hollywood crapola from the same era such as *Barry Lyndon* (1975) or *Apocalypse Now* (1979). The local colour in the form of a lion dance in the Portuguese colony of Macao is just as bad as the James Bond stylings—most obvious in the opening credit sequence to the international edit—and the gruesome soundtrack by John Barry, which really gets in the way during the fights. While the official *Game of Death* clearly belongs to the core of the Brucesploitation genre, it is markedly inferior to other versions, most notably *Enter the Game of Death* (1978) and *The True Game of Death* (1979).

22 Bruce the Super Hero — 1979
Directed by Bruce Le

Bruce Le's sister Susan Chang is an antiques dealer in Manila. She's attacked by thugs from the Black Dragon Society. Lito Lapid, a pedicab driver called Rocky in the movie steps in to help her. This intervention comes too late. Before Susan dies she gives Lapid a key, saying he must pass it on to her brother Bruce. Le flies into Manila and hooks up with his uncle. On the way into town from the airport he stops the car so that he can have a fight with some thugs who'd been following them. Bruce goes to a nightclub with his uncle. You can tell it's a groovy gaff because the band mime to Donna Summer's *Hot Stuff* and there are go-go dancers. Bruce notices the gang he had the run in with earlier and tells his uncle to go; then he takes out the hoods.

The Black Dragon Society are part of an unlikely mafia consortium of Italian, Japanese, Chinese and local Filipino mobsters. They want a treasure map that was in the hilt of a samurai sword which was bought at auction by Susan Chang. Hot on the trail are the United Nations Intelligence Bureau, later we find out Interpol are on the case too. There is a billion dollars in gold bullion hidden near Manila that the Japanese took from the Americans during World War Two. We see Rocky boxing and his father murdered by Black Dragon thugs who are looking for the map. Rocky hooks up with a woman called Marlene who is pretending to be a sports reporter but is actually a United Nations undercover cop. Rocky isn't phased by Marlene's real identity or the fact that her idea of classy food is fried chicken. Bruce finds Rocky sneaking about his uncle's house and they get in a fight. Bruce is wearing a yellow tracksuit with black stripes just like Bruce Lee in the footage he filmed for *Game of Death* (1978). Bruce is chided by his uncle for fighting the guy who helped his sister, so they stop sparring and become friends.

Le is repeatedly referred to as 'The Kung Fu King from Hong Kong'. He's a tough nut to crack so the mafia bring in Bolo Yeung and Chiang Tao to deal with him. Bolo is supposed to be a Japanese karate fighter known as The Bull Killer, he's shown in flashback killing a very tired and dopey looking ox. Anyone into seventies martial arts movies will recognise this as an attempt to position Bolo as real life karate 'legend' Masutatsu Oyama who was portrayed onscreen by Sonny Chiba in a triology of bio-pics beginning with *Karate Bullfighter* (1975). That said, Bolo doesn't look Japanese and doesn't move like Sonny Chiba. After a few twists and turns,

Bruce, Rocky and a couple of female undercover cops find the treasure map in the safety deposit box that Susan Chang had passed Lapid the key to. Map in hand they troop off to retrieve the treasure not realising they are being followed by the mobsters. They find the bullion and as they drag it away in a couple of sacks they are attacked by the bad guys. There are a bunch of fights but the key action is Bruce against Bolo. The two b-movie stars have a kind of muscle off before Bolo is beaten. You'd have thought this was the climax but Bruce still has to battle Chiang Tao. When Tao starts to lose he runs away, and then out of nowhere attacks Bruce with a rubber snake puppet that he's stuck over his right arm. Bruce counters snake fist with eagle claw—there are some cuts to footage of an eagle—and thereby wins. Meanwhile the army has shown up to capture all the stray bad guys. At least it seems to be the army; it's a bunch of guys in combat gear. They might be the United Nations Intelligence Bureau or even Interpol—or just a bunch of Filipino extras led by an American—but whoever they are they are good guys coz they're on the same side as Bruce, Rocky and the undercover cops.

This flick has some similarities to the earlier *Return of Bruce,* murdered relatives in Manila—and the later *Bruce and the Shaolin Bronzemen,* the search for missing treasure. Other repetitions include Bruce Le endlessly fighting the same actors including Bolo Yeung and Chiang Tao. These infernal returns invite us to view these films not as individual works but rather as a larger serial piece with unreliable narrators and a vague similarity to the French nouveau roman, especially the work of Alain Robbe-Grillet in both written and cinematic form. With Bruce appearing in a yellow and black tracksuit, music cues from *Enter the Dragon,* those doing the English dubbing at one time forgetting the main character is called Bruce Chang and referring to Le as Bruce Lee, not to mention the fight choreography, this has to be a core Brucesploitation movie. But what a shame it wasn't directed by Joseph Velasco who would have given us a complete and unapologetic departure from logic and sense! Le takes his film making a little too seriously and without the guiding hand of a more relaxed director in places gets bogged down in tedious attempts at realism.

23 KUNG FU FEVER 1979

AKA *BLACK DRAGON FEVER*

AKA *BRUCE LEE STRIKES BACK*

DIRECTED BY KIM SI-HYEON AND/OR DAVID POON

At the start of the movie there is a montage of Bruce Lee PR footage. Film of the Little Dragon is unconvincingly edited/redubbed to make it look like he's having telephone conversations about his kung fu finger technique. Then Bruce Lee dies and no one understands why. However, various gangs of good guys and bad guys—including Ron Van Clief as a villain—want to get hold of the mater's secret *Kung Fu Finger Book*. Amy Chum is a leather clad biker chick desperate to lay her hands on this manual, but because she wants to please her father she eventually joins the side of Bruce Lee's good ex-students led by Dragon Lee.

Inevitably, for parts of the movie, Dragon is clad is a yellow jump suit with a black stripe down the side just like Bruce Lee in the official *Game of Death* (1978). Once again Dragon does his hilariously over the top Bruce Lee facial ticks and hand gestures. There is also an incredibly poorly choreographed car chase involving Dragon Lee and Ron Van Clief. The film is a lot more fun when Amy Chum—or rather what is obviously her stunt double—is knocking people down and running over them on her motorbike. In the end Dragon defeats all the baddies including Ron Van Clief. While not quite as groovy or sleazy as *Bruce's Deadly Fingers* with Bruce Le, like that slightly earlier film the point of this one—at least in the English dub—seems to be to get the characters to use the words 'Kung Fu Finger Book' as many times as possible.

24 THEY CALL HIM BRUCE LEE — 1979
DIRECTED BY JUN POSADAS

A martial arts instructor takes a phone call and discovers Jack Lee is coming to Manila with Bruce Lee's secret *Ninjitsu Fighting Techniques* manual. Evil martial artist Tom Higgins is told to get the book—because if he doesn't it will be bad for business.

A sloppy shot of the flight tower at Manila airport slides down to people milling about, cut with close ups of the bad guys. Jack isn't actually shown at the airport but the hoods still track him to his hotel room where he easily defeats the mobsters. This scene includes Jack teasing one gang-banger by repeatedly putting Bruce Lee's *Ninjitsu Fighting Techniques* manual within his reach and then snatching it away again. After being battered by Jack Lee, these dojo dummies are chewed out by arch-villain Tom for failing to beat one man. Meanwhile Jack is hanging out with and training Rey Malonzo. They get chased to some wasteland by a huge gang and having creamed most of them, Jack has dirt thrown in his eyes and would have been badly beaten if Rey hadn't saved the day.

There is also a lot of comedy based around Rey's life, he gets himself and his dad sacked from their jobs by insulting the company president—who he thinks is a salesman—and has further trouble with his father when he beats him with nunchaku without realising it's his papa who has approached him from behind. However Rey's main comedy action is with his womanising buddy Tito. Rey saves his pal from a beating and to say thanks, Tito wants to paint the town red with his best friend. They go to a cheap café where one of Tito's girlfriends works and Rey is less than impressed. When the fat café owner emerges it turns out Tito owes him money. There is an argument that ends in Rey and Tito leaving without paying and the gutbucket creditor shouting: "You snake. May herpes infect your toes!" Rey and Tito go on to beat up a gang who they see mugging a girl and they return her stolen handbag.

The grateful girl, Nita, invites them home. It turns out she is the daughter of the company president who fired Rey and his dad, so when they fall in love things don't go smoothly.

In the main plotline, the evil martial arts gang observe Jack Lee giving Rey Bruce Lee's *Ninjitsu Fighting Techniques* as he leaves Manila. The bad guys scheme against Rey and send a girl called Susan to join his martial arts club and seduce him. Nita is tipped off and when she sees Rey and Susan together an instrumental section of *Sky High* by Jigsaw blasts onto the soundtrack—presumably in part because it was used in the opening credits of the big budget international martial arts film *The Man from Hong Kong* (1975).

When Rey and Susan are rumbled by Nita, the bad girl runs off and is nearly run down. Fortunately Rey saves her. After this Susan realises she's fallen in love with Rey and confesses that she was sent to set him up. The baddies then decide to kidnap Nita, and her father blames Rey. Pops grabs his shotgun before heading out after our comedy hero. Nita's dad finds Tito at the fat man's café and threatens him and the owner with his gun, cue a piece of slapstick with the obese chef getting stuck in a doorway.

Next the angry father goes to Rey's house. The walls are covered with posters of Bruce Lee. After threatening everyone in the house, Nita's dad is eventually convinced Rey doesn't know where his daughter is. Rey remembers what Susan told him about setting him up and realises that Tom and his evil martial arts school have kidnapped Nita and want to exchange her for Bruce Lee's *Ninjitsu Fighting Techniques* manual. Rey dons a yellow tracksuit to look ever-so-slightly like Bruce Lee in the official *Game of Death* (1978), and goes all out for revenge.

In a long sequence of fights, Rey takes out the gang and frees Nita. Tito is on hand to grab back Bruce Lee's *Ninjitsu Fighting Techniques* book after Rey throws it at Tom, and also to help Nita. In the film's best joke, during these fights the theme from *Enter the Dragon* (1973) is played over and over again to remind us that Rey neither looks like nor fights like Bruce Lee. His yellow tracksuit doesn't even resemble Bruce Lee's in *Game of Death*—it is just close enough to signify the requisite movie icon! The Little Dragon wore a jumpsuit, Rey dons a two piece tracksuit with a separate top and bottom; Bruce Lee's suit zips up at the back, Rey's from the front on the upper garment. Lee's has a thick black stripe on the side, Rey's two thinner black stripes.

The idea of a lead character obsessed with Bruce Lee crops up in earlier martial arts comedies including *They Call Him Chop Suey* (1975) with Ramon Zamora and *Enter the Fat Dragon* (1978) with Sammo Hung. A plot that hangs on a secret kung fu manual likewise links this movie to other fare such as *Bruce's Deadly Fingers* (1976), *Kung Fu Fever* (1979) and *Bruce's Fists of Vengeance* (1980). The last of these takes both plot elements and literal footage of Jack Lee from *They Call Him Bruce Lee* and recycles it; both films had the same producer K.Y. Lim. Although *They Call Him Bruce Lee* takes a detour into Filipino comedy in the middle section—a digression that I greatly enjoyed for its blatant stupidity—it still has more than sufficient references to the Little Dragon to make the core of the Brucesploitation genre. This was an early film from director Jun Posadas (AKA Francis Posadas), who had a long career and made something like 75 movies, including in 2014's *Magnum Muslim .357*.

25 THE TRUE GAME OF DEATH   1979
DIRECTED BY CHAN SAN-YAT AND/OR STEVE HARRIES

The credits are a montage of Bruce Lee photos. This is followed by footage of Lee at the *Fist of Unicorn* (1973) press conference and his Hong Kong funeral. The sickest, slickest and most cynical transition in the movie is a shift from a still of Lee's corpse lying in his coffin, to an exercise montage of Lung Tien-Hsiang. A narrator announces the young man we're watching hopes to step into the stiff's shoes; although it isn't phrased like this on the soundtrack, the visuals tell it that way. The sequence shows the actor failing to achieve the correct weight training form Bruce Lee deployed so successfully for his muscular and strength development. At first Lung attempts a medium grip lat pull down with a cable. As the bar goes up his backside rises away from the seat he's perched on, and he uses his bodyweight to assist him bring the weight back down—which is particularly comic as the pin is near the top of the weight stack and it looks like he's pulling about 25kg! Intercut with this are images of a huge stack of weights moving but it's obvious it isn't Lung lifting them since we can see he's not working hard. Just as ridiculous are the lying leg curls Lung does with virtually no weight at all; he goes super-fast on the reps because he's only working with about 5kg! For his bench press Lung deploys a studio bar without much weight on it. It seems likely that the exercise montage I've just described was scripted as comedy.

Shifting from the pseudo-documentary opening to the even more obviously fictional story, we see Lung acting out on a movie set. Lung is a big film star and the mob want to manage him but he refuses to be bullied into this. Since this film is a parody of the official *Game of Death* (1978), a lot of the mobsters are Caucasian and uniformly dressed in black suits and red ties. The fact this is a critique of cultural imperialism and the Hollywoodisation of the kung fu genre in films like *Enter the Dragon* (1973) and *Game of Death* (1978) is underscored by local mob boss George being Asian and not Caucasian like the top criminals in the official *Game of Death*. Alice Meyer plays Lung's wife, a Caucasian mix of Lee's wife and his lover Betty Ting Pei. After hanging with Lung on set as he makes his latest film, and watching him fight various gangbangers, Alice goes home alone. A couple of goons sent by the mobsters who want to act as Lung's agents are waiting for her. They threaten Alice and insist she spike Lung's drink with their 'medicine' so that he'll be unconscious for three days. When Lung returns, Alice stays mum about being heavied, and her husband relaxes and day dreams about being Bruce Lee—with footage from *Way of the Dragon* cut in to illustrate his fantasies. This is followed by a short city montage, and a long night out sequence including two songs performed by different singers. Lung is lured to a pay phone by the mobsters, so they can get Alice alone and threaten her some more, while also suggesting her husband is having an affair with the singer who is on stage. This long scene reflects the way the official *Game of Death* is padded out with boring non-sequiturs involving a load of b-list Hollywood actors, and it succeeds at satirising the plodding nature of the earlier flick without being anywhere near as dull!

Back at home Lung asks Alice to make him a cup of coffee. While Lung takes a shower, one of the mobsters enters the house with a gun to make sure Alice gives him a drugged drink. We see a very phallic gun barrel shoved through a crack in the curtains as the gangbanger hides prior to Lung emerging from the bathroom. The coffee cup shakes in Alice's hands as her husband takes it from her. After consuming the drugged beverage, Lung wants sex and *Don't Cry for Me Argentina* kicks in on the soundtrack. At first we see the clothed Caucasian actress in bed with Lung, then when her garments come off she is replaced by a South East Asian body-double. When shooting with body-doubles film-makers generally don't show the faces of the stand-ins. In this case we see the double's face several times, to parody the badly edited stand-ins for Bruce Lee in the official *Game of Death*; while simultaneously being a joke about the western media's obsessive reporting of the alleged fact Lee's Hong Kong fans wished he had a Chinese wife.

The sex is awkward, and Lung pushes his fingers into the double's bum crack while the humanoid head on a plastic toy placed in the background bobs up and down. The absurdity and bad taste of this sequence are a dig at the 'quality film' signifers in Clouse's 1978 movie. Their juxtaposition with the best-known tune from the musical *Evita* is truly surreal. During the softcore anti-action Lung is shown to have hairy legs, which suggests that kung fu movie actors are as keen as bodybuilders to remove hair from the torso and arms. The awkward foreplay ends abruptly when the effects of the poison Lung's consumed kick in. He flings himself off the bed and onto the floor, then back onto the bed. While Lung throws himself around, Alice pathetically flails her arms, giving the impression that the nude stand-in isn't an actress but is simply trying her best to do what the director wants. Alice believes Lung is dead but actually he survives and the fictional film star comes back disguised as an old man to watch over her. It isn't an accident that he looks a bit like one of Bruce Lee's incognito personas in *Fist of Fury*. The disguised Lung eventually asks Alice how he died, and when she says she poisoned him he reveals who he really is. They have an argument and Alice storms off and is kidnapped by the mobsters who have also discovered that Lung faked his death.

After this the film moves ever closer to the script of the official *Game of Death*. Lung gets a note telling him to go to a container port, where he is ambushed by motorcyclists in colour-coded jumpsuits. Fighting and losing against Lung, one of the motorcycle thugs even crashes into some boxes and out spill wind up toys (exactly as happens in the official *Game of Death*). Having dressed himself in a yellow jumpsuit with black stripes, Lung goes to a pagoda. Inside he fights a Dan Inosanto clone dressed identically to Bruce Lee's top student in the official *Game of Death*. However, while Lung's opponent uses eskrima sticks like Inosanto in the earlier part of his staged fight with Lee, here only the Bruce simulation switches from his initial weapon—a bamboo cane—to nunchaku. Since the nunchaku dual between Lee and Inosanto is probably the best known element of *Game of Death* after the Little Dragon's battle with Kareem Abdul-Jabbar, having only one man using nunchucks is a great way to massively let down viewer expectations. For me the laughs this generates more than compensate for the loss of the nunchaku duel, which I found stupidly stylised—but funny—in the original. Lung finishes his cloned opponent off in the same way Lee does in the 'official' version of this film, by strangling him with his nunchucks. On the next level rather than engaging in mortal combat with a hapkido master like Ji Han-Jae, Lung kills of a couple of guys who come across like out-of-condition wrestlers. This is perfect as bathos. The payoff, and surely the giveaway that this entire movie is a really vicious parody of the official *Game of Death*, is the final fight in the 'pagoda'. In the earlier film, Lee is made to look like a dwarf as he fights the enormously tall Kareem Abdul-Jabbar. In *True Game of Death,* Lung fights an Afro-American boxer—at least his accent indicates this is his ethnicity in the English dub—and they appear reasonably evenly matched in weight and height. Since this boxer looks like he should have retired some time ago, the fisticuffs are singularly lacking as cinematic spectacle—and spectacle was the whole point of this final pagoda encounter in the earlier film.

After beating the boxer, Lung jumps down to ground level from what is clearly not a pagoda, although there was a stock shot of one before he entered the building. This satirises Robert Clouse changing the location of Bruce Lee's pagoda fights to the floors above a Chinese restaurant. Lung fights a few guys around a car, then breaks into a building where he frees Alice and terrifies boss mobster George. Rather than killing George, Lung simply leaves him for the cops to pick up; which neatly illustrates the difference between Bruce Lee's TV work in the *Green Hornet* in the 1960s—when the Little Dragon playing Kato would deal with the bad guys in the same way as Lung does here—and the fact that the mobsters are murdered by a vigilante clone composite Bruce Lee in the official *Game of Death.*

This parody movie is a laugh-out-loud funny but merciless demolition job on Clouse and the doubles he deployed in 'Bruce Lee's final film'—final, that is, until Golden Harvest released *Game of Death II* AKA *Tower of Death.* A double stands in for Lung in a couple of scenes, and there are deliberate continuity errors in the use of cars in *True Game of Death.* Likewise the footage of Bruce Lee from *Way of the Dragon* edited into this movie aims a below the belt blow at Clouse for his use of archive reels in the official *Game of Death.* As far as Bruce Lee clones go, Lung isn't cut like a bodybuilder with a super-low body fat ratio in the way that Dragon Lee, Bruce Le or even the Little Dragon are in at least some of their flicks; instead his reasonably bulky and athletic physique makes him seem more like Bruce Li but minus the blandness. The write-ups I've seen of *The True Game of Death* miss the whole point of the film; since these 'critics' don't understand it as parody, they slate it as a truly awful bottom-of-the-barrel Brucesploitation!

26 BRUCE KING OF KUNG FU 1980
AKA *LEGEND OF BRUCE LEE*

DIRECTED BY BRUCE LE

A completely fictionalised account of Bruce Lee's street fighting days as a youth in Hong Kong. Bruce keeps losing the tear-ups he gets into, so his father sends him to learn Wing Chun with Master Yip. Bruce's two pals are as prone to scrapping as he is, and the Little Dragon intervenes when his friend gets his ass whipped by a blind kung fu master; only to find himself defeated too. When Bruce speaks to Master Yip about this, his sifu teaches him blindfolded boxing. Bruce alone, and his two friends elsewhere, are ambushed and badly beaten by members of a kung fu school they'd bested in earlier punch-ups. As the ultimate in humiliation, Bruce is strung upside down and flown as a human flag of defeat from the apartment building in which he lives. Bruce recovers but one of his friends dies from the injuries he received. Whereas in real life Bruce Lee moved away from traditional kung fu styles as his practice developed, in this movie he gravitates towards them and becomes a student of a snake fist master. His new sifu tells him to watch real snakes. He tries training with three real cobras. Bruce tests his techniques on the snakes, lunging and feinting with them to see how they react to his shapes. I assume that like the real shark with the zombie stuntman in Lucio Fulci's *Zombie Flesh Eaters* (1979), the cobras had been drugged. Nonetheless, Le's session with them is impressively weird. Le is bitten but drinks wine and forces one of the snakes to try the beverage, so that he can practice drunken snake fist. After this training Bruce is unstoppable. Bolo Yeung from *Enter the Dragon* (1973) turns up to fight Le with a couple of other thugs but they are quickly dispatched. In an earlier fight Bruce had injured the son of Master Kim; Sek Kin, who as Han had the climatic battle with Bruce Lee in *Enter the Dragon*. Kin keeps sending men out to get Bruce, but they're all defeated by his snake fist. When Bruce and Kin are the last men standing they face off. Kin seems to be getting the better of Le, but then Bruce switches from straightforward snake fist to drunken snake fist and wins the fight. Kin admits defeat and Bruce and Kin express admiration for each other's martial skills. Then Bruce leaps up into a flying kick and the frame freezes on roughly the same pose that ended Bruce Lee's *Fist of Fury* (1972). The movie is hugely enjoyable for its wackiness and many action scenes, but it isn't really a bio-pic, it's a batshit insane kung fu flick!

27 BRUCE'S FISTS OF VENGEANCE   1980
DIRECTED BY BILL JAMES

The credits are cut with Bruce Le doing a kung fu workout and showing off his small but perfectly defined muscles. As the camera pulls back we see that there's a poster of Bruce Lee behind him and that he's teaching a class in what we learn is a taekwondo dojo. The gym looks like it could be in apartment block and we stay there watching the training until Jack Lee phones Bruce from Hong Kong to say he'll arrive the following afternoon.

This conversation doesn't make sense. Jack says he will be on the 9 o'clock flight. It takes about two hours to fly from Hong Kong to Manila, so if Lee was on a flight at nine he'd either arrive around 11am in the morning or 11pm at night.

We then cut to Romano Kristoff and his bad guys training in their gym. Just as Bruce's students continue training as he takes a phone call, Kristoff leaves his men working out when the Filipino Ken Watanabe (not the Japanese/Hollywood actor with the same name) arrives. The two men sit down for a conversation and Watanabe reveals that the man with Bruce Lee's secret kung fu book will be arriving in Manila in the morning. An intense Kristoff tells Watanabe: "Very good! I've been trying to locate the whereabouts of that book for years. Now I have my chance to get it!"

Cut to the next day at Manila airport. The camera pans down from the control tower to arrivals and we are introduced to a bad guy who is spying on Bruce Le and Jack Lee. He watches them get into a car and then follows in his own vehicle. Bruce and Jack chat in the back of their car, while the villain follows them along the Manila seafront. To orientate us there is a shot of the Cultural Centre of The Philippines. Sadly the water fountains are turned off. The CCP looks much more impressive with them on. Bruce drops Jack off at Hotel Frederic so he can rest until he is picked up at 3pm to go to the martial arts tournament. Baddies follow Lee into the hotel, they seem to have multiplied and one of them phones Kristoff to tell him where the guy with Bruce Lee's kung fu book is.

Once he's alone in his hotel room, Lee opens Bruce Lee's book while we get to see a still of the Little Dragon—with spinning camera effects—and hear the theme from *Enter the Dragon* (1973). Later, Bruce Le is defeated by Kristoff at the martial arts tournament. When Jack returns to his hotel room he is attacked by Kristoff's men after opening the door to them. He teases one guy with Bruce Lee's secret kung fu manual, holding it out for him and snatching it away while fighting. This scene is cut in from the slightly earlier *They Call Him Bruce Lee* (1979).

The next day Jack goes to Bruce's taekwondo school but pisses off one student, while impressing many others. To teach the mouthy student a lesson,

Jack pulls down his pants and everyone laughs at him. Before leaving the dojo, Jack Lee gives Bruce Le a surprise present, the Little Dragon's kung fu manual. Later Jack meets up with another of Bruce's students to talk about teaching him Bruce Lee's Jeet Kune Do. However, Jack and the student are distracted by a couple of women from Kristoff's gang, who are out to seduce them. They end up having dinner with the women, and one gets Jack drunk and takes him back to her room in the hotel, which looks just like Jack's. While in bed they are attacked by the student Jack debagged and some of his friends. Jack with a little help from his villainous lady acquaintance easily defeats these novices. Jack tells the lady he has to go back to his students in Hong Kong. She realises she's not going to get Bruce Lee's secret kung fu book. She phones Kristoff who is mad at her for this failure, and not long after she is strangled. There is a cut to a shot of this henchwoman dead and underwater—the tiling makes it look like she's in a shower.

Bruce's Fists of Vengeance is hypnotic because the same things keep happening again and again and at the same locations. There are endless spy scenes in the lobby of Hotel Frederic, endless fight scenes in Jack Lee's hotel bedroom, and endless training scenes at the same two dojos. Eventually one of Kristoff's gang kidnaps Jack by pointing a revolver at him. Jack is made to turn around and then whacked unconscious from behind. Despite being tortured Jack won't reveal the whereabouts of Bruce Lee's kung fu book. Jack uses his legs to kick the gang, and so they tie his feet behind his head. Jack is impressively flexible and when left alone, he wriggles out of his bonds, this is enthralling; as are Lee's high kicks, although they're hardly in keeping with the martial art he is supposed to practice, Bruce Lee's Jeet Kune Do. Meanwhile Bruce Le is out watching cockfights with his girlfriend. Le looks like he's one hundred and one percent into betting, and has a huge grin on his face as he wins lots of money. These scenes of animal abuse rather spoil this otherwise great piece of schlock.

After escaping Jack goes to Bruce Le's taekwondo gym. He talks to James, the student he'd debagged. James apologises for his bad behaviour and is forgiven. One of Kristoff's gang sees Jack emerging from the gym and follows him to his hotel. Kristoff with support busts into Jack's room yet again. He thinks he is going to take Jack out with his fists and feet but gets the worst of it in an unarmed fight; he is only saved from death or at least serious injury when his gunman shoots Jack. Meanwhile Bruce Le has turned up at his gym and after learning Jack had been there but has gone back to his hotel leaves to find his friend. After exiting Hotel Frederic the bad guys realise Bruce Lee's secret kung fu manual must be at the taekwondo gym, which they attack and take apart. They not only get the book, they kidnap Bruce Le's girlfriend. Le finds Jack dying but his friend lives long enough to have a discussion with him about Bruce Lee's secret kung fu manual. Bruce then goes back to his gym to discover his students either unconscious or dead. He rouses James, the bad student whose turned good, to consciousness and discovers what happened. Bruce makes his way to Kristoff's HQ where he takes out various henchmen, frees his girlfriend and finally has the climatic fight with Kristoff.

The last battle seems to go on forever and ends up with the two men brawling in a fountain. Eventually Le wins and crawls out of the water. While the first part of the movie with its mesmeric repetitions is better than the climax, aside from the animal cruelty this is a classic piece of sleaze. Secret kung fu manuals in movies like this seem akin to grimoires in that both invest those who get to read them with incredible powers. This movie not only uses footage from producer K.Y. Lim's earlier *They Call Him Bruce Lee,* but also recycles much of its plot. However, *Bruce's Fists of Vengeance* has more action and less comedy, and would seem to be aimed at an international audience; whereas the earlier film appears to have been made to appeal to Filipino film-goers. According to an internet source I've yet to verify, director Bill James was born in the USA and had previously been employed by the Bates Alcantara Advertising Agency, where his job entailed promoting corporations such as McDonalds and Adidas in The Philippines. This may be the only film Bill James directed.

28 THE CLONES OF BRUCE LEE — 1980
DIRECTED BY JOSEPH VELASCO AND/OR NAM GI-NAM AND PRACHA POONVIVAT

Bruce Lee dies but Jon T. Benn (as Professor Lucas) is able to use cells from the Little Dragon's body to create three clones—who don't look like each other, let alone Bruce Lee—to fight crime. The clones are trained by martial arts masters Bolo Yeung *(Enter the Dragon)* and Chiang Tao. Dragon Lee plays clone one who is sent off to investigate crooks using a movie studio as a front for their gold smuggling operation. Thus we get a theme common to the Brucesploitation genre, corruption in the film business. Possibly this section draws on the official *Game of Death* (1978), which in its turn took the trope from earlier Brucesploitation flicks.

One of the crooks suggests killing Dragon Lee on set as he's filmed because then they can then exploit his death for monetary purposes. There are also attempts to kill the Bruce Lee clone off camera, but in the end Dragon Lee smashes the criminal gang. Next clones two and three (Bruce Le and Bruce Lai) meet up with CIA operative Chuck Lee (played by Bruce Thai) in Bangkok. There follow typical tourists shots of the Thai capital and nude girls on a local beach.

After some fun the two Bruce Lee clones and Bruce Lee lookalike (Chuck/Bruce Thai) take on Dr. Ngai, an evil scientist with a maniacal laugh who plans to take over the world with an army of invincible bronzemen he's created from ordinary mortals by injecting them with his special formula. In other words a bunch of extras who've been sprayed gold, and supposedly feel no pain when hit because their skin is as tough as metal. The clones and their CIA ally discover a poisonous plant—it looks like grass—that they stuff in the mouths of the otherwise invincible bronzemen to stop them and defeat Dr. Ngai. The Thai location if not the plotline draws on *The Big Boss* (1971), although here better use is made of local colour than in the earlier Lo Wei/Bruce Lee movie. Bruce Le and Bruce Lai return to Hong Kong for the final section of the flick, where Professor Lucas feels insufficiently rewarded for his efforts and orders the three Bruce Lee clones to fight each other so that he can take over the world with the survivor. He is foiled by a horrified assistant, who cuts the lines to the kit Benn uses to control the clones. The three Little Dragon simulations then battle Benn's henchmen and a death ray; leading to the demise of Bruce Lai and the eventual arrest of the mad scientist.

Clones of Bruce Lee was produced by Dick Randall, an American notorious for the threadbare wackiness of his exploitation flicks; here he's hedging his bets with a mix of sex, sci-fi, bronzemen and Brucesploitation. The craze for bronzemen in martial arts movies was kicked off by Joesph Kuo's 1976 movie *18 Bronzemen,* which was quickly followed with a sequel *Return of the 18 Bronzemen.* How much, if any, of *Clones of Bruce Lee* Joseph Velasco actually directed is open to speculation. An entry on the Korean Movie Database for *Sahyeong-samgeol* (literal translation *Death Penalty on Three Robots)* lists Nam Gi-Nam as director of what seems to be a different edit of the same film; this appears to be more focused on Dragon Lee and has a plotline about two rival crime organisations fighting for control of Incheon Wharf. The Thai section of this film was probably directed by Pracha Poonvivat; 'Supervisor of Thailand shooting' according to the English credits. Some sources give The Philippines as a shooting location, although much of the Dragon Lee material looks as if it is Korean. A few shots, for example external views of Queen Elizabeth Hospital, were clearly filmed in Hong Kong but these are generic and could be stock footage. Velasco may have helmed the scenes set in Hong Kong but much of the Dragon Lee footage appears to be lifted from a Korean movie. There is little agreement about its release date, some sources saying 1977, although 1980 seems more probable.

A number of fu fans have complained that this flick is boring because it consists of mostly of identical fight scenes, allegedly all choreographed by Bruce Le. Such whinging misses the point that the endless Bruce Lee and snake fu style brawling is an over-signified counterpoint to a final fight in which Bruce Le—after being freed from Benn's mind control, and thus no longer a Little Dragon clone, uses monkey kung fu against a snake stylist. Many viewers have only seen this flick in a very bad pan and scan English language version. I found it far more enjoyable in its original aspect ration than with a cropped picture, and would rate it as an absolutely crucial entry at the core of the Brucesploitation genre.

29 FIST OF FEAR, TOUCH OF DEATH 1980

AKA *THE DRAGON AND THE COBRA*

DIRECTED BY MATTHEW MALLINSON

This is a mockumentary produced by Aquarius Releasing and it demonstrates their complete contempt for Bruce Lee fanboys after their earlier success at marketing fare such as *Visitors In America*, a Korean film that had nothing to do with the Little Dragon but that this distributor nonetheless retitled *Bruce Lee Fights Back from the Grave* in order to draw in English speaking audiences.

Based in the Selwyn Theater building on Manhattan's 42nd Street, Aquarius were the leading distributor of grindhouse cinema in New York before the video market and Hollywood blockbusters killed off most of the independents in the industry. Aquarius handled sex films including *Deep Throat* (1972) alongside Eurosleaze from directors such as Joe D'Amato and Umberto Lenzi; for a time they were also the New York sub-distributor for the movies produced by Roger Corman. The firm and its boss Terry Levene specialised in tongue-in-cheek hucksterism, and if you're not laughing along with him, you're probably the butt of the joke; that's certainly the case with Bruce Lee fanboys and this movie.

After some generic shots of New York, *Fist of Fear* begins with the camera showing a marquee promoting 'The Oriental World of Self Defense' while on the soundtrack actor Adolph Caesar tells us we're outside the '1979 World Karate Championships'. Next comes Aaron Banks informing Caesar—whose playing the role of a TV reporter—that he believes Bruce Lee was killed by the death touch or vibrating palm, and that both Bruce Lee and he were working on perfecting this mythical technique; it exists only in wuxia novels and movies. Cut to footage of Bruce Lee speaking in the *Longstreet* TV show, over which is dubbed in a very camp and boyish accent: "The secret of karate is power, internal power from the ear." And then just to confirm that we're watching a satire, Banks goes on to make this absurd claim about the coroner's verdict that Bruce Lee's death was the result of misadventure: "now all misadventure means is that they really don't know what happened to the man…" The inquest into Lee's death was held in Hong Kong when it was under colonial British rule, and what misadventure means in legal terms in this context is a planned action—in this case taking a strong headache pill—that had an unintended consequence, viz an allergic reaction that caused Lee's brain to swell and killed him. Under the British legal system if the coroner felt unable to determine the cause of death then an open verdict should have been recorded. Banks is talking out of his arse and it is impossible to know whether he believed his own bullshit or if this is just huckster-ism to promote his Karate Academy and martial arts shows; as an educated guess I'd say it's probably a bit of both but overwhelmingly the latter. Not just in this film but elsewhere Banks has drummed up publicity for himself by repeating these stupid claims. However, Aquarius don't just point a camera at Banks and let him go into his rant, they make it clear they wouldn't want any sane viewer to think they buy his line on Bruce Lee. That's why later on there's a running gag about Fred Williamson being mistaken for Harry Belafonte; after Banks attempted and failed to make a career for himself as an actor, he switched to singing and allegedly studied music under Alan Green, who was simultaneously a vocal coach for Harry Belafonte.

Aquarius and at least some of their viewers will know the official Banks biography, most of which is probably baloney, but it has our martial arts promoter as a young man tanking at acting, singing, and various other pursuits, before discovering karate and almost instantly curing himself of substance abuse; although watching Banks talk about Bruce Lee, you'd swear he has to be on drugs if what he says isn't just a promotional put on. There are a few clips of karate fights, including Bill Louie pulling a crowd pleaser by poking out the eyes of his opponent and throwing them into the ringside seats. This is staged and faked, but then so was so much else at Aaron Banks' martial arts shows—which relied heavily on feats of strength and at times even appearances by stage conjurer Ralf Bialla who did the superannuated magic trick of catching a bullet with his teeth. What Banks was promoting with much board breaking and similar stunts, was more carnival than martial arts, and that's probably what attracted Aquarius to it. However it seems likely the Bill Louie stunt was an idea the film-makers came up with, since Aquarius were keen on eye-gouging in their exploitation offerings (Luis Buñuel anyone?): director Lucio Fulci is notorious for such scenes and one can be found in *The Beyond* (1981) which Aquarius distributed in butchered form under the title *7 Doors of Death;* Terry Levene also promoted *Queen Boxer* (1972) with a poster featuring a woman who is not in the movie holding a pair of eyeballs in the palm of her hand and the tagline 'the newest look, the oldest law, an eye for an eye'.

Returning to *Fist of Fear,* it moves on to cuts between Bruce Lee talking on *Longstreet* but redubbed with the scriptwriter's satirical bullshit, and Adolph Caesar filmed nearly a decade later allegedly interviewing him. This is obviously fake with the man conducting it clearly recorded at a different time and place to the Little Dragon. Throughout this section and wherever else Lee is redubbed, a super-camp voice is used to intimate that hyper-masculinity will ultimately be transformed into its opposite. After more touch of death bollocks featuring Caesar and Banks, we cut to a series of skits with blaxsploitation star Fred 'The Hammer' Williamson. These include a sequence where scriptwriter Ron Harvey (AKA Jasper Milktoast)—Levene's right-hand man at Aquarius—gets into an argument with The Hammer on the street, having mistaken him for Harry Belafonte. Here and everywhere else, the scriptwriter and director are playing this feature for laughs.

For those that get the insider jokes, the very inclusion of Williamson is another two fingers to Banks. This martial arts promoter never quite gave up on his ambitions to become an actor and was rather publicly humiliated over a speaking role he thought he was getting but didn't in *Three the Hard Way* (1974), which starred Williamson, Jim Brown and Jim Kelly; Banks did get a small part in the poorly received 1982 follow up *One Down, Two to Go.* Aside from his b-movie star appeal, the main point of having Williamson in the movie is to undermine Banks.

After Williamson, there's more Bill Louie fight footage before Ron Van Clief gets to confirm—because this is a satire and it's in the script—that Bruce Lee was murdered. Obviously, Van Clief is one of a number of martial artists—Chuck Norris's speech at the *1975 San Diego Comic-Con* convention provides another example—who believed Lee to be in poor health prior to his death, and that there was nothing mysterious about his demise. Van Clief's take on this can be found on his commentary for the DVD reissue of his film *Black Dragon's Revenge* AKA *Death of Bruce Lee* (1975). Van Clief's scripted lines are another indication that nothing anyone says about Bruce Lee in *Fist of Fear* should be taken seriously.

As the film moves on, Van Clief saves a girl from a gang of New York rapists—in a martial arts parody of flicks like *The Warriors* (1979). Twenty minutes in we come to the core of the movie, a completely fictional biography of Bruce Lee in which it is claimed his great grandfather was one of the greatest samurai master swordsmen in nineteenth century China (yeah, right!). This section is largely built around footage of a 16 year-old Bruce Lee in the 1957 Cantonese film version of *The Thunderstorm*. This is one of several movies based on a play by Cao Yu that tells the tale of a rich man who has two sons with his family's maid, then goes on to have a third in a subsequent marriage. The maid later has a daughter, but when this girl and the oldest son fall in love with each other they don't know they are half-siblings. This son also has an affair with his stepmother. Cao Yu was known as 'China's Ibsen' and this early Little Dragon film amounts to little more than bourgeois literary crap captured on celluloid. Fortunately the Aquarius team understood the need to demolish serious culture and reworked this self-conscious exercise in theatrical tedium into the tale of karate crazy Bruce pissing off his family with his martial arts obsession.

Cut into this black and white archive footage of a teenage Bruce Lee are colour scenes from *Forced to Fight* (1971), supposedly representing flashbacks to the antics of the Little Dragon's great grandfather as a master swordsman in nineteenth-century China. Actually *Forced to Fight* is a film from Taiwan for which Aquarius happened to hold rights because they'd distributed it in the USA; these days the flick is probably better known under its later video title of *Invincible Super Chan*. It is mind boggling that Bruce Lee fanboys are so lacking in humour that they complain about *Fist of Fear* being disrespectful to their idol and whinge the film-makers didn't know the facts about his life, or the difference between various forms of Chinese and Japanese martial arts. This is a satire, not a documentary, and the fanboys might as well complain that *Life of Brian* (1979) is not a historically accurate representation of Jesus Christ! The humour in *Fist of Fear* may be off the wall and zany, but clearly the treatment of Chinese and Japanese culture as interchangeable is a joke; which is not to defend this film against any charges of Orientalism that others might level at it, but simply an insistence that the film-makers knew exactly what they were doing and where the material they were deploying came from.

As a piece of detournement I would rank *Fist of Fear* alongside René Viénet's widely acclaimed *Can Dialectics Break Bricks?* (1973); it is also an important work in the evolution of cut-and-paste martial arts movies, pre-empting as it does many of the techniques used by Godfrey Ho and Joseph Lai in their ninja flicks. After the section dedicated to Bruce Lee, we have Bill Louie dressed up as Kato saving a couple of girls from rape in Battery Park. The slow pace at which Louie approaches the gang appears to be a piss-take that takes a kick at another Brucesploitation comedy classic, *Bruce Against Supermen* (1975). After this Aaron Banks explains that when he got together with Bruce Lee, the two of them would spend most of their time complementing each other about their various accomplishments. Then it's back to more martial arts demonstrations and finally a fight between Louis Neglia and John "Cyclone" Flood to decide who will be the next Bruce Lee. Neglia wins but doesn't become the new Little Dragon. Adolph Caesar then wraps everything up from an empty stadium by parodying the conventions of sports reporting and documentary film.

This movie belongs at core of the Brucesploitation genre, while at the same time it also neatly fits into the world of mockumentary flicks. While the archive footage of the teenage 'king of kung fu' is not as tedious as that featured in *The Real Bruce Lee* (1977), even detourned early Little Dragon footage doesn't merit multiple viewings; like most child actors the young Bruce Lee is excruciatingly boring to watch unless you're an obsessed fan. Aquarius were no doubt copying the moves of the producers of *The Real Bruce Lee* (Dick Randall and Serafim Karalexis) to an extent, but are also running down these rivals by making a mockumentary rather than a documentary; briefly but very explicitly dissing Bruce Li by name in their feature, as well as by having footage of Bill Louie as Kato parodying similar scenes of Li in *The Real Bruce Lee* and *Bruce Against Supermen*. The sheer crappiness of the Louie's Kato scenes as a finger up to Bruce Li is almost funny the first time it is viewed, but it isn't nearly good enough to work on repeat visits. It's ironic Levene should take a pop at Karalexis in this way because it was the Greek bringing *I Am Curious Yellow* (1967) to the USA and the resultant court case he won against its censorship that opened the floodgates to the tidal wave of seventies sexploitation movies that Aquarius—among others—made so much money distributing. That said, while Levene and Aquarius were satirising a variety of targets, like Randall and Karalexis they also wanted to make money.

Finally, it is also worth nothing when Aquarius distributed the English language version of *The Bodyguard* AKA *Karate Kiba* (1976), they tacked on a ridiculous opening sequence in which Aaron Banks and Bill Louie discuss and demonstrate the relative merits of—and differences between—Sonny Chiba and Bruce Lee.

30 GOLDEN DRAGON SILVER SNAKE 1980
AKA *DRAGONEER 5: THE INDOMITABLE*
AKA *A FIGHT AT HONG KONG RANCH*
DIRECTED BY GODFREY HO AND/OR KIM SI-HYEON

Three guys on motorcycles ride into some woodland for a meeting with Dragon Lee's brother Han. They expect him to say sorry for organising a protest against the protection racket they're involved in, when he says he's nothing to apologise about they start a fight and are beaten.

After the leader of the motorcycle gang reports to the big boss—whose face we don't see until its 'shock' revelation at the end—he is told he has screwed up and his cheek is scratched by a cat that is thrown at him. Some non-motorcycle riding members of the syndicate go to what is apparently Han's apartment building. They follow him into the lift and while two hold knives at his throat, a third plunges an electric drill into his body, shades of *Frightmare* (1974) and *Driller Killer* (1979).

Next there is a fight between Samuel Walls and Bruce Lee clone Bruce Lai. This switches to a differently attired Walls battling Cheung Lik. Some shots of a grinning Dragon Lee in a one-piece yellow tracksuit are also cut into this. Since Walls didn't have much of a film career, his fight scenes are probably out-takes from Joseph Velasco's *Enter Three Dragons* (1978), on which Godfrey Ho is credited as co-director.

After this detour, which doesn't relate in any way to the rest of the film, we return to what there is of a plot. The hoods double the protection money they are demanding from those who supported Han's protest. A rickshaw driving kung fu master takes Dragon Lee to a restaurant owner and gets him a job as a cook. Soon the gangsters are demanding that a family who own a farm sell up so that the area can be turned into a tourist resort.

At the farm there is a fight with the heavies involving darts sent bow and arrow style from the strings of an acoustic guitar, and then the guitar being used as a weapon. The rickshaw driver turns up and after a few plot twists and turns, one farm worker in the shape of Johnny Chan—a flash in the pan Jackie Chan clone best known for his starring role in *Revenge of the Drunken Master* (1984)—becomes his student. Inevitably some *Drunken Master* (1978) style training follows.

Moving back to the city, Dragon Lee trashes the protection racketeers when they turn up at his boss's restaurant but he loses his job because the gangsbangers say he must go. Dragon is confronted by a tall American fighter working for the criminals, but he creams him and his two side kicks. Dragon goes to the farm and gets a job there. It turns out the rickshaw driver was his brother's best friend, so they know each other. They are trying to find the men who killed Dragon's brother. By this time Chiang Tao has turned up as a second in command boss and we've had a scene of him being massaged by swimsuit clad young women. After the young female farm owner and her uncle are kidnapped by the hoods, Dragon rescues the girl from the criminals gym HQ; this has men working out in it throughout gangland meetings. Only the girl is saved, the uncle is killed by the gangbangers. A 'cop' is ineffectually investigating the kidnap.

Finally it all becomes too much for Dragon, who dresses up in a yellow one-piece tracksuit—but with red stripes and a horrible lace up front, so it isn't nearly as cool as Bruce Lee's in *Game of Death*—and races off with Johnny Chan to take revenge. By this time Dragon and the rickshaw driver have worked out the gangsters they are having trouble with are the same men who killed Lee's brother.

In a classic b-movie trope, Dragon disrupts Chiang's birthday by bringing him a coffin as a 'present'. Then Dragon battles and ultimately triumphs over Tao, a part of their fight takes place on a speedboat. Finally Dragon has to defeat the big boss who until the start of their fight is pretending to be a blind cripple. He turns out to have been the fake cop who'd investigated the kidnappings. Dragon eventually triumphs with the aid of a steel baseball bat that he'd hidden in a sling over his back!

There are quite a few Bruce Lee-like elements. Dragon Lee protecting a restaurant and other businesses parallels the plot of *Way of the Dragon* (1972). He also infiltrates the gym HQ of the gangsters by saying he's a telephone engineer, and the hoods don't realise who he is until he takes his hat off. Bruce Lee pulls a similar stunt in *Fist of Fury* (1972). Bruce Lee also disguises himself as a rickshaw driver and old man in *Fist of Fury*, so the rickshaw driver in *Golden Dragon, Silver Snake* might be taken as invoking this. For the climatic fight Dragon Lee dons a yellow tracksuit to emulate Bruce Lee and also during his fight with the big boss receives cuts to his face—from blades in his opponent's shoes—these look a bit like those Bruce Lee receives from Han in the climatic fight in *Enter the Dragon* (1973). Dragon goes over the top with his Bruce Lee impersonations in terms of facial and hand gestures; although his fighting rarely resembles the way Bruce Lee choreographed himself in his kung fu vehicles.

Golden Dragon, Silver Snake clearly belongs to the core of the Brucesploitation genre—even if it is just as much a comedy martial arts film riffing on Jackie Chan. The Korean Internet Movie Database lists this film as being 11 minutes longer than the English language cut and Kim Si-Hyun (AKA Kim Si-Hyeon) as the director. What the producers at Asso Asia seem to have done is taken a Korean film they may have partially funded, edited more than 11 minutes out of it, inserted the fight scene with Samuel Walls, redubbed it and released it as their own work with direction credits given to Godfrey Ho.

31 MUSCLE OF THE DRAGON 1981

AKA *DRAGON LEE FIGHTS BACK*

DIRECTED BY TO MAN-BO

This opens with the credits running over seven-plus minutes of cut-and-paste footage from *The Clones of Bruce Lee* (1980). From the climax of *Clones* we have Dragon Lee fighting Bruce Lai, then Dragon against Bruce Le. This is followed by Dragon battling it out with Chiang Tao. Finally Bruce Le takes on Cheng Kei-Ying and again this is from the climax of *Clones*. We then cut to a police station in Korea where a message comes through about Hong Kong cops wanting help with a heroin investigation, and sending Cheung Lik (Agent Q-101) to do undercover work.

Simultaneously the Korean cops are asked to look for a man who has vanished after being released from prison. The fuzz tell Kim An Chu's son to go home and wait for him but it turns out his disappearance is linked to the heroin being sent to Hong Kong and Japan from Korea. The first seven minutes of recycled action is in heavy contrast to these four minutes of static plot setting—told between a telex machine and talking heads. Cut to downtown and one of *Muscle's* silly jokes: Dragon in a payphone hanging up on someone and dialing again, so we expect more conversation, but our hero doesn't get through and all we hear on the soundtrack is traffic à la Godard's *Weekend* (1967). Dragon walks away, cut to him getting out of a taxi, cut again to a woman emerging from a flat in a tower block. She's answering the door to Dragon, who is fuzz investigating the matters brought up earlier at the cop shop. Chu's son isn't home, but Dragon finds him in a local bar and finally gets to ask him about his missing father, a chemist skilled at making heroin. The son says no one went to see his father in prison but recently a man had visited him, and he gives Dragon the geezer's card. Dragon explains to his boss at the police station that the dude who'd visited the missing man is involved in some kind of religion. Dragon is shown a photograph and told to check the guy out. The cops stage a fake mugging of this target with Dragon intervening and saving the guy's briefcase. The grateful criminal cum religious leader decides to recruit Dragon into his organisation, which we later learn is called the Moon Church. Dragon has to do some Bruce Lee mugging as he beats some other men in a fight, to prove he is good enough to join the church, and then wait until the full moon to become a member.

The sect only accepts powerful men and beautiful women. Dragon is put in a room and told not to leave it and not to tell anyone about anything he sees. The Moon Church elders are equally heavy with a girl called Kin whose father is the Bishop—or head—of their organisation. We see Dragon on a boat and Cheung Lik appears for the first time. He gets into a fight with other passengers—foreigners who belong to the Moon Church—and throws them overboard. Kin comes up from a lower deck and compliments Lik on his fighting skill. Lik blows it by telling the girl: "I can handle men but I can't handle women though." When Kin walks away, Dragon who was lurking in the background turns to Lik and addresses him saying: "You certainly don't have a way with women." Lik replies: "But I do with men." Unfortunately they aren't about to get it on, not in this movie, they only reach a tacit understanding to help each other out!

The boat arrives at its destination and the Moon worshippers go to a cave. The ceremony starts almost at once, with those present given a drugged drink. As they queue for the holy water Lik passes Dragon a handful of pills which are an antidote to what they're about to be spiked with. At the moon worshipping ceremony it quickly gets happy-clappy and then just as fast looks so trippy and loved out that you'd think those stumbling around must be 72 hours into a three-day rave! Of course, Lik and Dragon who've taken the antidote are faking drug-induced euphoria. A sloppy fight breaks out with Dragon at the centre, until Moon Church henchman Kim Dong-Ho orders the brawlers to stop and they obey.

Kin is forced to drink the drugged water, which she's so far avoided. Transformed into a zombie-like sex slave, Kin enters Dragon's room. When the girl starts to take her nightie off, Dragon is horrified but plays along after Kin says: "Why do they watch us all the time?" There is coy foreplay on the bed until Dragon manages to drop an antidote pill into Kin's mouth. Kin sobers up and freaks but Dragon pins her down beneath him and explains she's been drugged. Kin replies: "My father wouldn't do this to me, so I think The Bishop is a fake." Kim Dong-Ho, Sim Sang-Hyeon and another Moon Church guy are watching CCTV of the sexual action going down in the various bedrooms of the lust crazed couples who drank the love brew.

There is a cut-and-paste scene of Bolo Yeung having softcore sex that must come from elsewhere because the producers—Dick Randall and friends—wouldn't have paid such a relatively big name kung fu star to perform nude for a few seconds in bed. Since all the other cut-and-paste footage seems to come from *Clones of Bruce Lee,* this may do so too. However, I've not clocked it in the various English language dubs of that film I've seen. I'm unsure when the English dub of *Muscle* was made, but because it was probably after the Korean release of the flick in 1981, it is also possible this cut-and-paste material is an out-take from *Ninja Strikes Back* (1982); the

English dub of that has a very brief Bolo sex scene. The long-shot of Bolo and a nude woman having sex on a bed is fogged in the centre to obscure a full view. Moving on, while Dragon fakes being a sex crazed heterosexual zombie very well, Cheung Lik is less cautious. Lik gets up, dresses hurriedly and races out of his room. The drugged woman he was in bed with whines: "Where are you going? Don't leave me!" In the hallway Lik is confronted by two women who tell him he can't walk around. He says his woman is no good and he needs to find another one, then suggests a threesome. The two female Moon Church functionaries tell him to follow them, but Lik is knocked unconscious by a blow to the back of the head after taking one or two steps, only to wake up imprisoned in a pit in the floor of the cave complex in which the Moon ceremony took place earlier. After this Lik is interrogated and rumbled as a Hong Kong cop, while Dragon has to act out the role of compliant Church zombie.

This is followed by more cut-and-paste footage from *The Clones of Bruce Lee*. First we have Dragon's climatic fight with Bolo from the earlier film, then his fight with three of Jon T. Benn's less impressive kung fu henchmen. The second piece of cut-and-paste from *Clones* in this section does at least give Dragon the chance to display his one stick nunchaku—with a piece of wood on one end of the chain and a ring on the other, so that it can be swung around a thumb or finger as a way of confusing and frightening opponents, not to mention hurting them if they get hit.

The next piece of cut-and-paste from *Clones of Bruce Lee* features Bruce Lai in a variant version of one of his climatic encounters with another of Jon T. Benn's kung fu fighters. This fight is utterly senseless and wonderfully surreal in *Muscle,* although Lai appears in cut-and-paste material at the start of this movie, he is completely absent from its main narrative—it is Dragon and Lik who have infiltrated the Moon Church, not Lai.

These collaged scenes add more than thirteen minutes to the running time of what is still a short feature film. At the end of the Bruce Lai fight, we cut to Dragon returning to his room. I guess we're supposed to assume Dragon's been prowling around like Bruce Lee on Han's island in *Enter the Dragon* (1973) and not realise we've been watching footage very jarringly edited in from *Clones*. After a conversion with Kin—who says Dragon must save Lik and find her father—our hero leaves but this time wearing a shirt and jacket, he'd returned topless. Dragon is supposed to be guarding Lik, but he throws the Hong Kong cop a knife so he can cut the ropes he's tied with, and tells him to wait until dark when he'll help him escape. Cut to the criminals who've taken over the Moon Church discussing the low quality of their heroin. To rectify this they need Kim An Chu to refine their opium for them, but despite being their hostage he refuses to go back to manufacturing drugs now he's got out of jail after doing fifteen years of bird. The bad guys decide they'll have to kidnap Chu's son and use him as leverage to force his old man to make high quality smack for them. Their reasons for refraining from using their zombie slave drug on Chu are never clarified, perhaps being dumb criminals it doesn't occur to them, or maybe it isn't evil enough and therefore sufficiently fun. If the bad guys used the drug on Chu there would be no need to kidnap his son, which is what their minions attempt to do next—only the foot soldiers carrying out this task are arrested by the cops when they try to lure Junior into a car with the promise they'll take him to see his dad. This causes their bosses to suspect a spy is amongst them and they blame Kin, as well as wondering if Dragon is in on this with her.

While Kin is interrogated, Dragon gets Lik out of the pit in which he's imprisoned. When Dragon returns to his room, Kin is bound and gagged on the bed, and he's set upon by Moon Church goons. The bad guys tie Dragon up and imprison him with Chu, getting clean away with Kin just before the cops bust in to arrest them. After too much talking head plot exposition in the cave between Dragon, his chief and Chu, we cut to downtown. Dragon disguised as a beggar has a discussion with Lik as they stake out a known haunt of the villains. They're convinced the fake Bishop is Wan Pin San (Sim Sang-Hyeon) who is wanted in Hong Kong on various drug charges. When one of the gang turns up, Dragon and Lik hire a taxi to follow his car. As the two cops close in on the criminals' hideout, one Moon Church leader gets angry at the attitude of the others. Somehow despite not getting Chu to raise the quality of the heroin they produce, they've made five million dollars and are ready to split and wind down their whole operation in Korea. The shocked Moon Church believer spits: "You bastards! You pretend you're religious! You cheated us into producing heroin to kill people! Then trick us! You're evil bastards! Garbage!"

After a fight the true believer is tied up and taken down to the basement where Kin and her father—at least I assume it is the real Bishop as I don't know who else this could be—are roped and gagged. Lik who was making his way towards Kin and her dad hides out of sight when two criminals enter with their latest prisoner. Front of house, Dragon takes out a couple of minions before their bosses arrive. A big fight ensures, Kim Dong-Ho is the first to jump in and the effect is surreal. In the cut-and-paste footage from *Clones* at the start, the tiny Bruce Le manages to make the small but muscular Dragon look tall; somehow Dong-Ho succeeds in making Lee look like Kareem Abdul-Jabbar fighting the 'king of kung fu' in the official *Game of Death* (1978). Dragon is winning the fight but when Lik turns up and says he'll take care of the lesser villains, our hero chases after big boss Sim Sang-Hyeon.

Once all the criminals—including Hyeon—are arrested and piled up in front of the house, Dragon's chief arrives with some other cops. Kin emerges out of nowhere with her father. Kin embraces Dragon and everyone realises they are in love. The Chief says he'll be best man and congratulations are offered all around. Wedding bells ring on the soundtrack and we have an image of a church bell with a Christian cross above it, followed by a zoom in to the cross which fills the screen; reminding us that Christianity was the most popular religion in South Korea at the time this film was made—and not Buddhism or the shamanistic beliefs of the fictional 'Moon Church'.

Then there is a final head shot of Dragon and Kin in love and totally absorbed in each other as the setting sun shimmers around them. With all the *Clones of Bruce Lee* footage cut into this, not to mention Dragon's Bruce Lee mugging in some of its original scenes, this flick clearly makes the core of the Brucesploitation genre. On the one poster I've seen for this film under the title *Dragon Lee Fights Back*, Cheung Lik is billed under his Chansploitation name of Jacky Chang; on the credits of this film as I've seen it under the *Muscle* title he is credited as Chang Lic. So the producers and distributors were selling this as both Brucesploitation and Chansploitation, a hedged bet rather than just a single throw of the dice on the continuing appeal of the Little Dragon; although anyone viewing this in the hope of seeing Chansploitation will be disappointed. Whether it was actually made by To Man-Bo—that is aside from *The Clones of Bruce Lee* material for which Joseph Velasco is nominally responsible but may have been another director's work—or some uncredited Korean director, is a question I can't properly answer.

32 TOWER OF DEATH 1981

AKA *GAME OF DEATH II*

DIRECTED BY NG SEE-YUEN

Bruce Lee and his unconvincing double(s) visit the Buddhist temple where his fictional younger brother is studying kung fu. He wants to pressure this sibling into working harder at becoming a truly great martial artist. This is a lot less enthralling than seeing Hwang Jang-Lee kick some 'foreigner' around after receiving a challenge from him, which is what happens before Bruce goes to Kim Tai-Jong's empty room and tosses away his brother's porno books, leaving in their place his deadly kung fu manual.

Lee writes a letter to Kim—his brother in the movie—saying he was sorry to have missed him and telling him to stay away from women. Lee goes home to his dad and discovers his friend Hwang has died. Before going to the funeral, Lee tracks down Hwang's illegitimate nightclub singer daughter. The daughter gives Lee a roll of film passed on to her during a rare and unexpected visit from her father just before he dropped dead. Immediately a bunch of goons burst into the dressing room where Lee is having his tête-à-tête with the daughter, and there is a fight over the celluloid. When Lee hits the streets there are further fights, and even an attempt to run him down with a car that ends up going through a shop window. Lee beats all comers and retains possession of the film.

At Hwang's funeral a helicopter swoops down and uses a wire mesh claw to scoop up the coffin before it can be buried. Lee, or rather his double, runs after the snatched corpse and jumping up grabs hold of the wire mesh securing the coffin. What is obviously a dummy doubling as Lee—we don't even get a stuntman here—is hoisted high into the air with the stolen stiff. A dart is thrown from the helicopter into 'Lee's' neck and losing its grip the dummy falls to its doom. Kim then turns up to investigate his brother's murder. The only clues are the reel of film and the dart that killed his brother. The footage he's inherited depicts The Castle of Death, so Kim goes there and befriends its eccentric master Roy Horan. Kim is attacked by a masked man and comes to suspect the culprit is his host's trusted manservant, who used to be a monk at the Fan Yu Temple. A woman comes to visit Kim at night, he tells her to leave but she strips off; cue flashback to images of the porno books Lee, or rather his double, threw away earlier in the film. Kim starts to get it on with the nude seductress, but he remembers in the nick of time that his brother warned him about women. Heeding this sage advice he moves just far enough away to block being stabbed with a needle that has emerged from a large ring his nekkid assassin is wearing on her finger. What is obviously a stuntman dressed in a lion costume leaps through the window. Kim fights off the guy in the animal suit but the fake big cat still manages to maul the naked assassin before jumping out of the room the same way it came in.

After Roy Horan is murdered, Kim decides to investigate the Fan Yu Temple. Here he discovers the secret entrance to the Tower of Death, supposedly an upside down pagoda buried underground. Breaking in, Kim fights his way to a lift and presses the down button, seemingly this buried and inverted pagoda only has two levels—bargain basement and ground floor. After more fights, our hero does a suspended rope crawl along the ceiling of a corridor with a high voltage electric floor designed to kill intruders, so if he falls—although predictably enough he doesn't—it means instant death.

Next Kim is confronted by and has to fight Lee Hoi-Sang who has a shaved head. By this time Kim has already defeated other lethal fighters including Horan's traitorous valet and Tiger Yang Cheng-Wu, who is supposed to be some kind of wild man but comes across more like a would-be circus performer having a costume malfunction. Returning to the anti-action at hand, Hwang's coffin is on a raised dias and eventually it spins around to reveal the 'dead man' alive and sitting in a chair on the other side. Hwang explains he is an international drug dealer and Interpol were hot on his trail, so he faked his own death and whisked the coffin away to prevent further investigation. Wow, that's novel. It's usually the Lee-alike character who cons everyone into thinking he's dead when this plot device is used in Brucesploitation movies. Likewise, a Bruce Lee kung fu manual, as seen earlier in this movie, normally results in everyone fighting over it, but not here; we're just left to assume Kim took five minutes out from looking at porn to study it and by this means turned himself into 'the deadliest man alive' before taking out the bad guys.

Moving on, Hwang wraps up the lose plot strands with some jive talk before the final fight—his friend Lee got in his way so he had to be killed despite the fact they were mates. Now Kim must cop it too because of his irrational insistence on avenging his murdered brother—if it wasn't for this obsession it seems Hwang would just let him go without even trying to part the hero from Bruce's secret kung fu manual. So what we get as a finale is mostly one on one combat between Hwang and Kim, with the already injured bald guardian occasionally attempting to grab the white hat's ankle. Hoi-Sang eventually gets up so that Kim can take out the last two bad guys with a homoerotic double impalement using a sword.

While way better than the official *Game of Death* (1978), this final 'Bruce Lee movie' still suffers from falling too obviously into three acts with the good bits being Hwang Jang-Lee fighting at the start and finish; unless you watch the international rather than the Hong Kong version, in which case you also get a nice set piece from Casanova Wong too. The three act plotting gives the proceedings a stagey and contrived feel, while the archive footage of Lee unconvincingly cut into the first third will only excite fanboys, since the king of kung fu isn't actually fighting in any of it.

33 THE CHINESE STUNTMAN — 1982

AKA *COUNTER ATTACK*

DIRECTED BY BRUCE LI

After some street scenes the super-ugly American John Ladalski walks into a kung fu gym and starts correcting the students' technique before taking a bunch of them on in combat. Ladalski is winning until Bruce Li joins in and kicks his ass. The fight ends with a phone call for Bruce Li, he's overjoyed to discover he's got what he always wanted, a job as an insurance salesman. Li gets assigned to a sleazy manager who shows him the ropes of the insurance business. Meanwhile Ladalski goes looking for Li, and ends up waiting for him at his apartment building. Bruce is having a hard day, when he goes to sell insurance at a kung fu gym he is forced to fight.

When Li gets home bushed and finds Ladalski lurking in the stairwell he thinks the American wants a rematch. When the Ladalski says he wants to be Li's student, Bruce takes him in and takes him on. They hang around together and talk through Li's problems as they workout. Li and Ladalski train by kicking eggs hung from pieces of thread—I'm not sure how effective this is as a martial arts exercise but it does mean they can splatter each other with yolk. As Li and Ladalski become bickering buddies, Li's insurance manager meets up with fictional movie producer/director Wei Pin-Ao (best known to international audiences from his appearances alongside Bruce Lee in *Fist of Fury* and *Way of the Dragon*) whose movies aren't making money and whose big star Sze-Ma Lung is in terminal career decline. The shady insurance manager and Wei agree a fat policy on Lung and plan to subject him to on set accidents to get big pay-offs; with backhanders for the insurance agent every time this happens.

Wei is so greedy that the insurance manager doesn't want to do the deal himself—although he's happy to take a cut of the profit—so he passes the job on to Li but persuades Bruce to give him the commission. When Li goes to see Lung there is sloppy weight training—with *The Chinese Stuntman's* chubby kung fu star doing super-fast bench presses, relying on momentum rather than muscular control. At first Lung isn't interested in signing the insurance policy taken out by his studio, but after he tears Bruce's suit apart with his eagle claw technique, Li strikes back.

The movie star decides he likes the insurance man because no one else has the guts to stand up to him. Not long afterwards Lung has an accident and the insurance company send Li on set to check up on this. In the process of trying to protect Lung from doing risky stunts, Li starts demonstrating how to do them and is soon employed by the film company to perform as Lung's danger man double. However the other stuntmen don't like Lung or Li and are constantly trying to cause accidents.

There are a lot of tedious staged and supposedly real fights on and off set. John and Bruce are often ambushed. The assaults are motivated by jealousy at the movie studio and the fact that Li's old kung fu school are angry at him for setting up a new martial arts gym on his own. There is a brief moment of excitement when Chiang Tao jumps Li, but the energy this generates fades quickly as Bruce routs him; leaving viewers like me wishing this was a fight between Tao and *The Chinese Stuntman's* action director Bruce Le, who sadly stays behind the camera throughout this movie. Eventually in one of the flick's big selling points, Bruce Lee's top student and official *Game of Death* co-star Dan Inosanto is wheeled on as a bad guy to action direct the kung fu at the corrupt move studio; he mostly sits around doing nothing and looking like a withered piece of fruit. Inosanto is far worse as an actor than his top pupil Ladalski, who is at least spectacularly ugly in the way that a number of actors used in 1970s Italian crime movies were. Inosanto has absolutely nothing going for him onscreen.

The fictional foreign distributors in *The Chinese Stuntman* think Li is great and want him as the star of the films they're buying after seeing him leap onto and then tumble off a moving car; despite this seemingly being cut in the movie rather than done as a single take as the plot necessitates. Unfortunately for shady producer/director Wei, Bruce is hospitalised after being impaled on a piece of metal other stuntmen hid in a mattress he had to fall onto. After Li recovers there are more fights and Lung takes out a really big insurance policy on his 'friend'.

The film concludes with a jealous Inosanto fighting and defeating Ladalski, then battling Li. Inosanto looks like he's doing well when he catches the receiver end of a landline Li was swinging around by its cord as an improvised weapon—however the star turns the tables by throwing the base of the phone in his face. Li finally confronts Lung and the fading fictional star declares that if Bruce won't work with him, he's gonna collect his insurance policy on Li instead. The two men engage in an over-long and stagey kung fu fight. This punch up and the film finish with Li walking away from the movie business while Lung and Wei beg him to reconsider this decision because he's so great; really?

The Chinese Stuntman is an insufferably dull last gasp of the old school kung fu film in Taiwan/Hong Kong. On the extras of the Film 2000 DVD (2003) reissue of the movie, John Ladalski claims that the film was originally his idea and it was intended as a vehicle for Dan Inosanto to showcase Bruce Lee's real fighting methods and some other Filipino martial arts—as opposed to the fake movie kung fu that was popular in Hong Kong/Taiwanese flicks at the time. Ladalaski claims he wrote the original script with Li when the latter also came onboard as producer, director and co-star. However, as the movie progressed Li edged Inosanto into a minor bad guy role and turned the realistic street fighting Ladalski and Inosanto wanted to feature into flash but fake screen moves. Some Bruce Li fans argue that *The Chinese Stuntman* proves their idol wasn't just a Little Dragon clone but it is unlikely someone wanting to break out of the copy mould would make a movie with two of the world's top exponents of Lee's fighting style, and also choose Bruce Lee co-star Wei Pin-Ao for one of the main supporting roles. Given that there are also images of Bruce Lee all over this flick, this is actually one of the very few late Bruce Li films that slots unambiguously into the core of the Brucesploitation genre.

The Chinese Stuntman is a tedious swansong from the least interesting of the Bruce Lee clones. Although Li went on to co-star in *Power Force* (1982), like the fictional kung fu star played by Lung in *The Chinese Stuntman,* his career was fading. If what Ladalski has to say about initially approaching Li's producers with this project, but Li ending up producing the film himself is true, then it seems likely that by taking this project away from those he'd been working with he probably pissed them off and killed his own career.

34 Jackie and Bruce to the Rescue 1982

aka *Jackie Vs Bruce to the Rescue*
aka *Fist of Death*

Directed by Ng Ka-Chun and/or Choe Dong-Joon

A group of gangsters want a secret document that an agent is delivering to the Japanese martial arts school in an unnamed town. The Japanese school have the initials YMGA on the back of their sweatshirts, but on the English dub they are always called the YMCA (so that's what I'll call them). Three YMCA students are sent to meet the agent at the train station but they are attacked and killed by gangbangers who've disguised themselves as members of the Ching Wu kung fu school. The agent gives the secret sign to these imposters and when they fail to give the correct return signal he refuses to pass on the papers; which we learn later is a list of YMCA members and a treasure map.

There is a fight, the agent runs off, he's caught and stabbed but gets away again. He enters a house and asks Yu Feng—who just happens to be the girlfriend of top Ching Wu student Kim Tai-Jong (Master Bruce)—to hide him. Yu Feng obliges seconds before the hoods appear. Despite Yu Feng telling the gangbangers to get out of her house, they start to search it but give up when her father Wong turns up, who they recognise as a rich and influential local dignitary. After hiding the documents in a piece of clothing in the girl's wardrobe, the agent disappears. Blaming the Ching Wu school for the murder of their friends and the disappearance of the agent, some YMCA students go and kill the other gym's master. Ching Wu members retaliate by beating up YMCA students.

Kim returns from a trip to discover his Ching Wu master is dead. There is conflict between Kim and Chang Kang who both want to take over as head of the school. Kang is the hot-headed student—like Bruce Lee in *Fist of Fury* (1972)—who wants revenge, while Kim urges restraint. Local dignitary Wong steps in to mediate between the YMCA and the Ching Wu gym. In the end this proves unnecessary because what seems to be an expelled YMCA student guns down his ex-master at the end of an unsuccessful conciliation meeting between the two martial arts schools.

Since both Ching Wu and YMCA students see the assassination, and both know Ching Wu aren't responsible, the YMCA disappear from the story. Meanwhile various sub-plots develop around the hoods and their casino. The most important of these is that a gangster's moll is instructed to pick up a Jackie Chan clone played by Lee Siu-Ming. The girl is being attacked when Ming—who is an undercover agent posing as an illiterate rickshaw driver—comes to her rescue. This provides an excuse for a bunch of would-be comedy scenes in which the fake rickshaw driver in his plebeian disguise gets to interact as a rustic character with the sophisticated gang girl. The moll starts to fall in love with her mark and her gangbanging lover gets jealous and subjects her to rough sex in the shower. She's wearing a white negligee and the water makes it cling to her flesh. While this rape plays out, Serge Gainsbourg's song *Je t'aime* is illegally sampled on the soundtrack—the music might be intended to counterpoint and undermine the onscreen sexual violence, but for me it feels like an attempt to legitimise domestic abuse in the name of love.

Shortly after this Kim—who wears a yellow tracksuit like Bruce Lee and was the fight double for the dead star in the official *Game of Death*—has a bust up in the casino. Meanwhile Ming is kidnapped and tortured by the gang but rescued by the police who know he is an undercover agent. Kim is attacked in his bed by a ninja but fights him off. Kang has gone to the dark side and is working with the gang but when he fails to get them the documents they want, they kill him.

The gangbangers think the Ching Wu school must have the secret papers so they attack it, but while it is being smashed up and its students killed, Kim comes in wearing his yellow jumpsuit and sees them off with his kung fu. The gangbangers booby trap the light next to the bed Ming and his moll are now sharing. Ming survives the resultant poison gas attack but the girl is killed. Ming is contacted by and contacts various agents using secret codes. Kim gets a letter telling him to meet Ming in the forest, where they have a friendly fight to check out each other's kung fu. The two men exchange codes as they battle and realise they are on the same side. This practice bout stops when one of the gangbangers shoots at the two men because he suspects they know each other and are in cahoots. Kim and Ming part unscathed and on good terms. Ming continues exchanging secret signals with others on his side, and eventually meets up with the agent who arrived in town with the documents everybody wants. The agent tells Ming where the paper are, and he in his turn tells Kim, who tells his girlfriend they're in her room. Kim and Feng go to retrieve the papers but when our hero finds them, his girl pulls a gun on him and makes him give her the documents. She tells him she has no choice, the hoods have kidnapped her father and they'll kill him unless she gives them the papers. They argue and make their way downstairs, where they encounter a heavy with an arm around the father's neck and a gun to the old man's head. The girl throws the hood the documents and her father picks them up, the gangbanger then takes the papers from his hostage. The hood tells Feng to move out of the way so that he can shoot Kim, she refuses saying he'd promised her there'd be no killing. Feng is shot but then the mobster discovers he's plum out of bullets.

Meanwhile Ming has entered the room out of nowhere and chases after the villain who is escaping with the documents. Kim and Feng's father comfort the dying girl. After a brief fight Ming recovers the papers but the boss of the gangbangers enters screen right and our undercover agent has to run away. Sprinting into the countryside, Ming is confronted by more gangbangers. He beats the minions but soon the big boss has caught up with him and he's getting the worst of it until Kim materialises from nowhere and takes up the battle against the master criminal. After Kim's nunchuks are broken, Ming steps in to help and together the two men defeat the top hood.

This film has all the elements necessary to make the core of the Brucesploitation genre; you'd have thought with Kim switching between a white 1920s *Fist of Fury*-style suit and yellow and black 1970s sportswear to invoke *Game of Death,* this would result in something fantastically surreal and bizarre like *Enter the Game of Death* (1978). Unfortunately the movie is just a bore; it appears that the fault lies between Kim Tai-Jong being as bland as Bruce Li and the flick being poorly re-edited for international audiences. Ng Ka-Chun—who gets a co-director credit on the English dub—may have done no more than oversee the creation of an international version from an initial Korean cut. While some sources say this is a co-production between Korea and Taiwan, it looks and feels more Korean than Chinese.

According to the Korean Movie Database the film is set in Shanghai — which isn't clear from the English dub, although given the *Fist of Fury* stylings many viewers will probably assume this. The KMDB also states that the heads of the two gyms—Koryo Martial Arts Training Hall and Chinese 18 Fighting Skills Training Hall in the Korean version—have set up an anti-Japanese organisation, and those after the documents are Japanese militarists rather than gangsters. Therefore the Korean version features a Chinese-Korean coalition to resist the Japanese, and at one point a Japanese gym that is attacked; in the English dub this is transformed into the YMCA gym. All of which makes the plot sound as if it hangs together much better in the Korean version, and makes more sense of who is working with who and why the documents are important; the information that they are both a membership list AND a treasure map is introduced into the English dub with a throwaway line that comes across as an afterthought about providing a reason as to why a criminal organisation would be after them, they'd presumably be more interested in treasure than the names.

The Korean version is seven minutes longer than the standard English cut, which probably gives the plot more room to breath. Kim Tai-Jong is the big selling point of this movie as Brucesploitation because he was Bruce Lee's fighting double in the official *Game of Death* (1978), and also stood in for Bruce Lee and played his brother in the follow up *Tower of Death* AKA *Game of Death II* (1981).

Finally unless you're deeply into détournement beware of the hour and nineteen minute English language edit of the film that I've watched on YouTube—this is nine minutes shorter than the versions I have on a region 1 DVD from VideoAsia and a region 2 DVD from Film 2000—since the additional cuts take out crucial plot exposition and thereby render the ending absolutely senseless. This chopped down version leaves in nudity that might get the film pulled from YouTube, and must be a really frustrating viewing experience for most of those who haven't seen a longer version. Hard to know with regard to this posting if somebody is having a laugh or just didn't know there is a better—if still compromised—English cut.

35 Ninja Strikes Back   1982

AKA *Bruce Strikes Back*
AKA *Bruce Fights Back*
AKA *Eye of the Dragon*

Directed by Joseph Velasco, Bruce Le and allegedly André Koob (uncredited) and Jean-Marie Pallardy (uncredited)

In a drawn out pre-credits sequence, Bruce Le catches one of the Italians he's playing cards against cheating, and so he beats up those he's been gambling with to get his money. Bruce tells his girlfriend who is playing snooker he has an errand to run and will be back shortly. He goes to a mobster's villa where topless women are cavorting around the pool. The boss tells Bruce and Hwang Jang-Lee to do a job. They exchange a suitcase full of money for a valise that when they check it is empty. A fight breaks out. Using just their fists and feet, Bruce and Hwang defeat a lot of mafioso foot soldiers who are tooled with automatic weapons. The unarmed martial artists win but as the cops turn up Bruce is hit by bullets sprayed at him by a dying mobster. Hwang wants Bruce to get in their car, but Le tells him to save himself. Bruce is arrested by the cops.

There follows an animated credits sequence of a cartoon Le fighting ninjas. Most of the pre-credits scenes I've described aren't required; what needs to be established could be achieved with just the gangland exchange that goes wrong, but since this is a Dick Randall production topless totty is thrown in regardless of how flabby it renders the narrative. After the credits Bruce gets out of jail and tells the boss he won't work for him any more. Meanwhile Dick Randall is playing an ambassador who won't do business with the boss either. Bruce's former mobster friends attempt to kill Le and successfully kidnap the ambassador's daughter Sophie (Fabienne Beze). One of the kidnappers is a dragged up as a woman to add some tranny interest. After a couple of cops save Le when he's losing a fight with Hwang, he reluctantly teams up with them. The filth are played by André Koob and Corliss Randall (billed as Chick Norris). A lot of pointless tourist shots of Rome are inserted into the completely unsatisfactory 'action'; it didn't take much of this to make me wish I was watching a poliziotteschi (Euro-crime) genre anti-classic directed by someone like Fernando di Leo or Enzo G. Castellari, rather than the half-baked crap that makes up the first half of *Ninja Strikes Back*.

Things go from bad to worse when Le accompanies Koob to Paris in an attempt to track down Sophie. There is the obligatory nightclub scene. Koob pulls a hood off the dance floor and into the john. Threatening the thug with a gun doesn't make him talk, so the cop pushes his head into a urinal and he sings like a canary! This torture doesn't even cut it on film, coz when Koob pushes the flush on the pisser water simply runs down the back of the lowlife's head; for a viable variant on waterboarding it would be necessary to shove the geezer's bonce into a proper crapper—or hold him upside down by his legs with his face facing forward into the urinal. Regardless, Koob and Le have a lead on the whereabouts of the next suspect they need to torture. Before you know it we've transitioned from night to day and they're busting up a porn film set. Bruce is kicking seven shades of shit out of both the crew and the heavies protecting them; he leaves the cast alone because they are doing a lesbian scene.

After this, Le attacks a guy having sex with a woman. Cut into these beatings is a tourist montage of Paris. Following a long chase that involves a child being held at knifepoint, Bruce and Koob catch up with the next hoodlum they're after, and using their usual interrogation technique of roughing him up, get the news that 'the ninja' have Sophie in Macao. Unfortunately before we can shift east, Bruce has to return to Italy, where his girlfriend Laura is killed by a mob gunman who missed while taking a pot shot at our hero. This assassination takes place on a topless beach. Le doesn't seem too upset about Laura passing on to that great nudist resort in the sky; after all he's hypermasculine, and shortly after this killing Dick pays him $50,000 to bring Sophie home from Macao. That's lucky because it means Joseph Velasco can take over as director and the audience get something worth watching!

By the time this was made, it was traditional to show Bruce Le arriving at an international airport in his movies, so here we have a generic shot of him emerging from a terminal in Hong Kong. Bruce goes on to Macao and has some fond flashbacks to good times he spent with his father. The family home is empty and Le is horrified to find a portrait of his father with candles burning on either side, indicating he is dead. Casanova Wong shows up to explain that a couple of months ago, ninjas (Harold Sakata and Bolo Yeung shown in flashback) turned up to kidnap Bruce's sister. His father tried to stop this and was killed. Shift to a hillside graveyard so Bruce can pay his respects to the author of his daze, and where he and Wong are attacked by ninjas. The fight is nicely handled with the black clad ninjas disap-

pearing into thin air as Le and Wong attempt to land blows on them. Eventually the almost invisible assassins are seen off. Wong gets a friend to show them the ninja HQ. Inside Sophie has been injected with a drug that turns her into a nymphomaniac. Bolo gets to sexually abuse the kidnap victim briefly but Sakata tells him to leave her alone. There is also a short but hilarious group orgy scene—which puts the fumbling soft porn efforts earlier in the movie to shame with its sheer whackiness and unapologetic stupidity.

Every time Sakata appears James Bond music is used on the soundtrack to remind us he played Oddjob in *Goldfinger* (1964); in this movie his razor-edged weapon hat is still with him after first appearing in that Guy Hamilton effort eighteen years earlier. But Sakata also has a ridiculous claw hand, a bit like Han in *Enter the Dragon.* Returning to the narrative, Casanova and Bruce leave their friend in the forest while they go into the ninja HQ. Sakata has just left with Sophie, but various flunkies including Bolo are quickly despatched by Le and Wong. Down in the forest Wong's friend is decapitated by a black clad ninja. The kidnapped girls in the mansion, including Le's sister, are freed. Wong leads the former sex slaves away to safety. One girl stays with Le to help him track down Sakata and Sophie. In the forest Bruce searches for the guy who was keeping lookout and is attacked by ninjas. There follows another groovy disappearing fighters sequence and it takes Bruce a while to get the better of foes who possess the secret of invisibility.

Since Joseph Velasco is now helming our sleaze fest, it isn't long before Le and his female helper are on a speedboat that is catching up with Sakata's sailing ship. Sophie is tied to the front mast with her naked breasts prominently displayed, a kind of living post-modern variant on a pirate ship's figurehead; at the same time a cross-gendered updating of Odysseus tied to the mast so that he could listen to the siren's song. Le climbs up onto the sailing boat, and takes out its crew before battling their boss Sakata. Having successfully killed all the bad guys, he frees Sophie and takes her home to Rome.

Back at the ambassador's residence, Le is waiting downstairs for Sophie and her dad when he hears screams. Hwang's gang have abducted Sophie and killed her dad. Le is told that if he wants Sophie returned he must be at the Colosseum at dawn. This is a trap but Bruce beats the gangbanging minions, there is even a little nunchuck action.

Finally we've reached the climatic fight with Hwang, which is a parody of—and improvement on—Bruce Lee's battle against Chuck Norris at the Colosseum in *Way of the Dragon* (1972). Hwang is a vastly superior bootmaster to Chuck. Since this is a Bruce Le film, ultimately Hwang has to lose this last fight.

The Ninja Strikes Back definitely belongs at the core of the Bruceploitation genre because from half-way through, with Velasco taking over as director, Le's Bruce Lee mannerism during fights come out in full effect. Whether intuitively or consciously, Velasco treated Le not as an actor but as a somnambulist and therefore provides a freak show worth watching. One assumes Le directed the Colsseum fight to Velasco's cloned script-writing instructions. There is some argument about who shot the other European scenes; some believe André Koob and Jean-Marie Pallardy deserve a finger pointed at them for the sub-par sections of this flick. The first half of *Ninja Strikes Back* is every bit of as bad as Le's earlier globe trotting James Bondish 'adventure' *Challenge of the Tiger* (1980). However once Joseph Velasco is in charge of direction—as well as the minimal script—we roar away!

36 NINJA VS BRUCE LEE   1982

AKA *CONCORD OF BRUCE*

DIRECTED BY JOSEPH VELASCO

This is one of the notorious cut-and-paste movies with which Velasco exposes Godfrey Ho as a rank amateur within the scissors-and-glue martial arts subgenre. Why go to the trouble and minimal expense of buying up other people's footage—as Ho and his producers did—when you can just recycle your own?

This movie is basically a chopped down version of Velasco's earlier *My Name Called Bruce* (1978) with lots of his *Return of Bruce* (1977) chopped into the middle of it alongside a mere snippet from *Enter the Game of Death* (1978). So just as in *My Name Called Bruce*, the Korean cops and Bruce Le as an undercover rozzer from Hong Kong are after some antique smuggling criminals.

Sadly in this version of the movie the rare vase that everyone is after isn't smashed part way through. The plot is simplified and Bruce goes to Manila because he and the cops are tricked into thinking the vase has been sent there; actually it's still in Seoul. It's action all the way in The Philippines as we get pretty much nothing but chopped down versions of the many fight scenes from *Return of Bruce,* including the climatic one with Lo Lieh. The plot from this latter flick is completely dumped, alongside the movie's most annoying character, the fat orphan kid Piggy.

Since Bruce is still after the vase, he returns to Korea for the climax of *My Name Called Bruce.* Sadly the instrumental section of Hawkwind's *Master of Universe* which was originally used in the final fight has been replaced with something that impressed me less.

My Name Called Bruce doesn't have many Brucesploitation elements but *Return of Bruce* is full of them, and Velasco has also cut in Bruce Le fighting in a yellow tracksuit from *Enter the Game of Death,* so this one definitely makes the core of the Brucesploitation genre. There are no ninjas in the movie despite the title of the American DVD release—again showing that Godfrey Ho and his producers were just throwing pennies around by filming original ninja scenes to cut into the non-ninja movies they bought from other people. This movie has ninja in the title and a ninja on the cover, so it would be picked up by ninja fans in video stores; who'd only discover after they'd watched the flick there were no ninjas in it. As a result, Velasco comes across as smarter, cheaper and more exploitative than Godfrey Ho!

37 THE YOUNG BRUCE LEE 1987
DIRECTED BY LARRY DOLGIN

This is a radical re-edit—or perhaps a remake—of producer Dick Randall's *The Real Bruce Lee* (1977). The best part of the original movie, the extensive Dragon Lee footage from *Real* is completely cut. The clips from Bruce Lee's work as a child actor in Hong Kong take up around three times as much of the running time as before, clocking in at nearly an hour. The Bruce Li material used to illustrate the Little Dragon's life is dropped into different places, as is the press conference footage of the 'king of kung fu' and documentary coverage of his death.

Overall this is really boring but it patchily covers Bruce Lee's life from birth to death using lots of grainy childhood films, and as such makes the core of the Brucesploitation genre for sheer chutzpah. If you want to watch a child actor you'd probably be better off catching a Shirley Temple movie.

I'm uncertain of the date this was made, since mostly it is simply treated as an alternate title/version of *The Real Bruce Lee.* On the extras of the Film 2000 double DVD of this and *The Real Bruce Lee*, the notes say it was made a decade after the first version. Other DVD versions I've looked at, such as that put out by Pegasus in the UK in 2002, give no production details.

38 BRUCE LEE IN G.O.D. 2000
DIRECTED BY TOSHI OHGUSHI, TOSHIKAZU ÔGUSHI AND BRUCE LEE (UNCREDITED)

Allegedly this is an attempt to present *Game of Death* as Bruce Lee intended it to be seen. It uses non-actors to recreate the last year of Lee's life and explore the ideas behind his unfinished *Game of Death* project. The dialogue is mostly spoken in stilted English by non-native speakers, but cut into this docu-drama about Bruce Lee starting work on his unfinished film are interviews with Yuen Wah, Chaplin Chang and Dan Inosanto; the first two interviews are in Cantonese with Japanese subtitles only, the final one is in English.

Yuen Wah was Bruce Lee's stunt double in *Fist of Fury* (1972) and *Enter the Dragon* (1973), so knowing who he is and watching him speak without even understanding what he's saying serves to undermine the idea that Bruce Lee was doing anything other than 'movie kung fu' in his films. Chaplin Chang was the production manager on *Way of the Dragon* (1972) and an assistant director on *Enter the Dragon*; while Dan Inosanto studied martial arts with Bruce Lee and is defeated by his sifu in a staged fight that constitutes a part of the 1972 *Game of Death* footage.

The second part of *G.O.D.* is the most extended version possible of the material that Bruce Lee shot for *Game of Death.* This is every bit as boring to watch as the preceding docu-drama, and I'm sure it isn't how Bruce Lee would have presented the climax of the film had he lived to complete it. The far shorter edit of some of this footage in the official *Game of Death* (1978) is vastly superior to what is presented here, despite the fact that movie as completed by Robert Clouse is a turkey. In *G.O.D.* the extended edit of the final fight with Kareem Abdul-Jabbar is even less convincing as 'real' martial arts than the 1978 version. Abdul-Jabbar looks like he'd fall over if he fully extended his legs, and the bend maintained at his knees when he kicks is extremely irritating from an aesthetic point of view—although it makes sense from a practical martial arts perspective. As spectacle this fight works better in a shorter edit. In film-making editing is a part of the creative process, and that entails choices about what footage is and isn't included. Those responsible for *G.O.D.* are trying to use as much of the 1972 footage shot by Bruce Lee as possible, and as a result what they've assembled is not going to interest anyone who doesn't have an unhealthy obsession with the Little Dragon. There is also an obvious contradiction here between Bruce Lee's claims about using *Game* of *Death* to showcase his martial arts philosophy, and his unwavering devotion to his career as a film star. The footage fails to match Lee's claims about it illustrating his fighting 'philosophy' for the simple reason that if he showcased realistic martial arts that were designed for street fighting rather than celluloid effect, he wouldn't reach the mass audience he lusted after.

Whether Lee was or was not a great martial artist isn't something that need detain me here, because for the majority of those who've watched—and still watch—his flicks he is basically an actor. One assumes it was not beyond Lee to continually reforge the passage between theory and practice by elucidating the shortcomings of what he shows onscreen as practical martial arts, and correcting it as he goes along. Approaching *Game of Death* in this way, and with greater didacticism, could have been used to give *G.O.D.* a more avant-garde feel but it wouldn't have served to cement Lee's status as a movie celebrity—and so wouldn't have appealed to him as an actor, director or human being. The short bursts of shit talk before the fights in *G.O.D.* just get in the way of the action without truly interrupting it, whereas far longer and more theoretical speeches would have achieved a genuine alienation effect and might have lifted the footage we have out of the action film rut it wallows in; excepting, of course, the final fight when Lee is up against an opponent who towers over him –this is not 'street real' martial arts, but it really is something else as spectacle.

The footage of Lee battling it out with Abdul-Jabbar is the very stuff of which cinematic dreams are made, and with this sequence—despite flawed execution, mostly due to his opponent's shortcomings—the Little Dragon achieves the kind of martial arts spectacle that Jimmy Wang-Yu more consistently realised in his film *Master of the Flying Guillotine* (1976).

If Lee had lived and dialectically resolved his desire to be internationally famous as both a film star and a 'serious' martial artist, then *Game of Death* might have evolved into a terrific film. What we have in *G.O.D.* is an interpretation of Lee's project that does its originator a massive disservice—and which unfairly assumes that as he worked on *Game of Death* he wouldn't have been able to reshape it into something a lot better than his initial idea, which is all we are left with here.

Rather unusually for an example of Brucesploitation, this is aimed squarely at obsessed fanboys rather than a mass audience. It clearly belongs at the core of the Brucesploitation genre, but it is also a film that should be avoided like the plague since it will bore casual viewers shitless. *G.O.D.* makes *Enter the Game of Death* (1978) look like Cocteau's *Orphée* (1950) by way of comparison. Indeed, *G.O.D.* is even worse than the official *Game of Death*! And maybe, just maybe, in it's own way that is some kind of achievement!

39 Dragon the Master   2001
Directed by Ray Wu Wai-Shing

Lily Chung is a young and successful games designer. She has a relationship bordering on romance with Roy Cheung, who also works for the company that employs her. Lilly's best friend is martial arts film actress Karen Cheung whose boyfriend is Edmond So. Lily's brother is martial arts instructor Dragon Sek. When Karen gets into a fight with a guy trying to pick her up in a nightclub, Billy Chow steps in and saves the day. Karen is always getting in fights but needs help to get out of them; she doesn't win on her own. Billy's wife has left him and now he's come from the country to the big city to try and win a martial arts tournament. The big city in the movie seems to be Shenzhen, although if the name of the place is mentioned in the English dub then I missed it. Edmond is hustling money any way he can so that he has the dough to get married to Karen. Roy is a double-crossing shit who has fallen in with Mr Tong's criminal gang who want to bootleg Lily's game before it is officially released. Dragon spends much of his time running around in a yellow jumpsuit like the one Bruce Lee wore in the official *Game of Death* (1978). Using two female ninjas, Mr Tong attempts to steal Lily's yet to be released computer game. However, because Lily understands cyber-security what they copy from her computer is useless to them. Roy hires Edmond to work for Mr. Tong, although So doesn't know at first their job is to steal his friend Lily's game. Roy also discovers Billy's wife is sick in hospital and in need of a $60,000 dollar operation to save her life so Billy has to work for Mr Tong too in order to raise the money needed to avert his estranged wife's death.

Eventually Mr Tong's gangbangers hold Lilly and her younger brother hostage in a pagoda in order to force the game designer to provide them with a useable copy of her work. Before this we have been introduced to a Jackie Chan clone in the form of Jacky Chen, a master of the drunken fist. It seems the producers were uncertain whether Brucesploitation alone was enough to sell a film in the 21st century, and so they've added a dash of Chansploitation to this one. Having had a fight with Dragon Sek the night before while drunk, Chen seeks him out to apologise. The two kung fu masters end up racing off to rescue Sek's siblings. It is Dragon Sek who does most of the onscreen combat, fighting his way up three floors of the pagoda. The third and final level is decorated with barbed wire and is Billy Chow's lair. Billy even has barbed wired wrapped around his knuckles so that when he punches Dragon Sek, our hero ends up with scars like those inflicted by Han on Bruce Lee in the climatic fight of *Enter the Dragon* (1973). Of course, Sek eventually beats Chow and that's the end of the movie.

This flick is stuffed full of Bruce Lee type imagery, such as Sek being attacked by guys with motorised go-carts which echoes the battle between the Bruce Lee stand-in and the motorcyclists in the official *Game of Death*. Sek also does a good imitation of Bruce Lee's fighting style. So this movie clearly belongs to the core of the Brucesploition genre. That said it is also filled to the brim with wuxia style sword fights and wirework, so it is in many ways a postmodern reimagining of Hong Kong and Taiwanese action cinema of the sixties and seventies. It certainly doesn't limit itself to invoking Bruce Lee or indeed kung fu films—although as the Chansploitation elements indicate, it is fairly broad in the range of hand to hand combat flicks it draws on for inspiration. The plot is unnecessarily convoluted but overall the film is fun.

40 HERO YOUNGSTER 2004

AKA *JUVENILE CHEN ZHEN*

DIRECTED BY LAW KEI AND HUNG KONG

This is an unofficial prequel to Bruce Lee's *Fist of Fury* (1972). A group of Chinese rebels are gunned down at night by Japanese invaders. The next day Xu Xiao-Long (Chen Zhen or Chen Jun depending on how the character name is transliterated) is looting the corpses when one revives. Chen runs away but is called back by the man. Another body moves. Marsha Yuen Chi-Wai, playing an imperial princess who has abandoned the court in favour of martial resistance against the invaders, was deliberately shielded by her father, who was the first person to stir. Before Chi-Wai's father snuffs it he tells her to take a map showing Japanese invasion plans to her uncle. Travelling by train she arrives in the area where her uncle was last known to be residing. However, hot on her trail are the Japanese led by Billy Chow playing essentially the same role he had in the *Fist of Fury* remakes *Fist of Legend* (1994) and *Dragon In Fury* (2004); viz a sadistic fascist military officer. When Marsha arrives at her destination she is saved by Yuen Biao, although we don't learn his identity until later; we're first properly introduced to Biao as the owner of the Happy Restaurant without it being revealed he is a Maoist resistance fighter with incredible kung fu skills. By chance Xu Xiao-Long is on hand to lead Chi-Wai to safety after Biao secretly saves her.

What follows are various encounters between these characters as Marsha looks for her uncle, who has been expelled from the Kuomintang forces. It is no surprise when he ultimately turns out to be a patriotic idiot played by Law Kar-Ying who we initially meet as a street performer known locally as Old Tramp. Through various encounters the patriots recognise each other and group together, with fifteen year-old Xu Xiao-Long's rebellion against the Japanese becoming far more effective when he is brought under the Maoist discipline and organising skills of apparatchik Yuen Biao. However, while Marsha is apparently a Maoist because she knows the code to identify herself as such, Law doesn't respond to it. Nonetheless, Billy Chow eventually realises that under his pathetic and unbelievably childish patriotic street performances, Law is actually a spy disguised as a tramp, and imprisons him. Since the Japanese plan to take Law and an ancient temple idol away, the resistance has to rescue both. Biao organises a link up between the Maoist guerrillas and the Kuomintang forces, and both Law and the idol are saved, although Xu's aunt is killed in the fight as she protects her son who is Xiao-Long's sidekick.

For the final battle Law and his men are dressed in full Maoist uniforms and the Japanese are completely trounced! The film is hilarious since it basically functions as a piece of Bolshevik propaganda, and in the process also demonstrates that rather than being communists the Communist Party of China were reactionary capitalists with a strong nationalist bent; of course we know that historically it was the Maoists, following in the footsteps of the Russian Bolsheviks, who oversaw the transition from the formal to the real domination of capital in China through a process of industrialising agriculture and freeing workers up from the land to work in factories. Chairman Mao is said to have viewed Bruce Lee as a hero and at the end of his life, *Fist of Fury* was allegedly this dictator's favourite film. Donnie Yen (among others) who has also played the Chen Zhen character, basically equates the fictional fighter with Bruce Lee, the first actor to play him. So *Hero Youngster* hilariously sees the makers of the film ingratiating themselves with Beijing authorities by claiming Bruce Lee for Maoism and the forms of Chinese nationalism promoted by this immensely powerful and reactionary state. Xu Xiao-Long's role appears have to been in part modelled on the scamp persona of Bruce Lee's childhood films. This not only places Bruce Lee in the service of authoritarian nationalism, it also puts the movie at the core of the Brucesploitation genre. For anyone who isn't a Maoist and who understands the propaganda message of *Hero Youngster*—and doesn't allow themselves to be too distracted by the adequate but very average martial arts—the result is hilarious. This cheap looking film is way more outrageous in its message than any previous entry in the genre, despite being made decades after the first full flowering of Brucesploitation. It also serves to demonstrate the ideological adaptability of the older members of its cast. From the little coverage I've found of this flick in English it seems that the fu fanboys hate it, but I laughed my cock off watching this absurd schlock. If you liked *Reefer Madness* (1936), you'll love *Hero Youngster!* It gives Bruce Lee's carpet chewing performance in the original *Fist of Fury* a run for its money by very effectively—if inadvertently—delivering the message that patriotism is just as stupid as religion, and that both stink up the planet. Or as The Occupation Committee of the People's Free Sorbonne University put it in a telegram they sent to Politburo of the Communist Party of China on 17 May 1968: "Shake in your shoes bureaucrats, the international power of the workers councils will soon wipe you out. Humanity won't be happy until the last bureaucrat is hung by the guts of the last capitalist. Long live the factory occupations. Long live the great Chinese proletarian revolution of 1927 betrayed by the Stalinist bureaucrats. Long live the proletarians of Canton and elsewhere who have taken up arms against the so-called People's Army. Long live the Chinese workers and students who have attacked the so-called cultural revolution and the bureaucratic Maoist order. Long live revolutionary Marxism. Down with the state."

Note: despite having an apparently reversed version of one of legendary Brucesploitation director

Joseph Velasco's many names, Hung Kong the co-director of this is NOT as far as I can tell Velasco.

41 THE REAL BRUCE LEE 2   2004
DIRECTED BY L. DOLGEN AND KANT LEUNG WANG-FAT (BIG BOSS UNTOUCHABLE SECTION)

This is an unofficial sequel to 1977's *The Real Bruce Lee*. It follows the same format, taking an existing Brucesploitation film and running it after some archive footage of Bruce Lee's boyhood Cantonese movies and his post-death imitators. Thankfully the Bruce Lee footage runs for less time than in the 1977 flick and without being fascinating is nonetheless more interesting.

The clips from *Guiding Light* show Lee as a schoolboy and the film looks like a very dull drama. *Wise Guys Fool Around* and *Sweet Lady* show the Little Dragon as an older teen suffering from unrequited love and as an ace cha-cha dancer; which he was, so he looks great in this footage. This is followed by clips of Bruce Li in *Deadly Strike* (1978), Bruce Le in *Ninja Strikes Back* (1982) and an aged looking Dragon Lee in *Emperor of the Underworld* (1994). Presumably the late period Dragon Lee clip was thrown in because he was the new Bruce Lee replacement in the film *Last Fist of Fury* which rounded out the 1977 *Real Bruce Lee*.

Next on *The Real Bruce Lee 2*, viewers are introduced to 'Sky Dragon' (AKA Dragon Sek) as the new Bruce Lee of the noughties. We then get the whole of the Dragon Sek/Tin-Lung vehicle *Big Boss Untouchable* (AKA *Dragon the Master 2*) from 2002. Dragon Sek (Lionel in the English dub) is looking for his fiancée and her mother who have disappeared in the town of Big River. Along the way Sek befriends a hopeless gambler (Karel Wong Chi-Yeung) and his kung fu fighting sister (Karen Cheung Bo-Man) who own a restaurant. Sek has a series of run-ins with the gang who run the town. Ben Ng Ngai-Cheung who heads the crime gang is into extortion, gambling rackets and enforced prostitution, among other things. His gang have kidnapped Sek's fiancée but because she looks like his dead wife, Ng wants her to marry her rather than sell her into prostitution. Before long Karen Cheung falls in love with Sek but helps him look for his fiancée anyway. Eventually Sek decides to check out the docks and this leads to a big showdown between him and Ng's bodyguard, and Karen and Ng. After hard fights, Sek and Karen triumph. Sek is reunited with his fiancée who had been imprisoned with other women at the docks and the way this is portrayed is vaguely reminiscent of Bruce Lee coming across Han's prisoners in *Enter the Dragon* (1973).

Obviously *Dragon the Master 2* owes more to Bruce Lee's earlier vehicle *The Big Boss* (1971) than his Warner Brothers outing with Jim Kelly, John Saxon and Sek Kin. *Big Boss Untouchable* is shot on video and looks awful. Sek is spectacularly inept when he deploys nunchaku, which is odd since he uses them with much more skill in *Dragon the Master 1* (2001). Likewise, Sek comes across as a stupidly 'good guy' with all the charisma of a not so fresh corpse. Although the story is very old school, the fights include trickery that would have been difficult to achieve in such a low-budget effort back in the 1970s. One of the producers of this Sek vehicle (and some others including *Dragon the Master 1*) is Joseph Lai, the man behind many Godfrey Ho flicks and the international versions of Dragon Lee epics; this film is distributed by his IFD Films & Arts Ltd. Despite the risible waste of time that *Big Boss Untouchable* undoubtedly is, I love the concept of producing an unofficial sequel to a thirty-year old rip-off in the form of *The Real Bruce Lee 2*.

The front cover of the VideoAsia 2004 DVD proclaims this release to be both a 'world exclusive' and the 'ultimate edition'; of course, a first edition of a film is always the ultimate edition until the company concerned or someone else releases another edition (VideoAsia did go on to include *Real Bruce Lee 2* in their 2009 box set *Top Fighters: 10 Film Collection*—meaning their first DVD release of it was no longer a world exclusive). The English dubbed version of *Big Boss Untouchable* had already appeared as a Region 2 DVD on the UK label MIA in 2003, the year before VideoAsia issued *The Real Bruce Lee 2*. The flick has incredible credits. Richard Randall is listed as executive producer, presumably film fans are meant to mistake him for the notorious exploitation film producer Dick Randall—who alongside Serafim Karalexis was the producer of 1977's *The Real Bruce Lee;* however, Dick Randall died of a stroke in 1996, eight years before *The Real Bruce Lee 2* was released. Likewise the credited director is L. Dolgen, who might be mistaken for Larry Dolgin (one letter different) who alongside the two producers I've just mentioned is credited with writing 1977's *The Real Bruce Lee*. The only L. Dolgen I could find on Internet Movie Database is Lauren Dolgen, a producer and writer on the TV show *Teen Mom* with no directorial credits and given her track record unlikely to make a martial arts flick.

In short *The Real Bruce Lee 2* is a classic example of exploitation film hucksterism that attempts to sucker its audience. But what makes the initial VideoAsia release particularly great are the extras, video interviews with three of Lee's students—who talk about him as a guy who really wanted to be seen as cool, and who when they first met him in the sixties knew very little about weight-training or bodybuilding. Such claims really get hardcore Bruce Lee fanboys riled up because those making them aren't fawning enough! The content of *The Real Bruce Lee 2*, and the fact it's exploiting an existing example of core Brucesploitation, also puts this at the heart of the genre. That said, Dragon Sek's loose riffing on Lee and *The Big Boss* came so late in the day it can only be considered peripheral to Brucesploitation, which is where I've placed that film as a stand alone in my scheme of Lee-like things.

SEMI-PERIPHERY

ブルース・リーのグリーン・ホーネット

BRUCE LEE IN GREEN HORNET

絶賛の歓呼を浴びてブルース・リー《アメリカ主演第1回作品》ついに登場！

全米で記録破りの大ヒット！炸裂するヌンチャク！ほとばしる怪鳥音！最新秘密兵器を駆使して悪に挑む黒衣の怪人グリーン・ホーネット！

カラー作品 ■ ブルース・リー／バン・ウイリアムズ／ロバート・ストロース／ウェンディ・ワグナー／岩松マコ 映倫
監督ノーマン・フォスター 製作リチャード・ブルール ウイリアム・ドリヤー 音楽ビリー・メイ テーマ演奏アル・ハート ■ 東和提供

42 FIST OF UNICORN — 1973

AKA *UNICORN PALM*
AKA *BRUCE LEE AND I*
DIRECTED BY TANG TI

In a cameo, writer and director Tang Ti kills his criminal associates so he doesn't have to split the loot from a crime they've recently committed. This is witnessed by a family who are picnicking on a riverbank. Tang stabs the father to death, attempts to rape the mother before murdering her, and kicks the son into the water. Next the credits exploit the fact that Bruce Lee did some choreographic work on the fights as a favour for his friend Unicorn Chan, who is the pseudo-star of this flick.

Fifteen years have passed since the pre-credit violence and Unicorn, who survived being kicked in the river by Tang, is an adult completing his martial arts training. Finally he learns the 'heaven and earth fists'. This entails him doing a superman-style flying leap through the air and landing his two palms on his opponent's chest. A body double shot from behind and some fast cuts to a few seconds of Bruce Lee action directing give us the big selling point of this movie; viz that Unicorn's Shaolin instructor is none other than the Little Dragon.

Unicorn and Bruce Lee had worked together as child actors in Hong Kong movies—but it is only in the fictional *Fist of Unicorn* that Lee teaches his friend kung fu. The footage of Lee is fleeting and was shot without his knowledge. Unicorn leaves the fictitious temple where he learnt fantasy kung fu and hooks up with a widow and her young son, living with them in return for doing chores. We learn that the village in which Unicorn has settled is terrorized by the Wong family. They smuggle opium and buy guns from the Japanese, who are represented here by Bruce Lee's *Fist of Fury* and *Way of the Dragon* co-star Wei Ping-Ao, the latter has been given a Hitler-style moustache to signify that he's a fascist cad. Ti Tang heads the crime clan but his daughter is supposedly the brains behind the family's operations. There is also an indulged idiot son who stutters badly unless women have been provided for his pleasure in which case he goes into a flowing low-grade imitation of Rudy Ray Moore's x-rated street raps. The imbecile son takes a shine to Kitty Meng Chui, the daughter of a travelling circus family visiting the village. The stuttering idiot's desire for Kitty leads to the murder of her kin and the widow who has given Unicorn a home. Inevitably Kitty teams up with Unicorn to take on all the bad guys who include Whang In-Shik and Kurata Yasuaki.

The climatic battle is between Unicorn and writer/director Ti Tang. Unicorn doesn't do much fighting because the monks who trained him taught him restraint—making him a bit like Bruce Lee in *The Big Boss*. That said the best thing in this flick is his heaven and earth fists move. It begins with him wiggling his ears, and when Unicorn does this a picture of Bruce Lee appears behind his head. Super-cheap graphic wiggles come from Unicorn's palms before he flies like Superman—but with arms spread wide and held aloft—onto his opponent's chest! It's a kill every time! Despite the bad acting and the uncharismatic lead, this is an old school classic because of the shameless exploitation of the Bruce Lee connection, milking for all they're worth about ten seconds of original footage of the Little Dragon in the international cut of the film, and less in the Hong Kong edit.

Despite the paucity of Lee material, *Fist of Unicorn* was sold on his name. It was one of several flicks to exploit the star aura of the Little Dragon while he was still alive; the Hong Kong first run of this movie began before his death but ended after it.

43 THE CHINESE GODFATHER — 1974

AKA *CHIVALROUS KNIGHT*
DIRECTED BY LUI GIN

Often tacked on to the beginning or end of the *Chinese Godfather* is a seven minute featurette entitled *Bruce Lee's Last Days,* which appears to have been made to accompany this flick, on a disk I have of the movie issued by Dragon DVD it is included in the bonus material. In this featurette Betty Ting Pei narrates the last days and death of Bruce Lee accompanied by footage of the *Fist of Unicorn* press conference, Bruce Lee's Hong Kong funeral, Betty's own apartment including the bed on which the Little Dragon died, plus a gathering of those who made *The Chinese Godfather*.

At the time of Lee's death Ting Pei was widely assumed to be his lover, something she confirmed forty years later in an autobiography and various media interviews. In the seventies movie producers were keen to capitalise on Ting Pei's status as 'Bruce Lee's girlfriend' and the starlet went along with their ploys despite never speaking openly about the relationship until the Little Dragon's widow Linda Emery had been married to her third husband (the second after Lee) for more than two decades. One of the main selling points of *The Chinese Godfather* to Bruce Lee fans when it was first released was that it featured Ting Pei.

The film proper opens with a fight and then Michael Chan Wai-Man—presumably cast here because he was known to the public as a friend of Bruce Lee—coming across a mortally wounded man. The injured geezer gives Wai-Man a bag of jewels and asks him to deliver them to his wife (Ting Pei). Wai-Man goes home and discusses what happened with his sidekick Charlie Chan Yiu-Lam, who tells him that the dying man must have been one of the gang of robbers who burgled local big boss Mr Kwan. Yiu-Lam explains Kwan is involved in brothels, drugs and money lending, and the jewels should be returned to those he took them from. Wai-Man insists on taking them to Miss Ting (Betty Ting Pei), who doesn't want them because she's playing a good woman in this movie. Moments later a gang of thugs turn up but Wai-Man and Yiu-Lam see them off. Wai-Man tracks them back to The Lucky Casino run by bad girl Woo Gam.

Through a window Wai-Man watches Woo using her sexual allure to calm and manipulate the anger of one of her men, who she ultimately stabs in the back. The wounded man still manages to throttle Woo until Wai-Man steps in to save her. Woo tells Wai-Man a sob story about her life, and given how manipulative she is the viewer has to assume it is a pack of lies, but our hero buys it. She is setting Wai-Man up to fight Kwan's gang and wants the jewels, which her own men stole and our hero now has. Wai-Man finds himself in a dynamic that is presumably intended to resonate with Bruce Lee's love life. He is attracted to both the good woman Miss Ting—Bruce Lee's real life lover here being used to metaphorically represent his wife Linda—and the bad girl Woo, who becomes a substitute for Ting Pei's media portrayal as his evil mistress.

After Ting Pei and Wai-Man, the next actor down on the rung of Bruce Lee signifiers is Paul Wei Pin-Ao, who appeared in supporting roles in *Fist of Fury* (1972) and *Way of the Dragon* (1972) with the 'king of kung fu'. Pin-Ao is one of Kwan's flunkies and is killed off with a dart for failing to protect the gang-banger's jewels while his boss was away. Even more of Woo's men go after Wai-Man, but he sees them off. By now Wai-Man and his sidekick seem to be living with Miss Ting and her daughter; although Miss Ting isn't sharing a bed or even a room with the men. Kwan connects the theft to The Lucky Casino, which he empties of customers when he goes there with his men to get the two robbers he's identified. When Wai-Man turns up shortly after Kwan's gang leave, Woo tells him the big boss wants to run her out of town. Wai-Man goes to Kwan's casino, makes trouble and takes the cash box. In the meantime Kwan's gang have connected Miss Ting to the jewels. They go to kidnap her and her daughter. First they have to fight Yiu-Lam, and during this battle three different stills of Bruce Lee from *Way of the Dragon* and *Enter the Dragon* (1973) are cut in for fractions of a second.

Despite support from this almost subliminal Bruce Lee imagery, Yiu-Lam is killed. Wai-Man gives Woo the money he's taken from Kwan, to make up for her losses after the big boss emptied her casino of marks. For Woo money is an aphrodisiac and Wai-

Man gets to bed the bad girl. Later Wai-Man goes looking for Miss Ting but Kwan's hoods surround him. Wai-Man is injured but wins the fight. Kwan's gang are torturing Miss Ting and threatening her daughter, this stops when a hood arrives to tell the boss that Wai-Man has killed more of their men. The gang are instructed to find our 'chivalrous knight' whatever the cost. Wai-Man is being patched up by and getting busy with Woo when Kwan's heavies arrive to search her place. He evades the gangbangers by hiding under her bed. Woo talks to Wai-Man about the jewels again and asks him where they're hidden. Kwan's gang are turning over Wai-Man's house looking for the sparklers but can't find them. For no reason, there is a curious montage of a statue of an erotic dancer, a sculpted Dragon or Lion's head with fangs, and Kwan having drunken sex with a woman—presumably a prostitute from his brothel. Wai-Man steps into the frame and kidnaps the big boss; he wants Miss Ting back from the gang in exchange for Kwan. We see Kwan in ropes being struck and falling down. There is an almost subliminal cut to a framed photo of Bruce Lee in sunglasses with funeral flowers around it. Cut to Woo searching for and finding the jewels. Kwan frees himself from his bonds.

Cut to Wai-Man with Miss Ting and her daughter in her house, discovering the jewels are missing. Miss Ting says she's glad the sparklers are gone. Later as Wai-Man, Ting Pei and her daughter, are walking through the countryside, they're ambushed by Kwan's gang. There is a fight involving poles as weapons, and during it one of the gang tries to molest Miss Ting; when she resists he stabs her to death. Cue image of Ting Pei's daughter crying over her dead body, then cut back to the combat, which Wai-Man wins. Shift to Woo looking like she's having an orgasm as she examines the stolen jewels with a magnifying glass. Kwan walks in, Woo tries to stab him and he savagely beats her. Cut to a very angry looking Wai-Man making his way to the Lucky Casino with a group of men; one of whom is carrying Miss Ting's daughter.

When they reach the entrance, Wai-Man goes in and the men split-off with the little girl. Wai-Man takes out Kwan's sole bodyguard. Cut to a topless Kwan pulling up his trousers with a dead Woo lying on the bed. The editing implies Kwan killed Woo and then raped her corpse. Wai-Man opens the door and walks in. Cue quick cuts between the eyes of the two men and the face of the dead woman before the climatic fight. This battle moves out of the casino and into the countryside. It concludes in a forest full of traps, which is an excuse for the filmmakers to indulge in unnecessary cruelty by having animals die in some of these to parallel the fictional mortal combat we're watching. Wai-Man manages to scratch Kwan across the chest so that our villain looks like Bruce Lee after he's been slashed by Han's claw in *Enter the Dragon.* The two men fall into a snake pit and get out again. The escape isn't very convincing; it looks like the camera has been tilted and the two actors are bouncing along the ground on all fours. Finally both men are caught by rope traps and find themselves suspended upside down. Kwan frees himself and laughs at Wai-Man, who he believes he's defeated. Then the big boss steps on yet another trap and is killed by darts.

This film belongs to the amplic phase of Brucesploitation, it was made before the genre had come into existence but played a role in conjuring it up. Despite using an *Enter the Dragon* music cue and featuring Betty Ting Pei, the complete lack of nose thumbing in *The Chinese Godfather* means I can't place it at the core of the Brucesploitation genre and must banish it to the semi-periphery. According to some sources *The Chinese Mack* is an alternative title for this movie, although I have yet to see compelling evidence for this; however *The Chinese Mack* does seem to be an alternate title for another 1974 Hong Kong flick called *Martial Arts* that has a cast that overlaps with this one but is directed by Chui Dai-Chuen. *Martial Arts* and *The Chinese Godfather* are two different films that are frequently conflated as being the same movie, and/or confused with each other.

44 THE GREEN HORNET — 1974
DIRECTED BY WILLIAM BEAUDINE, DARRELL HALLENBECK AND NORMAN FOSTER

A cut-and-paste movie incorporating various episodes of the 1966/1967 TV series *The Green Hornet* with Bruce Lee appearing as Kato in a supporting role to Van Williams, who played the eponymous hero of the show.

In order to infiltrate the underworld, The Green Hornet and Kato pretend they are criminals, but in their fictional bubble they are really 'crime-fighters' who take out hoods and then leave them for the cops to arrest after they have given them a beating. Which gives the whole series a mildly postmodern spin, although the vigilante character Van Williams plays is a conservative capitalist authoritarian.

The first act is based around a TV episode entitled *The Hunters and the Hunted,* in which a group of rich big game hunters decide to take out all the criminal scum in their city including The Green Hornet and Kato. Despite the big gamers setting traps and using silent weapons such as the bow and arrow, they are easily outwitted our deadly duo. Here we have Bruce Lee's first onscreen use of nunchaku, later to become his signature weapon. In these sixties clips, the Little Dragon fails to display anything like the same skill with nunchaku that he developed for his 1970s movies. In short while this early use of nunchaku may excite Lee obsessives, it will disappoint nearly everyone else familiar with his Hong Kong films.

The middle part of this feature is made up of a story split across two episodes of *The Green Hornet* entitled *Invasion from Outer Space Parts 1 and 2*. These were the final two episodes of the first and only season of the series, which was abandoned after twenty-six instalments due to disappointing ratings. Dr. Mabuse (played by Larry D. Mann) is your typical carpet-chewing mad scientist who a decade earlier was sacked from his job by the US government for making unauthorised nuclear tests. Mabuse fakes a UFO crash, while unconvincingly disguising himself and his lackies as wankers from outer space. Mabuse and his gang crash Van Williams's pad as he plies his secretary Lenore Case (played by Wende Wagner) with drinks in what looks like a seduction attempt. Bruce Lee takes an instant dislike to the uninvited house-guests but when he moves to throw a Hornet Dart at them, he is zapped and knocked unconscious by an electrical device Vama (Linda Gaye Scott) has in her spacesuit. Gaye Scott is the only female in Mabuse's nuclear terror gang, and so she wears a skin-tight gold metallic outfit, while the men are dressed in silver.

Mabuse forces Van Williams to make an appeal for calm on a TV channel he owns; when he's not The Green Hornet, Williams is Britt Reid, a right-wing media mogul playboy. The mad scientist also demands that a highway is cleared of civilian traffic, giving the excuse this is the only way his non-existent mother ship can pick him up, and then departs with Wagner as a hostage. Williams soon works out Mabuse wants the highway cleared so that he can intercept a government convoy and steal an H-Bomb.

Before Van and Bruce save the day, there is a car and truck chase involving Williams (or more likely a stuntman) jumping from the back of The Black Beauty (the Hornet's equivalent of the Batmobile) into Mabuse's mobile laboratory as it speeds along the highway. Larry D. Mann's character is apparently named in homage to the fictional character in Norbert Jacques's novel *Dr. Mabuse, der Spieler* and the subsequent Fritz Lang films based on this. While this section of our cut-and-paste movie is probably the most appealing part to fans of pulp and noir serials—since it is amusing in a 1950s b-movie kinda way—it doesn't have nearly as much to interest martial arts mavens as the start and finish of the hack-and-slash job under review.

The final section of the film comes from a TV episode entitled *The Preying Mantis*, in which the mob use young martial arts fighters to muscle into the protection rackets of Chinatown. Mako Iwamatsu appears as Lo Sing, the leader of a motley crew of

Tong heavies who practice the Preying Mantis style of kung fu. What particularly excites the Lee fanboys about this is that it seems that Dan Inosanto stunt doubled for Mako. So in some parts of Kato's two fights with Lo Sing (or at least in the second), it is actually Lee brawling with his top student six years before they shot their 1972-staged battle which is featured at the climax of the official *Game of Death* (1978). That said, *The Green Hornet* fights are very short.

In the first, Lo Sing tosses Bruce Lee head first into a trashcan, giving viewers the comic sight of the Little Dragon's legs sticking out of a rubbish bin. The climatic and longer 'battle' is an honour bout staged in front of an audience in a Buddhist temple. Lee wins this time but even so the combat only lasts about thirty-five seconds; there must be at least as much of Mako in this as Inosanto, so while some Lee obsessives are prone to wetting their knickers about this first filmed encounter between Lee and his top student, it doesn't amount to much more than a few seconds of footage. With Lo Sing's defeat the occidental racketeers are forced out of Chinatown.

Since there isn't much footage of Bruce Lee fighting in any individual *Green Hornet* TV show, the producers of the flick tried to beef it up by randomly inserting combat from otherwise unrecycled episodes. This gives the film a surreal quality it shares with many collage concoctions. Likewise, as others have already observed, there are a plethora of unconvincing day-for-night scenes, the sets are terrible and there is way too much driving around what are obviously Hollywood movie lots. There is also a problem with a loss of information since what was a TV show has been cropped at the top and bottom to make it fit a widescreen cinema format. That said, I don't think there can be much doubt that *The Green Hornet* is exploiting public interest in Bruce Lee (after his death), so it is definitely Brucesploitation. The persona Lee put across in his kung fu films of the seventies isn't really present, so we can reach the blindingly obvious conclusion that this was something constructed at a later date.

45 THEY CALL HIM CHOP SUEY — 1975
DIRECTED BY JUN GALLARDO

The movie begins with a dream sequence in which Ramon Zamora beats up a load of thugs in a nightclub and gets to kiss the female singer of the house band. In waking life he's a Bruce Lee super-fan who dreams of being a great fighter. He works in a Hong Kong restaurant with his grandfather. Zamora is called Chop Suey because he's half-Chinese and half-Filipino (in the movie), and his grandpa teaches him how to make a superb version of this dish of mixed ingredients. His guardian dies so Zamora goes to Manila to work in his aunt's restaurant. Here he gets in fights with gangsters who are extorting protection money from his aunt. Jackson and his men are also involved in prostitution rackets and kidnap girls to use as sex slaves in their brothels. The boss hood is also given to knocking his girlfriend Jenny around; she has been imprisoned against her will. Eventually Jackson's men kill Zamora's aunt and kidnap the blind girl who works in the restaurant with him. Jenny, who Zamora had tried to help in an earlier scene, phones the restaurant and tells Zamora and the bald headed waiter Pugak to come and rescue the blind girl Jackson is attempting to rape.

After a few complications all three restaurant workers and Jenny flee Manila with the documentary proof of Jackson's gang activities. The police are also on Jackson's case looking for evidence against him before they charge him as a crime lord. Jackson discovers where those running from him are and goes after them with his men, while the police are in their turn on his tail.

The blind girl is murdered by the bad guys, which makes life easier for Zamora because she was in love with him but he's in love with Jenny. There is a battle in the jungle with Pugak getting killed. Jackson snatches the briefcase full of incriminating documents but falls into quicksand and dies. The cops shoot loads of gangsters and round up a few live hoods. Zamora and Jenny survive and presumably get to live happily ever after.

While there are several good sequences, especially the opening nightclub dream and a scene where Jackson kills a gangland rival in a massage parlour, in places this film drags. There are too many conversations either on the telephone or with characters just standing around. This is an action comedy that needs more excitement and laughs. The conceit of Zamora being an obsessed Bruce Lee fan disappears from the plot fairly early on in the film. I wouldn't put this at the core of the Brucesploitation genre because it wanders away from its interest in the Little Dragon, but because Lee is ritually invoked it makes the semi-periphery.

46 FURY OF THE DRAGON — 1976

DIRECTED BY WILLIAM BEAUDINE, ROBERT L. FRIEND (UNCREDITED) AND SEYMOUR ROBBIE (UNCREDITED)

This is a follow up cut-and-paste movie to *The Green Hornet* (1974). After an animated credit sequence featuring cartoons of Bruce Lee, various episodes of the mid-sixties TV series *The Green Hornet* are collaged together to create something resembling a feature film. Bruce Lee appears in a supporting role as Kato, with Van Williams as the star playing the eponymous hero of the show.

We start with *Trouble for Prince Charming*. In this a dickhead monarch called Prince Rafi (Edmund Hashim)—who is the unelected leader of some fictional principality (he has a grating fake French accent so presumably this is modelled on somewhere like Monaco)—arrives in the USA to perform state duties and visit his American fiancée Janet Prescott (Susan Flannery). Van Williams and Bruce Lee foil an assassination attempt when Rafi arrives at the airport. Next Janet Prescott is kidnapped from inside Rafi's consulate. The Prince is told he must abdicate or Janet will be killed. Van and Bruce kidnap Rafi to prevent him giving up his position of privilege. Van works out that Janet is being held captive inside the consulate. He uses a ransom he demands for Rafi as a ruse to get into the heavily guarded compound. Williams and Lee free the kidnapped Princess-to-be and Rafi is ever so grateful.

In *Bad Bet on a 459-Silent,* Williams and Lee take on a couple of bent cops, and the script protests just a little too much that this is a case of the odd bad apple tarnishing the city's 'finest'. Williams is shot in the shoulder early on in this episode, so the fighting falls slightly more heavily than usual on Lee. The bad apples come to a bad end, so thanks to Van and his sidekick Bruce, the police are no longer tainted by corruption but only in this story, not in the real world.

In *The Ray Is for Killing,* Bruce and Van take on a gang who are demanding a ransom for some prize items they've stolen from Britt Reid's art collection: a bad move as the right-wing media mogul and playboy they're trying to extort is secretly The Green Hornet. The gang have a deadly ray gun but Van uses his political connections to score a top-secret tin of special paint being developed to aid the re-entry of spacecraft into the atmosphere. As Van's dogsbody, Bruce has the task of covering every inch of their car with this ray gun resistant paint. Lee seems to have been a bit of a slacker on the spray job since the car looks no different after he's supposedly repainted it, and we—and our anti-heroes—can still see through the windows too. Unless this is invisible ray resistant paint... and it must be because Van, Bruce and The Black Beauty survive being blasted with the laser gun, and proceed to beat the shit out of the bad guys! The ransom money for the paintings is recovered, but we never learn if the artworks are saved—but who cares? These masterpieces are only the MacGuffin.

Finally in *The Secret of the Sally Bell*, Van and Bruce take on gun toting international drug smugglers and win yet again, with the usual close calls along the way. To increase the martial arts content in *Fury of the Dragon,* fights from other episodes are randomly inserted; including one already seen in

Bruce and Van's previous cut-and-paste adventures together in 1974's *The Green Hornet*. Even with these inserts there isn't that much martial arts, and Lee's fights are considerably less spectacular than in his later films. Nonetheless, this time around the producers have really let rip with the collage elements, so *Fury of the Dragon* is way more accidentally avant-garde than 1974's *The Green Hornet*, and its feral incoherence makes it more enjoyable than the previous outing. *Fury of the Dragon* is definitely Brucesploitation but the lacklustre martial arts results in it only making the semi-periphery of the genre.

47 BRUCE AND SHAOLIN KUNG FU   1977

AKA *CHING WU AND SHAOLIN KUNG FU*

DIRECTED BY JAMES NAM

This is set in 1930s occupied China and Korea. The Japanese want to close all the Chinese kung fu gyms which they view as centres for patriotic resistance. They decide to start with the Ching Wu school because it produces the best fighters. In charge of this repression is Bae Su-Cheon who plays General Yae Ho as a carpet chewing Japanese fascist; who might as well be a German Nazi since he has the same stereotypical characteristics one would find in a generic British movie depicting the latter. Su-Cheon decides no guns should be used against the Chinese fighters because he wants to demonstrate the superiority of Japanese martial arts to kung fu. As a top fighter, Bae's lieutenant son is supposed to lead the other karatekas to victory. Bruce Le as Lee Ching Lung—there is no Bruce in the movie—seeks the son out and easily defeats him. The Japanese lieutenant is so ashamed about being beaten that he commits suicide by disembowelling himself with his sword. Bae decides Bruce must be killed but Le's master sends his top student off to Korea to learn taekwondo and avoid being murdered. Everyone is of the opinion that when Bruce combines his Shaolin kung fu with Korean martial arts he'll be undefeatable.

Bruce's master is killed by the top fighters gathered together by the Japanese—including Bolo Yeung doing gorilla style kung fu—but only because the assassins looking for his student deploy trickery. After the humiliating defeat of his son, Bae decides he needs the best fighters, including a kung fu expert, to defeat the Ching Wu school. The Japanese follow Bruce Le to Korea. Aided by the female lead Kim Jeong-Nan, Le defeats all the fighters the fascist general throws at him. After overcoming a father and son albino karate duo who fight with what look like metal hands attached to chains, Bruce Le tells Bae he's gonna walk away and if Japanese use guns against him then the general is no samurai. Having had the superiority of Chinese kung fu to Japanese martial arts repeatedly demonstrated to him, Bae lets his men shoot Bruce down.

The retarded nature of all nationalisms is illustrated by this movie being peppered with Bruce Le speeches about 'glorious' Chinese patriotism—made all the more peculiar by the fact that he was born in Burma. While Bruce Le is in part avenging the death of his brother who we are led to believe is Bruce Lee's character Chen Zhen from *Fist of Fury* (1972), the connection isn't enough to put this at the core of the Brucesploitation genre. There is a lot of Bruce Lee-style nose thumbing and a few scenes that resemble parts of *Fist of Fury*, as well as a guest staring role for Bolo Yeung from *Enter the Dragon* (1973), but this movie plays fast and loose with its supposed inspiration. In places it seems closer to *When Taekwondo Strikes* (1973) than the Bruce Lee vehicle that is more generally taken to have (partially) inspired both of these later tales of Japanese military oppression. Likewise, as the weapons deployed get weirder and fights are run partly in slow-motion toward the end, this movie starts to feels closer to *Master of the Flying Guillotine* (1976) than *Fist of Fury*. Le uses a variety of techniques but iron finger is the predominant one in this movie and features heavily in the early demonstration and training sections.

48 BRUCE AND THE GOLDEN CHAKU 1977

AKA *GOLDEN CHAKU*

DIRECTED BY RONALDO SAN JUAN

The movie opens with a Cathay Pacific plane coming in to land at Manila International Airport. Rey Malonzo (billed as Bruce Ly in the English language dub of the movie—so I'll call him Bruce from now on) emerges from the plane dressed in a white Chinese suit like the one worn by Bruce Lee in *Fist of Fury* (1972). When Bruce grabs a cab he is lucky enough to be picked up by Ramon Zamora. They go to a martial arts club where Bruce (in the movie his character is called Jessie Hu) delivers a suitcase filled with $30,000 dollars to buy a pair of golden chaku, a lost family heirloom. Bruce hands over the cash but when he's given the nunchucks he discovers he's been conned, these aren't the golden chaku he was after but a cheap fake. A fight breaks out and while Bruce is distracted by the fisticuffs, the gang bosses run away with his suitcase full of money. Meanwhile Zamora has lumbered into the room with Bruce's luggage and backs up his passenger, so between the two of them they easily defeat the hoods.

The plot basically hinges around the fact that Bruce believes his uncle Chang Hu stole the golden chaku from his father, and he's now come to Manila to retrieve them. He'd sent the mob information about his uncle and offered them a hefty payment to retrieve his family's legendary weapon. Chang hasn't died as Bruce believes, he's faked his death and hidden the golden chaku in his otherwise empty grave. This unoccupied tomb is in the cemetery at which Zamora's father works as a caretaker; Zamora's father and Bruce's uncle are best friends. Chang Hu is living under the assumed identity of Tan, but the only person who knows this is Zamora's dad.

A further unlikely twist is that Bruce has been in The Philippines before and is romantically involved with Zamora's sister Emily; however her father disapproves because he knows that Bruce is his best friend's nephew and that there is a family feud one generation up from our anti-clone. To further force the hand of chance the gangbangers decide that ripping off Bruce's money isn't enough, they want the golden chaku too because the weapon is so valuable. Bruce wants the extra-special nunchaku because his father was undefeatable with them, but after his uncle took them pops was killed. One of the hoods is suspicious of Tan/Hu and with a few others follows him. Noticing he is being tailed, Hu walks distractedly into the road and is knocked down by Zamora's taxi. Zamora has to beat up the gangbangers before he can help the injured man. He goes with Hu and two cops to the hospital, and when the injured man's daughter Loita turns up he's immediately smitten with her. Hu insists the accident was his fault and he won't press charges. Zamora takes the whole thing as an introduction to Loita and is soon in a romantic relationship with her. There's even a double beach date with Zamora, Loita, Bruce and Emily. Meanwhile the gangbangers are still after Hu and the golden chaku. They eventually realise Zamora's dad is Hu's best friend and try to beat information out of him.

When Zamora finds the old man dead he blames Bruce, thinking that his sister's boyfriend must really be Hu because his father was uncomfortable around him. Emily protests to her brother that he is wrong but Zamora won't listen. Eventually Zamora tracks Bruce down to the graveyard and attacks him. During the course of the fight Bruce manages to convince Zamora that he isn't Hu, so they make up. Emily and Loita have become close friends and while they are together at the Tan house, the hoods turn up and beat Chang unconscious in an attempt to get him to tell them where he's hidden the golden chaku. Loita is grabbed by the gang. Emily manages to leg it while a couple of men employed by Tan/Hu fight the mobsters and are eventually killed. Emily is running home just as Zamora and Bruce are driving the same way. Malonzo is wearing a black Chinese suit with big white cuffs like Bruce Lee in *Enter the Dragon* (1973). Emily gets in her brother's taxi and they go back to Tan/Hu's house. Hu is dying but he explains who he is and that he had to take the golden chaku from Bruce's father because his brother had misused them and this resulted in the death of his (Chang's) wife. After he was widowed, Hu escaped to The Philippines with his baby daughter and the deadly weapon. He also reveals that he's hidden the golden chaku in his fake tomb. Bruce and Zamora rush to the grave and start to break into it, but by this time the gangbangers have also realised this is where the priceless weapon is hidden and turn up before our heroes have retrieved the golden chaku.

A big fight breaks out, with cuts between Bruce and Zamora each taking out the opposition. Although much of this bust up is unarmed combat, Bruce also uses the spade with which he was attempting to open the grave as a weapon, and later a broom. One of the hoods pulls up a white wooden cross and tires to use that to batter Zamora. Eventually Bruce manages to pull the golden chaku out of the fake grave and uses them to battle his way to victory; then when he's finished he throws the weapon to Zamora who uses it to take out the last remaining hood.

To wrap things up, Loita, Emily and Zamora, see Bruce off at Manila International Airport. In a loop back to the film's opening, Bruce catches a Cathay Pacific international flight. Despite the loose and unlikely plotting, the fast and furious action makes this movie fun viewing. There are enough Bruce Lee references to put *Golden Chaku* in the semi-periphery of the genre but the groovers who made this movie seem at least as interested in doing their own thing as ripping off the Little Dragon.

49 FIST OF FURY II   1977
DIRECTED BY LEE TSO NAM, IKSAN LAHARDI AND JIMMY SHAW

As an unofficial sequel to the earlier Bruce Lee movie, the plot of this flick revolves around the Japanese abusing all the kung fu schools in Shanghai. Almost a third of the way in Bruce Li appears to play Bruce Lee's brother. Li must avenge his sibling (who died in a hail of bullets at the end of the first *Fist of Fury*) and restore the honour of Chinese kung fu. He does this by systematically defeating all the Japanese fighters he encounters. Li beats the best 'Japanese' martial artist at the end, *King Boxer* star Lo Lieh. Rather than being finished off by the kung fu clone, Lieh as the dishonoured loser of the fight is left to commit suicide by hara-kiri; this idea is lifted from an earlier *Fist of Fury* knockoff *Chinese Iron Man*, and would be used again in *Fist of Fury III*. Li is arrested by the police rather than killed, leaving the way open for another sequel.

Like most of the films that riff on the 'original' *Fist of Fury*, this one contains a strong Chinese nationalist message. Of course the Japanese (or for that matter the British) imperialists in China were completely obnoxious—but it is possible to respond to this with progressive proletarian internationalism as well as reactionary nationalism.

■ THE LAST FIST OF FURY   1977
AKA *THE ULTIMATE LEE*
AKA *DRAGON LEE DOES DALLAS*
DIRECTED BY KIM SI-HYEON

See the entry for *The Real Bruce Lee* in the core section, since this film is incorporated into that movie.

50 SOUL BROTHERS OF KING FU   1977
AKA *THE TIGER STRIKES AGAIN*
AKA *THE LAST STRIKE*
AKA *KUNG FU AVENGERS*
DIRECTED BY HUA SHAN

Bruce Li is an immigrant in Hong Kong struggling to survive. He and two companions arrived on a small boat that was adrift at sea for days. The two guys practice kung fu and the woman who came with them falls for Bruce, so that eventually they are engaged. They help out Carl Scott, who is being racially abused and beaten up by both whites and Chinese. Bruce takes Scott under his wing and adds some kung fu to his karate chops, so that the black kid can defeat the racist bullies who have been picking on him. Bruce's immigrant friend (Lo Meng) has a gambling problem and gets into a fight with bookies, but is helped out of this sticky situation by Bruce and Carl. The criminal boss whose runners have been beaten up feels he's lost face, so this leads to endless attacks on Bruce and Lo. Bruce goes into competitive martial arts and when he wins a televised world championship the gang boss gets really mad and hires three top fighters to defeat him. They hospitalise Bruce and for good measure rape and murder his fiancée. Bruce is told he will never battle again but he decides he must, and so puts himself through strenuous training. He learns the iron finger technique, practicing on a special dummy and eventually he is smashing beer bottles with a single finger. To get his revenge Bruce attacks and kills the men who'd hospitalised him. Meanwhile, the gang have deployed a bar girl to seduce Lo and get him onto their side, so Bruce has to defeat his former best friend. He then wins a battle with the big boss. In one ending to this film the racism is taken to a dismal conclusion with Scott being lynched. In an alternate version, Scott lives. Throughout Bruce Li is a Little Dragon fan and his fighting style is compared to Bruce Lee. He also dons a yellow tracksuit with black stripes for the climatic fights and undergoes electric shocks as part of his training.

51 SOUL OF BRUCE LEE — 1977

AKA *SOUL OF CHIBA*

DIRECTED BY CHAN TUNG-MAN AND NODA YUKIO

Sonny Chiba's sifu appears to have been murdered by another top pupil and Chiba wants revenge. Chiba has to train hard to become a better fighter than his rival, and uses an electric shock machine to do this. The heavy voltage he subjects himself to is a nod to Bruce Lee, who it is widely believed used mild electric shocks to make his muscles work while he slept. Other Brucesploitations elements in *Soul of Bruce Lee* are a lead role for Tadashi Yamashita—who some unconvincingly argue was a Bruce Lee clone because of his role as Bronson Lee in a trilogy of Japanese karate films—and a relatively brief appearance from Bolo Yeung, a supporting actor in *Enter the Dragon* (1973). Beyond these elements *Soul of Bruce Lee* has little to do with Lee, but Sonny Chiba does have an incredible fight with a group of kung fu experts possessed by monkey spirits. Because of the pain of his training, Chiba is shown as being addicted to drugs—and this might be seen as a nod to rumours about Bruce Lee, whose autopsy indicated he used cannabis; it's also been claimed he abused steroids and cocaine. The twist at the end of this tale is that Chiba's master is a criminal drug dealer who faked his own death; a much loved Brucesploitation plot device that is even deployed in the official *Game of Death* (1978). Tadashi Yamashita plays a narcotics cop whose investigation into Chiba's master intertwines with Chiba's quest for revenge. This movie is beautifully inept and definitely worth seeing once despite not making much of talents of either Chiba or Yeung.

52 STEEL FISTED DRAGON — 1977

AKA *FISTFUL OF DRAGONS*

AKA *DUEL MAUT (DEADLY DUEL)*

DIRECTED BY IKSAN LAHARDI AND LEE TSO NAM

Steve Lee's father killed Junus's dad when they had an argument over how to split their profits. So Junus's gang kill Lee's mother and burn her hut in revenge. Steve vows to avenge his mom; his girlfriend Titin points out they don't know who murdered her. Titin also insists a gang killed the old lady so her boyfriend can't take on that many men. One of Junus's hoods overhears Lee swearing he'll get revenge and the gang decide to go after Steve. Junus runs an operation kidnapping girls and selling them into prostitution abroad. Inevitably there are caged women and cat-fights. Junus tells his hoods to bring Steve's girlfriend Titin to him. When the men try to abduct Titin she resists them, which sends them into a sexual frenzy.

The subsequent two-man rape is leeringly and unpleasantly shot. Steve's retarded sidekick Sandy watches some of it in horror. Her murder isn't shown but Titin is dead when Sandy cries over her body. Lee uses Sandy to lure four gang members to him. He kills one of them before the action switches to a bridge by a waterfall with a huge drop from it. Here a hood plunges to his death. Steve confronts another man and demands to know who murdered Titin, the guy says Junus. When our anti-hero turns his back on him, the hood tries to kill him, so Lee gouges out his eyes, which gives the editor an excuse for a freeze frame. The surviving gang member from the earlier part of the fight turns up at the bridge as Lee throws the gouged eyes down beside the body of his defeated foe; seeing this the surviving sex trafficker turns and flees. He doesn't want to end up dead like his three buddies. Because Lee's kung fu is too good for his men, Junus hires a killer called Radley. The gang grab Sandy and to save his retarded friend from being hurt, Lee agrees to meet the gang's boss the next day at The Temple. However, rather than wait twenty-four hours, Steve goes and confronts the hoods at the factory that is a front for their sex trafficking operation. A sign outside the building reads 'KANDAG NYAWA' and there is an outline drawing of a skull and crossbones beneath these words. Steve's plan is to go in and beat the crap out of the gang. He doesn't know that they've now got a hired killer to help them take him out. A sidekick who'd been with Lee is concerned the odds are against his friend and persuades another guy called Punto to back Steve up. Thus we have Lee fighting it out with dozens of men, while Punto races to the rescue. One opponent disappears into a vat of bubbling fluid. Inevitably there is a nunchaku battle.

Once Punto arrives at the factory shorter bursts of his fights are cut into Lee's longer combat scenes. The two men never fight together and when Punto does catch up with Steve, our anti-hero is injured and Sandy is called to help him limp away to safety. Punto defends a door so that the gangbangers can't catch our anti-hero. Eventually Punto is impaled on a shovel. Junus who has been injured by Lee and lost his hired killer tells one of his men to get Chan Lau (Wong Sung in the movie) while being patched up by a woman. Junus and the woman start making out. With the sex scene music still playing there is a cut to another woman who we later learn is Junus's sister Lora. She opens her door to find Sandy and Steve outside. Sandy says Lee has fallen from a tree and Lora agrees to help him out. Almost immediately a bunch of gang members come to search the house, but Lora sends them packing without letting them in. Lora and Steve quickly fall in love; our hero seems to have forgotten about Titin. A couple of sex traffickers are impressed when they see Lau demonstrating kung fu to his students. Lau agrees to go and see their boss. Junus knows Lau's weakness is women, so in come three girls with trays of fruit and alcohol, providing an excuse for the Hong Kong actor to deliver the line: "You sure got good looking apples lady!" To which he gets the reply: "Help yourself!" Not long after this Lau and the lady with the 'good looking apples' are alone in a bedroom with a CCTV camera trained on them. Lau is dressed down in nothing but his black pants, the woman is still fully clothed and she swings her legs in the air a couple of times to give Lau a flash of her white knickers. Cut to Lee cementing his love with Lora by being rude to her. His new girlfriend tells him her brother is after him and he'd better go somewhere that's safe. Because this is true love Lora goes with Steve and Sandy, while Junus's men search for them. Intercut is footage of armed police moving towards the sex traffickers' HQ.

A lookout spots the cops, an alarm sounds and the gang evacuate the premises; we see eight of them including the boss escape. The cops grab a fat naked john and free the trafficked women. Lora fuses over Lee and tells him his wound is nearly healed and that they should move on. She clearly likes abusive men because he snaps at her and invokes his father's death, apparently Steve's dad is now being avenged, Lora just wants to go and live somewhere in peace.

On the soundtrack we hear romantic music. Steve seems to accept Lora's point. Before running away, Lora wants to go and get something from her house. Her brother and his gang are holed up there and they lock Lora in her room. Leaving one man to guard Lora, the rest of the gang go after Lee. Steve and Sandy decide Lora has been away so long that something bad must have happened, so they agree they should move on. Before they can do so some hoods catch up with them, Lee takes them out but not before they've killed Sandy. Steve wanders away but Lau finds him. Lee kills the killer. Lora locates Steve and explains her brother imprisoned her but she was freed by the police. Now she wants to get away from her sibling's gang and live happily ever after. What Lora hasn't taken into account is Lee's feelings for his retarded buddy Sandy, and her boyfriend indicates he can't go anywhere yet by saying: "Now I've got to take my revenge for two deaths. Only then will I be satisfied." Sandy means so much to Steve that he's forgotten about his father, Titin, and even Punto—who presumably didn't look up to Lee quite as lovingly as his retarded sidekick. Sandy and Steve's mom mean more to our anti-hero than Lora ever will. But Lora is a woman who is prepared to fight for her man, and tells it like it is: "Forget about your revenge, you'll only go and get yourself killed." Cut to one of the gang telling Junus the police have a warrant to arrest him. The boss doesn't care; by falling in love with his enemy, his sister has dishonoured his family, so he must kill her and Steve! Lee is about to get on a boat with Lora and slip away when Junus and his remaining men catch up with them. Steve fights off the men who grab Lora, but while he's trying to protect his woman from them, Junus throws a bamboo spear into her stomach. Lee then takes out the remaining members of the gang, with Junus holding out the longest. The boss finally succumbs to Steve's blows and dies on the beach. Steve picks up Lora's body and carries the stiff off into the sunset.

While there are some Indonesian touches, the movie under review was clearly made with an international audience in mind—and some effort was put into making a simulation of a Hong Kong kung fu flick, which is why Lau was used as action director (as well as a villain) and Lee Tso Nam as an 'advisory' director. Iksan Lahardi also worked alongside Lee Tso Nam on *Fist of Fury II* in 1977. Here once the fighting starts it never really lets up, and that becomes tedious.

While *Steel Fisted Dragon* is sloppily edited it lacks the truly nutty splicing of Lee's other star vehicle *Cobra*; likewise while the music cues here seem mostly stolen from other movies, it avoids the totally in your face illegal sampling of pop hits found in *Cobra*. That said, Steve still gears up in some funky seventies threads, and he does a mean Bruce Lee imitation. While there are the usual nose thumbings, come on gestures, stompings and Bruce Lee-style screams, there are no obvious attempts to cop other elements from specific Bruce Lee movies, unless the imprisoned women are meant to invoke *Enter the Dragon* (1973).

53 BRUCE LEE'S GREATEST REVENGE 1978
AKA *BRUCE LE'S GREATEST REVENGE*
AKA *WAY OF THE DRAGON 2*
DIRECTED BY TO MAN-BO

Bruce Le plays a Chen Zhen-like character that riffs on Bruce Lee in *Fist of Fury* (1972) but this flick also has a few tropes from *The Big Boss* (1971).

Le's mother sends him off to learn kung fu from his Uncle Ho. The Japanese are running the town in which Ho has his martial arts school and are mistreating the dock workers unloading the guns they're secretly importing into China. Ho refuses to teach the workers kung fu because he wants to avoid trouble with the Japanese rapists and murderers. Le can't restrain himself and fights back against the colonialists; of course he beats them. Aside from a bunch of samurai and karate fighters, the Japanese also have Bolo Yeung as hired help; he looks very silly dressed up as a top Mongolian fighter. Uncle Ho refuses a challenge from Bolo but accepts a dinner invitation from the Japanese, and is poisoned by them. While the Ching Wu students are mourning the death of their teacher Ho, the Japanese attack them, killing many and injuring others.

Le returns to the school and after seeing the scene of slaughter goes to the Japanese HQ where he takes out everyone including Bolo. The Japanese boss is out on his boat so Le has to track him down there. They fight but the top man escapes from Le after falling into the water; however there are three Ching Wu students on the shore and they take him out.

When Le attacks the Japanese HQ and fights on the boat he's using a martial arts style based on Bruce Lee's movie moves, with plenty of nose thumbing thrown in. I prefer Le when he does animal kung fu, particularly snake. Here he is briefly shown copying a cobra and a monkey to master moves. I've watched both a supposedly widescreen region 2 copy of *Bruce Lee's Greatest Revenge* put out by CMV as *Seine tödliche Rache* with both German and English language soundtracks, and the region 1 full screen version issued by VideoAsia. If part of the image isn't missing from the German widescreen version, then the cinematography is horribly tight in terms of framing. The CMV DVD looks like it has been mastered from a widescreen VHS tape and while the overall quality is better than on the VideoAsia release, the night scenes are still too dark. I prefer the VideoAsia DVD because the extra cropping makes the film appear more avant-garde. That said, the flick is slow and boring, so it isn't worth watching unless you're a Brucesploitation completist.

54 Dragon Lee Vs the 5 Brothers 1978

AKA *The Five Brothers*
AKA *The Angry Dragon*
Directed by Kim Si-Hyeon

A dying man gives Dragon Lee a list of anti-Ching rebels that he is to deliver to a man in the south through a series of intermediaries. Hoping for monetary rewards and promotion, various government functionaries are desperate to get the list. Dragon Lee moves from contact to contact with the Ching forces hot on his heels. Bobbing in and out of the action is a mysterious woman dressed in white (Yuen Qiu). After Yuen steps in to help Dragon at a food stall, Dragon steals her horse because he is in a hurry to move on. At one point Yuen masks up as a 'silver ninja', but more usually she is wearing her special weapon—a hat with retractable blades.

The chief adversaries of the rebels are four Shaolin monks who are highly skilled in kung fu. One of them is Silver Hand (Martin Chui Man-Kwai), who wears a silver glove supposedly representing a part of his anatomy that has been amputated and replaced with metal. Eventually we learn that Yuen is the fifth monk of the title—the only good 'brother'. Her cool tricks include running across treetops in a forest when she wants to make herself scarce. The monks are all scheming amongst themselves for preferment, or in Yuen's case to free her 'reel' brother from jail. When Dragon refuses to cover the bribe Yuen requires to rescue her sibling—because he doesn't believe in having dealings with the Chings—she offers her brother monks something more valuable, a rebel. They agree but plan to trick her, substituting one of their own men for Yuen's jailed sibling. Meanwhile the rebels have bribed a spy to tell them what is going on, and discover that Yuen will deliver their man to the Chings in the morning. When Yuen turns up with the prisoner, Dragon and two other rebel fighters infiltrate the Ching HQ in disguise. When Yuen realises she has been tricked, she goes into battle mode in one part of the fortress, while Dragon and his men fight it out in another room. Eventually the two fights merge into one with Yuen and Dragon both attacking boss monk Lee Ye-Min. The Ching leader is so dazed from the blows of his opponents that he starts seeing Dragon and Yuen as fragmented multiple reflections; these resemble the mirror shots in the climatic fight between Han and Bruce Lee in *Enter the Dragon* (1973). After the defeat of the four bad 'brothers', we see Dragon and the surviving rebels saying goodbye to Yuen on a pass near a river.

Although mediocre to begin with the flick improves as it progresses. If the online sources stating the Korean title of this is *Odaejeja (The Five Disciples)* are correct, then the English dub tells a somewhat different story to the synopsis of the film to be found on the Korean Movie Database. This might account for some of the senseless plot elements in the English version, such as Silver Hand disguising himself for no discernable reason at all. On the KMDB the story is given as Dragon Lee going to China from Korea, and the conflict being between Korean and Japanese forces. This, of course, invites comparisons with the translation that went on in Rene Vienet's *Can Dialectics Break Bricks?* (1973). Vienet's flick took the movie *Crush* (1972) about a Korean anti-colonialist revolt against the Japanese, and detourned it via French dubbing into a revolutionary conflict between proletarians and bureaucrats (or the bourgeoisie).

55 ENTER THE FAT DRAGON 1978
DIRECTED BY SAMMO HUNG KAM-BO

Hung directs himself playing a fat country boy who is an obsessed Bruce Lee fan. Having been reassured by his father that his pigs will be fine without him, Sammo goes to Hong Kong where he works at his uncle's street restaurant. Gangbangers are trying to extort money from the business but Sammo beats them all up with his excellent kung fu. These fighting skills surprise everyone because Hung is porky and gets called Fatty a lot in the movie. The hoods come back when Sammo isn't around and smash his uncle's business up, resulting in its temporary closure. Hung secures work at another catering operation where he ends up in more fights; including one with two French-speaking men who are dissing Chinese kung fu over a restaurant meal. However, Sammo can't escape the hoods who plague his family—even when he gets a job as an extra on a Bruceploitation film, the guys who trashed his uncle's street kitchen are on set as actors too. Sammo thinks the Bruce Lee clone starring in the fake movie is pathetic and beats him up. Triads hassle Sammo's cousin to make counterfeit antique paintings for their boss. Later Hung and the cousin are doing the catering at a party and the hoods are there too. During this sequence Sammo gets tipsy and so there is some drunken boxing.

The climax of the movie has Sammo rescuing a family friend from the gangbangers. She's been kidnapped because an eccentric antique collector played by Peter Yang Kwan wants to abuse her; he helps the hoods offload their counterfeit goods, so they've grabbed the girl for him. Hung fails to get in a taxi with his cousin and has to chase after it all the way to the gangbangers HQ. Sammo fights Kwan's three bodyguards, who use karate, boxing and kung fu respectively as their combat styles. The karateka is a Chinese actor blacked up to look vaguely like an Afro-American; allegedly this was done as a critique of Hollywood movies that used Caucasian actors to play Chinese characters—presumably working on the principle that two wrongs make a right. Hung wins the fights and frees the girl. Since there is no romantic interest between Sammo and the woman he's rescued, Fatty returns to the countryside and his beloved pigs.

While the title might indicate an affinity with the world's most famous martial arts movie *Enter the Dragon* (1973), this flick more closely resembles *They Call Him Chop Suey* (1975), in which Ramon Zamora plays an obsessed Bruce Lee fan. *Enter the Fat Dragon* is superior to the Zamora vehicle because of the spectacle of the obese but incredibly agile Hung doing an excellent Bruce Lee impersonation in terms of fighting technique. Sammo's comedy sometimes draws the flick away from its Little Dragon super-fan premise, and so it belongs to the semi-periphery of the Brucesploitation genre.

In terms of Bruce Lee, *Enter the Fat Dragon* draws on his country bumpkin character in *The Big Boss* (1971) and *Way of the Dragon* (1972). Hung is an affectionate parody of the Little Dragon and not a clone. It is worth noting that producer Florence Yu Fung-Chi was involved in one of the earliest Chinese attempts to exploit South East Asian interest in Bruce Lee in the form of *Queen Boxer* (1972).

56 ENTER THREE DRAGONS — 1978

AKA *DRAGON ON FIRE*

DIRECTED BY JOSEPH VELASCO

Two brothers are swindling the Hong Kong mob boss one works for out of a stash of valuable diamonds, but they've framed an American called Sammy (Samuel Walls) for the theft. Sammy's friend Dragon Hung (Bruce Lai) is called in to help out but due to a mix up at the airport by those picking up the kung fu expert they collect Dragon Yeung (Bruce Thai) by accident. This causes a great deal of confusion, which only multiplies when Dragon Hung's brother Bruce Hung (Dragon Lee) turns up looking for his sibling. Sammy's friends eventually fight both the diamond smuggling gang and the double-crossers bent on diddling it to a standstill. Bruce Lai is killed by the skilled fighter directing the diamond scam but this warrior is no match for Dragon Lee in the climatic battle!

Amidst kidnaps, comedy scenes, gang fights and advice on correct living from a Buddhist monk—which amounts to beat the shit out of the bad guys—this movie is exactly the kind of whacky post-modern fun fans of Joseph Velasco have come to expect. The plot is of no consequence; instead we are dropped into a dreamlike art film atmosphere re-imagined from a low-brow proletarian perspective. Three of the four Bruce Lee simulators from *Clones of Bruce Lee* (Bruce Le is absent) are either re-united or perhaps appear together for the first time. Bruce Lai is the lucky clone getting to wear a yellow with black stripes jumpsuit like 'Bruce Lee' in his pagoda scenes from the official *Game of Death* (1978). Bolo Yeung from *Enter the Dragon* (1973) and *Clones of Bruce Lee* (1980) is present for a cameo appearance. Brucesploitation regulars Cheung Lik, Chiang Tao and Phillip Ko occupy their usual good guy (Lik) and bad guy (Tao and Ko) roles.

What some martial arts movie fans deride as 'over-acting' on Dragon Lee's part is in fact not acting at all—it is a deconstruction of cinematic spectacle every bit as effective as that seen in lettrist films of the 1950s. This is what makes Dragon Lee—at least when he is directed by Joseph Velasco—so much more fun than Bruce Li; the latter was a saddo ensnared by cinematic and modernist notions of naturalism into deluding both himself and naïve fans that he was copying Bruce Lee. Whereas for Dragon Lee becoming 'Bruce Lee' is a matter of simulation and/or actual cloning because there is no original to copy! 'Bruce Lee' is a cinematic construction who copped his moves from others. Like all great post-modern cinema, *Enter Three Dragons* represents a complete departure from logic and sense; any theorising about trash classics of this type should adopt a similarly insane modus operandi. Note: Bruce Li is credited as appearing in the movie although he is nowhere to be seen. Likewise Godfrey Ho is thought by some to be a co-director. This flick is sometimes confused with Dragon Lee's *The Dragon, the Hero* (1979) because both have the alternate title *Dragon on Fire*.

57 IMAGE OF BRUCE LEE — 1978

AKA *STORMING ATTACKS*

DIRECTED BY RICHARD YEUNG KUEN

Bruce Li dressed in a yellow jumpsuit like Bruce Lee in *Game of Death* (1978) uses a rope to climb to the roof of a tall building and tries to stop a diddled diamond trader from jumping. Li grabs hold of the guy's arm but it is a prosthetic limb and the trader falls to his death. Li then goes after the counterfeiters whose fake money triggered the suicide; in an office he's checking out he gets into a fight with a geezer who turns out to be a fellow undercover cop. The two agents spend a lot of time following the gang and in particular Dana Tsen, possibly because she's the best-looking suspect. The boss counterfeiter is played by Han Ying-Chieh; who was Housekeeper Feng in *Fist of Fury* (1972). Bolo Yeung from *Enter the Dragon* (1973) plays a Japanese guy doing deals with the triad gang but he falls out with them and is killed. Dana tells Bruce Li he looks just like Bruce Lee, hence the film title. The mob have an opportunity to shoot Li but decide to tie him up with the other undercover cop and gas them both in a kitchen. This gives Dana the opportunity to free them and reveal that she's an undercover agent too—by this point she must have been really bored of being naked and/or flirting with the men she encountered in this film. All three agents proceed to defeat the gang. Bruce Li is as bland as processed cheese but Dana lifts the film and takes it away from Brucesploitation.

58 Bruce Against Iron Hand — 1979

AKA *Bruce Against Iron Finger*
AKA *Iron Finger*
DIRECTED BY TO MAN-BO

Before the credits there is some night time skulduggery. After them Bruce Li arrives in Hong Kong on holiday from Singapore. We see him emerging from the airport and cut to him arriving at a nightclub with some Hong Kong cops while the house band mime to The Incredible Bongo Band's *Bongolia*. The Brucesploitation genre is stuffed full of these utterly surreal and badly mimed nightclub scenes that accidently adhere to the Isidore Isou's avant-garde cinematic dictum of dissociating sound and image. That said, *Bongolia* really provides a choice ninety second break as Bruce exchanges small talk with his friends from the Hong Kong filth. The nightclub entertainment progresses with a martial artist coming on stage and doing some feats of strength, then beating up a member of the audience who agrees to fight him. The girl who was with the guy who got the drubbing is impressed and invites the performer to her place. When they get back to the woman's pad the martial artist is hot, so his host suggests he takes his jacket off, and then says he should take his shirt off too. The kung fu master proposes they take a shower, the girl agrees. The fighter says he doesn't know the girl's name, she says its Lulu; actually she is Japanese actress Lee Hoi-Gei. After getting out of the shower, Hoi-Gei has sex with the martial artist. As the man makes his way to wherever he's going afterwards, he is attacked by a masked fighter who kills him using the iron finger technique.

The Hong Kong police are puzzled by this murder, one of a series, but Li realises a top-flight kung fu master must be responsible. When Li goes to interview Hoi-Gei—as she was seen leaving the nightclub with the murder victim—she tries to seduce him. Li makes his excuses and leaves. There follow a series of scenes featuring Li interacting and/or fighting with martial artists from a kung fu school effectively run by Ku Feng (the master of the school is sick) and another gym headed by Bruce Liang. Feng and Liang have mastered the iron finger technique so both have fallen under suspicion as the killer. Cut against this are the escapades of Lee Hoi-Gei. She is a nymphomaniac and Feng her jealous boyfriend. Because of his kung fu training if Feng has sex with anyone it will kill him. When Hoi-Gei tries to turn a massage she's giving Feng into something more erotic, he gets so steamed up the only way he can relieve himself is to go off and kill a girl using his deadly iron finger moves. At just under the hour mark there is a kinky sex scene. Hoi-Gei in her underwear orders a guy wearing black swimming trunks and nothing else to get on his hands and knees so that she can ride him like a horse. There is a thirty second break from Curtis Mayfield's *Pusherman* as Hoi-Gei sits on the masochist's back while pulling his hair with her right hand and spanking his bottom with the left, and all the while he shuffles around the room on his hands and knees. Hoi-Gei tells her slave to open his mouth and stubs her lit cigarette out in it. After the pony-play, Hoi-Gei and the masochist roll around on the floor. Although the curtains are drawn outside it is daylight and Feng turns up unexpectedly. Hoi-Gei tells the masochist to run. He jumps from the balcony into the garden wearing just his swimming trunks but is caught by Feng who beats him up and kills him. A jealous Feng then smacks Hoi-Gei around. Earlier there was a bit of plot about the trafficking of Vietnamese boat people, and when the cops find the murdered masochist and dying Hoi-Gei, the Japanese nymphomaniac tells Li that Feng has gone to the harbour to escape on a boat with some Vietnamese women he's going to sell into prostitution in The Philippines. Rather than going with the Hong Kong police, Li arrives to confront Feng and his men with Bruce Liang. There is a long and stereotypical kung fu scene among cargo containers in which Li and Liang eventually triumph over Feng.

This is definitely one Bruce Li's better films, even if both he and Bruce Liang are both completely overshadowed by Lee Hoi-Gei. Li and Liang get to wear a red tracksuit similar to the one Bruce Lee sported in the TV show *Longstreet,* but beyond that there aren't too many Little Dragon-like elements.

59 THE DRAGON'S SNAKE FIST   1979

DIRECTED BY GODFREY HO AND/OR KIM SI-HYEON

Dragon Lee is the top student of The Snake Fist school, and early on mugs a few Bruce Lee poses over *Enter the Dragon* music cues. The plot revolves around the evil Crane gym being jealous of the good Snake Fist school. Dragon Lee's master has taught him not to fight without a reason and not to kill. So when the Crane school murders his sifu and most of his fellow students, Dragon feels taking revenge would be wrong. In this he is a little like Bruce Lee in *The Big Boss*, he wants to fight but feels obliged to control his emotions. When Dragon's fiancée is kidnapped, he abducts the daughter of the Crane master and organises an exchange; however he is tricked and doesn't get his girl back. At this point Dragon loses it and proceeds to wipe out the entire Crane school—apart from the master's daughter who kills herself, presumably as a matter of honour. There is plenty of gore since Dragon's foes are prone to spitting gouts of blood as they die; there is even a fight with a fire eating and breathing dude.

The Dragon's Snake Fist is a very average old school Korean martial arts flick. It is unlikely Godfrey Ho had anything to do with this other than in a production/distribution capacity; especially given that the cast includes Si-Hyeon regulars Martin Chui Man-Kwai, Gam Kei-Chu and Lee Ye-Min. The conflict between the Snake Fist and the Crane schools might be seen as paralleling the karate versus kung fu rivalry in Bruce Lee's *Fist of Fury*, but beyond that and Dragon Lee's endless imitations of the Little Dragon's hand and facial ticks, there isn't enough here to place the film at the core of the Brucesploitation genre. Dragon looks like Bruce Lee on steroids and does wonderfully exaggerated versions of his mannerisms, but his fight shapes look nothing like those of the 'king of kung fu'.

60 FIST OF FURY III   1979

AKA *FIST OF FURY 3*
AKA *CHINESE CONNECTION III*
AKA *AVENGING FURY*
AKA *FIST OF FURY II*
AKA *FIST OF FURY*

DIRECTED BY TO MAN-BO

Bruce Li arrives in Macao from Shanghai. Those who have seen *Fist of Fury II* (1977) know that Li had been arrested by the police after avenging his brother Chen Zhen and defending the honour of the Ching Wu school. As soon as he's in Macao, Li encounters Wei Pin-Ao—the interpreter from *Fist of Fury* (1972)—and a bunch of Japanese thugs. Wei orders the karateka to beat Li up but the clone defeats them easily, all the while holding a bag in one hand. Li then locates his mother and goofy brother played by Hon Gwok Choi. Li's mother is blind from crying her eyes out over the death of Chen Zhen. The Japanese have opened a casino in the colony and want to kill Li, but because Macao is run by the Portuguese, they have to provoke him so that they can justify his murder as self-defence. Since Li exercises self-restrain the Japanese become particularly wily.

Bruce and his brother visit their uncle's kung fu school and his cousin takes a shine to him. This doesn't go down well with his uncle's top pupil Tong Yim Chaan who quickly becomes jealous—although Li is his usual bland asexual self and doesn't really reciprocate his cousin's obvious love interest. Chaan takes to drinking and his hatred escalates when Li intervenes to stop him fighting with a street performer called Miss Yu. Li goes on to invite Yu and her father to stay with his family while they are in Macao, and calls a doctor to help the old man who is sick. Meanwhile Wei as a comic Iago is winding up the cut-price Othello played by Chaan. After being banished from his kung fu school for attempting to sexually assault Li's cousin, Chaan throws his lot in with the Japanese. They murder an ambassador's daughter and then dressed in Li's clothes—stolen from his house—a masked Chan kills his old kung fu master. The attack is witnessed by the sifu's daughter. She tells the police the man she was in love with is the murderer.

The Japanese have already planted garments from the embassy murder in Li's house, so when he is arrested for killing his uncle, the cops find false evidence that he killed the ambassador's daughter too. Li is locked up prior to his trial. Miss Yu and her father overhear Wei, Chaan and the Japanese discussing how they framed Li, so they go and free him from jail. The Yu's want Li to leave Macao but he insists on going to see his mother first. We've already seen the Japanese beating up Li's brother and his mother dragging him back in the house. By the time Li gets there his mom has also been murdered. Li goes apeshit and busts up the Japanese casino. Chaan has made up with Li's cousin—she's forgiven him for attempting to rape her because he's sworn revenge on the man she thinks killed her father. When Li bursts in on them and reveals that Chaan is the killer, Miss Yu kills herself and Chaan is left to mourn her. Li catches up with Wei at a brothel and in not much longer than it takes to say 'I have Bruce Lee's secret kung fu finger book', the translator and his bodyguards are dead. As Li is confronting the Japanese big boss, Chaan bursts into the room so the chief villain tells him to prove how good his kung fu is by killing Li. Chaan having lost the love of his life takes on the Japanese boss in an attempted act of revenge, but he is defeated. It is then left to Li to take out this fighter, who despite having a samurai sword is neutralised when Li spits a couple of needles into his eyes. The big boss begs Li to kill him but just as in *Chinese Iron Man* (1974) and *Fist of Fury II*, Li leaves the top Japanese colonialist to commit seppuku.

As was also the case with *Fist of Fury II*, Bruce Li is a co-star here. It is an improvement on *Fist of Fury II* thanks to the comedy from Wei Pin-Ao and Hon Gwok Choi; both of whom have a lot more charisma than Li. The pouring rain throughout the final third of the movie lends it a gothic quality, and Li looks almost psychotic mugging it up as the Little Dragon.

61 THREE AVENGERS — 1979

AKA *THE LAMA AVENGER*

DIRECTED BY WONG WA-KEI

Bruce Li and a friend who I'll call Goofy because he provides a comic element, get sacked from a Chinese opera troop for beating up gang members who heckled their act. They have another fight with the hoods when the mobsters turn up at Goofy's shack to get their revenge. Goofy's house is destroyed, so the two men go to stay with Bruce Li's aunt who is having trouble with property developers who want her house. For want of anything better to do, Bruce and Goofy start a kung fu school. The son of the main real estate boss sends his American friend John to beat up the martial arts instructors, but Bruce easily defeats him and he becomes Li's student. There are more fights with the gang resulting in the property developer's son suffering brain damage, and Goofy's legs getting smashed. The cops catch Goofy and he goes to jail for six months for turning the gangbanger into a vegetable. Meanwhile Bruce Li becomes a martial arts movie star. When Goofy gets out of jail he goes with Bruce and others to a screening of Bruce's new film—it appears to be *Dynamo* (1978). At the screening, Goofy and Bruce get into an argument with a heckler. The real estate mogul then hires a top lama style fighter to kill Bruce and Goofy. In the final fight, Bruce with help from Goofy and John defeats the lama fighter. Li gives us a few desultory Bruce Lee mannerisms and in the final battle he wears a red tracksuit with white stripes similar to the one the Little Dragon wore in the TV series *Longstreet*. Earlier Li wears yellow tracksuit bottoms with a wife beater top, which has a vague similarity to the famous Bruce Lee yellow jumpsuit from *Game of Death* (1978). These elements along with the kung fu film icon strand put the flick in the semi-periphery of the Brucesploitation genre. Be warned, this is another Bruce Li turkey.

62 CHALLENGE OF THE TIGER   1980

AKA *GYMKATA KILLER*
AKA *SEIZE THE FORMULA*

DIRECTED BY BRUCE LE AND LUIGI BATZELLA (UNCREDITED)

Moments after perfecting a formula to render both animals and men sterile, a Spanish scientist and his assistant are shot dead by masked gunmen who steal the formula. The CIA's top undercover agents, Bruce Le and Richard Harrison, are called in by Jon T. Benn *(Way of the Dragon/Clones of Bruce Lee)* to prevent this dangerous information circulating among terrorists, criminals and rogue states. Viewers are introduced to Bruce as he is caught up in a street fight while bodyguarding what appears to be a top politician.

Harrison makes his first appearance in a large garden with topless models hanging on his every word. Much commented on by those reviewing this flick is a tennis match in which the boobs of Harrison's companions are shown bouncing about in slow motion. In interviews Harrison claims to have improvised this scene himself, although it could easily be the work of uncredited Italian director Luigi Batzella; it also resembles the endless jiggling titties in the Category III version of Bruce Le's later *Ghost of the Fox* (1990), so even the credited director might be the culprit here. The topless tennis is accompanied by The Bar-Kays version of *Montego Bay*, a super-phat and groovy music cue. Aside from The Bar-Kays, Dick's introduction as a cut-price James Bond is dull and formulaic; it also features urination jokes and a nude actress jumping into a swimming pool in slow motion. Moving on, Bruce Le has the wrong info on where the formula will be sold, and is lured into a trap where he does some kung fu fighting with thugs and is then shot at by gunman. Harrison dressed as a bellboy takes the killers out with his gun since he's waiting outside what we're told is City Hall. We seem to be somewhere on the outskirts of Madrid. Our undercover agents move onto a tiny and unimpressive bullring where the sale of the formula is really taking place. The auctioned papers are thrown in a hat to the highest bidder but Le jumps up and catches it, before sending it Frisbee-style to Harrison, who drops it. Le then does some uninspired kung fu fighting in the bullring with thugs, while Harrison has a gunfight. Once Le defeats the hoods someone lets a bull into the ring. Rather than jumping into the stands, Le wants us to know he's seen Sonny Chiba playing Masutatsu Oyama in *Karate Bullfighter* (1975), so he pretends to battle the bull. When Le is visibly in the ring with an animal it is a baby bull to minimise the danger of the 'stunt' but cut into this are shots of an adult bull both on its own and with a double for Le. Also mixed in are close-ups of Bruce with what is obviously a model of a bull's head and not a live animal at all! Eventually Le pulverises the model animal head. There is an animation to show Le killing the bull but it isn't even on a par with Sonny Chiba's low-tech (human) skull x-ray punch in *The Streetfighter* (1974).

Bullfighting is repulsive and cruel but presumably it is included here to give us the 'local colour' of Spain, as well as to reprise what is arguably Sonny

Chiba's least interesting screen fight. Bad girl Nadiuska, makes off with the formula as instructed by her bosses in Hong Kong. Richard and Bruce catch up with her in a nightclub where we get more local colour in the form of a shoddy flamenco act. Shortly after being introduced to Richard, Nadiuska develops a headache, so he gets to take her home. She decides it's hot and wants a bath, and as Harrison doesn't want to be alone he joins her in the tub. Le breaks into the house and watches his buddy getting it on with the villainess. When Richard spots him, Le does his Bruce Lee nose thumbing routine—about the only time we get it in this flick. Le finds the hat he believes the formula is hidden in, so he takes it. Nadiuska knew all along Harrison was a CIA agent and so planted a phoney formula for the spies to steal and also fakes her own death. She only got it on with Richard to manipulate him. The CIA get on the case and quickly discover the formula Le and Harrison stole is for Spanish Fly and not a deadly fertility suppressant. As a result our not so dynamic duo are soon hot on Nadiuska's trail in Hong Kong but so are some spies working for the Vietnamese government led by Hwang Jang-Lee. Here our 'men' are teamed with female CIA operative Sharon Shira. Before long our undercover agents are sunbathing on a beach and Richard is picked up by a pseudo-communist spy wearing a red bikini. This leads Bruce to observe: "He thinks he's Don Juan!" Sharon replies: "All men are the same." Le laughs nervously since he is way too hypermasculine to be straight!

After some bedroom athletics between Harrison and the 'Vietnamese' spy, we cut to one of the bad guys' safe houses where Nadiuska is supposed to be secure. The 'Vietnamese' in the form of Bolo Yeung *(Enter the Dragon/Bloodsport)* and a sidekick get to Nadiuska in her bathroom/bedroom, while her minders Brad Harris and Chiang Tao hang out downstairs. Harris is working out and we see him doing upright rows, bicep curls, and shoulder presses. Chiang Tao just chills listening to music on headphones. When the noise of Nadiuska struggling against her would-be kidnappers alerts the men to her plight, they rush upstairs and Chaing makes short work of the sidekick while Harris fights Bolo. With one man defeated, Tao gets a couple of chops at Bolo before the big man follows his colleague out of the window. We cut to the 'Vietnamese' spy who has seduced Dick searching through his papers because she thinks he is asleep. Harrison grabs her but she kicks him in the balls and escapes. Dick chases but Hwang is waiting in the hotel corridor and gives him a beating, Then Bruce turns up and he gets kicked around a bit before the 'Vietnamese' leader escapes too. After some buddy banter between Le and Harrison, Bolo stumbles upon the corpse of his sidekick who has been killed because their side doesn't tolerate failure. Bolo protests against the death sentence imposed upon him but in an all too brief fight is eliminated by Hwang. The action then shifts from the British colony of Hong Kong to the Portuguese colony of Macao, where the bad guys with the formula have a castle filled with martial arts fighters; shades of Han's island in *Enter the Dragon* (1973). Nadiuska finally arrives at the office used by the number one and two bosses. Producer Dick Randall's bit part is playing one chief, the other is handled by Spanish actor Tito Garica. The boss villains make Nazi salutes when the formula is handed over; there is nothing else to indicate they are fascists. Of more interest to the film-makers than whether they should include a neo-Nazi subplot, is the second anniversary bash at the Macao Trotting Club, where the crew grab fly-on-the-wall shots of celebrity trash.

Since I have no interest in Hollywood or American TV, I didn't recognise Jack Klugman, Morgan Fairchild or Jane Seymour; however some fu fans make excited noises about seeing them in these scenes. The footage of horses drawing buggies around a racetrack didn't excite me either. And I was frankly appalled by Dick Randall getting up from his ringside seat alongside Nadiuska, Garcia, Tao and Harris. Randall is clearly in such poor condition that he should be at a health farm losing weight rather than playing a bit part in one of his own movies. This abominable sequence is made even worse by the use of the *Radetzky March* by Johann Strauss on the soundtrack.

After this Chiang Tao catches a minion giving Hwang a map of the criminal compound. He attacks the 'Vietnamese' but Hwang is as good as he is, and the minion holds him back while his boss runs away. Tao kills the minion but Hwang has legged it. Hwang then has the spy who seduced Harrison tell her conquest that the formula gang have taken his colleague Shira captive and give him a copy of the map of the fortress HQ. When the spy meets her controller dialogue is used to let us know the Vietnamese plan is to get the CIA and the criminals to kill each other off. But Hwang also says there is something even more surprising to be revealed, the spy looks puzzled so her comrade spells it out: "…you know too much about us so I can't let you live." And then she is choked to death. Cut to Chiang Tao beating up Sharon Shira to get her to tell him who else is working with her, while Brad Harris and a couple of extra hoods stand by watching. Sharon kills herself with a suicide pill rather than divulge the secrets of the CIA. Bruce and Dick fight their way into the bad guys HQ. Garcia and Nadiuska are cuddling up together. When they're informed the castle is under attack, the boss decides to leave with his porn starlet friend, but tells his top bodyguards to stay and fight the CIA. By this point Dick Randall has disappeared without explanation, he was either off to a health farm or overseeing some other movie; he also produced *Pleasure Island* (1980), *Emmanuelle Goes to Cannes* (1980) and *Emmanuelle 3* (1980) around the time this one was made.

Having forced the crime boss to flee, Harrison doesn't have much to do, since there are no women seducing him for sinister reasons. It's Bruce who takes out Brad Harris. The winning blows shatter Brad's shades and send shards of glass into his eyes before a flurry of punches to the chest accompanied by a silly sound effect and a flying kick finish him off. Bruce deals with Chiang Tao next, this entails the wearing down of a skilful opponent, and we get an out-of-focus subjective shot from the perspective of the losing fighter—a bit like what happens as Bruce Lee defeats Chuck Norris in *Way of the Dragon* (1972). Tao is mostly despatched with kicks. Garcia and Nadiuska are still fleeing the complex when Hwang appears from nowhere, he kills the lady first and then her swain. Hwang picks up the papers he'd come to steal and is all ready to take them back to Vietnam but Bruce jumps into the frame and snarls "Give me the formula!" The 'Vietnamese' agent replies with kicks rather than words. Luckily for Bruce, Hwang is clearly more interested in getting away with the formula than beating him in hand-to-hand combat, so the action moves from place to place; at one point pausing in front of a wall on which someone has graffitied 'Pink Floyd rule'.

Eventually Hwang makes it into his less than impressive getaway car. Bruce manages to jump in through the open passenger window as the vehicle moves off. The struggle continues, the car stops, Hwang gives Bruce a good whack then accelerates and goes off the road down a hill. We see Le no longer in the vehicle tumbling down a verdant hill. The car explodes in flames with both Hwang and the formula incinerated. Richard looking down from the hilltop thinks Bruce is dead too. When Le asks Dick to help him up, Harrison is surprised but happy, and his chiding words are belied by the act of putting his arm around his buddy. Bruce has a radiant smile, at last he's got what he always wanted, some affectionate physical contact with Dick.

This isn't full-on Brucesploitation but you can see the baleful influence of the Hollywood version of Bruce Lee all over it. *Enter the Dragon* (1973) was a blockbuster crossover kung fu/spy thriller and it's the success of that formula that Le and Batzella are attempting to replicate here, much more than Bruce Lee as an actor. Luigi Batzella helmed some sleaze classics including *Nude for Satan* (1974), but it looks like he wasn't interested in this one. If I'd co-directed it I wouldn't have wanted to be credited either!

63 SKINNY TIGER AND FATTY DRAGON 1990
DIRECTED LAU KAR-WING

A martial arts comedy that riffs on a lot of earlier Hong Kong flicks, and takes it's cue for it's fight scenes from Bruce Lee's movies. Sammo Hung (Fatty) and Karl Maka (Baldy AKA Skinny) play a pair of buddy cops who refuse to follow the rule-book. They come into conflict with drug smuggling triads with a penchant for deploying transvestites in their operations. Sammo and Karl can't tell the difference between a man in a dress and a woman, so they end up groping women when looking for a transvestite with drugs hidden in his bra. The conflicts escalate and they ruin the wedding of the deputy commissioner of police as they battle gangbangers. To allow things to cool down, their immediate boss places them on leave. Fatty and Baldy go to Singapore, which they like so much they decide to jack in their day jobs and set up a karaoke business in the city state and hang with a couple of girls they've met there. They return to Hong Kong to resign but after Sammo's father and Karl's British colony girlfriend are hospitalised by the triads they'd been fighting, they decide they will have to confront the gang if they are to live in peace. The entire triad society is lured to an old chemical factory where the ex-cops intend to record them incriminating themselves, but things go wrong and the hoods are battled and blown up, with only Fatty and Baldy escaping the flames inside the exploding factory. Much commentary is already available about exactly what elements of various Bruce Lee films are being invoked here. Suffice to say the main joke is that while Sammo fights gracefully like Bruce Lee, being fat he looks nothing like him. Since this is a mix of action and comedy, the Brucesploitation element is played for laughs as much as anything else, and isn't a dominant part of the flick.

64 LEGEND OF THE FIST: THE RETURN OF CHEN ZHEN 2010
AKA *FIST OF FURY: THE LEGEND OF CHEN ZHEN*
AKA *THE LEGEND OF CHEN ZHEN*
DIRECTED BY ANDREW LAU WAI-KEUNG

This is a big budget sequel to Bruce Lee's *Fist of Fury* (1972). In the alternate universe it occupies, Bruce's Lee's Chen Zhen character survived jumping into a hail of bullets at the end of the earlier film and finds himself—alongside many Chinese labourers—on the allied side during World War I. The allies are unable to beat the Germans, but Donnie Yen as Chen Zhen can do this singlehanded, with the French coming in behind him to mop up. Having won WWI for the allies, Yen returns to Shanghai in disguise so the Japanese won't know he is Chen Zhen. He hooks up with the resistance who spout People's Republic of China propaganda lines. That means a heavy-handed emphasis on 'unity' and 'patriotism'. More irritating than the ridiculous political line, which might have been amusing had it been allowed to really disrupt the already convoluted narrative, are the over-blown blockbuster production values that left me feeling I might as well have wasted my time watching a piece of Hollywood crapola. Yen becomes a partner in the Casablanca nightclub where way too much time is spent on the dull as ditchwater Shu Qui as a pseudo-Shanghai sing song girl doing tedious big production stage numbers. Yen develops a relationship with Qui and this is doomed because he works for the resistance and she is a spy for the Japanese. Yen becomes a symbol of anti-Japanese rebellion by acting out as the Masked Warrior; a superhero modelled on Bruce Lee's Kato character from *The Green Hornet* TV series. Geared up like Lee in his chauffeur role, Yen is a generic costumed avenger; by the end of the film he is mimicking Bruce Lee's fight at the Japanese dojo from *Fist of Fury*. Yen's version of this is even more ridiculous than the Little Dragon's since it involves more karatekas being defeated by one man. While this climax is stupid, it isn't nearly as dumb as the way in which Yen defeats the Germans in WWI. Being more ridiculous the opening scene is also much better than the anti-climatic 'climax'.

This flick is definitely Brucesploitation but since it comes over as a cross between the awful *Lust, Caution* (2007) and *Watchmen* (2009)—with a lots of Bruce Lee tropes thrown in on top —it belongs to the semi-periphery of the genre. Donnie Yen had previously played the role of Chen Zhen in two Hong Kong television series, which I don't cover because TV falls outside my remit. Yen has also played Bruce Lee's Wing Chun teacher Ip Man in a series of films that are far more enjoyable than this abomination: but I don't cover these either because they are not Brucesploitation. The fight scenes in *Legend of the Fist* seem to be modelled on a mix of what Yen did in the Ip Man movies, Jet Li's version of the Chen Zhen character in *Fist of Legend* (1994), and Bruce Lee moves. There are a couple of almost decent kung fu scenes but overall the flick stinks.

HIS POWERFUL ENEMIES... HIS BEAUTIFUL WOMEN...
HIS UNMATCHED MARTIAL ARTS SKILLS...
THE MOST EXCITING KUNG-FU ADVENTURE OF ALL TIMES!

THE IMAGE OF BRUCE LEE

Starring
BRUCE LI
as the Dragon

YANG SZU
(star of "Enter the Dragon")

CHANG WU LANG
as the Tiger

and introducing the beautiful **LEI DANA**

21st CENTURY DISTRIBUTION · COLOR · R RESTRICTED — UNDER 17 REQUIRES ACCOMPANYING PARENT OR ADULT GUARDIAN

"THE IMAGE OF BRUCE LEE"

PERIPHERY

RAGE OF THE DRAGON

STARRING DRAGON LEE

COPYRIGHT 1980 TRANS CONTINENTAL FILM CORP. ALL RIGHTS RESERVED

"RAGE OF THE DRAGON"

65 ON THE VERGE OF DEATH — 1973

AKA *LINE OF DEATH*
AKA *BRUCE LEE VS CHINESE FRANKENSTEIN*
DIRECTED BY LI FAI-MON

A bounty hunter played by the Taiwanese actor Tang Lung is searching for a fugitive identifiable by a facial scar in the Old Hill district. The area has a reputation as a haunt for ghosts and zombies who kill the unwary. A band of martial artists from the Sun Wei gym claim to be able to defeat the zombies, and offer an escort service through the zone. Those who don't want their services are asked to pay a toll, but these extortionists are shown getting beaten up by the travellers they demand payment from.

Lung teams up with a one-armed swordsman he meets at the local inn. The Jimmy Wang-Yu knockoff wants to avenge the slaughter of his family but pretends that he is a ghost hunter. A girl and her cousin are looking for her father who has disappeared in the area; they end up being helped by a man with a scar on his face. Scarface is looking for his brother in Old Hill. The local zombies look more like Chinese vampires and even do a little hopping early on.

When the ghouls are engaged in combat with the out-of-town fighters they bleed because they are actually men made up to look like the living dead. The Sun Wei gym members are actually a gang of drug smugglers who try to keep people away from the district in which they operate by pretending it is haunted. One-Arm and Lung fight the head of the gang, a master of zombie-style kung fu. The former knows the only way to defeat the living dead stylist is to keep him fighting until daybreak when his kung fu powers dissipate. But the ghoul is wise to this strategy and makes a quick getaway when the sun comes up. Scarface and his two new friends penetrate the gang headquarters and uncover the possessions of the missing father. They're discovered and after a battle escape. Meanwhile Lung and One-Arm have taken possession of two cartfuls of drugs being transported by the gang. Scarface and his sidekicks run into them. One-Arm is the brother Scarface has been looking for but also the fugitive Lung is tracking. Scarface explains that he was framed for robbing a casino and he's innocent, his sidekicks back him up by telling Lung he's a good guy. Lung attempts to arrest Scarface saying the fugitive can explain all this to the magistrate. However, when Lung realises that the gang will fetch him a bigger bounty, he decides to let Scarface be and battle the smugglers.

Leaving everyone else behind, Lung penetrates the hood's HQ and his climatic battle with the zombie kung fu master takes him into a dungeon in which local villagers are incarcerated. This scene appears designed to invoke the imprisoned wretches on Han's island in *Enter the Dragon* (1973). To further underline that this part of the movie is an *Enter the Dragon* rip-off, the big boss grabs a metal claw and makes parallel cuts across one of Lung's pectoral muscles. Lung seems to be getting the worst of it, but between his use of a flaming torch and the imprisoned villagers shoving their arms through the bars of their cells and grabbing the gang leader, he wins through.

Finally the bounty hunter ties a rope around the zombie kung fu master's neck and kills him. Lung frees the grateful villagers but he is mortally wounded. Before he dies the girl who was looking for her father has to rush in and have a brief conversation with him to tie up some loose plot strands. Tang Lung has same name as Bruce Lee's character in *Way of the Dragon* (1972). Despite this as far as I'm aware his only really significant entry in the Brucesploitation genre is *Black Dragon Vs Yellow Tiger* (1974). It is also worth noting that *On the Verge of Death* is not the only film also known as *Bruce Lee Vs [The] Chinese Frankenstein*. There is another movie circulating among English-speaking fu fans under this title (see 114).

66 MARTIAL ARTS — 1974
AKA *THE CHINESE MACK*
DIRECTED BY CHUI DAI-CHUEN

This begins with a shot of a boy's head and an overlong homily about kung fu righteousness. Then a homeless kid and his mother are resting, he gets up to watch a kung fu master instructing some rich boys; the spoilt brats beat him senseless. Both their father and the sifu are horrified. The unconscious kid is revived and the father of the offenders offers the victim's mother a job working as his servant.

The abusers continue to bully the boy as he grows up, but he develops an intimate friendship with their sister Lee Fung-Lan. He watches the kung fu instructor and copies his techniques, until eventually he gets formal instruction and becomes a much better fighter than the brothers who are bullying him. The kid transforms into Michael Chan Wai-Man. The brothers still bully Wai-Man; he doesn't fight back because he and his mother are servants. Eventually his sifu is so appalled by the behaviour of the bullies, who say he mustn't teach their flunky, that he takes Wai-Man to his master for instruction. This old man insists that the bad can't win and martial arts should only be used to do good!

After perfecting his kung fu, Wai-Man returns to the house in which he grew up. The owner has just been attacked by The Three Tigers; when he was younger the master defeated them, but he is now too frail to win. The Tigers have also beaten up the sons and are in the process of kidnapping Lee when Wai-Man intervenes and creams them. Out of gratitude to Wai-Man for saving Lee's life, her father sends him off to a town with a letter of introduction for a job, so he can make money and then come home to marry the girl he defended and who just happens to love him. When Wai-Man arrives at his destination he goes to an inn where the owner Woo Gam takes an instant liking to him. When some street performers working outside the inn are threatened by hoods, Wai-Man steps in and beats up the bullies. Afterwards, Gam gets him to come inside to his room and tells him the gang will soon be looking for him. Later Wai-Man goes to the gang headquarters, a sort of combined gym and gambling den, and duffs everyone up. The gang is running a gaming operation elsewhere; which the film-makers use as an opportunity to indulge in gratuitous animal cruelty by showing a dog fight. Wai-Man savages the remaining hoods and kills their chief. When he goes back to the inn he finds Gam in his bed and they get it on. The next day the gang members ask Wai-Man to be their new boss. He also collects a lot of money and this makes our flawed hero and his coquette very happy. Although he's now running protection rackets in the town, Wai-Man won't allow his men to extort poor street traders, and beats a hood up for doing just that. Eventually Wai-Man decides to go home to see his mother and Fung-Lan. However they've left to visit him. While Wai-Man is away friends of the gang boss he killed arrive in town seeking revenge; they beat up his gang and kill Gam. When Wai-Man finds Gam dead he's distraught, he catches up with the men responsible for her death at their friend's grave.

Everyone wants revenge but it's Wai-Man who wins through to victory. His men discourage him from mourning Gam and shove him into the arms of two hookers for solace. Because Wai-Man's mother and fiancée want to know what's happened to him, the adopted son of the man he was supposed to work for is sent to look for him. The boy had admired Wai-Man for being a good gang boss and not exploiting the poor, and tells him he shouldn't be staying at the brothel. Then the boy leads Wai-Man's mother and fiancée to the bawdy house where they find him cavorting with naked hookers. They are mortified and disown him. The kid challenges his former idol to a fight. As this is kicking off, a discussion between the boy's adoptive father and Wai-Man's mother leads to the revelation that the combatants are brothers. The kid is the long lost son Wai-Man's mother had expressed heartbreak over losing in the early part of the film. She and the Fung-Lan rush to break up the fight by telling the combatants they are brothers. Wai-Man is contrite about his transgressions and the whole family is happily reunited. Wai-Man's brother has taught him he can't win at martial arts if he's bad. While there are a couple of nose-thumbings during fights, there are barely enough Bruce Lee-like moments from Wai-Man to even place this on the periphery of the Brucesploitation genre. Its melodrama and homilies make it tiresome to watch. Allegedly an alternative Hong Kong title of this movie was *Fists Like Lee*. The movie is sometimes confused with *The Chinese Godfather* (1974), which allegedly also went out under the alternative title of *The Chinese Mack*.

67 THE DRAGON LIVES — 1976

AKA *HE'S A LEGEND, HE'S A HERO*

DIRECTED BY WONG SING-LOY

Bruce Li stars in yet another fictional Bruce Lee bio-pic. The shots of San Francisco and other aspects of this film (such as Bruce Lee's training equipment) are similar to their depiction in *Bruce Lee: The Man, the Myth* (1976) and *Story of the Dragon* (1977). Obviously all three movies starred Bruce Li as Bruce Lee but even beyond this *The Dragon Lives* gives off a tedious sense of déjà vu. That said, in this flick Bruce is goofy and on more than one occasion comes very close to losing a fight. After Bruce's birth and some scenes of him getting into trouble as a child, we are shuttled forward to around 1964 with Lee barely able to speak English, but he's a fast learner and is soon having arguments with movie-makers about their racism. He also participates in the Long Beach tournament, where with a lot of effort and after staring defeat in the face, Bruce beats Afro-American boxer Sam Curtis. Then after picking up a role in *The Green Hornet*, Bruce gets totally pissed off with Hollywood bigotry and heads off to Hong Kong. Lee meets Betty Ting Pei and quickly makes his mark as an actor with his Chinese action movies. Bruce's wife Linda turns up and the kung fu superstar lives with her in a house that is way bigger than their actual home in Hong Kong. The American movie producer Bruce had already argued with appears again and Lee pulls him into a swimming pool.

When not playing pranks, Lee is depicted as mentally unbalanced via obsessive training. Bruce makes the movie *Enter the Dragon* but also spends days at a time practicing martial arts, while any other spare moments seem to be passed in the company of Betty Ting Pei. There is an extended non-explicit sex scene between Bruce and Betty with rain running down the bedroom window cut with shots in which filter coffee can be seen splashing into a glass jug.

The film ends with Bruce talking in a philosophical way to Betty as they lie on her bed. Then Bruce sits up and starts laughing, cuing us to the fact he is dying. To make the ending upbeat we go back to the Long Beach contest of 1964 and see the audience there burst into applause when Bruce defeats Sam Curtis. *The Dragon Lives* is more of a drama than a martial arts film, despite the fairly frequent fights. It is also the South East Asian Bruce bio-pic that seems to have most influenced the Hollywood movie *Dragon: The Bruce Lee Story* (1993). It is a snore fest.

68 SUPER DRAGON — 1976

AKA *THE YOUNG BRUCE LEE*

DIRECTOR LIN BING

This is a fictionalised bio-pic that shows childhood friends Bruce Lee (played by Bruce Li) and Hsiao Hu learning kung fu together. Their first master isn't very good but they find a new one and as he trains them they transition from being about six years old to around eighteen. Bruce is always getting into fights and this upsets his childhood sweetheart Chow Ming, her mother and his parents. Bruce goes to America and opens a kung fu school but continues with his street scraps. He returns to Hong Kong and finds that Hu is doing well as an actor/acrobat in the Chinese opera. He asks about Ming and Hu is evasive. Then Lee sees her and discovers she is married. This shouldn't matter since the Little Dragon has been fooling around with one of his US kung fu students. A movie producer wants Hu to star in a martial arts film. Hu isn't interested and suggests Lee. The producer says Lee doesn't look like a fighter. Then Bruce goes on local television to demonstrate the new style of kung fu he's developed. After this the producer wants to sign him, but Lee has already inked a contract with another studio. The Little Dragon becomes a celebrity. Hu gets sick and gives up on his stage career. Lee encourages Hu to practice his tumbling, and with some coaxing his friend regains both his confidence and success within Chinese opera.

Despite his film star status, marriage and children, towards the end of this flick Bruce begins to doubt whether what he's achieved was worthwhile, and worries about his death. In his final fight he defeats the student of an old kung fu master. The sifu tells Lee despite his victory there are still things he doesn't know, and then the old codger applies a death touch to Lee's back. Shortly afterwards, Bruce kicks the bucket. Some reviewers claim Lee's death isn't explained, but it is clear enough in this flick that it is attributed to dim mak.

Throughout the film, even those portions set in the fifties and sixties, the characters wear seventies clothing. The fights are really poor and Li looks much happier doing gymnastics than kung fu. There is also the standard training sequence showing Li using weights in a really jerky and uncontrolled fashion; presumably the director thought this poor form conveyed intensity since the reps are done way too fast. *Super Dragon* also features the almost mandatory scene of 'gweilo' bullies getting their just deserts for picking on the Chinese.

This is more of a melodrama than a kung fu film and so it belongs to the periphery of the Brucesploitation genre; making this placement mainly because of the lead actor's association with exploitation films, and so it becomes one by proxy. According to an unsubstantiated online source on WordPress dating from 30 April 2011, there is an alternative Dick Randall cut of this movie, which pastes in superior fighting sequences from *Wang Yu, King of Boxers* (1973) and *The Chase* (1971) AKA *Shanghai Killers*. David Arrate, the blogger who makes these claims seems to be saying this was the US cinematic version, and also the cut used for an early US home video release by Allied Artists. There are a few details in Arrate's post—particularly the statement the home video version was released in 1976 (rather early in the game)—that lead me to suspect it may be a hoax. Regardless, the possibly fictional cut-and-paste flick Arrate describes sounds considerably better than the version of *Super Dragon* I've seen.

69 RETURN OF THE TIGER 1977

AKA *SILENT KILLER FROM ETERNITY*
DIRECTED BY JIMMY SHAW

This starts well with Angela Mao beating up tumbling karatekas in a gymnasium; she makes good use of a trampoline and beams to achieve this. Unfortunately Angela is only Bruce Li's assistant and is sidelined for much of the movie. Li plays two gangs off against each other, while they try and work out what he's really up to; being dumb they fail to figure out he and Mao are undercover cops. While the story is apparently set in Bangkok, one gang is led by a Chinese national and the other by an American, and both want to control the local heroin trade.

The plot develops via endless scenes of men sitting around having long conversations and arguing about how much they should pay Bruce Li to knock off their rivals. Because information and disinformation is constantly being bandied about, there are a lot of shots of 1970s telephones. There are a few groovy nightclub scenes. In the first cabaret segment the house 'band', a singer and a guy with maracas, mime to Wild Cherry's *Play That Funky Music*. Later the same act pretends to hammer out *Ninety-Nine and a Half* and *Nowhere to Run.* Unfortunately when Bruce Li oils up like a bodybuilder for a fight there isn't a gay disco act like The Village People on the soundtrack. The drug gang led by Paul L. Smith decides to sell ten kilograms of smack they have lying around to their rivals. The mob leaders try to diddle each other when they do this heroin deal, only to be trumped by Bruce and Angela bursting in and announcing they are the filth.

The climatic battle between Li and Paul L. Smith is super tedious. The American has no grace and his punching is weak. Our clone electrocutes the gangbanger to eliminate him. Li does a bit of nose thumbing but remains his usual bland self.

70 BRUCE AND SHAOLIN KUNG FU 2 1978

AKA *CHING WU AND SHAOLIN KUNG FU 2*

DIRECTED BY JAMES NAM

This picks up where part 1 left off; Bae Su-Cheon (General Kawazaki here, General Yae Ho in the English dubs I've seen of *Part 1*) is sitting at his desk mentally ranting about the loss of his son, which is all Bruce Le's fault (Ching Lung in both *Parts 1 and 2*). Su-Cheon is still playing a carpet chewing Japanese fascist, and he goes up a gear from full-on nutzoid to two hundred percent schizo when he gets the news that Le survived being shot multiple times in the back at the end of the last movie. Su-Cheon decides Bruce must die, and to help him he has Chiang Tao (ridiculously made up as an old man called Shi Shaw in the movie) who is introduced retelling the story of the blind men and the elephant. This is after a Japanese secret agent suggests it was a Chinese who helped Le escape.

Having retold the folk tale, Tao corrects the agent and insists it was Korean Po Su Pi who assisted Le because a dart recovered from the scene is of a type only this taekwondo master uses. Since taekwondo wasn't actually developed until after the Japanese occupation of Korea ended, this discrepancy has to be explained away. None of the (fake) Japanese have heard of taekwondo because in this movie it is a secret style invented by Po that only Tao knows about. Tao is familiar with taekwondo because twenty years earlier he was defeated by its inventor; which is why he is now so desperate to find, fight and kill him. Su-Cheon wants to capture Le, and Tao wants to kill Po, now both men are conveniently linked. Tao rants about Po's four highly trained students who've been assigned to protect Le, and the hunchback looking after him. In fact the four students are on hand to defend their sifu's hideout a hundred and sixty kilometres away from where Le is recuperating. Likewise, both the hunchback and his coyly flirtatious daughter Lotus are nursing Le back to health. Once he's well, Bruce needs to find Po to pass on secret documents and to up his martial arts game.

Po's four students make mincemeat of the first Japanese sent after their master. When the Japanese track Le to the hunchback's hovel, the old man tells him that to find Po he should turn left when he leaves the house and to keep walking for a hundred miles (160km). Lotus is to show Le the way but when she looks back and sees the Japanese shooting her father, she runs to him and is killed too. Bruce swears to avenge this death alongside that of his kung fu teacher.

When Le hooks up with Po his desire for revenge annoys the old man, who thinks martial arts should be used to help people and not for personal motives. Le repents by sitting next to a waterfall, and Po eventually takes him on as a student; which pleases his two daughters who both flirt with Bruce. Initially Po only gives Le chores to perform, but once he's proved he's sincere in his desire to use martial arts to defend righteousness, Bruce is taught taekwondo.

Before long Chiang Tao and his top fighters close in on Po and Le, killing two of Po's students, but when our clone takes on the Japanese he creams them. Tao tries to run away but Bruce catches and kills him. Su-Cheon is now marching on the Buddhist temple where Po is in hiding—and to show what a fascist creep he is there is a scene where his men have to form a human bridge by bowing down knee deep in water, so that the General can walk across their backs to avoid getting his feet wet. Outside the temple there is a sacred Buddhist shrine and to flush Le out, Su-Cheon has his men set fire to it. He laughs his cock off like the homicidal maniac he obviously is while jumping up and down screaming: "Chinese kung fu is finished. Long live the samurai. Long live the samurai!"

Bruce appears—as the General knew he would—to avenge this affront to the Buddha and Chinese kung fu. Su-Cheon watches in disbelief as Le proceeds to take out his top karateka with some ridiculous wirework. In anger, the sword wielding general jumps into the fight as his best man is despatched by Chinese kung fu cum Korean taekwondo. Su-Cheon quickly succeeds in plunging his sword all the way through Le, so that it goes in through Bruce's back with a metre of blade sticking out of our hero's stomach on the other side; like an extra phallus! Not even this stops Le. By leaping at Su-Cheon front on and holding him in an embrace, Bruce impales the general! It's the perfect homoerotic act—a double penetration without so much as the need for a woman! This ending demonstrates yet again how hypermasculinity is often just a cover for repressed homosexuality. And when the type of penetration favoured in martial arts films—the kind achieved with an offensive weapon—sends the general into the ultimate ecstasy, the psychedelic fight music ceases and in comes a more romantic theme that plays over a freeze frame of Le and Su-Cheon in each other's arms. This frozen moment is heroically shot from below with tree branches in the background to signify that gay sex is perfectly natural. Needless to say many viewers will have seen such double penetrations before, for instance in *Revenge of the Ming Patriots* (1976), but it must be said that here the stunt is used to much greater effect.

This movie manages to be stridently against Japanese military imperialism, while extolling patriotism as a virtue as long as it isn't being practiced by the enemies of China. In the English dub there is definitely some cultural imperialism going on in the treatment of taekwondo as an offshoot of Shaolin kung fu; that said, this is pretty minor in comparison to what the Japanese military did when it invaded the Korean peninsula. Nonetheless, like all martial arts taekwondo is a product of hybridity, and in the case of this particular style it probably owes more to karate than anything else. Although Bruce Le mugs a few Bruce Lee gestures, there isn't much else in this hilarious movie that relates to the king of kung fu; it moves even further away from its alleged inspiration in *Fist of Fury* (1972) than its predecessor.

71 BRUCE LEE IN NEW GUINEA   1978

AKA *BRUCE LI IN NEW GUINEA*
AKA *BRUCE LI IN SNAKE ISLAND*
DIRECTED YEUNG GAT-AAU AND/OR JOSEPH VELASCO

This starts well with Bruce Li and Chan Sing throwing kung fu shapes to *Bongo Rock* by The Incredible Bongo Band. After this breakbeat classic—there is a reprise nearly an hour into the movie—things fall away fast. Bruce Li and his mate Larry Lee Gam-Kwan decide to leave Hong Kong and go to Snake Worship Island. Larry wants to study the local martial arts, while Bruce will pursue his anthropological interests. Li's views seem overly proscriptive for his profession, viz: "The devil sect is a particularly cruel and vicious sect. They deal in black magic and they use snake style martial arts."

With a couple of comedy guides, Bruce and Larry wander around what looks like a nature trail in Taiwan or the New Territories. On their first night in the 'wilds', they rescue a girl being chased by some tribesmen, but she dies anyway because she's been poisoned; the locals had wanted to sacrifice her in a religious ceremony. Bruce and Larry soon discover that Chan Sing, the Great Wizard of the devil sect, is lording it over the snake people. They also run into Cheung Lik, who is after a sacred artefact, the valuable snake pearl. There is a fight, then they team up, but Lik tries to double-cross Larry and Bruce so he is seen off; shortly after this he is mortally wounded by Chan Sing. Fortunately before Lik dies, Li stumbles across him and is tipped off about the Grand Wizard's three secret fighting tricks. Bruce and Larry get into a fight with some tribesmen and win. Before turning on his tail, head warrior Bolo Yeung tells Bruce: "Alright you. I dare you to fight my master though." Li chases after the retreating tribesmen and disappears, leaving Larry to go home alone.

Shortly after in screen time, but apparently weeks or months later in the narrative, Li gets back to Hong Kong. Using flashbacks, he tells Larry about his adventures, of how he lost a fight against Chan Sing, but was saved by Dana Tsen the snake princess. Li and Dana proceeded to fall in love. When Sing discovered Bruce with Dana, there was another fight and Li lost again. Dana saved him from certain death by promising to do whatever Sing wanted. Bruce was allowed to leave but before he went Dana put a spell on him that caused women who found him sexually attractive to believe he'd turned into a snake. Obviously Dana doesn't know too much about hypermasculinity or she'd have been more worried about men! Bruce and Larry practice snake kung fu in preparation for battling Sing. When the two friends return to Snake Island to rescue Dana, they run into three outsiders looking for the valuable snake pearl. These adventurers have guns and kill Larry but Li beats them off.

Reunited with Dana, Bruce discovers he is the father of a one year-old boy who is about to die because of the curse put on him by Sing and his son. The only way to save the kid is to get the snake pearl from the Grand Wizard. Dana tries to take the pearl but is molested by Sing's son; there is a subplot about attempts to get her to marry him. Fortunately Bruce arrives and kicks the Junior Wizard into a snake pit. Then he battles Sing and this time he triumphs, ending up with nothing worse than some cuts across his torso as if he'd been battling Han at the end of *Enter the Dragon* (1973). Clutching the snake pearl, Dana runs off to her handmaidens who are looking after the baby. Two of the outsiders who want the pearl attack the women in order to gain possession of it, but when Bruce turns up he sorts them out. Once the baby is cured, Li hands the pearl back to the snake tribe and he and Dana wander away to a perfect future with their baby.

Because so much time is spent walking around a nature trail the movie comes across a bit like a seventies Italian cannibal flick gone wrong, with half-baked kung fu fights substituted for the gore. Dana (stage name of Shum Shuk-Yee) is great but wasted in her fake leopard skin duds. There are hot and cool versions of this flick. In the hot version Dana and other women do full frontal nude scenes; in the cool variation these sequences are done clothed. Although Joseph Velasco (as Kong Hung) is credited as the director on at least some prints of this, it seems more probable Yeung Gat-Aau is mostly or entirely responsible for the tedious waste of time.

72 DEADLY STRIKE 1978

AKA *WANTED! BRUCE LI, DEAD OR ALIVE*
AKA *BRUCE HAS RISEN*

DIRECTED BY WONG FEI-LUNG

Bruce Li is the new police chief in a hick town. His deputies are lazy and there aren't very many of them. He wants to free the area from the grip of bandits, so he offers prisoners skilled in different martial arts the chance of a pardon if they'll march out into the countryside to fight the gangs. The lags accept this offer and so off they go to be constantly attacked by outlaws. The first half of the film comes across like a really boring western but with martial arts instead of gunfights. Things liven up when Li has to fight two bald-headed bandits dressed in leopard skin circus strongman drag. One performer stands on the other's shoulders for much of the encounter. Li wins by attacking the legs of the fighter whose feet are on the ground. Other enjoyable bouts follow this, including one with a whip; it isn't as good as similar scenes in the Shaw Brothers flick *The Shadow Whip* (1971) that may have inspired it. There are fighters who crawl along the ground like centipedes, and some snake style kung fu too. In the final fight, the chief bandit uses claw style to gouge lines on Li's face and body that look very similar to the marks left by Han's metal hand on Bruce Lee's skin at the end of *Enter the Dragon*.

73 My Name Called Bruce — 1978
Directed by Joseph Velasco

The film begins with a fake medical team rushing to the premises of an antique dealer. They spray the area around the shop and insist on giving the owner an injection since they claim he's been identified as infected. The men are actually crooks who steal a rare vase after giving its guardian an anaesthetic. The antique is placed in a coffin and taken to Chiang Tao who has offered to buy it. Tao doesn't want to pay for the vase, so rather than handing over cash he has his hoods wipe out the thieves.

Meanwhile two South Korean detectives are put on the case. The cops don't believe the antique dealer when he tells them nothing was stolen, they're convinced he was smuggling national treasures out of the country for foreign buyers. Bruce Le arrives from Hong Kong. He poses as a criminal buyer for the vase but at the same time wants to avenge the death of his brother. He has fights and is followed around by undercover agent Pearl Lin. This cop is also tailing Valerie, who's come in from Manila and may be double-crossing the bad guys. Eventually Valerie pretty much gets it on with Bruce, and sends him off to steal the vase from Chiang. Valerie appears with a gun at an upstairs window of Tao's HQ once Le has grabbed the antique and demands he hand it over. Having got the McGuffin in her hands she slips and is left for dead next to the broken vase.

The noise alerts Tao's gang to Bruce's presence. After he is captured we learn he is actually an Interpol agent. He'd simply assumed the identity of an imprisoned criminal buyer of antiques. The Korean authorities are closing in, so Chiang is planning his escape abroad on a hired boat. However Tao's plans are thwarted when Pearl Lin bursts in. She seems to be losing her fight against the gang until Le who is blindfolded and tied to a chair joins in by kicking out with his legs. Chiang escapes by car taking with him the empty case he'd kept the smashed vase in! Riding a motorcycle, Lin gives chase. Eventually she causes Tao to crash and when he runs off on foot she parks her bike and sprints after him. When Lin catches up with Chiang they fight, she looks like she's losing but Bruce appears and jumps in, and eventually Tao is defeated.

What makes this climatic fight so surreal is that part way through an instrumental section from *Master of the Universe* by London space rockers Hawkwind kicks in! Back in the day kung fu filmmakers would plunder some unlikely grooves, and this instrumental section from the *X in Search of Space* album wouldn't have sounded out of place on the soundtrack of *Master of the Flying Guillotine* (1976) which used a lot of krautrock, but placed where it is within *My Name Called Bruce* it serves to underline the dream-like qualities of the film; for most of the flick the beats are either generic plundered movie cues or funky 1970s disco sounds, so Hawkwind are quite a contrast. What makes Velasco's movies groovy is his refusal to adopt Hollywood realist tropes and his ability to create a dream-like ambience by placing strong set pieces into loose and incoherent narratives. This film doesn't even feature a character called Bruce and after the vase is smashed the characters in it continue to act as if it is undamaged! A variant version of this movie with cut-and-paste material added from elsewhere can be found under the title *Ninja Vs Bruce Lee* (1982).

74 Return of Fist of Fury — 1978
Directed by James Nam and/or Joseph Velasco

This is a follow up to *Bruce and Shaolin Kung Fu Parts 1 and 2*. At the end of *Part 2* (1978) Bruce Le and General Kawazaki killed each other in a duel to the death. Now the brothers of both men are in Korea to seek revenge. Le's brother is played by Kwak Mu Seong who is billed as Bruce Pak, so that's what I'll call him. General Kawazaki's sibling is apparently named Sapio but on the English soundtrack this sounds like Chow, so that's good enough for me. Chow is portrayed as a clone of Chiang Tao's Japanese samurai character in the previous flick. The dead general's name was Kawazaki in the second film in this series, here it appears to have reverted to what it was in the first movie—Yae Ho. Chow is inferior to Chiang Tao, and Bruce Pak isn't as entertaining as Bruce Le.

Pak is at his best at the beginning of the movie when he comes across as a Korean version of Clint Eastwood's Man With No Name character from *A Fistful of Dollars* (1964, but in its turn based on the 1961 Japanese movie *Yojimbo*). Bruce is wandering around getting into fights and trying to find out what happened to his brother, knowing that to do so he has to find Po Su Pi. Meanwhile Chow, like Chiang Tao in the previous episode, desperately wants to kill Po. Pak and Chow's Japanese gang get to hang out and fight each other in a restaurant run by resistance agent Yi. After a battle with Chow and his men in the countryside, Pak proudly tells the 'samurai' he's from the Ching Wu gymnasium; this despite his brother Le having been portrayed as the last surviving member of the Ching Wu school prior to his death in *Part 2*. In the previous episode Chiang Tao got to tell the top ranking Japanese officers the parable of the blind men and the elephant, this time Po recounts it to his surviving students.

Pretty much everything in this instalment feels like a cut down version of what's in the previous episodes; in *Part 2* Po had four top students and two daughters, now he has two top students and one daughter called Ching Chi. Pak asks the abbot of a Buddhist temple where to find the resolution he seeks about his brother's fate, and is told to go to the Japanese dojo. So Pak jumps through the window and beats up all the students, a bit like Bruce Lee in *Fist of Fury* (1972). Eventually Pak gets Yi to tell him where to find Po, but the Japanese are a step ahead of him. Po's top students are getting a beating when Pak arrives and jumps in to save the day. After this introductions are made to Po and his one remaining daughter. Pak is told that his brother is dead but will never be forgotten because he was a great hero and patriot. Cue a sepia replay of Le's death at the climax of the previous movie; there's already been a sepia replay of Le sitting by a Korean waterfall from the earlier entry, supposedly representing Pak's memories of his brother, but since in the story he hadn't been to Korean prior to his brother's death this isn't actually credible. With Pak's arrival Po becomes hopeful that the resistance will rise up against the Japanese. However the invaders are plotting to kidnap Yi from her restaurant, to use her as a hostage to flush Po out. Po sends his daughter and Pak to Yi's eatery to meet a resistance contact. When the Japanese arrest the contact a fight breaks out, Bruce frees the man and sends him outside while he takes on the enemy. Unfortunately the Japanese top brass are lurking in the shadows and shoot the contact as he emerges from the restaurant. Pak and Ching escape but soon afterwards Chow and his men are making their way to the resistance hideout. On the way the Japanese cross a river where Chow's brother made his men stand knee deep in water and bow so that he could stay dry by walking across their backs; the sibling merely has two guys carry him so he doesn't get wet. The Japanese have kidnapped Yi and say they will kill her unless Po shows himself; however the restaurant owner grabs a sword and kills herself harikari style to prevent the foreigners using her in this way. This cues the long final fight, first with Po's two top students, then with Pak and finally Po. Gradually the Japanese are eliminated until just Chow is left. Like Chiang Tao in the previous entry, Chow tries to run from Bruce but is soon cornered. Chow uses a mirror on his chest to blind Pak, but Bruce breaks out his nunchaku and smashes it.

Pak's use of this weapon is really pathetic, as is his Bruce Lee impersonation. He does the odd shuffle but his moves look more like badly executed lunge jumps than a trick the Little Dragon copped from Muhammad Ali. Pak is also severely deficient in the nose thumbing and come on hand gesture department. Despite these insufficiencies Pak soon despatches Chow. Po gives Pak his daughter's hand in marriage, because China and Korean are both suffering under the Japanese; no shit Sherlock, but is that any reason to marry? Before Pak and Chi wander off together, leaving the old man behind, Po hands his son-in-law the secret documents Le delivered to him in the previous flick.

On English language dubs I've seen the director is listed as Joseph Velasco but this may just be another instance of shameless credit grabbing. It seems more likely all three of the made in Korea 'Ching Wu' flicks were directed by James Nam.

75 BRUCE AGAINST SNAKE IN THE EAGLE'S SHADOW   1979

AKA *BRUCE VS SNAKE IN THE EAGLE'S SHADOW*

DIRECTED BY WU CHIA-CHUN

After a pre-credits fight, we see Lung Tien-Hsiang dressed in a white suit vaguely resembling Bruce Lee in *Fist of Fury* (1972) on a ferry returning home from prison. He sees a large 'midget' played by Hsiao Wang AKA Little Wang stealing watches from passengers' wrists. Lung takes the timepieces from Wang and returns them to the passengers; without the victims realising they were ever stolen. This is done to a muzak version of The Beatles' *Ob-La-Di, Ob-La-Da*.

Wang exits the boat ahead of Lung and is waylaid by some gangbangers who want a cut of his pickpocketing spoils. Lung intervenes because he knows Wang has nothing to give the hoods. When a fight kicks off Lung defends himself with unarmed combat, but once two gangbangers deploy chains as weapons our hero pulls out his nunchucks to defeat the bad guys. Wang and Lung become buddies, but then the midget disappears from the flick for a while as Lung's 'character' is fully established.

The daughters of two families who own pearl farms are both in love with Lung. Wei Lang was Lung's girlfriend but while he was locked up she got engaged to someone else, but she did look after the hero's mother, and so he accepts a job with her family. It transpires Lung was banged up after saving Wei from being raped; he accidentally killed one of the guys molesting her. Lung becomes romantically involved with Ming Chew, which Wei doesn't like. Meanwhile it looks like Ming's father and those around him are trying to take over all the pearl beds in the area. Someone sabotages the baskets of the family Lung works for. Simultaneously the lazy son of the good family racks up huge gambling debts, and the bad guys have an inside man spying on them.

While these conflicts provide plot logic for kung fu fights, they simultaneously 'justify' footage of female pearl divers in swimwear getting changed, working in the water and engaging in catfights. The women employed by Wei's family wear short red swimming trunks; those working for the Mings wear the same style of trunks but in blue. All the female workers wear white blouse style swimming tops. The main purpose of the seashore scenes is sexual titillation, even if it is rather demure. In a typical example of hypermasculine cross-dressing, heavies who appear to be working for Ming's father disguise themselves as female pearl divers to cause trouble; one is caught. An inside man spying on the Wei family frees the tranny. Lung infiltrates the Ming family home looking a little like Bruce Lee disguised as a telephone engineer in *Fist of Fury* (1972). Soon our hero and the freed tranny are battling on a tower; the set-up looks rather like a fight in Lung's other Brucesploitation vehicle *The True Game of Death* (1979). Lung wins the combat and Little Wang appears to help tie up the man and take him back to the Wei family as their prisoner. Wang is eventually able to identify the inside man too. Lung and Wang want to swap the spy for the lazy son's debts but hoods have taken the gambler prisoner. So the two hostages are exchanged and Lung still needs to find a way to cancel the kid's liabilities. Fortuitously Ming volunteers to bet against Lung for the debt. Ming loses.

It is revealed that neither family is trying to create a pearl monopoly. There is a bad guy who wants all the pearl beds in the hands of the family prepared to sell them to him, so that he can acquire exclusive control of the trade. This big boss is responsible for and funding all the bad behaviour of people supposedly working for the two pearl bed owning families, who are both basically honest. The exposition, at least in the English dub, is rather muddled about this. Since Lung is able to beat up all the local fighters working for the bad guy, the big boss has to hire more lethal martial artists from further afield. Since the first of these is a foreigner whose boxing and wrestling moves are piss poor, it isn't exactly exciting when Lung defeats him. Ming becomes convinced the foreigners have bought Lung off, but Wang is able to sort out their love life. Wei's father has changed his mind about selling his pearl bed and so she is kidnapped by the bad guys to force him to part with it. The hoods rough up Ming and her father, but Lung bursts in and saves them. Next, Lung has to rescue Wei but as he gets to the hut where she's being held, he's confronted by a kung fu killer whose been hired to eliminate him. Lung breaks out his nunchucks and kills his opponent by strangling him with them; just like Bruce Lee at the conclusion of his fight with Dan Inosanto in the official *Game of Death* (1978). Immediately after this the cops turn up and arrest the bad guys. Wei fleetingly thinks that as Lung's rescued her, they can get it on. But her joy evaporates when Ming appears and runs into Lung's waiting arms. The final shot is a freeze frame of Ming literally lifted off her feet by a happy Lung.

There are various other Brucesploitation elements in this movie such as *Game of Death*-style yellow tracksuit bottoms, albeit combined with a white wife-beater. There is also the odd come-on gesture and Bruce Lee-style scream, but not too much effort on Lung's part to make the fighting look like The Little Dragon's martial antics. Ultimately Lung's shapes are eclipsed by the even worse choreography on the catfights. The Chansploitation element doesn't go much beyond the title of the film. Director Wu Chia-Chun seems to have had a hand in *Jackie and Bruce to the Rescue* (1982). But nothing I've seen by him is as stupidly groovy as his first Brucesploitation effort *Bruce Lee Against Supermen* (1975).

76 THE DRAGON, THE HERO 1979

AKA *DRAGON ON FIRE*

DIRECTED BY GODFREY HO

John Liu and Tino Wong are Shaolin masters who fall out and become rivals despite having developed the double strike rock fist style together. Phillip Ko is their master, he wears a ridiculous wig and is supposed to be an old man. The three stars give a demonstration of their fighting style that runs through the credits, then reappear as different men twenty years later with Liu and Wong playing the disciples of the original bickering masters. Dragon Lee is Tino Wong's sidekick and is also skilled at strike rock fist. Dragon also deploys his one-stick nunchaku novelty weapon in this movie. The single stick has a chain with a ring on the end of it that can slip loosely over the thumb or finger. It works pretty much like a regular nunchaku, it just looks a bit odd. Liu admires Lee and Wong, but they are antagonistic towards him. Meanwhile Bolo Yeung sporting ridiculous fake chest hair—and with very hairy toes too—does gorilla style kung fu.

Bolo is one of the men wheelchair bound Chan Lau deploys against those who want to earn the twenty dollars he offers to martial artists who can win a fight against his man. We see Bolo beat an opponent easily, but Mars challenges Yeung and then gets the better of him. First he pulls off some of Bolo's chest hair in imitation of what Bruce Lee does to Chuck Norris in *Way of the Dragon* (1972); then he deploys a nail clawing tiger style that leaves flesh cuts on Yeung similar to those inflicted by Han on Bruce Lee in *Enter the Dragon* (1973). The other way in which Bruce Lee is cinematically channelled in this movie is by Dragon Lee doing his over the top king of kung fu facial and hand ticks.

The challenge fights for Lau's twenty-bucks are watched from a hidden and subjective perspective by Phillip Ko; he can learn and absorb the styles of other fighters simply by observing them. Although Bolo is defeated, Ko follows Mars and kills him using the tiger fist. Ko's kink in this movie is that he has an hourglass style timer with sand running through it, and he sets himself the challenge of defeating his opponents before all the grains have fallen to the bottom. After Mars is despatched, John Liu turns up to challenge Chan Lau's men. He takes on three of them at once and wins but he doesn't want the sixty dollars he's earned, instead he wants a job. As Liu is a top fighter, he's taken on. Lau and his men are selling antiques to western smugglers, and Liu is an undercover government agent investigating them. Lau wears strange white facial make up and is prone to fits of madness. In flashback we learn that when Lau was younger he attempted to ravish a woman but her Alsatian dog bit off his cock, and this is how he became a cripple. Lau practices mad dog kung fu—which involves biting—copied from the animal that emasculated him. Ko gets to learn the strike rock fist style by observing Liu and Wong fight. Liu always wins with his mysterious hand technique that hypnotises his opponents. Because he keeps losing fights, Wong undergoes some insane training with his fat and drunken master who we first see with multiple lit cigarettes in each hand, dragging on four or so fags at once. Eventually Liu and Wong—with back up from Dragon—team up, and the three of them defeat the bad guys, with some spectacular puking taking place as the villains die.

What really makes this film great is the insane camerawork and soundtrack; partly plundered Ennio Morricone spaghetti western scores. There are plenty of crazy zooms in the style of Jess Franco and other Eurosleaze masters. Not to mention good use of film run backwards; at it's funniest when Lau retreats into some bushes doing his mad dog kung fu before he's killed by Dragon. While not quite as good as Ho's cut-and-paste masterpiece *Scorpion Thunderbolt* (1984), this is still one of his best movies with it's tripped out mix of comedy, kung fu, horror, and sex. Note that *Dragon on Fire* is an alternative title for *Enter Three Dragons* (1978) also featuring Dragon Lee; resulting in this film and that one sometimes being confused.

77 FISTS OF BRUCE LEE   1979

AKA *INTERPOL*

DIRECTED BY BRUCE LI

The king of blandness plays an undercover cop called Lee investigating various gang activities. The credit sequence has Li sparring blindfolded to the seventies white funk hit *Pick Up the Pieces*. He is wearing yellow tracksuit bottoms with black stripes that look like the bottom half of the jump suit Bruce Lee wears in *Game of Death* (1978). Li travels to Hong Kong where he's been hired by a Mr Lo to install an electronic surveillance system around his house. There are already booby traps in the grounds to prevent intruders getting close to Mr Lo. This shady businessman has a list of secret societies that he won't sell, despite some gangs desperately wanting it. He also has an attractive daughter Miss Lo who Li gets romantically involved with. Miss Lo is subjected to two attempted rapes, their staging suggests that in the worst possible way they are intended as comic; both perpetrators are portrayed as effeminate. Despite Miss Lo being in her twenties, she's shown playing with dolls that double as weapons capable of firing deadly darts, and even kissing a huge teddy bear. The hoods are knocking each other off, with the leader of one gang faking his own death. Despite Li defending himself and Miss Lo using his kung fu skills, she is eventually kidnapped. Her father is forced to leave his fortress home in order to exchange his secret society list for his daughter. Li is simultaneously racing to the rescue, at first on a bicycle and when this breaks, by foot. At the final showdown Lo Lieh *(King Boxer*

AKA *Five Fingers of Death, 1972*) is defeated despite his 'deadly' chain punch weapon. This is a glove attached to a long chain. An American gang member played by Robert Kerver has another unusual weapon—a pole that has flick knife-style blades inside it and that can be broken apart to become nunchaku. Kerver is clumsy with the Little Dragon's signature weapon.

At the end of the movie Li looks like he is going to be shot dead by the surviving gang leader, but he's saved by an undercover cop who has infiltrated the mob. Miss Lo is not impressed to discover Li is the filth and slaps him, but the necessary arrests are made. For his directorial debut it seems Li wanted to move away from his reputation as a Bruce Lee clone and make a spy spoof with lots of stolen music cues from a variety of James Bond flicks. The convoluted plot and over-the-top spy gadgetry provide further indications that the director has his tongue firmly in his cheek, despite the comedy never being signalled loudly, nor allowed to get in the way of the fights.

78 THE TREASURE OF BRUCE LEE   1979
DIRECTED BY JOSEPH VELASCO

The film is set in China around 1930. A supposedly 'old' martial arts master is teaching four students the five animal styles of Shaolin kung fu. Each student learns a different style —Bruce Le gets dragon, the others panther, tiger and crane. The sifu is saving snake for later. The secrets of these techniques are detailed in a kung fu manual that the Japanese are after. The master claims that karate is just a Japanese version of Chinese snake boxing, since the Shogun's men have already stolen a secret book detailing this style from its Shaolin inventors and plagiarised it.

During the course of this movie the Japanese steal a fake version of the secret kung fu manual that has been created as a decoy to keep the real one safe. It transpires that Chiang Tao, the student learning panther style, is a Japanese infiltrator and he gives this away when he uses some snake moves in a fight. When the sifu reveals he knows Tao is an infiltrator the master is killed. Tao convinces Cheung Lik who has learnt tiger that the other two students are responsible for their master's death. However, Le soon gets the truth across to him. Lik pretends he doesn't know the score so he can keep an eye on Tao. Le learns some leaping tricks from the crane student. The Japanese track them down and the crane student is killed, and Bruce is captured. Lik frees Bruce and together they learn different animal styles so that they can defeat Tao. When another Japanese sweep for the surviving students is successful, Lik is killed. Before Bruce successfully escapes, Tao snatches the secret kung fu manual from him. Tao then spends his time learning more about the Shaolin animal styles.

From this point on much of the footage is spliced in from an earlier movie featuring many of the same actors. Characters appear out of nowhere including Bolo Yeung because much of the material we're seeing is cut in from *Bruce and Shaolin Kung Fu* (1977). Bruce is taught the iron finger technique by an old sifu. Eventually Le defeats Tao and rescues the secret kung fu manual. The Hong Kong Movie Database says *Treasure of Bruce Lee* was lensed in Korea—the footage spliced in from *Bruce and Shaolin Kung Fu* certainly was—but the original footage seems to have been created elsewhere. Much of the action takes place in what looks like a nature reserve. It looks similar to the park and forest settings shot around Baguio City, Benguet, in *Bruce and the Shaolin Bronzemen* (1982), so it may have been filmed in The Philippines.

Much commented upon in relation to the new footage is the fact that many shots are out of focus; in particular close ups of Bruce Le. *Treasure of Bruce Lee* is sometimes wrongly identified as a variant title of *Bruce and the Shaolin Bronzemen*. I have sourced two different releases of *Treasure of Bruce Lee* and three versions of *Bruce and the Shaolin Bronzemen* in order to compare them and they are definitely not the same film. *Treasure of Bruce*

Lee doesn't have much to do with the Little Dragon beyond the title and a few elements spliced in from *Bruce and Shaolin Kung Fu*.

79 THE DRAGON'S INFERNAL SHOWDOWN — 1980

AKA *DRAGON'S SHOWDOWN*

DIRECTED BY KIM SI-HYEON AND/OR GODFREY HO

Dragon Lee's parents are threatened by bandits. The father grabs a sword to defend himself but three unarmed guys easily defeat him. Dragon has two siblings and one is described in the English dub as being asleep. During the murder there are two fast cuts to what seem to be two different boys watching from two difference vantage points. Before embracing her dead husband Dragon's mother puts down a baby girl. The wife is dispatched with her husband's sword as she weeps over his dead body. Head bandit Martin Chui Man-Kwai wants the baby killed but Lee Ye-Min refuses because she's an innocent kid. Man-Kwai tells Ming he'll have to look after her and the more junior bandit scoops up the baby and carries her off as the criminals depart. Dragon is brought up by one of his aunts. We see a child practicing martial arts and this transforms into the adult Dragon Lee doing the same thing.

Cheryl Meng is in love with Dragon but he's more interested in using her as a sparring partner, as she's good with her fists and feet too. When his auntie dies, Dragon decides it's time to go looking for the bandits who murdered his parents. He tries to leave Cheryl Meng behind but she follows him. Meng is more in love with Dragon than he is with her, and one of the comic strands in the film is his role as hen pecked and underwhelmed boyfriend.

Dragon and Meng travel to the village where the earlier slaughter took place but the bandits shifted their base of operations a hundred miles (160km) away shortly after this. When they get to the village Man-Kwai and his men currently rule with an iron fist, Dragon can't find the head bandit because he's asking for him under his old name and only a few of his men know him by this moniker. Dragon and Meng get into a load of fights and end up destitute. Also wandering around the village and getting into trouble are Dragon's long-lost brother (Lim Ja-Ho) and his sister (Peggy Min Bok-Ki). Peggy has been adopted by Man-Kwai, although how this happened isn't elaborated upon.

When Dragon and his sister first encounter each other they don't know they're siblings but quickly establish a bickering relationship rather like the one the male lead already has with Meng. Dragon rants about girls like Meng and his sister and the need to vomit. Long-lost bro knows who Man-Kwai is and seeks revenge. First bro attacks Man-Kwai's men when they are taking protection money to the bank, then he redistributes the dough to those it was stolen from; next he attacks Man-Kwai's right-hand man Lee. It looks like long-lost bro will win the fight, until Lee electrifies his magnetic sword and disables Lim Ja-Ho's metal weapon; a tube that shoots out a cord with a hook on the end of it. Badly wounded bro is found by Dragon and Meng who nurse him. He reveals the secret of Lee's weapon, so Dragon gets a couple of magnets to strap around his wrists to repel the sword; he also makes sure he isn't wearing anything made of metal. When bandit Lee attempts to deploy this magnetic blade against Dragon, our hero uses his lodestones to control it and kills him. Kwai-Man has his men tie up Dragon's sister and lock her in a room so she is 'safe' until her brother has been dealt with. Grieving after long lost bro dies from his earlier wounds, Dragon forgets to take his magnets when he goes to fight Man-Kwai. Once the magnetic sword is electrified Dragon looks like a goner. Even his trouser belt gets sliced up so he has to use one hand to stop his pants from falling down. Meng turns up with the lodestones and also throws Dragon a belt for his trousers. Together Dragon and Meng defeat Kwai-Man.

The film ends with the Dragon, Little Sister, Meng and her mother, weeping over long-lost bro's grave. The three members of the younger generation say goodbye to Meng's mother, and Dragon and Meng walk away to enjoy their married life with little sister in tow. During the film Dragon mugs a few Bruce Lee facial and hand mannerism but does many more things the Little Dragon wouldn't do, such as use a recently cooked hot chicken as a weapon. This is a pretty typical Korean martial arts comedy flick of the time, notable mainly for the natty cloth cap Dragon sports in it.

80 MISSION FOR THE DRAGON   1980

AKA *RAGE OF THE DRAGON*

DIRECTED BY KIM SI-HYEON AND/OR GODFREY HO

During a late-night argument over whether Master Wong is a grave robber, this man's son beats up the guy who makes the allegation. Junior hopes to talk to his dad about the claim, but pops goes off to the woods to get Master Lee to value a dodgy antique he's acquired. Lee says the artefact was stolen from the temple a decade ago, so it must be returned. Before a full-on row develops, Wong and his men are attacked and murdered by a guy geared up in a red suit and ghost mask. Lee senior runs into a cave with the antique but the killer follows and despatches him too. After Master Wong's body is found, his son and some men attack Lee senior's servants. The Wongs want to know where Lee senior is but the retainers don't know. Dragon Lee trains by a waterfall and is attacked by a masked man. They fight until the assailant reveals he's Dragon's teacher making a final test of his martial arts skills, which the student has passed. A servant with a huge wart on his face turns up to tell Dragon his father Master Lee is missing. They go back to Lee's village but on the way are attacked by Wong's gang. Dragon easily defeats them. Carter Wong playing Master Kwan steps in to try to stop the fighting between the families. The Wongs are so overcome by grief they won't listen to reason and are convinced the Lees are responsible for their father's death.

While Dragon and Carter's sister (Mai Ling) are searching the haunted cave for Lee senior, one of Carter's men turns up to propose marriage to her. Mai Ling rejects this proposal and slaps his face because she's in love with Dragon. The man claims to be wealthy but at the same time he appears to be working for Carter so I'll call him Rich Flunky. Sometimes Carter is shown in darkened rooms or in dark glasses because he is extremely sensitive to light, and yet at others he walks around without a problem in daylight without shades. There are more fights between the Wongs and Dragon, alongside the capture and kidnapping of men. Suspicion falls on various parties including Master Wong's brother. It turns out this brother colluded with Carter to kill and rob Master Wong. When he demands his share of the loot with a pair of knives, Carter kills him. Dragon goes to see Carter after seeing off an attacker in the haunted cave. When talking to Carter and Rich Flunky, Dragon notices mud on the latter's shoes and realises he was the man who just attacked him in the cave. Carter clocks Dragon taking note of this, and when the kung fu clone leaves he tells Rich Flunky to go back to the cave to move Master Lee's body. Dragon hides outside the grotto and sees Rich Flunky dressed in his red killer suit pulling on a ghost mask. Meanwhile Wong Junior decides to kill Carter. The latter is mad at Wong Junior for hurting his sister in an earlier confrontation. Dragon confronts Rich Flunky in the cave; they fight and before he dies the fake ghost tells our hero where his father's body is hidden under the rocks. Wong Junior and his men confront Carter and Junior is killed in the ensuing fight. Knowing now that Carter killed his father, Dragon races off to confront him. Mai Lung begs her brother and the man she loves not to fight. Carter is winning the battle so his sister begs him not to kill Dragon. Carter reluctantly lets Dragon go. Mai Lung just wants to marry Dragon but our hero insists he must fight again. He realises that Carter's weakness is his sensitivity to light. He gets the worst of it in his second face-off with Carter until he rips off his shirt to reveal a vest made of mirrors that blind his adversary with reflected sunlight. Dragon defeats and kills Carter.

Some might see Carter's weakness as a reference to Kareem Abdul-Jabbar's sensitivity to light when he fights Bruce lee in the official *Game of Death* (1978). Beyond this and the odd bit of nose thumbing from Dragon, there aren't really any Bruce Lee-like elements in *Mission for the Dragon*. It's a pedestrian Korean martial arts movie, the best things about it are the hilariously bad dubbing, the surreal early eighties computer game sound effects added to the fight scenes and a verging on krautrock soundtrack.

81 Bruce and the Shaolin Bronzemen   1982

AKA *Enter the Game of Shaolin Bronzemen*
AKA *King Boxer II*

DIRECTED BY JOSEPH VELASCO

This is the *Citizen Kane* (1941) of exploitation film! Velasco's ultimate anti-classic is a holy grail for trash cinema enthusiasts.

In the credit sequence Bruce Le does a solo kung fu demonstration against a red background. Switch to Bruce training in front of a waterfall somewhere near Baguio City. Bruce's master gives him half a silver coin, which is one half of a treasure map, and sends him on his way. Before Bruce arrives in Manila, he has a few random fights and passes some Baguio tourist sites. Bruce meets a girl who takes him to a hotel that looks like someone's home. Le wants to find his uncle but his companion slips him a date rape drug with his coffee. Bruce lies down as he feels dizzy and has a headache; shades of the Little Dragon's final hours in Betty Ting Pei's apartment. The woman he's with says she'll do some chores and slips into a nightdress.

She takes a huge knife and tries to stab Bruce but he dodges the blade. A couple of gunmen come in but Bruce evades the bullets and kicks one of the assassins headfirst into a nearby toilet, the second is slammed down on top of him.

A fat guy, possibly Filipino action movie director Teddy Page, comes out of a shop with a huge tub of vanilla ice cream. Two thugs rob Teddy of his treat and start to strip him. Teddy moans for the snack but he might as well be building up towards orgasm. As one thug fumbles with Teddy's trousers, Velasco cuts to the other hood with white ice cream all around his mouth as if he's just given Teddy a blowjob and the money shot was still splattered across his face.

Bruce turns up and deals with the bullies. While this is going on, Bruce's uncle and cousin are being menaced by a midget in flash seventies gear backed up by hoods who want to know where the treasure is. Bruce and Teddy run into the two thugs Le just gave a dressing down, only now they're with their whole gang. Bruce takes them all on in a very surreal fight during which members of the gang hang back and act like spectators until it's their turn to get kicked in the crotch and/or arse. The hoods are only in the film to be hit and so they don't act like credible combatants. In this way the one man against an army of kung fu fighters cliché scene is both ironised and exposed as a metaphor for a gay gangbang. By the time Bruce gets to his uncle his elderly relative is dying from gunshot wounds. Bruce accompanies his cousin to the funeral but he clearly couldn't give a shit about the dead man. The film is ultra-camp and avoids deep emotion.

The head of the treasure seeking mob is Lita Vasquez and naturally she has a really effeminate assistant because so many of those attracted to hard as nails kung fu culture also long to be soft and feminine. Lita runs into Bruce on a beach and tries to get him to go swimming with her. He refuses saying he hasn't got his bathing costume. Her initial ploy foiled, Lita switches to plan b, she goes into the water and pretends she is downing. Bruce jumps in to save her and is attacked by a bunch of knife wielding chicks who emerge from the depths of the sea.

After a fight with Lita that Bruce wins, our anti-hero kisses her; which serves to underscore the fact that fisticuffs in this and similar flicks are a substitute for sex. There is also a scene where a morbidly obese masseuse gives Bruce some stress relief, then tries to kill him. However he successfully fights back and the comic fat chick acts as if she enjoys being knocked about. Like all the other queens of kung fu who appear in Brucesploitation movies, the masseur is obviously into sado-masochism. Bruce also engages in combat with a gang of sickle wielding dwarfs dressed in loincloths and a platoon of Shaolin bronzemen; i.e. guys who look like they've been badly spray-painted.

Bruce literally runs into a transvestite while he's chasing someone else and rips the guy's top and false breasts off. The tranny is outraged but Bruce doesn't even react, it's as if Le is really used to unwrapping women's garments and discovering ladyboys underneath. Bruce and his cousin are captured by Lita's gang but fortunately one of the women working for the female big boss has the other half of the silver coin Bruce got from his sifu and wants to help the captives. They escape and having put the coin together figure the treasure is buried at the finish line of the Philippine Racing Club. The track is in Makati City, the posh part of Metro Manila, but we don't get to see much of it; Velasco has already given us a tourist montage of downtown so we ain't about to get one of Makati.

After digging up a box, Bruce has to fight off endless gang members. The three holders of the coin get away safely but when they examine the chest they've recovered they discover it is empty and entirely bereft of clues about where the treasure can be found. Cheung Lik appears at various points wanting a fight with Bruce. When they finally get down to doing the dirty, or at least a tear-up as a substitute for it, Le watches the first couple of moves Lik makes and in the English dub announces in a super-camp voice: "Ooohhh tiger kung fu!" Bruce's dubbing is at some points so groovily-gay it makes Kenneth Williams sound straight. To return to the 'plot', Le goes home and discovers his cousin and the girl who had the other half of the silver coin have been murdered. This makes him really mad so he gets proactive and tackles the gang.

He fights a load of karateka, a Filipino stick fighter, and a guy with a samurai sword. There are some really stylised Bruce Lee type moves, including Le tasting his own blood and freezing into what are almost voguing poses every time he indulges in what he's wanting to pass off as a particularly effective piece of ultra-violence. The effect is to underscore how ridiculously stupid it would be to fight the way Bruce Lee does on screen in a street confrontation.

The two different British DVD releases of the movie I've viewed are considerably more surreal than American editions since a nunchaku sequence is cut from the ongoing series of fights towards the end, making it literally impossible for the viewer to understand how Le wins these penultimate confrontations.

At the end Bruce busts into Lita's mansion for a final showdown. She hasn't lost interest in the treasure but Bruce has and makes it quite clear he thinks it belongs to the country. Le's fight with Lita concludes with her throwing poison darts at him. Bruce removes them from his torso and flings them into Lita's eyes. This ends with Bruce and Lita collapsed over each other like two dead lovers. Throughout, Le is like a somnambulist who only wakes up when he gets in a fight. And a zombie was exactly what was needed to enhance the surreal quality and accidental avant-gardism of *Bruce and the Shaolin Bronzemen*. Le's character isn't even called Bruce—he's named Wong Lung in the English dub! A variant version of this movie with cut-and-paste material added from elsewhere can be found under the title *Bruce's Ninja Secret* (1988).

82 THE SUPERGANG — 1984

AKA *THE SUPER GANG*

DIRECTED BY WONG SIU-JUN

Big Brother has been murdered by a masked killer in Hong Kong. Bruce Le returns from Holland to get revenge. The dead man's gang is now headed by Kwan Yung-Moon. Bruce speaks to Kenneth who is a member of a rival gang headed by Piggy Ming. Kenneth warns Bruce not to rush to judgement. Bruce and Kenneth have been friends since childhood and Kenny is dating Jenny, Bruce's sister. Piggy's gang are coining it from human trafficking and enforced prostitution. Both organisations are involved in theft, gambling and protection rackets.

Inspector Tang is taking bribes from both gangs and telling them not to let their territorial disputes escalate and cause trouble. Nonetheless, relations between them deteriorate. When Ming's triads attack Moon's club, the rival gang are lying in wait. Appearing for the first time among the fighters is Bolo Yeung. He pops up again later and when his requests for money are rebuffed by Moon, Bolo threatens to tell Bruce who killed Big Brother. Moon attacks and easily defeats Bolo. As Moon jumps at Yeung the camera cuts to what is obviously a watermelon that has been painted black, and we see this splatter all over the screen as it is smashed. Moon blames Bolo's death on Piggy and Bruce believes him. Thinking Ming has gone too far Bruce leaves a pig's head on his car as a warning. Piggy hires a deadly Thai killer to take Le out. The assassin is Chiang Tao. Ming's gang protest that they want the $10,000 that Tao is being paid to kill Bruce. So Tao fights and easily defeats these hoods. Then in a fight that is every bit as perfunctory as that between Bolo and Moon, Bruce triumphs over Tao.

What the director seems to be doing is building up our expectations and then letting us down. Kung fu movie viewers had already seen so many long climatic fights between Le and Tao that this short one seems brutally silly and shocking. Bruce kills Piggy and then discovers from Kenneth that Moon killed Big Brother. Bruce goes after another gang member who was involved in the murder, but this man is shot dead by a motorcycle riding assassin before he can fess up. Le confronts Moon with the Halloween mask he wore when killing Big Brother. They fight but Bruce is slashed with a machete and kicked to his death off a cliff. It transpires Inspector Tang has been orchestrating all the feuding so that he can run organised crime in Hong Kong his way. He even had Moon killing fellow gang members. Finally Tang sends Moon off to murder Kenneth. But the tables are turned and Kenneth shoots Moon. Tang thinks he has Hong Kong sewn up but Kenneth drives up to him as he emerges jubilantly from a club and puts a bullet in his head. The film freezes and ends with Tang's death.

Two versions of this flick are available in English, one seems to have been edited for the American market and is roughly twelve minutes shorter than the other. The cuts seem to have been made to get a PG rating by removing sex but they also completely ruin the film and make it look like hackwork rather than the inspired piece of cinematic insanity it is in the uncensored version. The worst cut is to a long sex scene towards the end involving a lot of nudity. Moon is on a mission to kill off one of his gang members. An utterly minor character is having sex with his girlfriend in a tent at night. Moon looms above them in his ridiculous rubber Halloween mask ogling the softcore 'action' for a long time before killing a minion on Inspector Tang's orders. In the uncensored version this scene is drawn out at a point where the plot, and clearly the director had already lost it, should be racing to a conclusion. From the perspective of conventional cinema this scene is stupid and gratuitous. But since this movie is all about transgressing the rules of 'quality' cinema, to lose this extended scene and have the flick transformed into something properly paced, is to render the entire film pointless.

You need the 'full' 85-minute English language edition of this flick to fully appreciate it; those versions that are closer to 70 minutes in length are a waste of time!

83 BRUCE'S NINJA SECRET — 1988

AKA *BRUCE'S SECRET KUNG FU*
AKA *BRUCE'S LAST BATTLE*
AKA *BRUCE THE TOP MASTER*

DIRECTED BY JOSEPH VELASCO

A cut-and-paste movie that is mostly made up of randomly reordered scenes from *Bruce and the Shaolin Bronzemen* (1982), into which an editor has inserted some material from *Bruce's Deadly Fingers* (1976). The MacGuffin of a search for hidden treasure is retained from *Bruce and the Shaolin Bronzemen,* but in this version Bruce Le is mostly called by his *Bruce's Deadly Fingers* 'character' name of Bruce Wong; there are occasional slippages to calling him Bruce Wang. Aside from the fight with the bronzemen which is dropped, this includes all the key episodes from the 1982 anti-classic; killer dwarfs, encounters with the deadly Lita Vasquez, the morbidly obese killer masseur, the tranny who gets his false titties ripped off, the notorious homoerotic ice cream incident, the empty treasure box in Makati City etc. But these events are rendered even more surreal and dreamlike by the dropping in of scenes from *Bruce's Deadly Fingers* with the backdrop suddenly switching from Manila to Hong Kong. The main point of the additions from the supplementary movie seems to be to add the star presence of Loh Leih, but this time around and like everyone else, he is searching for the treasure rather than Bruce Lee's *Kung Fu Finger Book*. These drop-ins make little sense and are poorly integrated into what was already a very loose narrative, making this yet another brilliantly absurd Velasco foray into accidental avant-gardism! While I prefer the original *Bruce and the Shaolin Bronzemen* to this cut, both are groove sensations.

84 NINJA OVER THE GREAT WALL — 1990

AKA *SHAOLIN FIST OF FURY*

DIRECTED BY BRUCE LE AND CHEUNG NING

Black and white footage of the Japanese invading China unconvincingly cuts to colour fictional film of a northern Chinese village being attacked in '1931'. Bruce Le tries to save his family and friends by helping them flee but his mother is killed. Eventually Bruce is captured by the Japanese and their take no prisoners attitude means Le ends up on a corpse truck. A girl who Bruce helped escape goes searching for him amid a mountain of the dead and finds him injured but alive. They go to Beijing. The girl stops with her uncle who is collaborating with the Japanese, while Le stays with a kung fu master he'd saved from a bunch of ninja. A Japanese samurai challenges the sifu to a fight, the latter throws the match to avoid trouble with the invaders. The Japanese know the Chinese boxer didn't try to win and the father of the samurai fighter has him poisoned. The Japanese father is a modern and pragmatic ultra-nationalist, whereas the son believes in the old samurai code of 'honour'. Bruce blames the son for the sifu's death and attacks him. Although he loses, the son still stops his father's ninja from attacking Le. Bruce tells the samurai that unless he leaves China he will personally kill him. Dishonoured by his defeat the samurai returns to Japan to train.

The film is really boring up to this point but it finally takes off as Bruce has a series of battles with ninjas, including one who is on fire! Tedium sets in again as we see the two warriors who embody Chinese and Japanese nationalism training: Le develops his skill by studying the movements of the Yellow River which supposedly embodies everything great about China, the samurai proves his martial skill by showing he is prepared to kill a baby when instructed to do so. The samurai then tracks Bruce down and they have a final fight on The Great Wall. This is expensively staged and tiresome aside from some cartoon shots of bone crunching; an old martial arts movie cliché that remains amusing. Le is winning so the samurai's fascist father kills this embodiment of everything Chinese by shooting him. The samurai then kills both his father and himself. The screen turns red and Bruce's body is carried aloft on the shoulders of Chinese spectators with his arms splayed and his head hanging down like a dead saint. This draws on both Bruce Lee's *Fist of Fury* (1972) and Japanese samurai movies but unfortunately uses the rubric of 'quality' cinema to mesh them. Some sources date this movie to 1987.

85 BLACK SPOT 1991

AKA *EARTH AND FIRE*

AKA *VICIOUS PASSAGEWAY*

DIRECTED BY BRUCE LE

Bruce Le is living the high life in the Mediterranean where he is teaching statuesque French women martial arts. To undermine the idea he is actually doing any serious training we see him messing around with a couple of dumbbells; with an EZ curl bar lying in the background. Le is being hassled by the French cops and gangland boss Mark. Both want him to return to his old drug smuggling ways, albeit as an undercover agent in the case of the filth. So Bruce jumps in a speedboat and escapes to Paris, cue generic shot of the Eiffel Tower. Le has a problem, he wants to go back to Hong Kong but he doesn't have any money. He calls his girlfriend Fanny to ask her to bring him some dough but she's being bothered by les flics. Fanny agrees to bring Bruce greenbacks but when she meets him she hasn't got any lettuce and the fuzz are with her. After a chase around Paris, Le is caught by the cops and beaten up. They have a thick file on him with information provided by his former gang boss Mark who is mad at Bruce for giving up his life of crime so our anti-hero has a choice between jail and working undercover for the filth. Having cut a deal with the authorities, Bruce goes to his former gangland bosses to ask for money to get to Hong Kong. He's offered moolah in return for taking part in a cage fight against a huge and vicious opponent. Bruce has no choice but to agree, since he can't admit he's working undercover. We see the giant pugilist brutalising another fighter and apparently killing him by biting into his neck and drawing a lot of blood. After a boxer refuses to get in the cage with this freak, the promoters put in a live sheep that the huge misfit kills and guts. Next it's Bruce's turn to battle this psychopath. There is a huge height difference between the two fighters that is vaguely reminiscent of Bruce Lee taking on Kareem Abdul-Jabbar in the official *Game of Death* (1978). Bruce Lee's fight against Chuck Norris in *Way of the Dragon* (1972) is invoked when Le pulls chest hair from his opponent. Bruce wins his fight in *Black Spot* by jumping onto his opponent's shoulders and poking out his eyes, then following through with a series of vicious blows.

After about 25 minutes of movie time in France, we shift to Taipei where the French mobsters want Le to take out a gang boss played by Chiang Tao. Bruce refuses the dosh Chiang tries to give him and there is a brief fight that ends with Chiang getting shot in the stomach with his own gun. Bruce takes the slow boat to Hong Kong and hangs out with the mobster friends he's infiltrating for les flics. Before you can say 'life's a gamble', Bruce is kidnapped by Chiang's men. Tao was only injured and not killed in Taipei. Le avoids getting done in and has a fight with Chiang and his gang, which he wins. Tao ends up impaled on a stick. With Chiang out of the picture we slip almost seamlessly into the smuggling narrative. Various international police forces are on the case as Bruce and his triad friends head into The Golden Triangle to open up a new smack smuggling route. The heroin is manufactured by The General, an old and brutal guy who has a small army to back him up. While hanging around waiting for the drugs to be packed up, Bruce saves a local boy from being run down and befriends his family. Le then muses on his growing belief that the local people are basically good and the only way they can survive is by growing opium. He feels that the authorities attack the drug trade but never address the poppy grower's problems. The cops show up to do some infiltration. Bruce sneaks into the huge heroin production plant with a bleached blond French policewoman. The factory is vaguely reminiscent of Han's underground facility in *Enter the Dragon* (1973), just as the Thai setting might remind some viewers of the background location of Bruce Lee's *The Big Boss* (1971). After Le and the French cop get out of the plant all hell breaks loose. The General's men realise there's been law enforcement infiltration, leading to Bruce and a male cop being tortured. The main body of smugglers are ambushed on their way back to China and get the worst of it in a gun and grenade fight with the fuzz. Around the world drug smuggling mobsters are arrested, this is intercut with the usual clichéd shots of the tops of police cars. The Thai army shows up with tanks and even a helicopter to take on the drug paramilitaries. Bruce and the French policewoman are running around the underground heroin factory once again as it is invaded by the Thai army. Bruce and the female cop get to fight one of the General's toughest men, who is kicked into stacked up boxes of heroin, and emerges covered in white powder and looking like some idiot in a 1930s Hollywood comedy whose had flour thrown over them. Eventually the authorities take control of the drugs compound and the heroin factory is destroyed. A high-ranking officer orders the villagers to watch while his men burn their opium harvest. The old lady from the family Bruce befriended is shot while begging the army commander to leave their poppy crop alone. Soon other members of the same family are shot dead including the small boy whose life was saved by our anti-hero. When Bruce sees the little boy and his relatives have been killed, he goes apeshit; shooting down the Thai soldiers responsible in a blaze of automatic fire until he's hit by bullets in a freeze frame ending that invokes *Fist of Fury*. Some fans complain about how aged Le looks in this but if he appears old, Chiang Tao is superannuated.

86 FIST OF FURY 1991 — 1991

DIRECTED BY RICO CHU TAK-ON

In this comedy, Stephen Chow revisits Bruce Lee and the golden age of kung fu cinema in general. Riffing on Lee's country bumpkin characters in *The Big Boss* (1971) and *Way of the Dragon* (1972), as well as Sammo Hung's slapstick reinterpretation of them in *Enter the Fat Dragon* (1978), Chow plays a fish out of water Chinese mainlander who has just arrived in Hong Kong.

After Kenny Bee tries to rob Chow, our bumbling hero with a very powerful right hand punch—his 'fist of fury'—discovers he's lost the address of the only person he knows in the colony. Chow tells Bee that he needs to stay with him, and so the would-be robber takes the mainland boy to see a prostitute. Re-envisioning a scene from *Way of the Dragon*, some very low-key laughs are mined from the fact Chow fails to realise he's with a sex worker. Later at Bee's flat Chow strips his new friend naked and throws his clothes away, and this provides an opportunity for some gay 'gags'. Chow tries to find a job but fails at everything he attempts to do. When Chow and his buddy become waiters, this serves to remind us of Bruce Lee's employment at Ruby Chow's restaurant in Seattle just after he left Hong Kong as a teenager; as well as the Chinese eatery setting of *Way of the Dragon*.

Aside from providing an excuse for slapstick fights, the restaurant scenes in *Fist of Fury 1991* introduce us to Sharla Cheung Man, who Chow and Bee fall in love with. Unable to make a living, Chow is eventually convinced by Bee that he must use his 'fist of fury' to win a martial arts competition with a ten million dollar prize. When they try to register for the tournament the two buddies are told Chow has to belong to a martial arts school if he wants to participate. They join a down-at-heel gym and soon find themselves part of a gang attacking Corey Yuen, who is the sifu of a rival kung fu operation. Chow feels impelled to prevent Yuen's murder and is injured as a result; fortunate indeed, as it turns out Cheung Man is Yuen's daughter! A grateful Yuen takes Chow into his home. Soon some Japanese martial artists turn up to cause trouble and in a re-working of a scene from the original *Fist of Fury*, Chow beats their top fighter and makes him eat a paper sign they've brought with them that declares the Chinese to be the sick men of Asia. Plot complications arise from the fact Chow, Bee and Yuen's top student Vincent Wan Yeung-Ming, are all in love with Cheung Man. Eventually Ming uses a chemical soaked cloth to knock Cheung Man unconscious but his rape attempt is foiled by Chow. Ming then frames Chow for the failed sex assault. Chow is thrown out of Yuen's house and has to join another kung fu gym so that he can win the martial arts prize. Just before his semi-final against Chow, Yuen discovers it was Ming who tried to rape his daughter and then framed his opponent. Yuen tells Chow he will throw the fight but they need to make it look good. When Chow looks nonplussed the master explains that he'll need the prize money if he's going to marry his daughter; she won't wed a poor guy. After the fight Yuen is exhausted and suffering from asthma but still tells Ming to go away and not come back. The bad student kills Yuen and makes out he died as a result of his competition fight with Chow, despite the murder being witnessed by another of the sifu's disciples. Yuen's death is announced just before the final between Ming and Chow. Our hero allows himself to be punched and kicked around the ring because he blames himself for Yuen's death. Eventually Cheung Man discovers the truth and tells Chow. Ming then confirms this while the two men are still in the ring as a way of taunting his rival. Chow now has the motivation to defeat his opponent and win the girl, which he proceeds to do with aplomb.

The nearly thrown and then won fight plotting is lifted from the climatic competitive battle in the Brucesploitation movie *Dynamo* (1978) and other places. Since *Fist of Fury 1991* spends as much time invoking Brucesploitation and generic tropes from kung fu movies as it does Bruce Lee, I'm placing it on the periphery of the genre. This is more obviously a comedy than the original *Fist of Fury*, but I've yet to see a kung fu film that features anything funnier than Bruce Lee's ridiculously over-the-top performance in that 1972 flick.

■ BIG BOSS UNTOUCHABLE 2002
AKA *DRAGON THE MASTER 2*

DIRECTED BY KANT LEUNG WANG-FAT

See *The Real Bruce Lee 2* in the core section since this film is incorporated in its entirety into that movie. On its own it only belongs in the periphery of the Brucesploitation genre but given a different setting it also made the core.

OUTER LIMITS

DRAGON FORCE

ORIGINAL ENGLISH VERSION

THIS BEAUTIFUL WOMAN IS ABDUCTED BY THE NINJAS... NOBODY CAN SAVE HER BUT **DRAGON FORCE**

THE MYSTERY
THE THRILL
THE EXCITEMENT
THE FUN

BRUCE BARON · MANDY MOORE
"DRAGON FORCE"
JAMES BARNETT   JOVY COULDRY   FRANCES FONG   OLIVIA JENG
RANDY CHANNEL   SEON BLAKE   SAM SORONO and **BRUCE LI**

Y W CHEUNG and JOHNNY MAK   Produced by GEORGE MASON   Associate Producer TERRY CHALMERS
BOB HUKE — ROBERT HOPE   Music by CHRIS BABIDA   Written by TERRY CHALMERS and DENNIS THOMPSETT   Directed by MICHAEL KING

87 Kung Fu Master— Bruce Lee Style 1972

AKA *Tough Guy*
AKA *Kung Fu the Head Crusher*
AKA *Revenge of the Dragon*
DIRECTED BY JOSEPH VELASCO

Chan Sing is an undercover cop who goes to jail in order to help San Kuai bust out. This is so that the escaped criminal will help get him a job with Suen Lam's gang and he can then smash their smuggling operation with support from Cheung Lik. All goes according to plan until a hood who is suspicious of Chan observes him throwing Cheung a matchbox with a message inside. Lik then tries to discover what is being smuggled by the gang but ends up in a big fight. Chan pretends to kill him. The gang aren't convinced of Sing's loyalty and set a trap for him; after catching him out they proceed to whip him. Cheung is attempting to get help.

Before Lik and the locals he's befriended can fetch reinforcements the gang catch up with them, resulting in chases and fights. Chan busts free of the shackles that bind him and acting like an insane maniac proceeds to beat up the gangbangers, using one of his chains as a weapon. Lam and his hoods are soon running from Chan. Lik and his friends take out most of those they are battling but are eventually killed. Chan breaks Lam's leg but Kuai keeps attacking him. Eventually the two men are fighting in mud, a sequence that will thrill sploshing fans. Chan eventually kills Kuai and the film ends with its star dragging an injured Lam to justice.

Although this was released in North American cinemas as *Kung Fu Master—Bruce Lee Style*, it is best known to English speaking audiences as *Kung Fu the Head Crusher* because Sing deploys a special eagle claw technique with which he surreally crushes opponent's skulls. The film has no Bruce Lee-alike elements although there's some great nunchaku action from Cheung Lik, which may have been a very quick off the mark riff on *Fist of Fury* (1972). This effective old school basher is apparently the first flick directed by the king of Brucesploitation Joseph Velasco. It features typically surreal Velasco touches such as mad zooms to show the landscape around figures in the movie, mildly masochistic massage and wacko sex scenes involving Lam and various women. The reuse of other people's music includes both Ennio Morricone's *Farewell to Cheyenne* from the soundtrack to *Once Upon a Time in the West* (1968) and Isaac Hayes' *Theme from Shaft* (1971). This was also an early outing for action director Yuen Woo-ping.

88 Queen Boxer 1972

AKA *Kung Fu Queen*
AKA *The Avenger*
DIRECTED BY FLORENCE YU FUNG-CHI

Pre-credits we have Ma Yung Chen arriving at a Shanghai teahouse to settle a dispute with the Axe Gang. He is invited upstairs but this is a trick, lime is thrown in his face. Blinded and with several axes in his back, Chen still manages to take out around three-dozen hoods before he is murdered. The credits sequence shows Judy Lee demonstrating various kung fu forms against a red background with the *Theme from Shaft* by Isaac Hayes on the soundtrack. Then for half the movie Peter Yang Kwan acts as the central character while Judy Lee wanders around Shanghai acting like the alienated heroine of a spaghetti western; she even orders a couple of coffins while she's at it—one for her brother Ma Yung Chen, and one for the man who killed him. Lee first encounters Kwan running a pancake stall and watches impassively as he sees off members of the Axe Gang who want protection money. Next Kwan and his sidekick from the stall go down to the docks to get work. Here Kwan deals with some hoods who are mistreating the workers and extorting half their wages. Finally Kwan uses his fighting skills and reputation to take over a casino. Kwan's family are arriving from Shantung by train and he sends his sidekick off to collect them. The big boss of the Axe Gang, Lee Ying, is worried that Ma Yung Chen's family are coming from Shantung to avenge his death; their reputation as fearsome fighters precedes them. The hoods mistake Kwan's family for Chen's and kill them in an ambush.

The only person to escape the massacre is Kwan's now mortally wounded sidekick, who alerts his friend to the slaughter. There follows a confrontation between Lee and Kwan, when Chen's sister asks if Ying is in the casino, Kwan makes it clear he wants to kill him. Lee leaves without telling Kwan she intends to take Ying out first! She has been sexually harassed throughout the film, and earlier beat up a bunch of hoods who attempted to molest her. When she passes Ying and his goons at their teahouse, she is admired for her good looks and the boss sends a man to offer money for her favours. When Lee realises the proposition comes from Ying she goes towards him and asks if he is Pi (his character name). This confrontation is made into something psychotic with lots of swaying handheld camera shots cutting between the faces—and ultimately the eyes—of Lee and Ying. When Ying confirms his identity, Lee attacks. The boss retreats and dozens of men take on the girl. We are now half-way through the movie and we've just got to the point of it, Lee's incredible acrobatic kung fu. Kwan turns up to take his revenge during the fight, so he and Lee reluctantly attack the gangbangers in tandem. When Kwan is shot and wounded by a foreign gunman hired by the gang, Lee takes out the gweilo by throwing a knife at him; she then helps the injured man to safety and performs brutal surgery by using one of her daggers to remove a bullet from his chest. Afterwards they argue about how best to kill Ying. Kwan just wants to go for it, but Lee insists on consulting her master first. While Lee is away, Kwan is killed by Ying's men. We don't hear the advice Lee gets from her sifu but when she comes back and finds Kwan's body, she makes an all out assault on the Axe Gang's teahouse, ducking whenever they try to throw lime in her eyes and using her hair to flick it back in their faces. Eventually every last minion is despatched, leaving only Ying. Lee throws six axes into him before we see she's badly wounded with blood dribbling from her mouth. She staggers towards Ying with two fingers extended to take out his eyes. There are fast zooms into each character's peepers and a reprise of the *Theme from Shaft*. One version of the film I've seen simply cuts out as Lee's fingers near Ying's face, another turns most of the screen black with a couple of spaces for eye holes, making it clear the villain's peepers are gouged out. As the tagline for the US release had it: 'an eye for an eye'.

The Bruce Lee connection here is that Chia Ling was renamed Judy Lee by her studio and briefly became famous as Bruce Lee's 'sister' but she wasn't and before long the actress was forced to apologise to pissed off Little Dragon fans. Ling was promoted as the female Bruce Lee by the US distributors of this film. These Lee connections aren't evident from simply watching the movie hence its placement in the outer limits of the Brucesploitation genre. It has a similarity to some of the unofficial *Fist of Fury* (1972) sequels in that Judy Lee plays the sister of the central character in *Boxer from Shantung* (1972), just as clones in the riffs on Bruce Lee's second adult starring role would sometimes play his brother. Allegedly this flick was shot in just eleven days.

89 LIGHTNING OF BRUCE LEE   1973
DIRECTED BY CHUNG GWOK-HANG

Two men are mourning over the grave of their kung fu master. One wants to escape poverty and make his way in the world, the other wants to stick to the path set for them by their sifu. These blood brothers fight and part. Both end up in the same town, one working for the local gang boss and the other fighting hoods to protect the honour of the daughter of the man who sponsored his kung fu studies. There is a lot of melodrama involving a woman seeking revenge against the gang boss for killing her husband, the threat of women—including the one the good kung fu expert wishes to defend—being forced into prostitution, and the volatile relationship between the blood brothers who've taken opposed paths. In the end the blood brothers unite to fight the gang boss, and together they defeat him, although the student who took the wrong path is killed in the process. Only the good kung fu student and the girl whose honour he has been defending survive. Basically this is a generic old school basher from Taiwan. It has nothing to do with Bruce Lee beyond the title given to it for its English language release.

90 Spirits of Bruce Lee   1973

AKA *Spirit of Bruce Lee*
AKA *Angry Tiger*

Directed by Heung Ling

Michael Chan Wai-Man investigates the death of his brother in Thailand, close to the border with Myanmar. Journeying to the town from which his sibling disappeared he clocks Pai Lot Chai Sing beating off a gang molesting two women, and wades in to help. The two men travel on together. Sing puts Wai-Man in a hotel and goes on to his job working for the local gang boss. Sing is an undercover cop but Wai-Man doesn't know that yet. The hotel turns out to be the one Wai-Man's brother stayed in a year earlier; the owner says the sibling ran up a bill and disappeared without paying it. The hotelier introduces Wai-Man to Ku Wen-Chung, the patriarch who runs the local Chinese teahouse. Wen-Chung has a kung fu fighting daughter Suen Ga-Lam, and a fat son played by Chan Fei-Lung. To cut out much exposition done via dialogue, Wai-Man moves in with the Wongs, romances the excruciatingly bashful daughter, and is told by his new love and her sibling that they stumbled across his missing brother dying in the woods a year ago. While wandering around town with Ga-Lam, Wai-Man spots a guy waving his brother's expensive Swiss watch around, pissed off no one will accept it as gambling collateral. Ga-Lam draws the guy away from his associates, then Wai-Man beats him up to find out where he got the ticker. Wai-Man and Ga-Lam go after the hood whose name they've jut got, and discover the missing man was killed by the local gang for the valuable jade he'd acquired.

The rat who took the watch from the Wai-Man's sibling is killed by being kicked off a cliff. Ga-Lam and her father counsel Wai-Man to be cautious in attacking the gangbangers who murdered his brother because their HQ is well protected by fighters. Our hero pretends to agree with this but sneaks away at night and kills some of the hoods. He is wounded by a knife thrown into his leg, and only escapes thanks to Sing's help. The next day Sing warns Wai-Man and the Wongs to disappear because the mob want to get them. When the hoods find the Wong teahouse empty they burn it down. Wai-Man quickly recovers from his wounds and learns the gang boss is giving his men a holiday, which provides the perfect opportunity to take him out. Fortunately the entire Wong family are expert kung fu fighters, even the fat son. Wai-Man and the Wongs kill the big boss, but his men who were enjoying themselves in town hear there is trouble at HQ. They stream back but fortunately Sing witnesses their return and calls in his uniformed men. Ku Wen-Chung is killed but as the gang surround Wai-Man and the two younger Wongs, armed cops arrive and save them. Sing finds the crates of guns the gang were smuggling and the Wong siblings wander off with Wai-Man carrying the body of their dead father.

The best thing about the flick is a couple of Japanese fighters—one with a whip—who appear without explanation during the climatic fight. I'm not aware of anyone having made a kung fu interpretation of *Last Year At Marienbad* (1961) but about the best thing I can say about *Spirits of Bruce Lee* is that the plot could easily be re-arranged to do just that. Suppose Wai-Man and his brother were the same person, and that our anti-hero came back a year later pretending to be a sibling investigating his own faked disappearance, while tricking locals out of their jade and modesty.... alongside much discussion of what happened last year in Wan Sen?

91 BRUCE TAKES DRAGON TOWN   1974

AKA *BRUCE TAKES THE DRAGON*
AKA *DARE YOU TOUCH ME?*

DIRECTED BY LIU HUNG-SHENG

A dude with a briefcase is chased by three guys. He fights and defeats them, and when he bashes them with his case, white powder flies out of it. You'd think he was involved in the drug trade but as the movie goes on the powders being smuggled are called 'stuff' and 'salt'. After fighting off three men, the salt smuggler is stabbed in the back. It is only after the credits that we are properly introduced to our hero Daredevil Alan (Yuen Si-Wo), who races into a gang HQ to beat up hoods. Eventually he confronts Boss Chin who is sitting at a desk. "Where's my mother?" Daredevil Alan demands. "Don't worry she's receiving our hospitality." Chin replies. "I want my mother!" Alan wails. Before you know it, Alan's mum is chiding him for being rude to Mr Chin. The gang may have kidnapped Mrs Fung but they are giving her a good time so when she tells mummy's boy Alan to do what Mr Chin wants he has to agree.

Daredevil Alan is a relatively average looking guy and when he flexes in a mirror we see a more muscular double in the close ups. Likewise, while Daredevil Alan looks like he knows his martial arts, he is not fluid in the way Bruce Lee was. On Mr Chin's instructions Daredevil Alan smashes up Boss Wen's brothel, and the next day tells the rival gang leader to return the goods he's stolen. Wen offers him twice the pay he's getting from Chin, and is puzzled when this offer is turned town. When Chin's men try to waylay Alan with a rope, he takes it from them and uses it to skip like a girl. Sadly rather than having male lovers, Alan has a girlfriend Susan. There are even flashbacks to them cutely playing together as kids. Susan's father wants Alan to get out of town and stay out of trouble before he will allow a marriage. These remonstrations lead Alan to have flashbacks to his two brothers being murdered by gangbangers. After doing a bit of investigation into the hood's operation, Daredevil Alan visits his friend Eddie The Cockerel. While talking to his mate, our hero notices that a kid employed by Wen is spying on him. Alan slaps the boy around until Lung Fei steps in and starts beating up our hero. Eddie The Cockerel breaks up the fight and tells Fei that Alan is his friend. Lung is Wen's number one fighter and at first he is called Wu in the English dub, but later on his name becomes William; just to confuse viewers William is also the name of Wen's number two henchman. When Wen discovers Chin has kidnapped Alan's mother, he tells his men to snatch her for him. The counter-kidnap goes wrong and when Wen's men bring Alan's mother to him she's dead. Wen doesn't want Daredevil Alan to know about this as he knows he'll go nutzoid when he finds out, so he tells his men to bury the stiff and kept quiet about what happened. A kid called Simon overhears this and tells Alan.

Our hero shouts 'mum' and throws himself around like a toddler having a tantrum. Daredevil Alan is all for running straight to Wen's HQ and killing everyone, but Susan persuades him to plan his revenge carefully. So each gang is sent a letter suggesting alternate compromises to their differences. They meet up, argue and are about to kill each other when the local magistrate shows up with a pistol and stops mass slaughter taking place. "Damn!" says Daredevil Alan who is observing this perched in a tree: "That means I'll have to kill them myself!" He then proceeds to butcher some of Wen's men. Wen blames Chin, but the rival boss insists he's not responsible. The magistrate says he'll investigate.

Susan gives the audience her perspective on this turn of events by play-acting with two dolls she uses to represent herself and Daredevil Alan. She chides her man as a 'naughty boy' but in a loving and admiring way! Wen's gang kidnap Eddie The Cockerel. Alan rescues him and The Cockerel is able to tip Daredevil off as to when Wen's gang are moving the goods they've stolen from Chin. Alan passes the news on to Chin, who tells Daredevil to go off with his men to take the stuff back. While they are waiting for their gangbanging rivals to turn up,

Alan makes his excuses and slips off to kill Chin. First Daredevil takes out the top bodyguard Chin still has with him, then he impales the gang boss on a swordstick. Having tricked the lesser gang members to kill each other off, Daredevil Alan takes on Lung Fei. Once Lung is defeated, Daredevil Alan jumps up and down on his back like a triumphant schoolboy. Daredevil Alan is now free to kill Wen, but the gang boss backs away in terror and falls to his death before our hero can murder him. Susan and Simon turn up and Daredevil Alan tells his girlfriend: "I'm sorry I disobeyed your father, I did it for mum!" Susan assures Daredevil she'll wait for him; this doesn't require any further explanation as we already know her father has told our hero to go away and become an honest citizen before returning to take his daughter's hand in marriage. On his way out of town Daredevil Alan runs into the magistrate who tells him to 'go'. They walk off together. The magistrate is apparently happy to turn a blind-eye to a spot of illegal vigilante action when it suits him!

Bruce Takes Dragon Town is an almost perfect example of a laugh-out-loud super-dumb old school basher, even if much of the comedy was introduced by the dubbing team and probably wasn't planned by the director. Beyond the title this movie has nothing to do with the Little Dragon. Nonetheless its angered certain Brucesploitation fans because it has been falsely marketed as a Bruce Le movie, although that clone doesn't appear in this Taiwanese production. The Good Times video I have of the flick (issued in 1999 and with the box giving the title as *Bruce Takes the Dragon*) features a drawing of a man who looks like Bruce Le on the front, and has a picture of the 'reel' Bruce Lee on the side. The flip-side blurb reads as follows: "Bruce Le cleans up corruption with flying fists in this variation on *The Dirty Dozen*, a dramatic martial arts exhibition in which the heir to the throne of Bruce Lee displays all his spectacular talents. When Chang Ching arrives at the town of Ching Fong to take his place as sheriff, his task of cleaning up mass corruption is a big one, and for this mission he selects seven prisoners from the local jail. Before they can succeed as a team, he must teach them lessons in humanity and cooperation, and only then will Chang Ching and his own *Magnificent Seven* be prepared to give evil the deadly strike." This is, of course, a summary of the plot of *Deadly Strike* (1978) starring Bruce Li (pronounced Lie).

According to some sources the Ocean Shores VHS release of *Bruce Takes Dragon Town* bills the lead actor as Bruce Lie; I've only seen front cover images of this particular edition of the flick and can't verify this. There is a 2015 documentary short by Emily Chao riffing on this flick entitled *Bruce Takes Dragon Town* in which having discovered: "...her uncle's lost kung fu film, the filmmaker travels to Taiwan during Ghost Month to uncover his past." This documentary doesn't have much to interest most fu fans; although it does demonstrate the ways in which the reception of martial arts films changes and mutates over time as they are absorbed by different audiences.

92 CHINESE IRON MAN — 1974

AKA *IRON MAN*
AKA *YOUNG HERO OF SHAOLIN II*
DIRECTED BY JOSEPH KUO NAM HUNG

This is a *Fist of Fury* knockoff. The Japanese are strutting around a Chinese town bullying people. In the restaurant where Wen Chiang-Long works as a chef, they get fresh with Nancy Yen Nan-See, who slaps one of them. This leads to the Japanese pushing around those who try to protect the girl, including her father. When the Japanese demand that one of the Chinese crawl on his hands and knees and bark like a dog, it is too much for Wen. Being the 'Chinese Iron Man' of the title, he creams the Japanese and makes them crawl out of the restaurant on their hands and knees, with one of them barking. The defeated Japanese fighters have failed their dojo and their nation, and this leads to a series of confrontations in which the violence between the kung fu students and the karatekas escalates. The Japanese are after Wen but he eludes them, although inevitably there is a confrontation in a park from which the Chinese are banned (a bit like *Fist of Fury* but run differently). The invincible 'Chinese Iron Man' always wins in these confrontations. When the Japanese attack the kung fu school, one of the students fetches Wen who takes care of the invaders but in the process a couple of them are killed. This is due to carelessness on the part of a sword wielding samurai rather than the Chinese, but nonetheless Wen is branded a murderer. Wen is forced to hide out in the mountains with support from his kung fu school and his fellow workers at the restaurant. An underplayed romance develops between Wen and Nancy. Eventually the Japanese lay a trap for a couple of kung fu students going out to see Wen, and kill one of them.

In the sequence that is closest to *Fist of Fury*, Wen invades the Japanese dojo and beats up lots of students, as well as killing the master responsible for the death of his friend. The chief karateka then emerges to confront Wen and finds himself defeated by Chinese kung fu. Wen spares the life of this sensei but the man has lost face and so feels compelled to commit ritual suicide by disembowelment. This seppuku motif would be recycled in the unofficial *Fist of Fury* sequels *Fist of Fury II* (1977) and *Fist of Fury III* (1979), which both feature defeated Japanese fighters committing harikari.

Wen is chased around a bit more and then the Japanese dojo insists on sorting out its differences with the kung fu school in a public mixed martial arts match. A ring is set up in the street between the two schools, and the Japanese come off worse. Wen is in the crowd disguised as an old man, which invokes one of Bruce Lee's comedic masquerades in *Fist of Fury*. Wen's master is getting the better of the top karateka present, until the Japanese fighter pulls a dirty trick and uses a weapon hidden on the inside of his ring to stab the man who is defeating him. The sifu is covered in blood and Wen somersaults into the ring to challenge the karateka. The 'Chinese Iron Man' pulls off his disguise to reveal who he really is, wins the fight and then meekly hands himself over to the cops.

Wen's fighting is brutal and closer—although not nearly as impressive or entertaining—to Sonny Chiba than Bruce Lee. There is no attempt on Wen's part to imitate Lee, what's being rerun here is the atavistic nationalism and basic plot dynamics of *Fist of Fury*. Wen lacks Bruce Lee's over-amped hammy acting skills and therefore fails to undermine the plot's patriotic bullshit with an over-the-top performance that makes anyone who claims to love their country look like a grade A nutjob. Rather than nunchucks, the weapons Wen deploys most effectively are a rolling pin and a length of rope, but he also does a lot of bare hand brawling. Ultimately the fights are slightly more convincing as fisticuffs than the bouts choreographed by Bruce Lee because they display considerably less skill and control than film footage of the Little Dragon. *Chinese Iron Man* features Bruce Li in a minor role as a Japanese bad guy.

93 THE FIERCE ONE — 1974

AKA *JAWS OF THE DRAGON*

DIRECTED BY JAMES NAM

Rival gangs are fighting for possession of two suitcases, one full of heroin and the other full of cash. The film focuses on star/director James Nam's character Junior and his role as a top enforcer for one mob. To complicate matters Nam runs into his childhood sweetheart. Rekindled love justifies a tourist montage of Seoul in which Nam and his girl walk the streets, go to the beach and indulge a taste for animal cruelty by visiting a dog-fight. The girl is kidnapped and viciously gang raped in front of a bound Junior so that Nam's character has the 'motivation' to go completely nutzoid in the climatic part of the movie when he takes out the rival hoods.

This being a 'gritty' seventies Korean movie, in the end everyone loses out, Nam's girlfriend is the sole survivor of the endless slaughter. Before that there are plenty of scenes of guys getting their faces stomped on, having car doors slammed into their heads, attacked with a claw hammer, burnt with a blowtorch or even subjected to Chinese water torture. The two gangs also blow up their rivals by tossing lighted sticks of dynamite at each other.

None of this has anything to do with Brucesploitation, but there are a number of reasons this movie might turn up in a discussion of the genre. Nam appeared in a several movies with Bruce Le, and also directed films featuring that clone. These director credits may or may not include *Return of Red Tiger* (1977), which incorporates copious amounts of cut and paste material from *The Fierce One*. This flick is also one of several DVDs issued in the USA by Kung Fu Theatre with claims from this gray market operation that the movie stars Bruce Le although he doesn't appear in it. From the back cover of the 2006 Kung Fu Theatre release: "Bruce Le is 'Junior'. A ruthless member of a Kung Fu gang. When the gang's leader 'Blackbeard' vows revenge on a rival gang, Le finds himself in a battle for both love and money. A classic film depicting the choice of battle between honor and lust." Of course, Bruce Le isn't Junior and doesn't appear in the film! Shorn of its animal cruelty *The Fierce One* would be an enjoyable piece of trash with its shamelessly lifted music cues from international blockbusters like *The Man With the Golden Gun* (1974) and *Shaft* (1971).

94 BRONSON LEE, CHAMPION 1975
DIRECTED BY NODA YUKIO

Tadashi Yamashita plays a Japanese American from Ohio who wants to take part in the world karate championships. He dresses in white, wears a cowboy hat and has a deep southern drawl on the English dub. In the movie his father was a famous karateka but his parents died when he was young. Bronson was raised by Granny, who loves him as much as he loves her. Arriving in Tokyo, Bronson befriends a family who run a restaurant; two siblings and their grandfather, their parents are dead, mirroring Lee's family situation. Bronson discovers all the places in the karate championship are taken. This provides him with an excuse to spend a lot of time eating in restaurants, where his sloppy table manners bring to mind the eponymous anti-hero of *Accattone* (1961). Bronson even eats badly while engaged in combat.

After Bronson gets into a brawl with the accredited Japanese karate championship challenger and beats him, the gangbangers backing this fighter decide Lee would be a better bet than the man they have and so switch them. Ignoring the true 'spirit of karate' embodied by Mr Suzuki who is running the tournament, two crime syndicates are backing different athletes and betting on the outcome.

At one point Bronson reveals that he's not only in the competition to develop his martial arts skills, he wants the prize money; the shocked reaction this elicits is appeased when he reveals he needs the cash for Granny because she's in debt and requires the wedge to get her farm back. Because Bronson doesn't stray too far from the true spirit of karate, some romantic interest develops between him and Suzuki's daughter. Bronson doesn't want to settle down and so the girl is the prime mover in their relationship. Bronson representing Japan and Black Tiger from Singapore reach the final and their match is declared a draw.

Along the way America's Gary Samson gets to demonstrate sportsmanship by being graceful in defeat, and to chide the Mexican entrant Gonzales for his 'sour grapes' as a sore loser. The gang backing Black Tiger want to fix the re-match by wounding Bronson. They kidnap Suzy, whose restaurant running family our hero has befriended, to lure him to their lair. The hoods try to hire Gary Samson to do the dirty work—since he's an expert knife fighter—but he refuses. Gary snatches Suzy from their clutches, they are chased and Bronson appears to help them out. The heavies are seen off but Gary is mortally wounded. Before he dies he instructs Lee to tell Suzuki the mob have huge bets placed on his tournament. Suzuki is outraged because gambling on a championship goes against the true spirit of karate. The sensei confronts the hoods and cancels the re-match. Black Tiger's gang attack those who believe in sportsmanship and although they are beaten off, Bronson is blinded in the process. Fortunately before Lee's father died the old man taught him how to fight blindfolded, so when Black Tiger challenges our hero to a death match, he can still rise to the challenge. Needless to say Bronson wins. Just before Black Tiger expires, all the friends Bronson has made in Japan turn up and are elated to see that the true spirit of karate has triumphed.

This flick is corny, the fights are too samey, while its construction and moral message make it as dull as ditchwater. Yamashita is considered a real life expert fighter, but on film he is stiff and unexciting. This exercise in tedium is considered to be Brucesploitation in some circles because its main character's moniker has at times been treated as a pseudonym of the actor who plays him. Bronson Lee is supposedly a merging of the film-star names Charles Bronson and Bruce Lee; therefore it might be a clone name. Karate expert Tadashi Yamashita as Bronson Lee comes over more like a cut-price Sonny Chiba morphed with 'cowboy' singer Randy Jones from The Village People. He could be a gay clone but he's definitely not imitating the Little Dragon.

This is one of a trilogy of karate films from the Toei Company, but the other two don't seem to have been issued in English dub; they are available with English subtitles.

95 BRUCE, D-DAY AT MACAO 1975

AKA *LITTLE SUPERMAN*
AKA *LITTLE HERO*
AKA *FIST OF VENGEANCE*
AKA *KUNG FU SUPERMAN*
DIRECTOR NG SEE-YUEN

During World War II troops surround a crashed Japanese plane. The war film vibe fades as James Nam (playing Japanese Colonel Kino) is sent undercover to Macao to recover the secret documents Chinese patriots have removed from the burning wreckage. Chinese Colonel Huang Yi-Qing (played by Wong Yuen-San) has gone to Hong Kong to recruit his friend Bruce Liang, who he wants to assist in the search for the Chinese resistance agent with the secret Japanese invasion plans. Bruce isn't interested until he is tossed a huge wad of cash, but he insists that if he's hired so are the four street kids he's adopted. Wong's partner Ho Kwong-Ming is clearly less than impressed by Liang and his urchins. Laing and his gang of delinquents are left behind in Hong Kong and shortly after Ming is killed by the Japanese in Macao. Wong gets away from the trap laid for him and his partner by Nam, but only with help from Liang's guttersnipes who appear from nowhere. At first the kids don't let on Liang is also in Macao—earning the money he's been paid—but eventually the truth comes out.

Also knocking about is Woo Gam, who plays a patriotic Chinese 'tart with a heart of gold'. There are fights between the Chinese and Japanese forces secretly operating in the Portuguese concession, with both sides eventually discovering they are looking for a musician. The Japanese grab hold of him first and kill him, but his kid sister played by Lau Lee-Lee gets away with the bango in which the Japanese invasion plans are hidden. After some more combat and help from Woo, Lau ends up with Wong and Liang. Lau doesn't realise these are the contacts her brother told her to deliver the documents to.

The urchins engage in a lot of argy-bargy over who should have the banjo until Lau rushes off with it to ensure her brother's mission is completed. She's grabbed by the Japanese, but they leave the banjo behind, which is found by one of Liang's adopted kids Mang Hoi. Eventually the rival groups both realise the documents must be in the banjo; which is endlessly used as a combat weapon and seems to be indestructible. The Japanese catch Hoi with the banjo and kill him. When the rest of his crew find his body, Liang is deeply upset and you know the Japanese are gonna catch it. Nam takes the documents and plans his escape by sea, while his men are sent by land as a decoy with the banjo sans the papers. The kids and Wong intercept and trounce the men with the decoy. Liang catches up with Nam and they have a bloody battle. When Liang achieves the upper hand, Nam attaches talons to his right fingers, and our kung fu superman ends up with three cuts across one cheek a bit like Bruce Lee at the end of *Enter the Dragon* (1973). Liang is wearing a white suit and it is soon drenched in fake blood. Eventually Wong turns up with the kids, Nam is defeated and the documents recovered by the Chinese. But Liang is mortally wounded and dies. Liang's kicking is truly spectacular in this movie, the fights are frenetic and relentless, so while the film takes a while to get going, once it lets go of its patriotic message it is fabulously entertaining. There aren't many Little Dragon tropes but the flick sometimes gets talked up as part of our genre because of its alternative title *Bruce, D-Day at Macao,* and the fact that as *Kung Fu Superman* it was included in the VideoAsia Brucesploitation box set *The Ultimate Dragon Collection.*

96 BRUCE HONG KONG MASTER — 1975

AKA *HONG KONG SUPERMAN*

DIRECTED BY TING SHAN-HSI

The first two thirds of this is a family melodrama involving marriage in a large working class family, and relationship stresses in a small bourgeois household consisting of a doctor, his wife and their son. Bruce Liang's girlfriend belongs to the large family, and he chauffeurs and bodyguards the head of the bourgeois household. Liang has some relationship problems too and for a portion of the movie his girlfriend doesn't speak to him, but they make up in the end. Both families feel threatened by a crime wave engulfing Hong Kong, with junkies mugging people and general assaults. This is cut up with tourist footage of the British colony and Christian imagery of crucifixes and Christmas. After the doctor's wife is assaulted and his girlfriend's sister is raped and dies, Liang decides to single-handedly cleanse Hong Kong of criminal lowlife. This makes for an explosive conclusion to the flick as Bruce takes on a drug dealing gang led by Bolo Yeung, whose members include a youthful Sammo Hung. There's also cross-dressing comedy when Laing disguises himself as a streetwalker to entrap scumbags and punks. Liang has the odd fight in the first fifty minutes or so but the film is extremely dull until he becomes a Charles Bronson-style vigilante known as The Superman.

This is more of a *Death Wish* (1974) knock-off than Brucesploitation, and beyond the title—which could be interpreted as referring to Liang rather than Lee—has nothing to do with the genre. The juxtaposition of a church service with a sexual assault prefigures the work of directors like John Woo and Abel Ferrara. The fights are great but there aren't enough of them to make the flick worth watching in its entirety.

97 BRUCE, KUNG FU GIRLS — 1975

AKA *FIVE PRETTY YOUNG LADIES*

DIRECTED BY SHUT DIK

A crime victim runs out of a bank and sees an unconscious cop. There is a cut to a flashing red light on top of an emergency vehicle. The credits kick in and we see newspapers rolling off a printing press, then a boy selling them. Throughout this the camera zooms and pans, while screaming psyche-garage fuzz guitar wails on the soundtrack. Cut to an upmarket apartment block, a couple of cop cars are parked outside so presumably we're meant to think this a police station. The camera pans up the building and then across to a window with a balcony. Inside the apartment a cop is interviewing the man we saw pre-credits, while a woman police officer takes notes and two of her male colleagues stand to attention. Plainclothes cop: "So you're saying when you took out the money you had no idea someone was there?" Victim: "That's right there was absolutely no sign, and so I knew it could only be the invisible thief, I tried various delaying tactics but he tumbled to that and then whacked me over the head. Ooocchh!" Rozzer: "But how did he take the money?" Victim: "I swear you're not going to believe it but before my very eyes the bag just flew through the air!"

As the credits are abbreviated, we're only one hundred and twelve seconds into the flick, so the speed of the movie is absolutely nuts. After a minute or so of police procedural we cut to a man running into a women only swimming pool. He's being chased by hoods, who start beating him when they catch him. Polly Shang-Kuan confronts the gangbangers with the words: "What do you think you're doing? Only girls are allowed into this pool." One of the thugs tells her: "You're just a girl! Stay out of it, or you'll get hurt!" Polly and her four sisters then proceed to make mincemeat of the men; since Shang-Kuan is the star of this flick she does most of the fighting. The saved man thanks the sisters for helping him. He turns out to be a physicist and the hoods were after a formula he'd created.

After this the cop who conducted the interview at the police headquarters visits the sisters at the gym they're running and we discover he's their uncle. Later the physicist visits this health club and brings each of the sisters a present to thank them for saving him from the gang. By this time all the girls are smitten with the handsome young man. They all call him independently and ask for a date. Four of the sisters appear to be stood up, although perhaps the physicist is there invisibly and is the cause of odd things happening between them and other dinners. This on-and-off invisible man does hook up with Polly at a nightclub where the house band mime unconvincingly to Joe Tex's *I Gotcha*. When the music changes to a slower and smoochier number, Polly and the nerd hold each other close as they dance. When Polly goes home her sisters are all mad because she got the man. When Polly leaves the room she blows her four sisters a kiss. Three other sisters do the same to a diminishing number of siblings as they depart individually. Finally it is the turn of the fifth sister to leave, but there's no one to blow a kiss to. Looking like an overgrown schoolgirl with her hair in bunches, the last sister breaks the fourth wall of the film and blows a kiss to the audience. For a few fractions of a second there is a cut to a white modernist sculpture of man's head. A lipstick outline of a kiss appears on the left cheek of the bust.

Shift to Miss FiFi, a female big boss and dialogue about a kidnap. Gangbangers are holding the physicist's mother hostage because he'll do anything to save her. Miss Fifi doesn't like the fact the nerd she's strong-armed has become friendly with Polly and her sisters. The girls are having a birthday party. First the physicist turns up with a present, next hoods appear. A comedy fight follows in which the gangbangers are creamed and pied with birthday cake. Once the thugs have been ritually humiliated, the cops arrive and the 'men' are hauled off to jail.

Next we see a guy in a silver suit go into what looks like a shower room, we hear his footsteps but can no longer see him, he was using an invisibility machine. Polly and her siblings hassle their superintendant uncle to let them help him catch the invisible thief. He agrees and takes Polly with him to talk to another victim. In a flashback we're shown a gun moving by itself through the air and wads of notes being removed as if by magic from a safe. We also hear a threatening male voice, which is that of the physicist. At a police meeting another tape is played, this time it's Miss Fifi's voice saying she's the invisible thief and telling the cops about the theft planned for that night that they won't be able to stop. The designated victim refuses police help so the cops decide to wait outside his house. Polly's uncle even allows her and her sisters to come along. The girls are dressed in their crime-busting all black leather uniforms of knee-high boots, skimpy shorts, short sleeved crop tops and studded leather wrist bands; in short they're done up like a male masochist's wet dream.

The victim has bodyguards but they're useless. Polly and her siblings snatch back a valuable picture the thief was stealing but the criminal gets away. The art the girls saved was stolen, which explains why the invisible thief's victim didn't want the authorities involved. Our head kicking kung fu girls don't just fight crime, they also like to have fun, so we see them playing ball games. Polly gets a call from her uncle asking her to help protect some valuable moon rocks being displayed locally. The rocks arrive by plane and are locked up, so the sisters can go away on a camping weekend. There's Asian pop on the soundtrack as they trek through the countryside. They sit around a campfire while Polly pretends to play acoustic guitar and sing. In the morning they're attacked by thugs but the girls cream the hoods. One gangbanger is caught and forced to cough up the name of the person who sent him. Polly realises the failed assault is connected to the moon rocks and that she and her sisters had better get back into town. Before the kung fu amazons reach their destination, the invisible thief strikes. Some cops are gassed and the main attraction is spirited away. But everything is okay, the authorities were exhibiting fake moon rocks. Once the real deal is put on view the sisters don their skimpy leather gear to protect it. When the invisible thief turns up the girls are ready with a high-tech trap. The captured man is rendered visible and turns out to be the nerd whose favours the sisters were fighting over. He insists he was forced into committing the crimes. The physicist tells Polly and her uncle about the gang's warehouse, as well as the mansion where the boss lives and his mother is being held hostage.

Polly disguises herself as a blind masseur to get into the chief's palatial home. Although the number two boss didn't call for Polly's services, he decides to have a massage anyway. The cops raid the hood's warehouse, and after a fight arrest the criminals there. When the thugs at the mansion learn of this they decide to kill the nerd's mother. Polly throws off her disguise to reveal her skimpy gang busting uniform, and launches herself into combat in order to save the old lady. Polly handcuffs various heavies while she fights. As the male number two boss tries to make off with the physicist's mother, Polly's sisters arrive by car, and there is a fight between him and these kung fu pseudo-Scythians; one girl guides the old lady to safety. The female big boss makes herself invisible and the cops turn up to cart hoods to jail. Our heroes rush to the moon rock vault to find Miss Fifi in the act of half-inching the McGuffin. A ray that counteracts invisibility is deployed. Throwing off her now useless invisibility garments, the criminal mastermind reveals she's dressed in a patent red vinyl cat suit and has dynamite strapped around her waist. She gets out of the vault with the moon rock in its protective suitcase by threatening to blow everyone up if they try to stop her. The cops and the sisters follow the female boss to her car and then the beach. When Miss Fifi puts down the suitcase, one of the sisters throws a chain lasso around the villain's legs. We see the suitcase being hauled to safety on another chain. Miss Fifi is yanked backwards, hits the sand, the dynamite around her waist is ignited and blows her to smithereens. All that's left for the superintendant to do is see his nieces off from Taiwan to their San Francisco home.

While *Bruce, Kung Fu Girls* comes across as a groovy update on light-hearted sixties spy thrillers and even older comic book characters like Wonder Woman, it has nothing to do with Brucesploitation. Director Shut Dik did contribute one bona fide entry to the genre in the shape of *Bruce Lee: A Dragon Story* (1974).

98 ENTER THE PANTHER — 1975

AKA *CONSPIRACY*

DIRECTED BY HON BO-CHEUNG

The discovery of gold leads to a fight between workers and their foremen at a mine. Two relatives of the mine owner poison their uncle and use the stricken man's hand to sign a document that will make them rich. A third relative is in bed with a figurative gold digger. The two poisoners take the mine owner to his wife telling her he's drunk too much wine. He promptly dies. Bruce Li turns up to teach alongside his uncle at a martial arts school. Li accidentally bumps into the mine owner's daughter and she isn't pleased when she learns Li has been assigned to drive her from his town to hers. Along the way, on a twisting dirt road in beautiful countryside, the murderous relatives turn up in a car and get their cousin to go with them. They trick her into entering an inn where they try to get her to drink wine but she refuses. Meanwhile Li takes the girl's bags to her house. The girl's mother insists Li and a female cousin find her. They take the mine owner's daughter home from the inn. The girl is a bit short with Li and gets mad when he decides to go. Next one of the murderous cousins proposes marriage to the mine owner's daughter. She declines and so her father's killers kidnap her. Bruce steps in and saves her just before she is about to be raped by the man whose offer of marriage she rejected. After this Bruce and the mine owner's daughter get romantically involved. One of the killer relatives runs off with the gold digger who'd been two-timing another family member with this beau. These runaways are caught by men who work for the cockold and are killed. The widow and daughter's suspicions have been aroused and they get an official exhumation order for the mine owner's body in order to see how he died. The killers and their henchmen turn up to prevent this happening. There is a standoff and then a long fight at the graveyard. Bruce easily beats all the henchmen, but one of the brothers turns out to be a great fighter and pretty much destroys Li. Bruce's uncle has to step in as the grave is still being dug up. Li eventually gets back into the fight and is losing until he throws dirt in the killer's eyes. After this Bruce and his uncle give the villain a kicking. Meanwhile a quick look at the disinterred stiff reveals he was poisoned. The two surviving villains are frog-marched off and the movie ends.

While *Enter the Panther* doesn't come close to scaling the heights of amnesiac surrealism attained by Joseph Velasco, there is still much to dig in the way it makes the viewer put the story together like a puzzle—rather than relying on a 'quality cinema' plot that all too neatly relays its narrative.

99 BRUCE LEE FIGHTS BACK FROM THE GRAVE 1976

AKA *VISITORS IN AMERICA*

DIRECTED BY LEE DOO-YONG

This starts with ten seconds of material put together by American distributor Aquarius, which shows an obviously fake tombstone with Bruce Lee's name on it, cuts to a stock shot of lightning, then to an unknown actor jumping out of the grave. After this there is a ten second credit sequence added by Aquarius which transitions into a close up of part of the art work they created to sell the movie to English speaking audiences. The rest of the film is an English language edit of a Korean flick originally entitled *Visitors In America*.

Jeong Jun—billed as Bruce K.L. Lea on the English dub—flies to LA to hook up with his buddy; his brother in the Korean version. When he gets to California a taxi driver tries to rob him but he uses taekwondo to get his own back. It seems Jun's buddy is dead but he's just in time for his funeral and cremation. Jun then carries what he thinks are his friend's remains around in a box suspended by a sling from his neck; with a photo of the deceased attached to the front. What Jun doesn't know is his buddy is now a big time drug dealer who has faked his own death and his 'ashes' are actually a million dollars worth of gear and money the friend wants smuggled to Taiwan. However, rather than taking the drugs to the non-deceased's family in Taipei, Jun goes looking for answers about how his friend died.

Along the way he gets arrested and released by the police and has fights with the five drug runners who his friend was last seen with. He also encounters Deborah Dutch—billed in the English dub as Deborah Chaplin—who helps him in his quest because she knows what the men he's searching for look like. Dutch provides an excuse for an awkward romantic subplot. Jun eventually uncovers the ruse of the faked death and box full of drugs, and fights the friend who tricked him. He loses but just before he's killed the cops show up and shoot the drug runner dead. The fuzz had been trailing Jun throughout the movie because they believed he'd lead them to the man they wanted.

This is a bog-standard Korean actioner of the mid-seventies helmed by a veteran director. The plot is easy enough to follow but is somewhat spoilt by poorly thought through re-edits and over-the-top dubbing. The butchery appears to have been done in Hong Kong where many Korean movies were hacked around and faked up as Chinese for international audiences. *Visitors In America* has a couple of accidental Bruce Lee-like moments when Jun throws down his coat, and then pulls facial hair out an opponent's beard during a fight. These occur because they are exploitation film tropes and not to specifically reference Bruce Lee. The signifers of cockiness and anger deployed by Lee—including coat throwing—were already well established as visual displays of such emotion before he used them, and are not in any way unique to the Little Dragon.

Due to the way this movie was aggressively retitled and marketed by Aquarius, *Visitors to America* is one of the best-known 'examples' of 'Brucesploitation'. Further contributing to the flick's notoriety is a rumour that it was helmed by cult Italian director Umberto Lenzi under a fake name; this isn't true. There are some plot similarities to *Game of Death II* (1981) but whether the latter movie was influenced by this one is hard to say.

100 NEW FIST OF FURY   1976

AKA *FISTS TO FIGHT*
DIRECTED BY LO WEI

Three refugees from the Ching Wu School are seen off from Shanghai harbour by Lo Wei; the director cameos again as a Chinese cop. When the survivors arrive in Taiwan, Jackie Chan steals Bruce Lee's nunchucks from them after wrongly assuming they must be valuable because they're in a fancy case. Chan spends much of the flick either being beaten up by or talking up his hatred of the cruel Japanese colonists; to give this a bit more 'depth', Jackie doesn't know who his mother is, but the viewer is let in on the secret she's a local Japanese madam. Meanwhile Nora Miao hooks up with her sifu grandfather Yi Ming, so that they and various other characters can spend yet more time saying negative things about the Japanese. Moving on, Chan Sing plays a Japanese karateka plotting to take over all the Chinese martial arts schools in Taiwan; when he isn't busy doing that, then he's putting down kung fu as inferior to his own fighting style. Cheng Siu-Siu is Sing's brutal karate-expert daughter, who is even more badass than her dad.

Sing, his daughter and some karatekas turn up at Ming's eightieth birthday to cause trouble, this starts with a suggestion that a mythical Chinese hero isn't as good as a legendary Japanese hero. Eventually the Japanese challenge the actor playing the Chinese hero to a fight, but as the embodiment of patriotic 'local' chivalry standing up to colonial barbarity, Ming somersaults onto the stage to take the place of the threatened thespian. Before battle can commence, Ming dies standing upright. The Japanese leave and after a typical graveside scene, Miao decides to replace her grandfather's kung fu training academy with a revived Ching Wu school. No one in Taiwan has heard of Ching Wu and the local collaborationist sifu soon gets into a barney with Miao and her students, only to find his followers arses badly beaten. The humiliated master falsely tells Sing that Ching Wu insulted the Japanese, so the next day the karatekas go and smash up this kung fu academy. Siu-Siu even pulls down the Ching Wu school sign. In town Sing tells everyone they're to have nothing to do with kung fu, and leaves the broken Ching Wu hoarding in the street.

Until now Jackie has refused to learn kung fu because it is too much like hard work, but hearing the Japanese are against Chinese martial arts, he makes a speech and with his dad nails the sign back together. Hoisting the hoarding on his shoulders, Jackie leads a crew of Chinese patriots to Miao's school. When Jackie arrives at his destination we get cuts between him holding the sign aloft and stills of Bruce Lee; this is to underscore that Chan—Jackie not Sing—really is 'the new fist of fury'. Everyone proceeds to get really good at kung fu in no time at all; which is lucky because before long Sing calls the heads of all the local martial arts schools and their top students into his dojo for a meeting. The Chinese are told if they don't want to drop their own names for Sing's Japanese school designation, then they must win a fight against his students. Those who attempt to leave are killed by sword-wielding thugs hidden in rooms they must pass on the way out. The other schools aren't tough enough to defeat Sing, Siu-Siu and their students, but Ching Wu kill off not only the visible opponents, but also the hidden assassins who try to ambush them on the way out. What Ching Wu hadn't foreseen is the Japanese army hiding outside the dojo, and after realising these kung fu fighters have beaten the karatekas, they gun Taiwan's top martial arts practitioners down—making the ending of this movie remarkably similar to director Wei's other riffs on the same anti-Japanese theme including *Fist of Fury* (1972) and *None But the Brave* (1973).

Given that Wei wrote and helmed the original *Fist of Fury*, this isn't so much Brucesploitation as a continuation of the nationalistic bullshit he'd been serving up for some time and which Bruce Lee slyly undermined—with his hybrid martial arts style and hilarious overacting—when he worked with this director. Only Sing and Siu-Siu come close to Bruce Lee's insane carpet-chewing performance in the original *Fist of Fury*, and since none of those playing Chinese characters appear to have completely lost their marbles, the film is very unbalanced in its depiction of nationalism (which is a repulsive European ideology). *New Fist of Fury* is way too long in its original 1976 cut; there is a shorter edit that knocked thirty minutes off the running time.

101 REVENGE OF THE MING PATRIOTS 1976

AKA *THE MING PATRIOTS*

DIRECTOR ULYSSES AU-YEUNG JUN

This is a typical 1970s fu film set at the end of the Ming Dynasty. Chased by the Chings, Bruce Li, Judy Lee and another guy escort a Ming Princess, her father's will and some treasure in the form of jewels, to safety. The Chings are close behind them, and so they have fights along the way. There is a pre-*Drunken Master* (1978) stumbling old man kung fu boozer who is secretly protecting the heroes of the film. Even better is one very nice fight sequence where a Ching fighter gets a sword stuck through his back and it comes out the other side through his stomach, so he leaps at an opponent using the blade that has gone through him to inflict a serious wound on a Ming foe; this 'double penetration' stunt was used to even better effect in *Bruce and Shaolin Kung Fu Part 2* (1978) a couple of years later. The Wu Tang Clan US DVD release of this film appears to have been mastered from more than one VHS tape and thus the picture and sound quality vary incredibly, making the viewing experience either a nightmare or truly avant-garde—depending on your perspective. The film's relationship to Brucesploitation consists of the fact that Bruce Li and Judy Lee are among its stars; alongside other Hong Kong/Brucesploitation regulars of the seventies including Carter Wong, Michael Chan Wai-Man and Lung Fei. This flick really isn't of any interest unless you like historical old school kung fu fodder, and even as an example of that it isn't exactly top drawer material.

102 BRUCE AGAINST THE ODDS — 1977

AKA *Big Boss 2*
AKA *The Mighty Four*
AKA *Four Brave Dragons*
AKA *Lone Shaolin Avenger*
DIRECTED BY KIM JUNG-YONG

Bruce Cheung Mong is furious that Casanova Wong's mother turned down his proposal of marriage. A decade after being told he wasn't conjugal material, he takes his revenge by turning up at her house with some henchmen and killing her husband (Wong's father). Mong tells the poor woman he still 'loves' her and that she and her son must live with him. Wong's mother kills herself while the boy watches from his hiding place in a cupboard. Shortly after this, Yeung Wai turns up too late to save the adults from Mong; all he can do is take the kid away and train him in taekwondo. The boy turns into the adult Casanova Wong and tells his uncle/master that he wants revenge. Wai tells his protégée he isn't yet ready to kill Mong. Wong also learns that as a baby he was married to Carrie Lee Ying-Ying whose father was murdered by the same tyrant. Each of them has half a jade amulet, so that they can recognise each other when they meet. Ying-Ying has disappeared but rather than searching for his wife which is his uncle's wish, Wong wants to take revenge for his parent's deaths.

In the vicinity of Mong's palace Wong runs into a girl who turns out to be Ying-Ying. This young woman knows who Wong is but he remains ignorant of her identity until the end of the flick. Wong is captured by Mong's men and tortured. Wai is wandering around and also runs into Ying-Ying, who asks for his help; she fake fights him to get on the good side of Mong's men and is taken into their compound. Ying-Ying frees Wong and reunites him with his master; the errant child groom now trains dutifully. Ying-Ying has disguised herself as an old woman to spy on Mong and his men, but is rumbled by them and caught. Wai and Wong then make their way into the palace, initially by the master dragging the student in a coffin. To ensure there is no one alive in the coffin, a guard plunges a sword into it, a device also used in *Bruce Lee's Ways of Kung Fu* (1977) but Wong is only nicked by the blade. After this the student, with his the master following him, battles his way through the compound. Eventually Wong kills Mong and Wai frees Ying-Ying. The master explains to his student that Ying-Ying is his wife, and then everyone walks off camera so that viewers are left with a view of Mong's chambers, which were partially destroyed in the climatic fight.

This has nothing to do with Brucesploitaion beyond having been put out under the titles *Bruce Against the Odds* and *Big Boss 2*; it is one of at least three films to be issued under the latter title. The fighting in this couldn't get much further from Bruce Lee's more fluid and 'realistic' movie kung fu, since there is some impressive wire work and lots of ridiculous jumping. The camerawork is often minimalistic during fights with the static cinematography serving to emphasise that Casanova Wong's incredible kicking skills require no trickery. The story is easy to follow but the film appears to have been extensively re-edited by Asso Asia Films in Hong Kong since some elements don't quite add up, and the English dub is seven minutes shorter than the Korean release. The brutality of the action reflects the repressive nature of the military dictatorship in South Korea when it was made, even if the flick itself has a historical setting. The guards wear masks that cover their entire heads and look extremely fascistic.

103 BRUCE AND THE DRAGON FIST — 1977

AKA *Furious Dragon's Rage*
DIRECTED BY SHIM WU-SEOB AND ZACKEY CHAN NGAI-WAI

A taekwondo gym defeats a karate school at a martial arts competition in a Chinese village. After the win, the taekwondo master receives news that his wife is arriving from Korea. The couple meet at the train station and drive off in a carriage as an instrumental version of *When a Child Is Born* plays on the soundtrack—in the distance at the bottom of a hill we can see a 1970s car drive by. Since the village is supposed to be in Northern Manchuria and isn't under Maoist rule, while taekwondo wasn't developed until the 1940s, we can assume the film is set in the 1940s. Bruce Le is bumbling around the village pretending to be a fortune-telling beggar, but actually he's an undercover cop trying to arrest a killer. Using monkey kung fu movements, Le presents himself as an annoying idiot who gets in everybody's way but is basically harmless. When he engages in combat he pretends he isn't fighting and it's just by chance that other's get hurt. The man Le is after has been hired by the karate school to kidnap the taekwondo master's wife. The killer played by Chiang Tao spends most of his time having sex with prostitutes in a brothel and hires three local men to carry out the kidnap for him. Once the Korean wife is held hostage in the basement of the karate school she is whipped and sexually menaced by the school's hunchbacked odd job man. The karatekas try to force the wife to write a letter to her husband telling him to close down his school, but she heroically refuses. The taekwondo master runs around looking for his missus and the local men who carried out the kidnapping are killed as he pursues them; we find out later this was done by a Shaolin fighter who loves prostitutes. Despite acting like an idiot, Bruce is actually doing a meticulous investigation and has tipped the taekwondo master off on who to pursue. Eventually the taekwondo master and Bruce Le have a big fight at the karate school, inching their way to where the captive wife is being held. The karate school is destroyed, the taekwondo master's missus is freed and Bruce Le captures Chiang Tao.

This flick is Bruce Le's greatest triumph as an actor, and it is so ridiculously over-the-top it is his second best movie overall after *Bruce and the Shaolin Bronzemen* (1982). But it has no Bruce Lee elements whatsoever unless one takes the idiotic beggar act as an extended riff on Bruce Lee's scene as a goofy but fake telephone engineer spying on his enemies in *Fist of Fury* (1972).

104 BRUCE AND THE SHAOLIN POLES 1977

AKA *SECRET OF THE SHAOLIN POLES*

DIRECTED BY ULYSSES AU-YEUNG JUN

Meng Fei plays folk hero Fong Sai-Yuk who defends the people against a corrupt Manchu government. Chang Yu is the local government official employing cross-dressing assassins—and eventually a Japanese fighter in the form of Kurata Yasuaki, called Dragon Lee in the English dub—to kill Fei's rebel character. There are all the standard anti-Japanese tropes with Kurata's character abusing the prostitute he's purchased, and bigoted disgust expressed about a Chinese woman having sex with him. Meanwhile Lau Kar-Wing is running around town and hanging out in the local brothel pretending to be Fong Sai-Yuk. When Meng catches up with Lau at the whorehouse they fight and then become friends. Kar-Wing has rescued the heads of Fei's kung fu brothers who've been killed by Yu. Having the whole body for burial is important to some of those who believe in Taoist reincarnation, so Meng is extremely grateful to Lau. Eventually Kurata challenges Fei to combat on the Shaolin poles, which the Japanese fighter has booby trapped. Beneath the poles—which look more like logs buried in the ground—are sharpened pieces of bamboo, so that whoever comes off them will be impaled and die. First Yasuaki defeats Lau on the poles. Meng is beaten on them too but various onlookers help the badly injured hero escape. He is revived with Shaolin herbs and spirited away to be trained by Dorian Tan who plays a crippled master. Since Yasuaki is threatening to rape Fei's love interest and then kill his mother if he doesn't turn up to fight him again on the poles, there is a rematch. This time with his extra training, Meng wins. Fei must now confront Yu and his men to save his mother. It looks like Yu is going to get the better of Meng, but Tan throws his pupil his crutch and this becomes the weapon with which he defeats his nemesis. Meng plays Fong as a typical thumbing sucking mummy's boy and his use of a fan as a weapon underscores his ambivalent sexuality. Fei is superior in the role of Fong Sai-Yuk to the utterly wooden Jet Li, but Fu Sheng's Shaw Brothers movies provide the most entertaining depictions of this folk legend; of course scenes of fighters on poles can be found in 1974's *The Men from the Monastery* in which Sheng plays Fong Sai-Yuk.

Beyond its alternative title of *Bruce and the Shaolin Poles*, this movie has nothing to do with Brucesploitation, it's much more of a Chang Cheh/Shaw Brothers rip-off.

105 BRUCE IS LOOSE — 1977

AKA *THE GREEN DRAGON INN*

DIRECTED BY WU MIN-HSIUNG

Wong Jun murders the family of a woman who refuses to marry him, believing he'll get away with this because his father is the local warlord. However, Yueh Hua—the marshal who is assigned the job of arresting the killer—is determined to live up to his name of Bold Dragon. On his way to arrest Jun, the marshal gets into a fight with Lo Lieh, they part without injuring each other. Despite Jun's father having sent men to protect him, Hua defeats them in a brothel and arrests the criminal. The warlord hires assassins to rescue his son. Hua has to transport his prisoner through territory controlled by the father. The marshal takes thirty men and where there is a choice of two routes, sends some men one way with a decoy disguised as the prisoner, while he goes another with his captive. The decoy and his escort are attacked but succeed in killing many of those trying to free Jun. Eventually they are overwhelmed but Polly Shang-Kuan jumps in and saves the last two of them. The guards and the prisoner travel on to Green Dragon Inn where they will stay the night.

The inn is now under the control of the warlord's men. Also present is Lieh, who offers the marshal's party his suite of rooms, as he has booked all the available accommodation. The warlord's men try to bribe Hua, and when he refuses the money fight him, but they are easily defeated. Three of the bandits stay inside the inn pretending they run it. They let a top fighter in but he can't beat Hua and has to escape. Lieh who has observed everything proceeds to kill the three remaining inn keeping imposters. The warlord and his fighters surround the inn. Next Shang-Kuan breaks into the inn and tires to reach the prisoner. She fights with Hua and when they end up on a bridge above the street between the two parts of the inn, the marshal is wounded by an arrow fired by the warlord's men. The combatants duck back inside the inn and Shang-Kuan tends to Hua's wounds; she reveals she wants to kill Jun to avenge her uncle's family. Hua sympathises but says his job is to keep Jun alive to be tried.

The warlord and his men make various attempts to rescue the prisoner, while Lieh reveals to Hua that he too has a beef with Jun. Eventually the combined forces of law and revenge make a break for a river crossing with their prisoner. Shang-Kuan takes on the warlord's top fighter who wounds her by throwing a knife in her stomach, but she still kills him with her sword. After breaking the prisoner's leg so he can't get away, Hua battles the warlord, while Lieh takes out some other men. Lieh then races to take over from Hua who is being worn down by the warlord. It is only when Lieh and Hua attack together that they manage to hold their opponent down on the ground. Shang-Kuan staggers up, pulls the dagger out of her stomach, leaps in the air and deploys the weapon that's mortally wounded her to kill the warlord. The film ends on a freeze-frame of Hua and Lieh holding a dying Shang-Kuan upright.

Although there is some unarmed combat, this isn't even a kung fu film, let alone Brucesploitation, it belongs to the wuxia genre. It is an attempt to take Shang-Kuan back to her 1960s swordswoman days, and draws on her debut flick *Dragon Inn* (1967). It was retitled *Bruce Is Loose* for North American audiences by legendary exploitation film outfit

William Mishkin Motion Pictures; although Lewis Mishkin rather than his father Bill was most likely responsible, as this was the distribution company's last release and Mishkin Senior had gradually withdrawn from the business to care for his sick wife Elaine.

A hand drawn poster for the English language version of the film shows Bruce Lee taking on and defeating four guys at the same time—the copy on this promo reads: "Deadlier than Chiba, quicker than 'The Juice,' look out baby, cause *Bruce Is Loose!* Starring Lee Bruce, the only star who could play the part written for Bruce Lee! 'The most violent, spectacular fighting we've ever seen!' *Kung Fu Express.*" 'The Juice' is a reference to American football player O. J. Simpson—who when this was released on the grindhouse circuit in 1983 was famous for his sporting achievements rather than as the principal suspect in a murder investigation.

The flick was also falsely marketed as a Bruce Le vehicle by Best Film and Video on VHS (1989) and Kung Fu Theatre on DVD (2006). The back cover of the Kung Fu Theatre release features the following blurb: "When an innocent family is brutally murdered, Bruce Le—Marshal Bold Dragon is sent to bring the killer to trial. As Bruce travels on this treacherous journey, his skill and cunning are challenged by a team of expert Kung Fu assassins sent to destroy him and rescue his prisoner. In a final spectacular confrontation, Bruce comes face to face with his powerful arch rival, The Master, who will stop at nothing for victory."

107 BRUCE LEE'S WAYS OF KUNG FU 1977

AKA *DRAGON LEE'S WAYS OF KUNG FU*
AKA *WAYS OF KUNG FU*

DIRECTED BY KIM JUNG-YONG

Seawater breaks over rocks at the bottom of a cliff, there is a pan upwards and a cut to an old man with an evil laugh accompanied by eighteen women wearing bright uniforms. The women gather around the man and demonstrate a couple of fighting moves. On the soundtrack further laughter is followed by a voiceover: "Kung Tien the master of the Castle of the Devil's Disciples has gathered eighteen girls together. Each possesses unique beauty and different deadly styles of kung fu. Listen, they trap their rivals by seducing them and then they kill them. When you two improve I want you to kill this Kung, right!" A cut reveals that this voice belongs to another aged sifu who is speaking to his pupils. They both agree to kill Kung. One of them wants to do this immediately but the master says he is not ready.

Cut to Kung in his cave HQ where he is confronted by a fighter called The Southern King who wants to kill him, but is easily defeated by the eighteen deadly amazons. These guards are geared up in long dresses and capes, with knee high boots. After the Southern King is killed, Tien is angry that the would-be assassin got into the cave at all. Those responsible for this lapse in security are blindfolded and beaten up by the other women as punishment. Cut back to the good kung fu master, one of the two pupils he's charged with killing Tien comes to him with Dragon Lee's hair. This leads to some flashbacks, with the master recalling his sifu telling him that he must deal with Tien, and memories of Kung poisoning other masters. The good sifu tells the remaining pupil that his parents were killed by Tien and he must learn the style of Master White Cloud in order to avenge his family. He is to go with Dragon and find the other girl—Miss Kim—so that they can 'mend the broken pendant'. Each of those who will kill Kung have one third of the same medallion. Dragon attempts to infiltrate Tien's cave HQ and as he does so he sees an undertaker boatman who has made more than seven hundred coffins for the fighters who have died in the castle.

The cave is garishly lit in colours reminiscent of a 1960s Italian horror movie, and much is made of the removal of the coffin carrying the corpse of the Southern King. Dragon is soon caught and subjected to mistreatment by the deadly amazons: including some boot on the throat shots. Our hero is wearing one third of the broken medallion around his neck and the brutality he is subjected to makes it visible to everyone present. Dragon is locked in a wooden cage on the cliffs, where he is to be starved to death. A male fighter is wandering around checking things out. A masked woman who looks like a ninja turns up, beats up Dragon's guards and frees him. Dragon gets away but nearly drowns; the masked woman is caught. She is Miss Kim, one of Tien's eighteen Amazon bodyguards.

Next Tien is getting it on in bed with his number one Amazon. The male fighter who was wandering around is soon caught and badly injured. Dragon washes up on a beach and is found barely alive by the undertaker boatman, who saves him. What follows is a lot of chopping between characters—including the second medallion wearing good pupil of Dragon's master and a fat comedy character waiting for his partner to turn up. A recovered Dragon infiltrates Tien's cave for a second time, and gets the undertaker boatman to agree to try and save Miss Kim. They place her in a coffin still alive, and although a spear is plunged into it by the guards to check Miss Kim is dead, she smears blood from her hand onto it and avoids being pierced by the weapon. Cut to Dragon wandering around outside, where he is attacked by some of Tien's men, who throw a spear in his stomach. Dragon stumbles away badly wounded and falls down where Master White Cloud is sleeping. This master intervenes to stop the bad guys finishing Dragon off, but one of them turns the tables by throwing sharpened fake fingernails in White Cloud's eyes. By this time Dragon has recovered enough to beat off the attackers and prevent the sifu being killed.

Afterwards White Cloud tells Dragon he came to kill Tien, but now that he's blind he hopes Dragon is the right man to learn his style and complete the mission. Meanwhile Dragon's fellow pupil with a part of the broken pendant is detained by Kung's men. Everyone who comes near the Castle of the Devil's Disciples is to be held for questioning because Kung fears an assassin is going to kill him. Already in detention is the skinny half of the comedy duo that have yet to team up. Number two pupil decides to fight his way to freedom and the skinny comic follows him. Master White Cloud is killed by Tien's bodyguards while Dragon is away, but fortunately he'd already told Dragon about his kung fu book, so the young avenger is able to learn his style from this secret manual. Skinny comic falls in with number two pupil, and eventually fat comic falls in with both of them. While the comics go off to the castle, Dragon and number two pupil accidentally meet at a street food concession in the forest, overhearing their conversation the waitress Miss Kim realises one of them is the guy she saved from Tien. They place the three parts of their medallion together in a kind of 'one for all and all for one' moment! The comedy duo overhear the three kung fu fighters discussing their plans and decide to surprise them by getting to Kung first. The fat comic drags up so that he can get close to Tien's male guards as a ladyboy, and then attack them. At the first watch post things go well but at the second the comics knock off one guard before being killed by another. This clears the way for the medallion wearing trio to race towards the castle. Our kung fu heroes battle their way through all the guards to Tien, where they take him on three against one. Tien murders Pupil Two and Miss Kim, but Dragon kills the boss bad guy and gets to live.

The movie has nothing to do with Brucesploitation. The three different DVD copies I have of this and the version I've seen online list Mark King as director in the opening credits, however many seem to think it is a Godfrey Ho film, despite that seeming improbable as it is so Korean in style. It has also been claimed that Godfrey Ho served as prop master on this film. The best name in the largely fake English language credits is Million Chong, photography. The overall feel with all the rocky shore views and choppy seas is of a Jean Rollin movie with kung fu amazons rather than lesbian vampires and, of course, minus Rollin's nudity and extended sex scenes. That said the gimmicky weapons used by the eighteen amazons—including dart-firing fans—also push us in the direction of Jess Franco's 1960s spy capers. And like so many martial arts films that English language viewers too often denounce as incomprehensible, this flick operates as a fairly simple puzzle, the viewer must put the plot together like the three parts of the broken pendant.

107 The Dragon, the Lizard, the Boxer   1977

Directed by Ngai Lai and/or Law Kei

All hell is breaking lose in Vietnam and so we can assume this movie is set in early 1975 at the time of the fall/liberation of Saigon. In Hong Kong Tan Tao has hired a boat so that he can bring his brother Meng Fei home from the conflict. Meanwhile Margarette needs a ship to collect gold from Vietnam and since every available boat has been hired, some gangbangers agree to sort out transportation for a cut of the loot. The hoods fight Tao for his boat and lose. Meanwhile Meng saves Edna Diaz from being raped and sweeps her off her feet to safety. Diaz explains she's a reporter from The Philippines and Meng takes her to meet his brother Tao. The brothers argue because Tao says they must leave immediately, whereas Meng wants to collect his goods first. Military activity forces them to leave without the unidentified goods. A crowd of Vietnamese refugees are trying to get on Tao's boat, and the captain is keeping them off. There is an argument about whether to let them on since they will overload the ship, but in the end they board. The last guy onboard is fat and greedy and claims to be a bank owner called See Kiat. The gut-bucket steals another guy's food after failing to buy it with a string of pearls. Margarette having arrived in Vietnam discovers her gold has been moved to a safer place—Dragon Island. Ramon Zamora goes to pick up his fiancée Edna Diaz but she's disappeared.

Later in some throwaway lines Ramon reveals he's an agent for The Philippines government, apparently investigating bullion smugglers. After rescuing his pet cat, Zamora makes his escape by stowing away on Margarette's boat. When Zamora is discovered there is a bit of a fight but Margarette takes a liking to him and lets him work for her alongside her hoods. The heavies are planning to double-cross their lady boss and take an instant dislike to the Filipino Bruce Lee. When Margarette and her team arrive on Dragon Island they're met by men guarding the gold. They are to wait for her husband Wong Yan before moving it. Tao's boat hits a storm—this involves a hilariously unconvincing model being tossed about in a tank of water—and everyone on it is shipwrecked on Dragon Island. There is instant drama when the brother of refugee Kitty Meng Chui dies, which means Tao can act sympathetically and romantic interest develop between them. This relationship is considerably more chaste than that between Diaz and Meng. While women from the shipwreck are bathing in a pool, three gangbangers stumble across them and are beaten off after they try to molest them. Margarette gets her men to investigate the other people on Dragon Island and Zamora insists on taking a look too in case Diaz is among them. She is and a priest and a nun have just conducted a marriage ceremony between her and Meng. After unarmed combat between the Filipino Bruce Lee and Meng, a tearful Diaz has to explain to Zamora that her feelings for him were just sisterly, and the man he was fighting is her true love. Edna's now ex-fiancé takes this on the chin and shows he's willing to be friends with everyone. The hoods attack Margarette but she escapes to the refugee encampment with knife wounds. Tao tends to Margarette's injuries but seeing another woman on his bed makes Kitty jealous, so she runs into the forest and hides. Tao can't find her but Diaz does, then they're both grabbed by heavies. See Kiat convinces Margarette that as well as being a bank owner he's the best fighter in Hong Kong and he'll help her out for a share of the loot, so they go back to the cave where the gold is hidden and confront the double-crossing gang. However, Kiat can't fight, so Margarette has to handle the hoods alone and is mortally wounded; while the gut-bucket saves his own skin by cowering on his knees. Tao and Zamora go to the cave, battle the gang and rescue Diaz and Kitty. What's happened to Kiat is left hanging until the climax. Margarette's husband Yan turns up with more men and is angry with the double-crossers for messing around with the gold, it shouldn't be moved without his permission. The double-crossers convince Yan the shipwrecked refugees killed his wife and stole the bullion. So the boss and his men go to burn down the huts the refugees are living in. Zamora, Tao and Meng take on the Yan and his hoods. While this is happening a couple of the Hong Kong double-crossers slip away to steal the gold. The bad guys fighting Zamora and his allies are taken out, while in the cave Kiat has added dynamite to the boxes of gold. When the double-crossers go to get the loot, the fat con artist blows them up. He's massively over-estimated the amount of explosive required and the entire underground cave complex is smashed to smithereens. Zamora observes that no one will get the gold now.

In the opening credits of the Hong Kong release of this movie Zamora is explicitly billed in English as the 'Philippine Bruce Lee'. The directors/scriptwriters Ngai Lai and Law Kei were knee-deep in Brucesploitation when they made this Hong Kong/Filipino co-production since they'd just completed *The Dragon Lives Again* (1977) and would go on to make *Bruce Lee the Invincible* (1978); that said, there aren't really any Bruce Lee-isms here.

108 THE FIERCE BOXER AND BRUCE   1977
AKA *THE FIERCE BOXER*
DIRECTED BY S. A. KARIM AND/OR JOSEPH VELASCO

Three men on horseback are winding their way through the Indonesian countryside and as they approach The White Lotus School one of them, Tony, says he's going to destroy it. Young students are practicing outside and Tony demands to see their martial arts master Peter. The sifu is shown a corpse and says he had to kill the man because he was a villain. Tony announces the stiff is his brother. The men with Tony start to fight Peter, but then the guy avenging his brother takes over and his men set a building alight. Peter tells one of the students to save his son Richard, who is a small boy. The kids are pursued by the two minions. Tony kills Peter. The men chasing the boys catch up and are attacking them when Sammy the White Stalk master appears from nowhere and chases Tony's sidekicks off. This intervention comes too late to save the older boy who dies, but Richard is adopted by Sammy.

Richard grows up with siblings Ricky, Michael and Amy. Michael too is adopted and he is mean to Richard. The boys practice martial arts and Amy grows into a woman. Michael is in love with Amy but she's attracted to Richard. When Richard and Michael have a practice fight it is Richard who wins. The White Stalk school takes part in an annual friendly competition with the Flying Tiger School at the Arena Persahabatan Silat (Friendship Arena). Richard and Ricky both beat fighters from the rival school, but Michael looses his match. Richard and Ricky have to fight each other for the championship. Richard is the better fighter but he throws the match because Ricky is his senior and so it would not be right to beat him. After this Michael attempts to rape Amy and is banished by Sammy. After a while it is decided Michael should be allowed back but it is too late. He's fallen in with the Black Eagle School. Michael and his new friends attack The White Stalk School, and an escalating conflict develops. Although Richard beats Michael when he encounters him in town, back at the school Ricky is badly injured and Sammy is mortally wounded by Tony the top Black Eagle fighter and an exponent of the secret style. On his deathbed, Sammy gives Richard The White Stalk book of the secret style. Richard, Amy and Ricky, go and hide in the mountains so that Black Eagle fighters can't find them until they have improved their martial arts using the secret style instruction manual.

After a year of hard training they're ready to take their revenge. Just after they've paid their respects at Sammy's grave, they are confronted by Michael and kill him. Tony then decides to chase down Richard and Ricky, and confronts them in a forest with his top two fighters. At this point Richard realises Tony was the man who killed his father. The other two fighters are the minions who chased after Richard until Sammy saw them off. Richard kills one of the support crew, and Ricky the other, then our two heroes must battle Tony to the death. Before long the master of the Black Eagle School seems to have the upper hand. We cut to an image of the sun breaking through the clouds, then to Amy looking concerned, then the Kung Fu Theatre DVD release of this film finishes although we haven't yet reached the conclusion of the climatic fight.

Since I've not come across another version of the film in English, I haven't watched it to the bitter end. The copy I have—and which seems to be the source for the online downloads I've found—lasts for 90 minutes before it cuts out; on the DVD disk the running time is given as 91 minutes. *The Fierce Boxer* is an Indonesian picture originally issued under the title *Pukulan Bangau Putih* with a 96 minute running time. Depending on whether the film was trimmed for English language release, the Region 1 DVD is missing something between one and six minutes at the end. Information on Indonesian film sites make it clear Richard avenges his father, so the tables must be turned in the climatic fight. Tony is killed, while both Richard and Ricky survive.

This flick only gets treated as belonging to the Brucesploitation genre because it was released in the USA under the title *The Fierce Boxer and Bruce* by Best Film and Video on VHS in 1988, and on DVD in 2006 by Kung Fu Theatre. Both these releases use their covers to sell the movie as a Bruce Le flick although that clone doesn't appear in it. I've only seen the DVD; the VHS may or may not contain a very slightly longer English language version.

The sole review I can find of the VHS is sketchy—it bemoans the false selling of the tape as a Bruce Le feature and the only plot summary it provides is an inaccurate one from the back cover of the release—but it does give the running time as 91 minutes so my best guess is the English dub is slightly shorter than the Indonesian original and my Region 1 DVD release is missing the last 60 seconds of the international cut.

On the Kung Fu Theatre release the title is just *The Fierce Boxer* when it comes up in the opening credits—but *And Bruce* has been added on the case and disk. This DVD appears to be 'mastered' from the earlier American VHS, the Best Film logo appears before the movie proper starts. Most of the English language credits are blatantly falsified, apparently in the hope of fooling viewers into thinking this is a Chinese rather than an Indonesian production. Judging by the sole English language review I found this wasn't entirely successful, since the disappointed Bruce Le fan who wrote it figured the movie had been made in 'Thailand or Manila or someplace'.

Although Joseph Velasco under his Chinese Kong Hung name is credited as director, this is clearly the work of veteran Indonesian film-maker S. A. Karim. The action is set in the Indonesian countryside and the production values are so low they make Hong Kong b-movies look lush by way of comparison. Nonetheless there are some nice touches such as Richard's father jumping through the roof of a burning building with his son in his arms; not that this hadn't been done before, but a fighter smashing through a roof always makes for good spectacle. Obviously it's better to enjoy this for what it is, one of relatively few old school Indonesian martial arts flicks accessible to English speaking audiences, than get angry about the fact Bruce Le isn't in it as promised on the boxes of the Region 1 releases. While the film is nothing special, I'm happy enough to have seen most of it!

109 RETURN OF RED TIGER 1977
DIRECTED BY NAM GI-NAM AND/OR JAMES NAM

After a tedious stills credit sequence that goes on way too long, masked and baseball bat wielding bad guys make a night time attack on members of a rival gang whose car they've stopped. Some viewers might experience a strange sense of déjà vu since this scene is pasted in from the opening of James Nam's film *The Fierce One* (1974).

After that and without rhyme or reason, the film switches to a daytime chase around trains and railway tracks (not lifted from *The Fierce One)*. From this point on *Return of Red Tiger* becomes deliriously incomprehensible, thanks to the juxtaposition of new material and cut-and-paste scenes from *The Fierce One.*

Two gangs want to get hold of a valuable microfilm with lots of attempts at double-crossing. A nightclub singer and her recently released from prison boyfriend want to snatch the valuable microfilm so they can move to another country. The couple are chased, attacked and beaten. Bruce Le plays a mute beggar who became mentally ill after being traumatised as a child; his mother's boyfriend hit him and tied him up for watching them have sex, then his mom abandoned him. Le is obsessed with both the nightclub singer and drinking milk. He does the latter very sloppily, spilling it all over himself. When the singer is attacked, Bruce jumps to her defence. He uses a cat style of kung fu and even mews like a moggy. Le claws his opponents and early on we see scratch marks on their faces when he does this, but in later fights these aren't shown. Le crawls on the ground while brawling and rather than being a genuine kung fu style this seems to be something made up for this movie.

What this 'martial art' most closely resembles is Jackie Chan's combination of snake style with 'cat's claw' in *Snake In the Eagle's Shadow* (1978) but, assuming the dating I have is correct, this movie appears to have been made before that one, so if there is influence it would seem to be Chan who is copying Le.

The climactic fight in *Return of Red Tige*r is, of course, between Bruce Le and James Nam—the latter plays two characters and directed at least some of the film. Prior to the final battle, Bruce betrays the singer's boyfriend to one gang; who may have been playing cops in a different cut of the movie, the boyfriend's handcuffing after capture certainly looks like stereotypical movie police work. The singer is so angry about this that Le eventually saves both her and her lover from the gangsters/fuzz. At the end the singer and her gangster boyfriend get the microfilm—which was hidden behind the eye patch of another hood who'd planned to double-cross his boss—and depart abroad. Bruce caterwauls over the loss of the woman he loves throwing his head back and screeching at the sky like the hurt pussy he very successfully portrays. True trash film aficionados won't be able to take their eyes off this train wreck of a movie!

There seem to be different versions of this film, since some online reviews detail plot elements not present in the three different Region 1 DVD releases I have of this movie which all feature the same cut. It is, of course, possible I've found English language reviews of non-English dubs that tell an entirely different story with the same images. On the copies of *Return of Red Tiger* I have, Joseph Velasco gets a script credit. However rather than being insanely surreal like a Velasco movie, this one just goes off the rails. My copies credit direction to James Nam who definitely helmed the cut-and-past material. However director credits on English language versions of these films are often unreliable, and while the Hong Kong Cinemagic website currently list James Nam as the sole director, the Hong Kong Movie Database suggests it was made by Nam Gi-Nam. These would appear to be two different filmmakers born in 1939 and 1942 respectively; the Korean Movie Database lists James Nam under the Korean name Nam Seok-Hun. *Return of Red Tiger* doesn't really have any Bruce Lee clone elements beyond the odd coat-throwing move by Bruce Le, and so despite it's radical incoherence making it a trash anti-classic, it must be banished to the outer limits of Brucesploitation.

110 RETURN OF THE DRAGON   1977
DIRECTED BY CELSO AD. CASTILLO

Ramon Zamora plays a former lawman who after growing sick of killing criminals, settles down to family life in a tribal setting. However his violent past catches up with him, and the primitive village he'd retired to is trashed and its inhabitants murdered by hoods. Zamora seeks revenge but when killing those who butchered his people he suffers agonies for what he's doing. The Catholic culture this anguish emerges from shows through in torture done crucifixion-style; endless extreme pain, cruelty and violence, something the director occasionally contrasts with bucolic pastoral shots. Part martial arts epic and part spaghetti western, this unabashedly violent movie is the best Zamora flick I've seen. That said, beyond the English title deliberately inviting confusion with Bruce Lee's *Way of the Dragon* (1972) due to that flick being released as *Return of the Dragon* in the USA, this doesn't have much to do with Brucesploitation. This only merits inclusion in the outer limits of our genre but is well worth seeking out as an ultra-violent exposition of the revenge is pointless trope in exploitation cinema.

111 10 COMMANDMENTS OF LEE   1978
AKA *MASTER AND THE KID*
AKA *SHAOLIN MASTER AND THE KID*
AKA *FURY OF THE SHAOLIN MASTER*
AKA *ONE MAN ARMY*
DIRECTED BY LIN FU-TI

Yueh Hua is a law enforcement officer whose family are slaughtered on the orders of Chan Sing and so he resigns from his post to avenge them. Sing had Hua's family killed in retribution for the beheading of his heir; our hero had arrested his son. To exact revenge, Hau must discover who murdered his kin. He dresses in white and tries to leave his nephew—who escaped Sing's men—with other people, but the kid keeps running away to follow his uncle; in the end the two of them hit the road together. The man in white must gradually work his way back to the mastermind behind the slaughter of his loved ones. Things are complicated by the bad guys putting a price on Hua's head so lots of people are trying to kill him in order to collect the reward. There are too many tedious scenes with the kid, who appears to have been dubbed by an adult woman. We get a cameo from Woo Gam who tries to kill Hua with a hairpin, unfortunately she fails and we see no more of her. Various scenes feature Phillip Ko, who is dressed in black to underscore he is Hua's nemesis. At first it isn't clear Ko is a villain, later we discover he's only knocking off top assassins and making it look like the hero's work so he can claim a higher reward for the man's head if he takes it! There are various plot twists involving other characters that need not detain us, before Hua confronts first Leung Kar-Yan, and at the climax defeats Chan Sing—with a little help from a lady who owes him a debt of gratitude. Unfortunately Chan Sing is dressed in period costume and made up like an old man, so he doesn't have his usual ugly in a cool way mofo presence, and like Woo Gam there isn't enough of him. This movie riffs on the Japanese samurai *Lone Wolf and Cub* series, but isn't nearly as good.

Since there are neither characters nor notable actors in this flick with the name Lee, it is probably safe to assume that the distributors who put it out in English under the *10 Commandments of Lee* title were attempting to cash in on interest in the Little Dragon. Nonetheless, beyond this variant title the flick has nothing to do with Brucesploitation and is really a samurai knock-off.

112 BRUCE LEE'S DUAL FLYING KICKS 1978
AKA *DUAL FLYING KICKS*
DIRECTED BY LIN BING

Lung Fei is a corrupt mayor who is instructed by Chan Sing to clean his town up. Since Sing is secretly Fie's underworld boss, as well as a higher ranking official, the mayor understands he is being instructed to take out two undercover cops known as the Double Kicks. This is easier said than done since their identity is unknown; the Double Kicks cover their faces with black gauze when they appear in public. Fie delegates the task of assassinating the plainclothes cops to two different gangs, offering his daughter's hand in marriage to the leader whose men succeed in killing them. When a bunch of heavies are wiped out by the kung fu cops, one gang enlists the aid of a sorcerer. However, since Fie's daughter doesn't want to marry an ugly hood, her maid—who is also an undercover cop—suggests they secretly help the Double Kicks. When the sorcerer is helping the hoods to get the better of the Kicks, the two women intervene and the boot masters survive. Dorian Tan plays the Double Kick who has infiltrated Fie's gang. In dialogue that makes little sense, Tan's putative father Wu had asked Fei to look after his son should anything happen to him just before he takes some men to kill the Double Kicks. Wu and all bar one of his men are killed, so Fei is obliged to look after Tan. Presumably, Tan substituted himself for the real son or used some other subterfuge to ingratiate himself with Wu and become an adopted son. There is stereotypical comedy training and fighting based around Tan pretending he doesn't know kung fu; having to act out exaggeratedly poor form when being instructed in martial arts, or make it look 'accidental' when he gets the better of other experts. The non-comedy combat is more enjoyable, and in places the high kicking cops having their faces obscured by black gauze makes the flick extremely surreal. It comes as no surprise when the Double Kicks eventually unmask Chan Sing as the mastermind behind the criminality they're investigating. Naturally, the Double Kicks triumph in their final battle with Sing.

Beyond the fact that some English language distributor added 'Bruce Lee's' to the title of this film, it has nothing whatsoever to do with Brucesploitation. *Dual Flying Kicks* has a handful of great scenes but overall it's a mess; nonetheless it is a lot more entertaining than director Lin Bing's core Brucesploitation effort *Goodbye Bruce Lee, His Last Game of Death* (1975). Star Dorian Tan was principally a taekwondo practitioner and famously taught his adaptation of the style to both John Liu and Bruce Lee's daughter Shannon Lee.

113 BRUCE LEE THE INVINCIBLE 1978

AKA *THE INVINCIBLE*
AKA *BRUCE LI THE INVINCIBLE CHINATOWN CONNECTION*

DIRECTED BY LAW KEI

Michael Chan Wai-Man is a bad Shaolin student who is banished by his master to Malaysia. Cheung Lik plays a good student of the same sifu who goes to Malaysia and discovers that Wai-Man is now terrorising the local population and leading a criminal gang who run the local mine, casino and brothel. The gang kidnap Lik's beautiful cousin and beat up his aunt and uncle who run a grocery store. Lik sends for his master and Bruce Li, who is the siu's number one student. So that Wai-Man doesn't recognise him, the master disguises himself with a 'mask' so that he looks like someone else, and a different actor plays the character for much of the movie. The three good Shaolin fighters battle Wai-Man, who not only has back up from his gang of local hoods but also Malaysian tribesmen. There is a chase through the jungle and the highlight of the film, a couple of one on one fights with killer apes who are trained in kung fu; these are very obviously actors in cheap gorilla suits. In the end the good Shaolin fighters save the girl by defeating Wai-Man, his gang and the Malaysian tribesmen.

This has nothing to do with Bruce Lee beyond the title. Nonetheless among some of those who couldn't tell the difference between the Little Dragon and Bruce Li, it did lead to the false rumour that Bruce Lee fought gorillas in one of his movies. There is also a cameo from Bolo Yeung. Director Law Kei had made a genuine Brucesploitation anti-classic in the form of *The Dragon Lives Again* (1977).

114 Bruce Lee Vs The Chinese Frankenstein — 1978

Directed by Kwok Shek Ske

A father and daughter who work as street performers turn up in a village looking for their long lost son/brother. To attract all the young men of the village a competition is announced in which the man who can defeat the daughter in a fight can marry her. The girl is such a good fighter no one can defeat her. In the woods around the village people are being murdered. This is done with classic horror movie subjective camera work from the perspective of the killer who we don't see at first—later it's revealed he's a young dude wearing a rubber monster mask. The lost son/brother is discovered amongst a group of buffoons who are constantly pulling silly pranks. Having learned he's not an orphan, the boy is trained in advanced kung fu techniques by his father and sister. His idiot friends watch his instruction and copy it, and their fighting skills improve too. Meanwhile a weird old sifu sits beneath a waterfall to clear the poison from his body while his killer student wanders around committing murder. The father, daughter and son have to defeat the evil master; the son's idiot friends take on his disciple. Ultimately good triumphs over evil.

Beyond the English language title the film has nothing to do with Bruce Lee, and there is no Victor Frankenstein and no monster either; the horror elements amount to a few minutes of screen time, this is actually a kung fu comedy. Despite one of the actors being credited in English as Bruce Yi, this movie is a refugee from the outer limits of Brucesploitation and makes it here only because of the English title. The incoherent story and editing, alongside the ultra low-brow comedy, can be viewed as skid row surrealism.

There are at least two films that have been marketed as *Bruce Lee Vs [The] Chinese Frankenstein*, the other I'm familiar with is a 1973 production (see 65) that has the alternative names of *On the Verge of Death* and *The Line of Death*. I could find no information about the director of the *Chinese Frankenstein* title under consideration here. The director's name is rendered Kwok Shek Ske in the film titles, and Kwok Shek Sze on sites selling the flick. I've yet to identify what this film was called before it was re-titled to sell it in English language markets. The year of production I give is a guess based on the look of the film and may be wildly inaccurate.

115 Bruce Li's Magnum Fist — 1978

AKA *Magnum Fist*
AKA *Great Hero*
Directed by Hon Bo-Cheung

This begins with what looks like vintage war footage of the Japanese attacking China. The strident music accompanying it comes across as a Taiwanese pisstake of the Nazi *Horst Wessel*. I've no idea what the song was about but the music made me think I was watching a comedy despite the ostensibly serious nature of the opening footage and the inclusion of some military style drumming on the instrumentation. The English credits don't include any music information, and Bruce Li is billed as Bruce Lai.

Post credits a group of Japanese soldiers steal a woman's chickens as she rants at them in impotent fury. Fortunately Bruce Li appears out of nowhere to save the chickens. The slapstick karate of the Japanese is no match for Li's droll kung fu. Other indications the fight is supposed to be funny are Bruce's posture before he starts kicking and punching, and over-the-top sound effects when people are hit. Moving on, partisans successfully attack the Japanese who are portrayed as comic fascist soldiers over-reacting to everything. There is a Japanese captain who is fat and has a Hitler moustache. He is driven around in a motorcycle sidecar and keeps having silly accidents; the buffoonery is often underscored by dumb music. Angry that the resistance are getting the better of his troops, the captain decides to occupy the village in which the partisans are based. Meanwhile partisan leader Li wants to marry Polly Shang-Kuan but her father is thinking of selling her—without her knowledge—as a concubine to the local innkeeper who has a harridan for a wife; cue typical seventies sexist 'comedy'—possibly exaggerated in the English dub which puts a British spin on it. This is followed by more 'laughs' with the Japanese captain ordering his stupid troops around and demonstrating his basically non-existent hand-to-hand combat skills, but his men have to let him beat them or they'll be in trouble. Taking the train to the partisan's village, the captain has a long *Billy Liar*-style flashback to the martial triumphs of one of his great samurai warrior ancestors. When the villagers realise the Japanese are going to occupy their homes and shops, the partisans go off into the mountains as they don't have enough men to fight the fascists head on. When he stops his troops outside the village to tell them to maintain good order, on the English dub the captain sounds more like a caricature of a British sergeant major than anything else. What appears to be a wedding celebration is going on and frightened by the sound of firecrackers the captain falls flat on his face. The partisans have a problem; the transmitter used to stay in touch with other Chinese fighters is hidden in a coffin in the village that is now occupied. They solve the issue by hiding their radio operator in the same way. So that their man can be fed, the partisans convince the Japanese the room in which the coffins are housed is haunted by a man who died of starvation; to appease the ghost they must feed it. The Japanese become frightened when they see the food left for the ghost gets eaten. The occupiers love the innkeeper's food and take to gorging themselves on the grub made by 'the stupid Chinese'. When Japanese soldiers attempt to rape Shang-Kuan and her friend, they are no match for Polly's kung fu, and accidentally kill one of their own men. Shang-Kuan is briefly imprisoned for this but escapes. When the Japanese attack the partisans in the mountains, they are the losers and have to retreat accompanied by 'comic' music. The captain only survives because Bruce doesn't want him replaced, he's an imbecile and therefore useful to the partisans. Since Polly's father has changed his mind about selling her to the innkeeper, who is in with the Japanese due to his skills as a chef, the cook decides to betray Li. Meanwhile Bruce is having relationship problems because Polly who is now with him in the mountains wants to go and fight the fascists and pays little heed to his objections. They even have a literal kung fu fight. However all is soon resolved because news comes through on the transmitter that the Japanese Emperor has ordered his army to surrender. The captain and his men don't believe this at first, and once they learn it is true they feel totally humiliated. The innkeeper gets a right scolding from his wife for trying to bag himself a concubine, and Bruce gets to marry Polly.

Bruce Li's Magnum Fist is basically a war comedy with some kung fu thrown in for good measure, and aside from the odd move by Li has few Bruce Lee-like elements. *Magnum Fist* is underwhelming, particularly when you consider it's director's previous movie with Bruce Li—*Enter the Panther* (1975)—was a bizarre anti-classic which managed to break pretty much all the rules of 'quality' cinema. The best thing here is Polly Shang-Kuan, but she's seen to much better effect in flicks like *Bruce, Kung Fu Girls* (1975).

116 DEATH DIMENSION 1978
DIRECTED BY AL ADAMSON

T.E. Foreman is a scientist who has invented a deadly 'freeze bomb'. Feeling a twinge of conscience over the fact that Harold Sakata funded his scientific investigations in order to make a weapon of mass destruction, Foreman implants a microdot containing his research findings in the forehead of his assistant Patch Mackenzie, destroys his laboratory and injects himself with a slow acting death drug. Soon both the criminals and the authorities are chasing Mackenzie.

George Lazenby plays a police captain who puts Jim Kelly on the freeze bomb case. Twenty-four minutes into the film Kelly meets up with his investigation partner, Myron Bruce Lee. There is a lot more of Kelly than Lazenby or Myron Bruce Lee in this flick. There are car chases, martial arts battles and gunfights. The villains always know where the cops are, and where Mackenzie is when she contacts the authorities hoping they'll pluck her to safety. Sakata's character started his criminal career as a pimp before moving into arms dealing, so there are lots of scenes in brothels.

Since this is a Dick Randall production some real sex workers seem to have been employed to show off their nude 'assets' alongside the actresses. Eventually we discover that Lazenby is the hood's inside man on the police force, tipping them off about everything and explaining how they always knew where to find Kelly. But just as the bad guys get their hands on the microdot containing the plans for the freeze bomb, Kelly and Myron Bruce Lee burst in on them and sort everything out; two uniformed cops arrive to back them up a bit later. Like *Challenge of the Tiger* (1980) and *The Ninja Strikes Back* (1982), this is basically one of several unsuccessful attempts by producer Dick Randall to cross the martial arts genre with a James Bond-style thriller. Here the 007 elements come from the use of the actors George Lazenby and Harold Sakata who were both famous for their roles in Bond films.

The Brucesploitation content is minimal; the biggest being that Bruce Lee's *Enter the Dragon* (1973) co-star Jim Kelly has a lead role. Myron Bruce Lee neither acts not looks like the Little Dragon; the closest he gets to being a 'king of kung fu' knock-off is practicing some southern Chinese hand strikes, which do resemble what Bruce Lee did in demonstrations when he was still practicing traditional Wing Chun, but this is not really specific to him. Presumably Randall had the idea of changing the actor's name to one similar to the Little Dragon after filming; beyond his moniker Myron Bruce Lee isn't actually a clone. *Death Dimension* sucks shit through a straw because it is slightly more competent, and therefore considerably less entertaining, than Al Adamson's usual schlock.

117 EDGE OF FURY 1978
DIRECTOR LEE TSO NAM

Bruce Li is a Hong Kong based chauffeur whose boss Mr Chen is arrested and then executed in Thailand for smuggling drugs. Why someone with a huge house and various business companies would courier their own drugs is beyond me—but apparently this was Chen's modus operandi. Both the police and the various gangsters believe Li must know where Mr Chen stashed a huge quantity of opium. But Li is just a nice boy who didn't even realise his wonderful boss was involved in criminal activity. A lot of time is wasted establishing what a good guy Li is; he wants to get married, he looks after his sick mother, he spends a lot of time playing with the bratty son of his boss. Despite too much downtime between fights there is the obligatory kung fu combat in a container port. Gang leader Yasuaki Kurata wants to get his hands on the drugs, so he gives Li a job and the deposit for a flat. When Li fails to show his gratitude by telling him where the opium is, the gang kidnap his girlfriend Michelle Yim and give Bruce twenty-four hours to provide them with the gear or the girl cops it. This makes Li really mad and he ransacks the home of his dead boss in front of the widow played by Dana Tsen. In *Edge of Fury* Dana is more concerned about her inheritance and her love affairs than her husband's fate. While getting mad at Dana and ransacking her house, Li sees a photograph that clues him in as to where the drugs are hidden. He finds the opium and calls up Kurata's gang to exchange it for his girlfriend. Once Michelle is safe, Li blows up the drugs and most of the gang. There follows a final fight in which Li defeats Kurata before the police arrive.

Edge of Fury has nothing to do with Bruce Lee and only gets included in Brucesploitation lists because the bland Bruce Li takes the lead role. It's a slow and boring seventies kung fu flick.

118 THE DRAGON, THE YOUNG MASTER 1978

AKA *DRAGON THE MASTER*
AKA *DRAGONEER 8—THE UNBEATABLE*
AKA *THE DEADLY SILVER NINJA*

DIRECTED BY GODFREY HO AND/OR KIM SI-HYEON

In a pre-credits sequence a man is attacked and left badly wounded by racketeers who want a treasure map; they find it in their victim's boot. After the bandits leave someone emerges from behind a tree, the stricken man asks for help but the mystery figure whose face we don't see finishes him off with a sword. Five years later the Silver Ninja attacks the gang who stole the treasure map and takes their gold from them. The Silver Ninja is masked but from what we can see of his eyes and build he would appear to be Dragon Lee.

Next Dragon turns up in the town run by the map stealing mob and gets into a series of fights with them. Various hoods accuse him of being the Silver Ninja but he denies this. Dragon uses his fists to save Qiu Yuen (a flower seller) from the gang; then he does the same for a blind man who turns out to be the father of the girl he helped earlier. Dragon moves in with Yuen and her father. Both Dragon and Yuen have more fights with the local gang. Qiu is even kidnapped by them but fights her way to freedom. Dragon reveals to the blind man that he is looking for the scumbag who killed his father. The old man reacts badly to this news. Dragon knows the name of the villain who killed his father, but he doesn't realise it belongs to the blind man.

Eventually the blind man approaches Dragon when he is sleeping with the intention of killing him, but can't carry through his plan. Dragon wakes up and the blind man confesses that he killed the hero's father. The old man explains why he brought his friend's life to an end—although in the English dub the reason really isn't too clear, it may have been: a) the blind man didn't realise who he was killing and thought Dragon's father was one of the bad guys; b) his friend had information neither of them wanted the bad guys to get and given his condition killing him was the best way of keeping this from them; c) Dragon's father was mortally wounded and would have died anyway, so his friend was just putting him out of his misery. Regardless, Dragon is about to take his revenge but Qiu rushes into the room saying she heard everything and successfully pleads for her father's life. By this time we know that Dragon really is the Silver Ninja. Meanwhile Ming, the head of the local gang has been joined by his brother who is an excellent martial artist. The brother has come to help deal with the Silver Ninja. The blind man decides to go off on his own and leaves a note for his daughter and Dragon, who when they find it go looking for him. The old man then realises he hasn't left his daughter and Dragon the copy of the treasure map he has to ensure their future. He returns to his house and is killed by the Ming brothers. Dragon and Yuen see the Ming gang marching out of their house. The racketeers have discovered the blind man's copy of the treasure map and decide to move the loot as they're convinced Dragon knows about these riches and will take them. Dressed in matching Silver Ninja costumes Dragon and Yuen take on the gang and avenge their fathers. While we get some Bruce Lee come on hand gestures from both Dragon and Yuen, beyond this there are few clone-like elements. As usual Dragon's fighting style is nothing like Bruce Lee's and contains acrobatics that would prove fatal if he was involved in real combat. *Dragon, the Young Master's* connection to Brucesploitation is mostly through the marketing methods of its international distributors. As part of that shilling Godfrey Ho has been listed as the director on the credits of the English language copy I have, but it seems much more likely that Kim Si-Hyeon actually helmed this generic and unenthralling Korean actioner.

119 BLIND FISTS OF BRUCE LEE — 1979
AKA *Blind Fist of Bruce*
DIRECTED BY KAM BO

Bruce Li gets to play second fiddle to Simon Yuen reprising his *Drunken Master* (1978) role. Li manages a bank in some backwater town in the early twentieth century. He imagines he is a good fighter and thinks he can protect his bank with his kung fu skills. However, Bruce's masters are imposters with no genuine martial arts ability and what they've taught him are useless—but comic—fake animal styles. To convince Li his kung fu in unbeatable, the conmen hire fake robbers to burst into his bank who then allow themselves to be beaten up by super-bland Bruce. When real thieves turn up, Li's kung fu is so poor he loses both his bank and his honour. Only one man in town can outfight the bandits, an old blind musician played by Yuen. Eventually Bruce persuades the sifu to teach him martial arts, and after many whacky training scenes, he's good enough to defeat the bandits who've stolen everything he has. However rather than accepting defeat, the villains of the film call in Tiger, Yuen's bad pupil who blinded the old master years earlier. Together Yeun and Li defeat Tiger. If you like Simon Yuen, you'll find this an enjoyable seventies kung fu movie but it has nothing to do with Bruce Lee.

120 THE GOLD CONNECTION — 1979
AKA *Iron Dragon Strikes Back*
DIRECTED BY KUEI CHIH HUNG

Bruce Li and his friends find Vietnamese gold while scuba diving. His chums think they are rich but kung fu sifu Bruce insists they put the gold back in the water and return for it later to avoid trouble. Bruce figures if the treasure belongs to some criminals it is better not to have it because being rich is of no use if you are killed. Bus driver Han Kwok Choi returns the next day and takes the gold for himself. Choi offloads a couple of bars to a fence. He's given a low price because the bars are marked and difficult to sell. The fence is soon kidnapped and viciously tortured by the people smuggling gang the gold belongs to. He gives them Choi's name before being killed and hung from a ceiling light and fan combo. This dangling from an electric flex image gives away where director Hung is coming from. He's heavily influenced by 1970s Italian exploitation films and would go on to make *Corpse Mania* (1981) which has been called the only Hong Kong giallo; although that isn't strictly true because *Gold Connection* is clearly a giallo crossed with a Fernando di Leo-style crime story and kung fu.

The hoods go to Choi's house and despite tearing the place apart don't find the gold there because the man they're after is burying it on a mountain. The gang decides to wait but one of Choi's scuba diving friends turns up first, so they fight and capture him. Upon returning, Choi sees blood outside his shantytown abode from the earlier battle and becomes suspicious. He enters the house cautiously and narrowly avoids being killed with a harpoon; here we see the influence of Mario Bava who featured a harpoon as a murder weapon in *Bay of Blood* (1971).

After fighting and a chase, Choi gets away and the gang become heavier in their attempts to retrieve the gold. Bruce Li's girlfriend has a burning sack thrown over her head in yet another scene drawing on giallo influences. She is attacked so that the mobsters can get keys that will enable them to make surprise attacks on Li and her scuba diving brother. The mobsters haven't figured out this is only a movie, and so Bruce gets the better of them with his fake kung fu. Eventually Li and his friends agree in a telephone conversation with the gang to swap the gold for a captured mate. Neither side trusts the other. Li's posse bring boxes filled with rocks, while the gang are planning to kill off the scuba diving fighters to prevent them going to the cops.

After a battle, Bruce's kidnapped friend and many of the hoods are dead, but Li and his other two chums escape. We are told they go to Macao but return to Hong Kong because they are broke; this isn't shown. Li takes up action directing kung fu films and a killer dressed up as the martial arts movie villain Silver Fox attempts to murder him on set. The scene is silly with many people getting slaughtered; it seems to be a nod to Brucesploitation movies in which there are attempts to kill a Bruce Lee-like star on set.

The crooked businessman whose gold has been swiped is fed up with his gang's inability to get the better of Li and company, so hires a professional killer. A scuba diver involved in dodgy business deals is the first to cop it from the hit man. First the victim is mugged as he takes money to the bank, then the killer knocks him off in murder you'll miss if you blink. Bruce thinks things have got so dangerous that Choi should move in with him, so they sit around his swanky pad drinking beers and watching a vintage—contemporary at the time—Watford Vs Nottingham Forest English football match on the TV. Choi then decides to have a bath; which as anyone who has watched a few giallo or slasher movies will know, is a bad move.

The killer crashes through a window and stabs Choi to death in the water, before proceeding to hang him from the shower hose. Li senses something is wrong. He grabs a sword from the collection he keeps at home and prepares to fight for his life. Bruce isn't doing badly in the martial stakes when the assassin kills the lights. Earlier Li had been toying with his new automatic camera—which we'd seen him using at the beginning of the movie to take photos of his girlfriend—and he deploys the repeat flash function to flood the room with light. Finally with a jump kick he flies through the air and breaks the hit man's neck; although the head which snaps from the body clearly belongs to a dummy. The next day we see Bruce in dark glasses emerging from his apartment building. A gunman is waiting in a car to assassinate him. Li falls dead in the street, and we learn the gang leaders are writing off the loss of their gold happy in the knowledge that those responsible for stealing it are dead.

Aside from the Italian elements already mentioned, there are some components taken from spaghetti westerns too! With a star as wooden as Li it clearly wasn't possible for director Hung to be as downbeat and dirty as a typical Eurosleaze crime flick of the same period. Hung did manage to make some good movies when he wasn't lumbered with Li, in particular *Boxer's Omen* (1983). *The Gold Connection* is definitely a very minor entry in Kuei Chih Hung's relatively long list of directorial credits including the notorious *The Bamboo House of Dolls* (1973). I noticed few differences in the picture quality and cropping between the Region 1 and Region 2 releases of this film that I've watched—but preferred the US issues put out under the *Iron Dragon Strikes Back* moniker because they were dubbed into English, rather than subtitled, as is the case with the UK Vengeance Video version.

121 CHAMP AGAINST CHAMP　　　1980

AKA *CHAMP VS CHAMP*
AKA *TWELVE GATES OF HELL*

DIRECTED BY GODFREY HO AND/OR LEE HYEOK-SU

Dragon Lee is attacked by a bunch of Master Kai's badass fighters on his way into a village. He defeats them all and Kai isn't happy when he learns this. However, he's even more wound up about Master Tai and the rebels plotting against him. Lee has returned to the village he'd left some time before to meet Tai's daughter Sing for their arranged marriage. Dragon's father has accompanied him on this trip. Everyone likes to hang out and fight at an inn owned by a red nosed old dude. One of the battles in the restaurant is accompanied by classical music on the soundtrack, although most of the time the score is what you'd expect to hear on a grindhouse release of this vintage.

Initially Dragon goes to the restaurant alone and then he takes his father there. Tai has been injured by Kai's men but while Dragon and his dad are talking in the restaurant, the injured rebel's right-hand man overhears them and takes them to his master. They then strike on the brilliant plan of hiding Tai at the inn because its already been searched by Kai's men, so they won't think of looking there again! Once Tai is in a room at the inn he tells his man to take his list of rebels to their friends in the south. Just as the messenger goes out, one of Kai's men chases a woman from a private room and recognises the good guy. Dragon has to intervene and although the messenger gets away with the list, after much fighting and with a switch to an outdoor location, Tai has been captured, Lee senior killed and our hero has a poison dart in his leg. Fortunately Sing comes across Dragon and despite not knowing her fiancé from Adam, gets a doctor to attend to him at the country retreat built by her grandfather. Although the dart landed in Dragon's thigh, the doctor only has to amputate him from the knee down in order to save him from a slow and painful poisoning death.

When Dragon realises who Sing is he decides not to reveal his identity because he thinks it would be wrong to make her marry a raspberry. Sing discovers who he is anyway because his fever leads him to talk in his sleep. Dragon is depressed about being a useless cripple until he has a flashback to being taught kung fu by Master Wai who told him never to give up or be depressed about his training. He was ready to top himself until he recalled being told about the legendary Steel Leg, a great fighter who only had one pin to walk about on and replaced his missing limb with a metal substitute.

When Dragon excitedly tells Sing this, she reveals that Steel Leg was her grandfather and that his gym is part of the complex they're living in. The training room is full of cobwebs but Dragon immediately finds Steel Leg's martial arts manual detailing the secrets of the eighteen kicks. Once the room is cleaned up, Dragon spends most of his time there reading the secret manual and constructing a steel leg in the furnace that's conveniently present. In a surrealist touch, while he's making himself his steel leg Dragon appears to have four normal limbs. With great effort Dragon learns to use his new steel limb and do the eighteen kicks. By the time Dragon leaves Sing, the young couple are deeply in love with each other. They even make the beast with two backs despite not yet having enjoyed their nuptials. Dragon then heads for Devil's Gate where Kai is torturing his soon to be father-in-law. After Dragon insults Kai and his merry band of badass followers by using his steel leg to break the Devil's Gate stone sign, there are several set piece battles. As Dragon fights Kai's men and uses his steel leg to deliver the eighteen kicks, they end up in the branches of trees or skidding twenty-metres along the ground.

When Dragon faces Kai's four deadly female fighters they make themselves invisible and start beating him up. Fortunately, Dragon is able to make his hands smoke and thanks to this magic the women become visible again. Lee then uses the sashes around their waists to tie them to a tree. There follows more wandering around the Korean countryside and fights with Kai's men; during the combat there are vaguely metallic bonging sounds whenever Dragon performs a deadly kick with his steel leg. Dragon humiliates one of Kai's men by pulling his pants down and exposing his bottom; the embarrassed warrior accuses Dragon of being a dirty fighter. Another of Kai's men is able to use his mouth as a flame-thrower. But fear not, this human torch is no match for Dragon's steel leg kung fu; even if what he's doing looks more like taekwondo than a Chinese animal style. After freeing Tai, Dragon has his climatic battle with Kai: during this kicks that miss his opponent result in the bad guy's cave HQ being demolished—and so we see cardboard rocks crashing down around them. Eventually Dragon chases Kai outside and defeats him.

Champ Against Champ is a tedious old school martial arts period drama and there are no Bruce Lee-like elements within it. The plot synopsis for *Twelve Gates of Hell* directed by Lee Hyeok-Su on the Korean Movie Database makes it sound like a different film. The most likely explanation for this is we have a badly butchered version faked up in Hong Kong to resemble something a complete idiot in the overdeveloped world might mistake for being 'Chinese'.

122 BRUCE VS BILL   1981
DIRECTED BY LAM KWOK-CHEUNG

Chinese American karate exponent Bill Louie ends up with a set of keys to a safe containing a huge amount of money intended for his country. Louie, a restaurant waiter in the movie, intervened when gang members attacked an old businessman who had the keys. The old man dies but before he does so he insists Louie gets the keys to the only man who knows the location of the safe. Alexander Grand, the Caucasian boss who heads the gang, is pissed at his underlings for failing to get the keys and killing one of only two men who know where the safe with all the money in it is. Grand tries both buying the keys from Louie and sending his men after him to take them—both ploys fail, at least initially. Bruce Le turns up when Louie and his sidekick Fung Yun-Chuen are fighting one of Grand's men—having already beaten off the rest of the gang. Le thinks Louie is bullying a beggar and attacks him. The fight is broken-up by Tin Ching who successfully appeals to their base patriotic and nationalistic sentiments by saying that Chinese shouldn't fight each other.

Next Grand tries to hire Le to kill Louie but Bruce turns him down. Through Grand, Le reconnects with his mistress (veteran actress Angela Yu Chien) a nightclub singer. In *Bruce Vs Bill* Chien looks at least twice Le's age, although in reality she was about 39 when it was shot. Chien is actually working for Grand and after spending a lot of time in bed with Le makes a really lame attempt to stab him. When Le first appears and at the end of the film, he has a talking parrot with him. The bird has all the best one-liners but it disappears for a long time; presumably replaced in Le's affections by Chien. The parrot and Le's white suit are two of the three best things in this movie; the third is Chiang Tao but more about him later. Despite not taking up Grand's offer of money for murder, Le seeks Louie out so that he can fight him. While Le battles Louie, Grand's men attempt to kill them both. Le realises he'll have to team up with the waiter if he wants to live. Grand's gang only ever gain the whip hand over Le and Louie by fighting dirty with burning chemicals and ropes.

However, even when captured by the gang and with his upper limbs bound, Le is able to kick their 'gweilo' boss face first into a handily located pile of poo! This makes Grand very cross, so he has Le and Louie chained to a railway track in the vain hope that a passing engine will kill them; a real old-time movie cliché. Using his legs, Le gets Grand into a headlock about 30 seconds before a train is about to run them down and the cowardly hood orders his gang to release the good guys from the tracks so that he isn't killed as well. Le and Louie hold onto the bottom of the moving train to get away. When they get inside a carriage they discover more hoods are onboard but successfully fight them off. Louie is desperate to give the key to the one man who should have it, but doesn't know how to get hold of him as he's only spoken to an emissary of this entrepreneur. Tin Ching tells Louie and his friend Fung Yun-Chuen he'll safe-house them in a property he has in the country. Louie stupidly gives the key to Chuen thinking it will be safer with him, despite the fact that his mate's kung fu is lousy!

When Tin Ching leaves them they hear him being beaten up. Chiang Tao has turned up with a big western fighter. Tin Ching is only pretending to be hurt, he's secretly working with Grand and the fighters who play act duffing him up. The villains set fire to the house. Louie manages to escape but Chuen is killed and the bad guys get the keys. When the dude the safe keys should have gone to turns up he sends his emissary to get Louie, but the hoods intercept the messenger and kill him. Then the ugliest heavy pretends to be Louie and asks the businessman to take him to the safe. He won't give the entrepreneur the keys until the besuited bourgeois proves to him he is their rightful owner by showing him they undo the lock. The hoods took the body of the entrepreneur's emissary to him alongside their cock and bull story. To keep his mark happy, the Louie impersonator orders three of the gang to bury the body. Even after the good guy they're successfully fooling into leading the gang to the safe disappears, they continue digging a grave until Louie turns up to kick their butts. Louie kills two of them and buries the third up to his neck in the grave he'd been digging, then sets fire to the grass and leaves around his head so that he'll reveal where the others have gone. Getting back on his bicycle, Louie peddles furiously to get to the house where the safe is. Bill takes out most of the gang but is having trouble with the top fighters until Bruce appears. Good prevails, the money is saved for Louie's country and even the parrot is happy because he is reunited with Bruce.

Le does make the odd Little Dragon-like gesture but these are few are far between. Alexander Grand was an extra in Bruce Lee's *Fist of Fury* and also appeared in a bunch of Brucesploitation movies including as 'James Bond" in *The Dragon Lives Again* (1977). The plot set up at the start of *Bruce Vs Bill* resembles Le's earlier *Bruce the Super Hero* (1979).

123 COLD BLOODED MURDER　　　1981
DIRECTED BY ALBERT LAW DO-BONG

Post credits Bruce Le fights crime boss Chiang Tao and some of his henchmen at a harbour. Le wins and since he's a cop he arrests the criminal. Cut to an unseen assailant murdering prostitutes. The butchery is depicted in a perfunctory fashion from the point of view of the killer. Each woman welcomes him and is quickly despatched. In the successive short sequences the otherwise unseen psychopath wears the same pair of bloodstained white gloves.

Following each of the three killings there is the same shot of the flashing top of a police car rushing through the streets. Next the film degenerates into soap opera with Michael Chan Wai-Man, his wife Yin and their baby, living in domestic hell. Life is hard, the baby is always crying and Wai-Man can't get a regular job so he takes whatever backbreaking work he can find. He does a bit of illegal street vending and gets busted by the cops. The baby is sick and Wai-Man's wife has trouble finding work too until she gets a break into prostitution. When Yin comes home from work she's 'too tired' to make love to Wai-Man. Soon after Wai-Man goes unannounced to Yin's work, taking their baby with him. She pushes him away so she can go off with a rich guy; to pile on the melodrama the baby is crying and gesturing for his momma to comfort him. Still holding the kid, Wai-Man is beaten by thugs who if they're not Yin's pimps, work for the guy she's with. Yin leaves Wai-Man to live with her boss or john. She decides she wants her baby so she goes with some thugs to collect him from Wai-Man.

In the ensuing fight Wai-Man is thrashed and a huge cupboard falls on the baby, as the tot doesn't appear again the accident must be fatal. A traumatised Wai-Man is instantly transformed into a nutzoid serial killer who murders any prostitute he can find called Yin. There follows a load of police procedural and cop shop politics. Carter Wong feels he's losing face because the chief has asked an old friend of his to help out with the prostitute killer case and his girlfriend is complaining she isn't seeing enough of him. Bruce Le is having clothing issues, in some scenes his dress sense drops so low he wears a white sweatshirt with the word 'Playboy' written across it. Judy the new girl is being subjected to sexual harassment and is forced to pose as a hooker in an attempt to lure the killer into a police trap. Wai-Man is enticed into the ambush but manages to escape. Meanwhile Chiang Tao is released from prison and has not only his gang but also Bolo Yeung—over from Thailand in the movie—waiting to greet him. Tao wants to get Bruce for busting him and sending him to jail, but Bolo says he'll take care of it. Bolo ambushes Bruce outside his home where an accomplice holds Judy at knifepoint. Just when Bruce looks like he's going to lose the fight, Judy frees herself from the thug and shoots at Bolo, who escapes in a car. A further distraction from the main plot thread in the central section is Wai-Man's wife Yin wanting to leave her new lover because he's lost all his money; they fight and the police are called.

Yin and her boyfriend fall to their deaths from a roof just as Bruce is about to jump in to save them.

When Carter Wong appears on TV to talk about the serial killer and presents the public with a photofit drawing of the suspect, Wai-Man goes apeshit. He not only smashes his TV, he stalks and kills Wong's girlfriend. The day after this murder Wong tells his colleagues he didn't sleep well the night before; he's presumably too buttoned up to admit that he's upset about the death of his girlfriend. The cops working on the prostitute murders go out together and Wong gets blind drunk. After this Wong spends a lot of time puking, which is graphically depicted.

When Bruce and Lau Dan take their boss back to his apartment the killer is waiting for him. Bruce and Dan hear a gunshot as they are leaving, so they race back to save Wong. A chase up the stairs to the roof of the building involves all three cops and gunfire. At the beginning of the movie the serial killer was a lousy fighter continually getting beaten up by low-level thugs, at the climax he is a skilled martial artist who looks like he'll get the better of the three cops in rooftop combat involving fists, feet and improvised weapons; by this point everyone seems to have run out of bullets. Pulling out all the stops and using a long metal pole as a spear, Bruce is able to snatch victory from the jaws of defeat and kill Wai Man. That would have made a good end but then there's the other plot strand about Chiang Tao to resolve. Bruce knows Tao and Bolo want to kill him, so he attacks Chiang's headquarters on his own. Le takes out some low-level thugs and defeats Bolo without any difficulty. Tao decides to run from Bruce but when the 'cop' catches up with him he puts up a good fight and is eventually defeated.

Despite the cameo from Bolo and Wai-Man sporting claw marks like Bruce Lee at the end of *Enter the Dragon*, inflicted by Wong's girlfriend before she's killed, *Cold Blooded Murder* has few clone-like moments. This flick is more notable for the number of times it portrays guys getting kicked in the nuts than as Brucesploitation!

124 ENTER THE INVINCIBLE HERO — 1981

AKA *DRAGONEER 13—THE SIGNIFICANT*

DIRECTED BY GODFREY HO AND/OR KIM SI-HYEON

The credit sequence features Dragon Lee's penultimate fight against Lee Hoi-Sang from *Enter Three Dragons* (1978) slightly altered by the insertion of freeze frames. Then bandits are robbing a convoy carrying money through rural Korea. The robbers' leader is a one-eyed hunchback. The raspberry is a great fighter who incorporates his deformity into his shapes as he cripples his opponents. Cut to Martin Chui Man-Kwai with a glowing medallion and a strange protrusion emerging from his belly button; he breaks a tree trunk in half by headbutting it as a demonstration of his martial arts skills. Lee Ye-Min comes to remonstrate with Man-Kwai. He wants the fighter—who fronts a transportation company—to compensate the villagers for their losses since his firm was paid to protect the money that was stolen by the bandits.

Cut to Ye-Min's daughter Seo Jeong-Ah who is inspecting the field in which the robbery took place. She wakes Dragon Lee who was apparently asleep in the pasture during the theft. Jeong-Ah jumps on her horse and canters away in fright. Dragon looks around and finds the type of knife used by his martial arts school, implicating someone connected with it to the robbery and attendant murders. Cut to Casanova Wong—with two topless musclemen bodyguards who accompany him everywhere—ordering Man-Kwai to pay the villagers the compensation he owes them. Man-Kwai acquiesces since Wong is the biggest and richest boss in the area.

Cut to Dragon Lee going into the village looking for a job. First he beats up some of Man-Kwai's goons after they start a fight with him, then he encounters Jeong-Ah again when he goes to her father's house to look for work; they argue and engage in some mutual face slapping. Dragon has a fight with another of boss number two's goons, this time in a restaurant rather than on the street.

Cut to Yi-Min counting his money, and then some bandits trying to rob him of the compensation he's just received. Jeong-Ah drags Dragon to her house and he beats up the bad guys. Man-Kwai turns up and offers Dragon a job, and they sign a contract specifying how our hero will defend the transportation company's convoys from bandits; he is to be well paid but if the goods are stolen he's financially responsible. On Dragon's first attempt at guard duty the hunchback and his gang turn up in the field where the previous robbery took place and there is a fight. The other guards cower in the background while Dragon takes on the bandits, he wins the battle but while he's engaged in combat the gang make off with the goods and money. Dragon is now massively in debt and he's told the only way he'll be able to come up with the necessary money is to offer himself in servitude to a local rich man—and number one mobster—Casanova Wong.

When Dragon goes to Wong's place he discovers this boss is a fellow student from his martial arts school who he'd helped out in the old days, and who still owes him a major favour. Wong gives Dragon the money he needs to pay back his debt. Casanova also recounts his own past, which includes a flashback—pasted in from *The Magnificent* (1979)—in which he performs an incredible series of continuous spinning kicks without a cut and involving no camera trickery! Everyone is happy and two men from the village collect the money from Wong. As they cross a bridge, Man-Kwai and his gang mortally wound the couriers and steal the dough. One of them makes it back to Yi-Min's house where Dragon is having tea with the village head and his daughter. The fatally wounded man manages to say the word 'bridge' before expiring. Dragon races to the crime scene where he finds one dead body and a valuable blue jewel that has fallen from Man-Kwai's belt.

Cut to Casanova Wong giving a kung fu demonstration; then discussing the recovery of the money he lent which he had his flunky steal from the villagers. Man-Kwai is working on Wong's orders. Dragon has a talk about the theft with Man-Kwai, and notices a blue jewel just like the one he found at the bridge is missing from the transportation company boss's belt. He stares at the girdle and the conversation shifts to it. Man-Kwai realises that Dragon knows he is responsible for the theft, and when he alerts Wong his boss is pissed off. Man-Kwai confronts Dragon at the bridge where the robbery took place and they fight. Despite Man-Kwai's seeming invulnerability, Dragon beats him by pulling on his belly button protrusion and about a metre of red chord comes out too.

After killing Man-Kwai, Dragon goes to confront Wong who he suspects of being the big boss. They have an argument and end up fighting. Wong wins the battle but doesn't kill Dragon. Since Dragon's kung fu is inferior to Wong's he is not a threat to him, and Casanova makes it clear his generosity in allowing his opponent to live finally repays the debt he owes him. Dragon hides in the hills and trains until he can punch through paper without any movement from the sheet, and smash his fist into a barrel of water without splashing. Having achieved his training goals, he rushes outside to tell Jeong-Ah and finds her skinny-dipping. Angry that Dragon hasn't left the area but is hiding in the hills, Wong has his goons murder Yi-Min. Next the hunchback and a few other men are sent to confront Dragon, but they end up dead. Dragon goes to Wong's HQ where he is confronted by what looks like an old man, who then pulls off his disguise to reveal that he's actually Wong's goon who sports a mohawk hairstyle. The English dub supplies no reason for this, but it presumably indicates a plot strand ditched from the English version of the flick. Dragon defeats this man and a whole series of other goons prior to his climatic fight with Wong. Despite some excellent kicking, including spinning kicks, Wong is defeated by Dragon. All in all a typical old school Korean actioner that has little to do with Bruce Lee!

125 ENTER THE KING OF KUNG FU — 1981

AKA *ZEN KWAN DO STRIKES PARIS*
AKA *KUNG FU LEUNG STRIKES EMMANUELLE*
AKA *KUNG FU EMMANUELLE*
DIRECTED BY JOHN LIU

Writer and director John Liu stars in this loosely autobiographical flick about a man who set up some Zen Kwan Do martial arts schools in Europe and has affairs with a series of women. Liu's real-life half-French daughter Natasha even appears as an extra. After a scandal brought on by his womanising—tediously recounted in voice-over and flashback—Liu moves to Hong Kong but when his scientist father is kidnapped, he returns to Paris to help the police search for pops.

The story is contrived and confused, and in the English cut a number of plot elements—like what happened to the kidnapped father—are never resolved. The flashbacks to Liu's womanising and his readiness to involve himself with any pretty face really draw out the relationship between martial arts and porn film actors in terms of the different but still repetitive and stereotypical physical performances expected from them.

One wonders what Liu's wife Marion Blank—who was a producer on this film—made of Liu's onscreen womanising given the flick's autobiographical nature and the fact that in the English cut he is playing himself as a former kung fu instructor turned movie 'star'.

There is no nudity in the English version I've seen, just some romantic fumbling, but Liu does his trademark splits and high kicking routines. The tourist shots of Paris are clichéd: Eiffel Tower, River Seine, Pompidou Centre etc. The acting and pacing are terrible too. Liu fights various Caucasian martial artists but doesn't do anything we haven't seen him do before; he creams Dan Schwartz playing an American karate champion in an absurd stars and stripes gi. Liu's gi is referred to as a kimono in the English dub. Liu would have looked far groovier in a dress than his taekwondo outfit! If Lui had been a tranny he may have been less prone to being suckered by 'seductive' women and had more fun with other men. Liu's master in Hong Kong sends a back up fighter to support him in Paris; this dude battles with a cane and looks like he might be using the hybrid oriental and European system of self-defence known as Bartitsu.

As well as being released *as Enter the King of Kung Fu*, this features a couple of shots of a hoarding with Bruce Lee in his *Game of Death* yellow jumpsuit, and a short discussion of Liu's Zen Kwan Do and the Little Dragon's Jeet Kune Do. Whether Zen Kwan Do was actually developed by Liu or his real life 'master' Dorian Tan is a moot point.

126 THE FURIOUS — 1981

AKA *THE FURIOUS KILLER*
DIRECTED BY JOSEPH VELASCO

This starts in Indonesia. The location is established by a panning city shot during the opening credits that shows a huge advertising hoarding for the 'milk champions' Indomilk; what can be read of the poster runs 'susu para juara Indomilk'. Next there are a couple of low level street drug sales, then a cut to another dealer who goes into a derelict building where he passes wraps around. Mixed in with the junkies are undercover cops who move to make arrests; there's a bit of a fight and the dealer runs off. Over funky beats there is a chase past rickety shacks to an open storage area where lots of large metal barrels are stacked up.

After a fight an undercover cop arrests the dealer. At the police station the hood is offered freedom for information about his boss. The cops then stake out a beach where their target Michael Chan Wai-Man is receiving a drug delivery from a boat. A bunch of children wander into the scene and to facilitate his getaway, Wai-Man grabs a chubby kid as a hostage and menaces him with a gun. A car chase with more funky beats results in the death of two motorcycle cops and the young hostage; Wai-Man gets out of his motor before it explodes, the kid doesn't. Our anti-hero has his gear but soon discovers things are two hot for him in Indonesia, so he skips to Hong Kong.

So far there's been an ever-changing array of cops and villains—including some recognisable Chinese film faces in an interior scene that was probably filmed in the British colony—now we can settle down to Wai-Man as the main criminal. Carter Wong and a visiting Indonesian sidekick become the chief law enforcement officers.

There are Jess Franco-style shaky camera shots from vehicles as Wai-Man travels around Hong Kong. While Velasco deploys speed and Franco utilises slowness, ultimately the narrative destroying effect of these opposed strategies leads to the same anti-cinematic nirvana. Wai-Man hooks up with Hong Kong crime boss Ku Feng. The fugitive not only wants to sell his drugs, he wants to join the gang buying them. Feng agrees to this if Wai-Man carries out three tasks for him, which is basically to wipe out Lo Lieh's rival organisation. So Wai-Man busts into a hotel and beats up some hoods who are gambling, then after dousing their room with petrol and setting a fire, he locks them in the inferno. One hood survives and this gives Velasco an excuse to include an exterior shot of Queen Elizabeth Hospital in Hong Kong, which is internationally famous for its dead Bruce Lee connection. The foot soldier is so badly burnt he can't talk. Wong tells the gangbanger to close his eyes to answer yes to questions. When shown a picture of Wai-Man the hood closes his peepers and the inspector learns this is the psychopath responsible for the attack. Next Wai-Man goes to a gym to murder a heavy. He gets the muscleman out of a shower and after some back and forth fight action, strangles him with cloth from a towel dispenser.

The final target is Lo Lieh himself, who we are introduced to having fun with a topless woman. Wai-Man breaks in on the sexual athletics by shimmying down a rope and climbing in through an open window, but Lieh is aware of the intruder before he strikes. With Lieh's men streaming in from the next room, Wai-Man has to escape back out through the window and haul himself onto the roof. Lieh and a goon run up the stairs to confront Wai-Man. The minion is taken out, and when Lieh seems to be getting the better of Wai-Man, the furious killer pulls a poisoned needle from the waistband of his trousers and stabs it into his opponent's throat. Wong and other cops arrive a few moments too late to catch Wai-Man; who they realise must be working with Ku Feng because he's going after the rival gang.

The cops try to get Wai-Man when he goes to meet Feng, he escapes but the gang are overwhelmed. In the process Wai-Man loses the money he'd just got from Feng for his drugs. With few options in Hong Kong, Wai-Man goes to Thailand. The authorities know he has a brother there, so Wong and his Indonesian sidekick go to Bangkok. After a nice exterior shot of the airport, there is a cute tourist montage that is similar but very much superior to the one seen in *Clones of Bruce Lee* (1980); it isn't the same footage and it may or may not have been shot at the same time as the Bangkok material in *Clones*.

Wong and the Indonesian cop take out and tie-up the gang led by Wai-Man's brother, then sit and wait for their prey to turn up. Despite being gagged, the gang leader creates a disturbance when his sibling arrives, so forewarned Wai-Man runs off. The two cops chase him and use their guns to total his car. A brief foot chase culminates in a fight and the fuzz emerge victorious. This is another classic slice of Velasco trashola; although I suspect he may not be responsible for the scenes shot in Indonesia or the Bangkok tourist montage. That said, this has nothing to do with Brucesploitation and I'm only providing an overview of it here because Kung Fu Theatre issued it on DVD in Region 1 in 2006 with a cover blurb claiming it was a Bruce Le movie: "The action is fast and furious as international police chase 'The Rattlesnake', a notorious drug lord, on a trail of death and destruction across South East Asia. Only Bruce Le can put an end to 'The Rattlesnake' when they meet in a deadly game of fierce Kung Fu action… Winner takes all!"

This release and an earlier VHS tape from Best Film & Video, with a cover that likewise falsely advertises the flick as a star vehicle for Bruce Le, have led to *The Furious* being invoked on odd occasions in discussions of Brucesploitation. The choreography here is at times of the ultra-old school basher variety with arms simply being swung and flailed at full extension. The only thing I didn't like was the dreadful soundtrack music when the cops busted up a nightclub. However this musical slip doesn't spoil the movie. I should also mention that there is a tracking flaw at the top of the picture throughout the film on the Kung Fu Theatre release; since the 2007 Canadian DVD version of the flick on Substance doesn't suffer from this fault it is superior, despite also being an absolutely shit full-screen transfer from a VHS tape.

127 Dragon Force — 1982

AKA *Power Force*

Directed by Michael Mak

A Bruce Baron work out is intercut with the titles. Afterwards Baron goes undercover on a crime syndicate in Rhode Island, and once they sell him diamonds he reveals he's a cop. There is a shoot out which Baron wins. Then we are in the lair of the chess-playing main villains as a newscast relays the death of the King of Mongrovia. Russian terrorists force the plane in which the king's heir 'Princess' Mandy Moore was travelling to make an emergency landing in Hong Kong. Moore goes to stay with former Miss Hong Kong Olivia Cheng and her brother Richard. The latter is a cokehead whose lines include: "You can call me Rich because I am."

Moore is kidnapped from her bath by masked ninjas. Some of her staff, most notably Jovy Coudrey are actually working undercover for the Russians. Baron is taking a break from undercover work but gets called in to sort things out. The geo-political significance of Mongrovia is explained to him by his boss. It is the only source for a special stainless steel that both the Americans and Russians are after. If he hadn't died the king would have signed a contract to provide this material—which is crucial to the construction of nuclear power plants—to the USA. Baron's contact in Hong Kong is Ah Chu at The Good Fu-King Flour Co. When shown a picture of the premises with the name written above it, Baron asks his boss how to pronounce it and gets the reply: "I wouldn't even begin to try." Presumably American secret agents don't use the f-word. There are also sneezing jokes with regard to Ah Chu's name; this contact offers to sell Baron some James Bond-style gadgets. The American agent isn't buying even when he's offered thirty percent off on bulletproof T-shirts. Baron is sent to meet local crime busters Dragon Force at the Tiptoe Forest. Before Dragon Force will work with Baron they want to test him to see if he's any good, so after a series of fights —and about a third of the way into the movie—Bruce Li pops up in a supporting role. Li is head of Dragon Force and Baron is initiated into this crime fighting fraternity in a ceremony that is so cheesy it makes Freemasonic rituals look sophisticated.

Aside from Li, the other members of Dragon Force are Si Ming, a bald kung fu fighter and a samurai. They take even more of a backseat in this movie than our clone. Dragon Force proceed to run around Hong Kong chasing people and having fights with ninjas. Baron gets hit by a poisoned ninja star, but unfortunately Li cures him with the kiss of a cobra, which sucks the badness out. In order to track down the villains, Dragon Force plant their female operative as a singer in a nightclub, where the bad guy's chief torturer and serial rapist Tong Tin Hei picks up showgirls. Tong is enraptured by Ming who tricks him into swallowing a bug so that he can be tracked. Tong tries hard to get it on with Ming, but she's too tough for him.

When Tong goes back to HQ a tracking device alarm alerts his Russian masters to the fact that Dragon Force know where they are. A bit later Tong is killed for his stupidity. Having the location of their HQ rumbled forces the bad guys to bring forward their mind control operation on Mandy Moore. Her hair shorn, she sits nude and drugged as a man paints Chinese characters over her body and then sticks acupuncture needles into her. Dragon Force bust into the secret HQ and get to fight more ninjas, but chief bad guy James Barnett gets away with the now totally zombified Moore.

There is some slapstick based around the fact that Barnett is fat and thus has to be pushed through a door by his underlings to escape. When he pretends to be trapped in the door of a helicopter, it is obvious he could easily get through it on his own if the script didn't demand otherwise. Dragon Force 'rescue' Jovy Coudrey who they think was kidnapped with the Princess. They wise up when Ming catches Coudrey using a transmitter to alert the Russians to where they are. Ming locks Coudrey up and goes to get Li. By the time she returns a ninja has broken into the room and killed Coudrey with a sword. The ninja leaves behind a printed invitation from Barnett for Dragon Force to come to his island for lunch. Li knows this is a trap but figures that attending is the best way to get the criminals. Li, Baron and the rest of Dragon Force get a polite reception until Sam Sorono—the ugliest bodybuilder among Barnett's henchmen, and possibly some kind of monster created by the Russians—challenges Li's bald kung fu fighting sidekick. The Dragon Force operative kills Sorono. Soon the team's samurai is fighting, and finally the whole crew are doing variations on the Ali shuffle. Ninjas throw bombs at Baron and Li but they bat them back with bamboo poles causing exploding masked men in orange suits to clutter up the screen. When Baron and Li grab Mandy Moore they have to knock her unconscious because the zombified princess tries to kill them with a knife. It looks like Barnett is going to escape on a speedboat, but Baron machine guns it, causing a big explosion. All that remains is for Li to undo the mind control on Moore using his acupuncture skills; not shown but spoken about afterwards.

One of the things that makes this film particularly shit are its light orchestral music cues, but actually everything about it is bad. By all rights it should have sunk without trace. Although he's the absolute pits, Bruce Baron has a cult following based on his work for Godfrey Ho; director Michael Mak went on to make the massively successful Hong Kong Category III (i.e. softcore porn) hit *Sex and Zen* (1991). Thankfully, after this there was no more cinematic cloning around for the bland Bruce Li, it was his last film. Beyond Barnett's island HQ—which vaguely resembles Han's Island in Bruce Lee's Hollywood vehicle—*Dragon Force* has little in the way of 'king of kung fu' references.

128 SECRET NINJA, ROARING TIGER 1982

AKA *SECRET NINJA*

DIRECTED BY GODFREY HO AND/OR KIM SI-HYEON

A man approaches Tiger's castle and after identifying himself as a ninja is taken to see Hwang Jang-Lee. The two men know each other and the visitor accuses Hwang of killing their master. The man starts fighting and is soon killed. Although others confront him at first, it's Hwang who eliminates the intruder. Simultaneously there is the semi-return of the barechested musclemen who were Casanova Wong's bodyguards in *Enter the Invincible Hero* (1981), but now they're acting as shadows to Hwang. The uglier of the two is a bodyguard from the earlier flick, the other bodybuilder looks like a new recruit. Hwang tells his best fighter Chew he is to take part in a contest for the hand of Lee Ye-Min's daughter Susan. At the marriage competition we catch glimpses of Lim Ja-Ho and Seo Jeong-Ah in the crowd, who will team up with Dragon later in the movie. Dragon arrives after Chew has been crowned the champion. While those officiating the competition insist it is over, Chew is so confident in his abilities as a fighter that he says he'll take on Dragon regardless. Chew does his trick of standing on one leg, while holding the other absolutely straight against his body so that he has a foot above his head, before bringing the limb down to heel kick his opponent. Despite Chew's incredible flexibility, he is beaten by Dragon. Chew tells his friends Dragon is a good fighter, and one of the ninjas present says: "We will have to get him!"

Dragon goes off to seek the permission of his sifu to marry. Meanwhile, Jeong-Ah sneaks into Susan's bedroom to tell her that they are sisters, and Ye-Min isn't really her father. Jeong-Ah also tells Susan that their pops was murdered ten years ago, and shows her a scar she got at that time. This exchange is interrupted by knocking sounds. We cut to the main gate being opened, no one is visible to the servant who answers, but ninjas sneak in. By the time two sword-wielding ninjas break into Susan's bedroom, Jeong-Ah has disappeared. The ninjas put Susan in a sack and carry her off. Later Jeong-Ah is in a roadside café where she overhears one of Yi-Min's men ask if the owner has seen anything strange. As soon as he leaves the servant is attacked and murdered by ninjas. Jeong-Ah starts a fight with the killers; after Lim Ja-Ho jumps in to help her, they triumph. Jeong-Ah persuades Ja-Ho to accompany her to Tiger's castle, then they battle some more ninjas. We cut to Dragon Lee being enticed into a restaurant by a ninja disguised as a ladyboy. Although Dragon plans to marry Susan, it seems he's open to other sexual adventures. He gets suspicious after feeling up the ladyboy and realising how rough and hairy his leg is. The ladyboy punches Dragon and then the tranny and a ninja comrade who is also in the restaurant, pull off their disguises and fight Susan's fiancé. As Dragon defeats them, Ja-Ho and Jeong-Ah turn up. When Ja-Ho tells the victor he is good, Dragon replies: "That hurt a lot, I was nearly beaten by a transvestite."

Apparently already knowing that Susan's been kidnapped, Dragon agrees to accompany his new friends to the ninja castle. We then cut to Hwang doing ritual magic, and two of his men sparring. One uses monkey style, the other has the tops of his index fingers missing and is able to tickle the animal fighter from a distance using a special technique. The monkey expert pulls down the pants of the tickle master, who has a pornographic text strapped to his leg. Hwang is angry because his society has nothing to do with women. Hwang has more success than Jeong-Ah in convincing Susan that Yi-Min isn't her father, but she still doesn't want to go along with the Ninja Society's plans for her and her fake dad's dosh.

Meanwhile Dragon, Ja-Ho and Jeong-Ah get into more battles with ninjas. While looking at Jeong-Ah's backside after lying down to sleep, Dragon goes into a reverie in which his comrade—who until this point he'd believed was a man—strips for him. He can now see she is a woman. Dragon and Ja-Ho confront Jeong-Ah but everything is resolved after she explains she's only dressing up as a young boy in order to save her sister. Ja-Ho insists that both he and Dragon prefer Jeong-Ah as a woman; some viewers may be less than convinced about this after watching Dragon's lustful response to the ninja ladyboy—and many westerners will lack sufficient immersion in South East Asian culture to read Jeong-Ah's character as a gender-bender until the point is explicitly explained through dialogue as her masquerade unravels.

The next day as our heroic trio make their way to Tiger's castle, there are more battles. The most notable of these occurs when Dragon is attacked after he emerges from bathing in a pool. Dragon has wrapped a towel around his lower regions, but we get a good view of his bum as he tries save both himself and his modesty. Ja-Ho jumps in and sees off the ninja. Dragon disappears and turns up again at the end of the fight fully dressed. Back at his castle, Hwang is holding Ye-Min, as well as Susan, captive. In front of both Susan and Hwang's men, Ye-Min reveals that he saw the current leader of the Ninja Society murder its old master ten years ago. Hwang is so angered about his duplicity being exposed to his minions that he kills Ye-Min on the spot.

Shortly afterwards, Susan seduces Hwang. She's hidden a knife in her bed and hopes to kill him; before she grabs the weapon there is a relatively long sex scene in which our two protagonists appear to enjoy getting busy with each other. This isn't very credible given that according to the plot Susan hates the man she's getting it on with, and his warrior ideology prohibits him becoming involved with women.

When Susan finally attempts to deploy the knife, Hwang quickly disarms her. Dragon and his crew are approaching the castle and getting into more fights with ninjas. A nude Susan is whipped by Hwang's musclemen, and then harangued by their master. Having fought their way into Hwang's stronghold, and defeated everyone except the boss ninja and his two musclemen, Jeong-Ah goes to free Susan while Dragon and Ja-Ho wait outside to confront the super-kicking villain in a final showdown. First the sword swinging musclemen are disposed of as Hwang watches from above. Then Dragon and Ja-Ho jump up into the room where the boss ninja has ensconced himself. Hwang seems to be getting the better of our two heroes, until Jeong-Ah and Susan turn up outside. Susan flashes her tits at Hwang, which distracts him sufficiently for Dragon and Ja-Ho to win the fight with a lot of acrobatics. The film ends with Dragon and Susan, and Jeong-Ah and Ja-Ho, walking off as two happy couples.

129 THEY CALL ME BRUCE 1982
DIRECTED BY ELLIOTT HONG

Johnny Yune plays a Korean working as a cook and waiter for mafia bosses in California. The mobsters are portrayed as stereotyped Italians and Yune is an everyman Asian (rather than Korean) who people associate with Bruce Lee and assume is a kung fu expert; he's actually hopeless at fighting. Yune joins a dojo but is kicked out; wandering off with a pair of nunchaku, he knocks himself out while simultaneously foiling a grocery store robbery. He is hailed a hero and seeing the media coverage of his cook as a deadly kung fu expert, his mafia employer decides to send Yune off with Raf Mauro to make cocaine deliveries across America. Yune thinks he's delivering special Chinese flour and doesn't realise he's transporting drugs. The martial arts trained girlfriend of a rival mafiosa and a head kicking female karate cop are on his trail; the rozzer secretly protects our man along the way. There are some drug jokes, and when Yune finally gets to New York, the cops bust the boss of bosses and reveal to our fish out of water hero that he was trafficking coke. Since the fuzz had Yune bugged and realise he wasn't knowingly involved in crime, he's free to go and find the lady his grandfather told him about. When Yune's grandpops visited the USA as a sailor, he fell in love with the Statue of Liberty, which represents America itself. Some think this movie funny. I found it a total bore. Gags involving nunchucks used as chopsticks failed to amuse me; as did jokes about the food Yune makes tasting good thanks to his use of dog meat. Bruce Lee functions as just another signifier among the many stereotypes deployed here. The many movies spoofed in this include *Saturday Night Fever* (1977), *From Russia With Love* (1963) and *The Godfather* (1972), and they aren't even martial arts flicks!

130 5 PATTERN DRAGON CLAWS 1983
AKA *FISTS OF LIGHTNING*
AKA *THUNDERFIST*
AKA *THUNDERING FIST*
DIRECTED BY GODFREY HO AND/OR KIM SI-HYEON

The Du Mar Temple has regular martial arts competitions with the best fighters getting to learn the secret Shaolin kung fu techniques contained in four heavily guarded instruction manuals. Local thugs laugh at the five new students. One of the winners is so keen to learn the secrets that he steals the books. The abbot guarding them wakes up during this audacious theft and the student murders him. While arguing with his girlfriend about what he's done because he wants her to flee with him, he is caught red handed by Master Kwok. While the girl sticks around, Kwok and the naughty student disappear. Since the Du Mar Temple now lacks leadership, local thugs make their move and kill monks and disciples. Kwok and the naughty student are engaged in existential self-torture over their transgressions. Kwok blames himself as much as the top student for the murder of the abbot. The remaining four students are told they should take one book each, but Dragon Lee is the best of them and he decides the books should stay together. The Du Mar Temple is under continual attack by the bad guys who eventually take it over after killing most of the students. Hwang Jang-Lee wants to prove he's the best fighter in the region, and have his brother ranked number two. Hwang defeats Dragon who is the top remaining student. Dragon is left for dead but he's discovered by an old hermit and nursed back to health. Although it is obvious the old man is Master Kwok, Dragon doesn't figure this out but it is eventually revealed to him. He learns that the naughty number one student was so overcome by remorse for killing the abbot that he's committed suicide. To counter Hwang's thunder foot kick, Kwok teaches Dragon the thunder fist. Eventually the two men go off to challenge the gang that are terrorising the Du Mar Temple and have stolen its gold Buddha. Kwok is killed in the showdown with Hwang but Dragon triumphs. A cheap lighting strike effect is shown on screen every time a thunder foot kick or thunder fist punch is used. These moves burn clothing too!

Dragon seems more subdued in this movie than usual and refrains from doing his trademark Bruce Lee nose thumbing muggings. Many of the actors are dubbed into English with extremely camp voices. While the simple plot line and training sequences make this a very generic old school Korean martial arts movie, the cheapness of the sets and Hwang's kicking lift it into a higher dimension of trash cinema.

131 LEE THE ANGRY MAN   1983

AKA *ANGRY YOUNG MAN*

DIRECTED BY WONG SING-LOY

A group of young men bicker among themselves. There are conflicts over girls and obscure events, which we gradually discover are due to a couple of the guys having involved themselves with a criminal gang. The men fight, although initially these are Jackie Chan style comedy battles, go bowling and to a disco with their 'gals'. In a generically sexist plot, the women play secondary roles. There is some discussion of martial arts and patriotism, but nonetheless these Taiwanese men decide to learn Japanese karate. The conflicts with the criminal gang escalate, the connections some of the friends have with it are exposed, there are kidnap attempts and torture. Eventually the friends—even those who joined the gang—unite against the criminals, and there is a showdown at a construction site involving much dodging of vehicles. The victorious but battered heroes are soon reminded that they are late for their karate grading. Hwang Jang-Lee turns up an hour into the movie as the main Japanese villain, and simply sits around for twenty minutes as the top banana observing gradings at a local karate dojo. The Japanese and some Taiwanese ass lickers pick on students and beat them up. Eventually the trio who have just triumphed against the criminal gang use kung fu to defeat karate. That said, with his trademark high kicking, Hwang Jang-Lee's moves look much more like taekwondo during his few minutes of screen fighting than the Japanese martial art he's supposedly deploying. Lee underlines that his Taiwanese opponents have switched from karate to kung fu by observing after an attack has been made on him: "It's the butterfly style!"

This has absolutely nothing to do with Bruce esploitation and belongs to the outer limits of the genre. To me not even the title suggests Bruce Lee, although I've dealt with the film here because some English language fu fans seem to think it does. Casey Scott on dvddrive-in.com (he's reviewing the Something Weird DVD *Karate: The Hand of Death* which includes the *Lee the Angry Man* trailer as an extra) rhetorically asks: "Guess who the title is supposed to be based on?" Scott deemed it unnecessary to answer this question, but as he describes neither the main character in the film called Lee—who emphasises in a speech that his is a 'Chinese' name—nor the guest star Hwang Jang-Lee, one can conclude that based on a viewing of the trailer and not the whole film, this online reviewer saw it as an attempt at Brucesploitation. I'd view it as closer to Hwangsploitation since fans of this martial arts actor who check out this flick because their favourite bootmaster is in it will be gravely disappointed by his modest role. Wong Sing-Loy also directed the Brucesploitation bio-pic *The Dragon Lives* (1976), and that film is also a turkey.

132 MARTIAL MONKS OF SHAOLIN TEMPLE   1983

DIRECTED BY GODFREY HO AND/OR AN UNIDENTIFIED SOUTH KOREAN AUTEUR

The evil Wu Dan gym led by Hwang Jang-Lee are murdering those Shaolin fighters who won't abandon their school to join the ranks of his killer elite. They even assassinate the Grand Abbot of the Shaolin Temple. Dragon Lee goes undercover to get revenge. Initially he pretends to be a travelling entertainer. His act is more or less the same as the fat comic in *Bruce Lee's Ways of Kung Fu* (1977), he offers people the chance to cut off his head and if they fail he keeps their money. Meanwhile to establish his credentials as a (fake) Buddhist monk, Martin Chui Man-Kwai intervenes when a fried chicken eating bad guy is trying to terrorise a rich man. The man with meat stuck in his beard battles Man-Kwai with an oversize sword; when he realises he is losing, this Korean Accattone gets his men to hold his giant weapon and he pulls a smaller and thinner sword out of his mega-blade. He is now able to fight more nimbly but Man-Kwai still trounces him.

Next Man-Kwai exposes Dragon's slice-my-head-off challenge as a worthless scam, so our hero becomes a waiter at the inn where the fake monk is staying. Also wandering around is pickpocket and Shaolin Temple fan Seo Jeong-Ah. She steals the winnings Man-Kwai makes from beating Dragon, then returns the money when she goes to see the great Buddhist monk at the inn and is fooled into believing she stole from a holy man. Dragon loses his job but Man-Kwai persuades the inn-keeper to let him have it back. Shortly afterwards, Jeong-Ah tells Dragon that Man-Kwai is the Grandmaster of the Shaolin Temple. He must know this isn't true but goes along with it so that he can find those who killed the Grand Abbot. Man-Kwai offers to make Dragon his student after seeing the young man's physical skills as he works; guessing, as he later reveals, that Dragon is an undercover Shaolin monk.

To decide the student issue, Dragon and Man-Kwai have a food eating competition; they have to see who can eat a bowl of rice laid before them by snatching the food from each other. Man-Kwai wins so Dragon becomes his disciple. Man-Kwai accompanied by Jeong-Ah has Dragon carry his things as they embark on a long journey. Along the way they encounter a man who says he's been travelling for three months to fight Man-Kwai. The challenger wins but since he is Man-Kwai's student from earlier on—who had fought and lost against Dragon—the result is rigged. Dragon says he'll fight the man but if he wins the defeated fake monk has to become his student. This comes to pass and so a role reversal ensues in which Dragon treats Man-Kwai as badly as he was when he'd been the disciple. All of this is a set up to lead Dragon into a Wu Dan trap. Eventually a bunch of bad guys attack Dragon in the street, with Man-Kwai assisting them in the assault. Dragon is tied up and taken to see Hwang Jang-Lee, who has him unbound so that they can fight; during the course of this combat Dragon ends up with scratches across his face a bit like Bruce Lee in *Enter the Dragon* (1973).

Dragon loses the brawl but is allowed to live if he licks the soul of Hwang's shoe—and this comes to pass in a sequence that should have gay foot fetish enthusiasts queuing up to see this movie. Dragon is put in a prison cell and Jeong-Ah is placed in service to Hwang. Then the guy who falsely claimed he'd travelled for months to have the earlier fight with Man-Kwai turns up; with Jeong-Ah's help he frees the imprisoned Dragon. Jeong-Ah nurses Dragon, while Man-Kwai and his goons search for him. When the bad guys approach the dwelling in which

Dragon has recuperated, Man-Kwai's ex-student confronts his ex-master and tells him he's decided to follow Dragon. Man-Kwai insists he threw the fight in the rice field, presumably thinking this victory is what turned the pupil against him. The two men battle and Man-Kwai's ex-student is killed. While this is going on, Dragon and Jeong-Ah escape.

A bit later, a different set of Hwang's goons catch up with Dragon and Jeong-Ah while they're doing their laundry. Dragon fights and beats the bad guys, but while he's doing this Jeong-Ah is kidnapped. Dragon has a flashback to training a student monk at the Shaolin Temple. We cut to Jeong-Ah tied up with her arms spread in a crucifixion pose and her clothes torn and disarrayed. Hwang figures that Dragon will have to come to his HQ in a bid to rescue Jeong-Ah; the girl reveals that the big boss of the bad guys killed her father ten years earlier. Moments later there is a commotion outside because Dragon is beating up Hwang's hoods. Convention dictates that the penultimate fight should be between Dragon and Man-Kwai, with the latter defeated. Before the final face off with Hwang, Dragon removes his shirt so that we can admire his cut upper body. Despite Dragon using spears and nunchaku, Hwang is getting the better of him until the student monk who was introduced in the flashback immediately after Jeong-Ah's kidnap suddenly jumps into the fight from nowhere. Together Dragon and his student defeat Hwang. The movie ends with this exchange between Dragon and Jeong-Ah. Girl: "So tell me where do we go from here?" Boy: "There's a temple on the hill, let's get married."

With regard to Godfrey Ho it seems improbable that he directed *Martial Monks of the Shaolin Temple*; the ensemble of actors used make Kim Si-Hyeon a likely candidate for being the 'auteur' at work here. Note the nunchucks sequence is cut from the one UK release I've watched of this film, it can be seen on US versions.

133 THE LAST DRAGON — 1985
DIRECTED BY MICHAEL SCHULTZ

This is a Motown production. It looks like a series of MTV promotional videos with a martial arts subplot to string them together into something resembling a movie. Taimak is a sexually naïve and Bruce Lee obsessed youngster with a hip beyond his years younger brother. Our hero wants to reach the final level of martial arts mastery that he calls 'the glow'. The sifu he hopes will teach him this ultimate kung fu technique turns out to be a computer in a fortune cookie factory; making the flick seem closer to *The Wiz* (1978) than *Enter the Dragon* (1973). Along the way there is a showdown in a cinema where Bruce Lee's Hollywood star vehicle is being screened, and other clips of Lee are worked in at other points; including Vanity teaching Taimak about adult love by screening the Little Dragon's only screen kiss, with Nora Miao. Given that when this was made Vanity was a crackhead who'd romantically involved herself with a series of rich pop stars ranging from Prince to Adam Ant, Billy Idol to Nikki Sixx, and eventually had a short lived marriage to professional American footballer and later convicted killer Anthony Smith, her attraction to straight-edged Taimak is hilariously unlikely. Julius Carry plays Taimak's nemesis and this evil character already has the glow. Fighting Carry at the end of the movie, Taimak finally realises how to look inside himself for true martial arts mastery, defeating his enemy and getting the girl. Vanity was still a decade away from cleaning up from drugs and finding her highs as a born again Christian. While this film is superior to *No Retreat, No Surrender* (1986), neither movie is likely to appeal to anyone who was already teenage at the start of eighties; the cheese and nostalgia factors will work best for those who hit puberty at the time these films were made, or perhaps later. Unless you were born between about 1972 and 1985, it's unlikely this flick will groove you. The real talent here—in the form of Norman Whitfield, Willie Hutch and other Motown veterans –manifests itself on the soundtrack rather than onscreen. For me this is a teen musical with some kung fu and a bunch of Little Dragon clips thrown in; since I don't view it as a martial arts movie I don't see it as Brucesploitation.

134 FUTURE HUNTERS — 1986
AKA *SPEAR OF DESTINY*
DIRECTED BY CIRIO H. SANTIAGO

This starts in a post-nuclear apocalypse scenario with Richard Norton being chased through the wasteland in 2025. The landscape looks more like the coast around Manila than the post-nuke Los Angeles it is supposed to be. Norton is captured and escapes. Ten minutes later he gets his hands on his own Holy Grail, a glow in the dark spearhead! This entire pre-credits section is a low-budget *Mad Max* rip-off. Cut to mid-eighties present where viewers are confronted by possibly the most repulsive screen couple of all time; Linda Carol as academically inclined heiress Michelle and Robert Patrick as her gold-digging ex-Marine boyfriend Slade. Linda is doing anthropological research in an old temple outside LA. Slade is whining that with her money Michelle doesn't need to bother with this shit. The temple Michelle is investigating is where Norton has recovered the Spear of Destiny; called the Spear of Longinus throughout the English dub of the movie. Longinus was the name of the soldier who is supposed to have pierced Jesus with his spear. Since the publication of Trevor Ravenscroft's *The Spear of Destiny* (1973), there has been much speculation among conspiracy theorists about the Nazis using Longinus's weapon as part of an occult programme to achieve power. Much of Ravenscroft's information supposedly came from a man called Walter Stein. About a decade after *The Spear of Destiny* was published, Ravenscroft admitted that he hadn't actually met Stein when he was alive, but rather he'd had conversations about Nazi occultism with Stein's spirit. This is of relevance because the plotline of *Future Hunters* is based in part on such crackpot speculation.

In the movie the bad guys who are after the Spear of Destiny are Nazis who want to exterminate in a nuclear holocaust what they stupidly configure as impure races. When Michelle and Slade emerge from the temple they are attacked by bikers. Presumably having used the mystic power of the Spear of Destiny, Norton emerges from the future just as Michelle is about to be raped and saves her. Unfortunately he's shot doing this. Before he dies, Norton entrusts Michelle with the head of the Spear of Destiny, saying she must get it to Professor Hightower. The next day Michelle is threatened by Nazis who are after the occult relic. She goes looking for Professor Hightower and discovers he was last heard of doing research in Hong Kong. After being chased and shot at by more fascist goons, Michelle flies from LA to Hong Kong with Slade. Slade's old buddy Bruce Le—wrongly credited as Bruce Li in the titles—is waiting to meet them. Leaving Michelle at a hotel, Bruce and Slade go looking for Professor Hightower at the last place he is known to have visited, a temple. Being a whining tosser, Slade gets in a fight with the Silver Fox guardian of the temple played by Hwang Jang-Lee. Bruce has to help Slade since this dork's marine combat training won't save him from Hwang's thunder kicks! Bruce also does some muscle flexing, which is a gay groove.

Unfortunately the fight scene between Le and Hwang is cut short by a sniper who kills the Silver Fox. Back at the hotel Michelle is under attack from Nazi thugs. She is saved from a serious sexual assault by the return of Bruce and Slade. It transpires that Professor Hightower has gone to Manila, so it's goodbye to Bruce Le and on to The Philippines. There are more scrapes with Nazi goons. Michelle is kidnapped and Slade has a car chase all the way to the fascist HQ.

Some of those who've reviewed this film think there is a continuity error here because the pursuit starts at night and concludes in daylight. To me it looks like the abrupt night to day change is supposed to suggest the chase went on for a long time. Slade is captured by the Nazis who now also have their hands on the pointy bit of the Spear of Destiny that Norton entrusted to Michelle. The fascists have also captured Professor Hightower and our two zeroes are imprisoned with him. Hightower dies but Michelle and Slade escape. They follow the Nazis to the Venus Valley where the other part of the Spear of Destiny is hidden.

On a remote island, Michelle and Slade are recaptured but they escape with the Spear of Destiny when the fascist encampment is attacked by Mogols on horseback. The Nazis give chase but Michelle and Slade evade them and hook up with a tribe of dwarfs. The midgets agree to show them where Venus Valley is if they'll help take out the Mogols first. After much joyous throwing of dynamite, the Mogols are defeated. The dwarfs show Michelle and Slade the way to Venus Valley, and shortly after the Nazis catch up with the Americans. Most of the fascists end up killed, but having got the better of the Nazis this couple are captured by the Amazonians. Michelle is told she has to fight the Amazonian wrestling champion over the pit of death. If she wins she can have the other half of the Spear of Destiny, if she loses the Amazon Queen will take her man. Michelle wins and it's the Amazonian pro who gets eaten by crocodiles. Then the boss Nazi shows up leading to a bit more fighting and an earthquake. After the dwarfs arrive, Michelle joins the two parts of the Spear of Destiny together and humanity is saved!

This film only makes the outer limits of the Brucesploitation genre because it gets covered on fan sites like *Many Bruces* due to a cameo from Bruce Le—but it has nothing to do with Bruce Lee and is just a regular Filipino exploitation flick. *Future Hunters* totally sucks because Robert Patrick and Linda Carol are awful leads. The film was written and produced by Anthony Maharaj who would go on to direct both Bruce Le and Richard Norton in *Mission Terminate* the year after this one came out.

135 NINJA CHAMPION 1986
DIRECTED BY GODFREY HO AND/OR KIM SI-HYEON

Another IFD cut-and-paste job, a pre-existing movie that has been chopped down with ninja sequences randomly sprinkled into an unrelated narrative. After some shots of Victoria Harbour in Hong Kong, we cut to Korea where Rose and her boyfriend George—an Interpol agent—are camping in the woods. Three men whose faces are plastered with clown make-up attack them; Rose is raped and tortured.

After undergoing an abortion, Rose flies to Taipei and meets up with some diamond smugglers. She seduces All Asia Boxing Champion William Wong, the brother of one of the diamond smugglers. After getting Wong to her room, Rose coats her nipples with poison and moments after sucking her tits, the boxer is very sick. Wong was one of the men who raped Rose and now she's taking her revenge.

Our heroine whips Wong to get information about the other two rapists from him. Then Rose dumps Wong in her hotel bath and waterboards him. Later we learn she castrated him but this isn't shown. Interrupting this are some talking head scenes involving Bruce Baron and Richard Harrison rapping with each other on the phone. Harrison's 'guest star' shots are lifted from *Ninja Terminator* (1985), and take up twenty seconds of screen time. Rose's ex-boyfriend George works with Richard and Bruce, so presumably they're all Interpol agents—Baron is also a ninja. George doesn't don a ninja uniform but he must have mystic powers since he's able to have face-to-face conversations with Baron when they're each in different rooms; the backgrounds behind them don't match. It may be that Godfrey Ho hoped viewers would believe George and Baron were in the same space, but it's more likely he didn't really care.

George explains to Baron that Rose would have used feminine intuition to identify her rapists, so the fact she knows who they are is no mystery. He also claims the police let the rapists off due to lack of evidence, and is very bitter that the authorities consider feminine intuition insufficient to secure criminal convictions.

At the conclusion of George's psychic conference with Baron, Rose calls him and arranges to meet up. Rose is angry with George for deserting her at a time of crisis and marrying Jenny, and tells him she's going to murder his crippled wife after she's killed her rapists. George wants to slaughter the rapists with her because he's an Interpol agent with a licence to kill, so if he takes responsibility she won't get into trouble with the police. Hoods who just happen to be passing assault Rose, so George fights them. Rose runs off but is picked up by another of her rapists Ronald, who is pretending to be a cop. Meanwhile red suited bad ninja boss Pierre Tremblay gives us some more talking head anti-action as he informs his men Rose is doing their work for them. Ronald drives Rose to a secluded dead end next to a warehouse building where he plans to shoot her. Rose asks if she can put some make-up on before she dies. Ronald agrees, which gives his victim the chance to get mace out of her bag and spray it in the rapist's face. In the melee that follows, Rose manages to smash Ronald several times with her stilettos, slam the car door on his wrist and trap him, then grab a knife and stab him. Rose even gets to knee Ronald in the bollocks before running him down with his car. After this Rose has to flee because the real cops turn up.

Next Jenny fails to get it on with her husband because he is still in love with Rose. Somehow Ronald has managed to survive, so our feminist avenger has to disguise herself as a nurse and kill him in hospital. Rose stabs Ronald a few times in the groin with a syringe to soften him up before getting him to reveal that Walter was the third man who raped her. As a coup de grâce, our feminist heroine shoots the second rapist in the head after saying: "You know what the greatest gift in the world is Ronald? Peace!" Then Rose meets up with George to ask him for money. George's proclamations of love seem to be rekindling their relationship. They obviously spend a long time together as we transition from day to night, and when George makes it clear he'll leave Jenny and his job for his not-so-ex, Rose swoons and falls into his arms.

Rose picks up Walter in a nightclub and suggests he takes her home. After Walter puts his hand up Rose's skirt and literally rips her pants off, we cut to George waiting for her at the airport. He rips up their plane tickets; Rose hasn't turned up in time for their flight back to Korea.

Cut to George in the Taiwanese countryside where he has a fight with goons from the diamond smuggling gang. One of the guys attacking him also appears Kim Si-Hyeon's earlier movies *Enter the Invincible Hero* (1981) and *Secret Ninja, Roaring Tiger* (1982), where he holds his foot above his head and then brings his heel down on his opponent. This bit part actor reappears during the climatic fight but doesn't perform his contortionist heel kick in this flick. George disappears into thin air while fighting him and reappears elsewhere, so although we never see George masked up, it seems he's had some serious ninja training.

When Rose thinks Walter isn't looking, she injects poison into grapes and smears the potion over her lips. Walter doesn't like the taste of lipstick, so he wipes Rose's mouth before kissing her. Rose gets a couple of grapes into Walter's mush, but he forces a snog and transfers them into her gob. Rose spits the grapes out because she knows they're deadly. Walter laughs and says she'd used the trick before; there is a brief fight during which the rapist kills the lights, and when they come back on we see he's stabbed Rose. After a scene with a coffin and more random ninja schlock, Rose's identical twin sister Cherry—same actress—lures Robert, Walter's mobster boss, to a very large ship. The big man is the bait to bring the third rapist to her lair. The sequence is accompanied by a sample from *Trans-Europe Express* by Kraftwerk. This may or may not be intended to remind us of Alain Robbe-Grillet's film *Trans-Europe Express* (1966), which includes sado-masochist sex scenes that in some ways parallel the content of *Ninja Champion*.

Because Cherry looks like Rose, the mobsters check the coffin in which they'd put their victim's corpse and find it is empty except for a cassette tape. Meanwhile George is wandering around Taipei. Walter is freaked by the taped message, which appears to be Rose saying she's always a step ahead of him and is going to send him to hell. Elsewhere George confronts his father-in-law over his involvement in the diamond scams. More random red versus white ninja footage follows. Then a few mobsters led by Walter make their way onto the boat where Cherry is holding Robert captive. Walter finds Robert tied up but rather than freeing him, the boss's number two stabs his superior so that he can take his place. After killing Robert, Walter goes to the next deck but is trapped by Cherry and her mute bodyguard Turner. The mobsters backing Walter up melt away but come back later with reinforcements. Walter is strung up by his arms from a motorised hook and the information that it was Larry—George's father-in-law—who came up with the plan to rape Rose is forced out of him. Turner pulls down Walter's pants so that Cherry can castrate him but a bunch of mobsters burst in brandishing guns to prevent this.

Walter's fate is an aspect of the story that is left dangling. We see Walter hanging with his pants around his ankles and his men pointing guns at Cherry and Turner, then there is a cut to a shot of George lurking in the shadows and we never see Walter again. The hoods shove Cherry and Turner into a different part of the ship. Larry confronts the now bound Cherry and Turner. He explains that his crippled daughter Jenny was hopelessly in love with George. Therefore Rose had to be gang raped to sully her in George's eyes, so that the Interpol agent would marry Jenny instead of his true love, who he'd view as spoilt goods. Larry orders one of his henchmen to kill Cherry by beheading her with a sword, but George shoots the killer, then after telling the hoods 'my gun shows no compassion', he frees Cherry. Rose's identical sister grabs the sword her would-be executioner dropped when he copped it and uses it to impale Larry. One of the lesser hoods shoots at George but only hits his leg. George kills the gunman and a full fire fight ensues. Turner manages to overpower a mobster and take a pistol from him.

As we hear police sirens signalling the arrival of the authorities, most of the mobsters on the ship have been killed. George, Cherry and the mute make their exit. Turner kills a mobster as they leave. Cut to the cops. Dragon Lee gets around thirty seconds of screen time as a policeman, half of it in long-shot with other characters moving around him. Dragon is wearing a white suit and has two words of dialogue. As the cops jump out of their bus with guns drawn he shouts: "Search!" Having raced through the ship with another cop, Dragon replies 'right' after his colleague observes: "Seems like they're all dead." That's it as far as Dragon Lee goes but this brief appearance leads to his name appearing in the truncated credits, and the inclusion of this film in some discussions of Brucesploitation.

Ninja Champion still has two plot strands to tie up. First Cherry leads George to Rose's corpse and the Interpol agent admits he's responsible for her death but declares he'll always love her. Finally, all the ninja sequences that have been added to Kim Si-Hycon's film *Poisonous Rose Stripping the Night* (1985) have to be resolved. So looking like a couple of overgrown schoolboy nerds, Bruce Baron and Pierre Tremblay confront each other in a Hong Kong children's playground. Tremblay explains to Baron that: "I wanted Larry to replace Robert but he was only worried about his crippled daughter, so I told him to send in his men to rape Rose, hoping that George the Interpol agent would marry his daughter. With her as a spy I'd know Interpol's every move in advance. But then Rose came back for vengeance and an even better plan presented itself…. So then Rose started her killing spree. So I thought to myself, why not clean my record, get rid of the old gang at the same time and start a new life? And it worked. Rose and George got rid of Larry and

Robert, while you (he's addressing Baron) got rid of my three heavies. Ha ha ha... And when you're dead nobody will know my secret and I can start all over again! Ha, ha, ha...." Baron and Tremblay then engage in some over-stylised fighting, until the white ninja stabs the red ninja to death on the monkey bars.

Kim Si-Hyeon's original version of this movie ran for eight minutes longer than *Ninja Champion,* and given the insertion of the scenes involving ninjas endlessly talking and occasionally fighting, around twenty minutes must have been cut from the original edit. The story also seems to have been altered, since it appears that in *Poisonous Rose Stripping the Night* the heroine faked her death and sought revenge using another identity; there was no twin sister. This no doubt accounts for why the body in the coffin towards the end looks so much like a dummy. *Ninja Champion* is a rape-revenge movie, think *I Spit on Your Grave* (1978) or *Ms. 45* (1981), disguised as a ninja flick. It has nothing to do with Brucesploitation.

136 No Retreat, No Surrender   1986
AKA *Karate Tiger*
Directed by Corey Yuen

Bruce Lee obsessed Kurt McKinney has difficult relationships with his dad and a girl called Kelly, and troubles with bullies too. After his pops is given a beating by Jean-Claude Van Damme, the family karate dojo in LA is closed down, with Kurt and the folks moving to Seattle. Van Damme is working for the mob who are taking over all the leading dojos in American to use them as fronts for organised crime; this is petty much forgotten in the mid-part of the movie that is a dull-as-ditchwater teen drama. In Seattle, McKinney quickly finds a new best friend in the form of hip-hop loving and Michael Jackson imitating J. W. Fails. Kurt visits the grave of the Little Dragon and because he's having a hard time, the ghost of Sifu Lee (stupidly called Sensei in this movie) deigns to train him. The ghost is played by Tang Lung, one of Bruce Lee's fight doubles in the official *Game of Death* (1978). Lung uses a can of Diet Coke to demonstrate his martial arts philosophy and to show how low he can go. There are the usual training sequences and a final showdown at a full contact karate competition, where a couple of the local bullies and their well-meaning sensei get flattened by Van Damme, before McKinney jumps into the ring to teach 'The Muscles From Brussels' the meaning of defeat. Seasonal Films and their Hong Kong director obviously went for the lowest common denominator in an attempt to break into the American market—a *Karate Kid* (1984) and *Rocky* (1976) crossover aimed at teenyboppers. The choreography and editing were handled by Hong Kong rather than Hollywood 'talent', so the fights look reasonable, but everything else about the film is so crap it isn't worth seeing. Mckinney is a dork and Van Damme comes across as a complete twerp. This is a teen movie with some martial arts elements, rather than an adult fight flick, so it isn't Brucesploitation.

137 Mission Terminate   1987
AKA *Return of the Kickfighter*
Directed by Anthony Maharaj

Pre-credits a bunch of American soldiers and their Vietnamese guide played by Bruce Le are trying to capture a village held by the Vietcong. The Americans seize a local woman and tie her up. They decide they need air support so they call in a helicopter to bomb the settlement. Bruce starts a one-man assault hoping to save women and children from being blown to smithereens. The soldiers think he'll be killed but as his attack is successful they follow him and take the village. Civilians are led to safety before their homes are destroyed. The GIs find gold. Later we later learn it was stolen by Le's bad brother Dick Wei. The soldiers hide the treasure so they can come back and get it later. Bruce is disgusted because he believes the gold belongs to his country. Dick and Bruce have a brief confrontation but don't actually fight; there is a flashback to a battle they had as boys under the supervision of their Japanese ninja master.

After the credits it is fifteen years later (1985) and we're in Thailand. Dick Wei is murdering the squaddies who stole the gold in Vietnam. They know why their buddies are being killed but they don't want to let anyone else in on the secret. Richard Norton is called in to deal with the case. He goes to Hong Kong to talk to Le about the murders, but our moptop isn't co-operative. The Japanese master who taught Bruce and Dick the deadly ninjutsu arts turns up to trail the bad student to a secret terrorist camp where Wei is in charge of combat training. The master is caught but escapes, so Wei has to track him down and kill him. The assassination is interrupted by the arrival of two Buddhist monks, so Wei leaves the master mortally wounded. Bruce arrives from Hong Kong and is told by his dying sensei to kill his brother. Bruce now teams up with Richard Norton and together they infiltrate the ninja terrorist camp. Bruce wants to take out his sibling then and there but Norton stops him. They leave and return later with members of the Queens Cobras. The latter are Thai soldiers who have been trained to stare down poisonous snakes; there is even a scene with one of these men doing this. As Wei takes out the highest ranking of the American soldiers who stole the gold, the elite Thai squaddies led by Norton and Le launch their assault on the ninja terrorists. Gun battles and a repeated diversion with ambush tactic follow. The good guys have just about cleaned up the abandoned cement factory the terrorists were using as their base when Wei returns. Le has a short fight with Wei, but Norton has to kill the chief villain because he's the lead actor. The Americans arrive at the last moment to transport Bruce and Richard back to base and blow up the now empty terrorist HQ.

One reason Brucesploitation fans talk about *Mission Terminate* is that a Bruce Le still from it is used on the American DVD cover of Joseph Velasco's cut-and-paste anti-classic *Ninja Vs Bruce Lee* (1982).

While there are ninjas in *Mission Terminate*, it seems the masked assassin on the cover of the aforementioned Velasco DVD has been collaged in from *Super Ninja* (1984). The *Many Bruces* website described *Mission Terminate* as far removed from Brucesploitation; while the *Clones of Bruce Lee* site has a 2010 interview with its star Richard Norton that doesn't question its 'Brucesploitation' genre status. This is a bog-standard eighties military action picture that only makes the outer limits of Brucesploitation due to the misplaced enthusiasm of fans such as Lee Holmes.

138 THEY STILL CALL ME BRUCE — 1987
DIRECTED BY JAMES ORR AND JOHNNY YUNE

Bruce Won (Johnny Yune) is walking past Green's Liquor Store in downtown Houston as the owner is thrown through the glass door by a couple of Mr B.'s thugs who are shaking him down for extortion money. Bruce confronts the men. The antique vase Yune was holding is thrown into the air and caught by a vigilante. The hoods run off because they've spotted this man and other members of the Neighbourhood Action Group (NAG). The shopkeeper tells the vigilantes that Yuen saved his life, and addressing our star informs him he's better than Bruce Lee.

That's this flick's main and repeated joke: because Yuen's character is Korean and called Bruce, he's constantly assumed to be a great martial artist and somehow linked to the Little Dragon. The other main motor for the flat comedy here is the fact Bruce isn't familiar with American culture and the subtleties of English usage.

Returning to the plot, the NAGs tell Bruce about their dojo and give him directions to the Veteran's Association because he's looking for Ernie Brown who saved his life during the Korean War. Bruce is then provided with a list of Korean War veterans called Brown in the Houston area who he proceeds to call on. A psychiatrist called Ernie Brown thinks Bruce is mentally disturbed. When Bruce visits Suzie's Massage Parlour to see head gangbanger Mr

B. he doesn't get as far as the veteran. He steps in to stop a hooker called Polly being slapped around and tries to frighten the hoods with the following dialogue: "With my right foot I can kick your face. With my left I can kick your nose. With my fingers I can poke your eyes out. Take a good look at my face. I'm an Oriental." Bruce Won isn't a master of taekwondo, kung fu or karate, and he gets his ass well and truly kicked by Mr B.'s thugs. Bruce exits Suzie's Massage Parlour via the window and without his vase—a five hundred year old family heirloom—that he wanted to present to Private Brown. The gangbangers give the vase to their boss who recognises it as a valuable antique.

Having been beaten up, Bruce goes to the dojo where the NAGs train. He spins a cock and bull story about his injuries and the vigilantes are impressed. Hearing about Bruce's combat expertise, their sensei Master McLean gives him a job and a place to live. McLean is being harassed by Mr B. because he owes him money, he wants Bruce to look after the dojo so he can take off. The gangbangers are demanding the sensei throws a big championship fight in the seventh round as repayment for his debt.

At the dojo Bruce fakes his fighting skills and by getting other people to do his job for him, the fact he doesn't know any martial arts isn't rumbled. He befriends an orphan kid called Billy and gets him to cover the children's classes. Billy has a pet dog called Kato, named after Bruce Lee's character in the *Green Hornet* TV series. Bruce returns to Suzie's Massage Parlour to try and get his vase back, he fails but drags Polly—a 'tart with a heart of gold'—out of the establishment. Before long the hooker wants to know Bruce intimately. At the same time an uncover cop is snooping around, trying to nail Mr B. and work out how Bruce fits in with the gang. Bruce mentors Billy by giving him a lucky odd sock so that the orphan will win a competition he fears he'll lose; this particular psychological trick works.

While Bruce is out trying to track down Private Brown—and having 'comedy' battles with Hell's Angels and a bull—Mr B.'s hoods kidnap Polly and slap Billy around, leaving the kid in a coma. After taking Billy to hospital, Bruce cross-dresses as a geisha girl so that he can infiltrate Suzie's Massage Parlour and rescue Polly. When Bruce is unmasked as a man masquerading as a female masseur, Mr. B. is told by his thugs that this is the karate master who has been causing them so much trouble. Since Sensei McLean isn't co-operating, Bruce is offered his place in the big televised fight as long as he throws it in the seventh round. Bruce agrees if the gangbangers will free Polly, write-off McLean's debt and pay Billy's hospital bill. Then he adds in broken English as an afterthought: "But the most important, bring my vase." Soon Bruce is being slaughtered in the ring by a fighter called The Executioner. Billy sees this on television and staggers from his hospital bed to the live match, and while Bruce is recuperating between the sixth and seventh rounds, he presents his friend with the lucky sock that enabled him to win an earlier competition.

Unable to let Billy's misplaced faith in his martial arts skills crumble, Bruce manages to knock The Executioner out. Mr B. and his thugs are about to attack Bruce with knives, but in the nick of time they are arrested for racketeering by uniformed cops. Polly and Billy get into the ring with the victorious Bruce who is upset because he thinks Mr B. is the Private Brown he was searching for. However there is a saccharine sweet turnaround when the undercover cop reveals he is the Ernie 'Slim' Brown who befriended Bruce as a child in Korea; something he had to keep secret until he'd closed the case against Mr. B. The vase Bruce brought from Korea is presented with thanks to Private Brown. Polly tells Bruce she wants to marry him and that makes him happy too. Bruce gets a medal and is made an honorary police inspector to thank him for the role he played in bringing Mr. B. to justice, and Billy is reunited with his dog Kato.

This is a sequel to the earlier *They Call Me Bruce* (1982) and it is truly awful; the comedy doesn't work and the fight scenes are even worse. Although others have praised this flick as an example of

Brucesploitation, it's a piss-poor comedy and not a martial arts film.

139 CHINATOWN CONNECTION 1990
DIRECTED BY JEAN-PAUL OUELLETTE

Someone is poisoning batches of cocaine resulting in drug deaths around LA. Meanwhile angry undercover cop Lee Majors II (the son of *The Six Million Dollar Man* actor) kills three gangbangers who've murdered a uniformed officer and are holding the priest and congregation of a church hostage. Returning to the first plot strand, Art Camacho shots dead a drug dealer called Scarface Man while working with Bruce Ly; actually Hong Kong actor Henry Yu Yung who has been renamed to make it sound like he might be Bruce Lee. The Scarface Man was Ly's only lead on the poisoned coke case and he needed to bring the suspect in alive. Aside from doing routine police work, Ly also runs an anger management course for out of control cops, which mostly consists of teaching them martial arts. Camacho is coerced into going on the scheme and while he's off duty, Ly is teamed up with Majors for the drug deaths investigation. At first the two cops don't get on, but gradually they grow to like each other. Majors has a stool pigeon who points out no one is dying in Chinatown. Ly enjoys a polite relationship with the big boss of Chinatown, who it turns out is connected to the poisoned coke deaths and has teamed up with an ex-CIA agent turned drug baron played by Fitz Houston. The CIA renegade is randomly poisoning the gear of Latino dealers to discredit their merchandise among LA drug users. The idea is to open up the cocaine market for the new syndicate Houston has set up using his 'Chinatown connection'.

Working with information from Majors' informer, Ly and his partner quickly bust the case wide open by investigating a cheese factory where the coke is stashed in waxed casing. The bad guys realise the cops are onto them and decide to warn Ly off by branding him. Despite falling into their trap, Ly's kung fu is so good he gets to brand Houston instead. The mob send a sword wielding ninja to take Majors out, but the assassin chops at the furniture instead of his target, giving the cop time to take him out with a gun. Having tied everything up, our two buddies get a warrant to arrest Houston, and decide to do it in the tower block owned by his partner in crime—so that they can take down the big boss of Chinatown at the same time. Backed up by the three cops (including Camacho) from Ly's anger management course, they storm the skyscraper in what might be a nod to the pagoda sequence in the official *Game of Death* (1978); except they don't fight masters of different styles on every level, just hoods with guns. First they break into the basement, where they knock some hoods around and take out the CCTV. Next they go to the ground floor and secure it. Leaving Camacho on the front desk, Ly and a white female cop take the lift to the penthouse office, while Majors and a white male cop take the stairs to the top. Our law enforcement avengers get delayed half way up by some hoods who are eventually taken out in a gun battle. Meanwhile the big boss of Chinatown is trying to double-cross Houston, but when the intruder alarm is sounded the gangbanger who is supposed to shoot the ex-CIA man gets distracted. Houston takes advantage of this and kills his criminal opposition. When Ly makes it to the top of the tower we get an anti-climatic fight between him and Houston. Eventually the bad guy is kicked out of a window and falls to his death. Ly then delivers a homily about how easily empires fall, echoing some earlier dialogue.

The fights here are not only slow, they are really lousy. Despite his name, there is nothing in Bruce Ly's performance to indicate he's a clone, ultimately I don't think he is. The worst thing about this super-dull movie is that despite its weak martial arts, it is competently put together; if it were a train wreck it might be more entertaining. Ouellette's earlier horror flick *The Unnamable* (1988) has something of a cult following. He also helmed *The Unnamable II: The Statement of Randolph Carter*.

140 GHOST OF THE FOX — 1990
AKA *WAY OF FOX*
DIRECTED BY BRUCE LE

Pre-credits there are a few horror scenes from later in the film. Depending of which version is viewed, next there is either an extended softcore sex scene with the God of the Snakes and female minions, or a cut straight into the Evil Gods attacking the Taoist priests protecting humanity from these deities. The latter sequence looks like a bog standard old school kung fu fight. The boss priest gets injured so he tells a child that they must be prepared to take over his role as protector of humanity. The child trains and transforms into the adult Bruce Le. When the boss priest dies he hands a sword to his successor and the mature Le goes off on his travels. Bruce protects a wandering scholar from bandits. The scholar goes into a town and saves a fox that was going to be slaughtered by purchasing it. Because the caged fox smells the scholar is refused a room at the inn. He's told he can get free accommodation at a temple outside the town. It's ruined and haunted; Le is hanging out there in his role of demon slayer.

The ghost daughters of the Fox God are banging around the temple seducing any passing men and then killing them. Depending on the edit viewed, there is either quite a lot of softcore sex and nudity before the killings, or not much at all. The scholar gets frightened and releases his fox, which is actually a ghost in animal form. Alongside the ghosts there is a hopping vampire. The fox the scholar bought has transformed into a beautiful ghost woman and she seduces him but he isn't killed because Le is rooting around. When the scholar turns up in town the next day the locals can't believe he's still alive. The following night the scholar goes back to see the ghost lady but is attacked by her sister, however the sibling he saved in fox form comes to his rescue. Meanwhile the father and sisters of these ghosts are getting mad at them for not making enough pills for the God of the Snakes. This deity is less than happy about the quality of the pills the ghost family have been making from dead men and he lets the God of Foxes know this. The guilty ghosts use the excuse that Le is making things difficult for them. True love develops between the scholar and the ghost he saved from the butchers slab, and the sympathetic sister helps this along. Eventually the love-sick ghost is locked up by her father. Le, the scholar and her sister set out to rescue her from the castle of the Evil Gods. The scholar is mortally wounded and taken to a Buddhist temple where prayers and occult rites are performed over him. The Evil Gods make what is obviously a small model of the temple sink beneath water but it rises again due to the power for Taoist magic and prayer. Goodness and love ultimately overcome evil.

The film is a low-budget rip-off of everything from *Boxer's Omen* (1983) via *Mr Vampire* (1985) to *Chinese Ghost Story* (1987). The lightning bolts of force that emanate from Le when he does his Buddhist prayers are cheap and cheesy. The kung fu is average. The softcore sex in the Category III version is hilariously bad; it is accompanied by awful lounge music, half-hearted orgasmic moans and jiggling breasts. These scenes are tedious and the flick is mercifully shortened when they're cut. Nonetheless, this is still one of Le's better efforts as a director because he isn't trying to push a 'patriotic' message or do 'proper' acting in what is obviously an exploitation film.

141 COMFORT WOMEN — 1992
DIRECTED BY BRUCE LE

It's 1931 and the Japanese are invading parts of China; the film opens with newsreel style footage of these events just like Bruce Le's earlier and marginally less tedious *Ninja Over the Great Wall* (1990). In *Comfort Women* there are no ninjas and no kung fu fights, just the odd kick and gun battle. After five long minutes during which we see troops and women being moved around, the story almost kicks in. Tomi Akiyama (Lily Lee) is a top female Japanese war reporter who is considered more powerful than an army by the military top brass because of the impact of the pieces she writes. Lily is a loyal supporter of Japanese imperialism until she hears allegations that her country is running brothels serviced by kidnapped women. She goes undercover disguised as a male soldier to investigate and is horrified by what she finds. Lily gets romantically involved with Bruce Le who plays the Japanese military man assigned to protect her. When she writes a story exposing the horrors of the kidnapped comfort women, General Kawasaki is really pissed off and after having her arrested he turns her out as a sex slave. Since this is a women in prison (WIP) movie we've already had the obligatory shower scene, and from this point on the film is focussed on rape and torture during non-filler segments. There are also escapes and recaptures.

The Chinese torture Le in an elongated sequence that allows the director to explore his own masochism in a wooden way. Lily attempts suicide at one point but is convinced by the other comfort women she is the only person who can tell their story so she has to live; this provides the director with an excuse to show her endlessly writing—which is very boring to watch. One comfort woman discovers after having sex with a soldier that he is her brother who she hasn't seen since he was eight years-old. She blows him and herself up with a hand grenade that is fortuitously hanging off his belt. There are inter-titles telling us about the Japanese attack on Pearl Harbour; indicating ten years have passed since the beginning of the film. Lily catches VD and deliberately infects 500 Japanese 'beasts' with this disease. When this is discovered she's sent to the Imperial Japanese Army's Unit 731 for bacteriological research. Here we see more prisoners tortured; the way VD has destroyed Lily's body is 'scientifically' explained and visually illustrated by 'doctors' who display her diseased carcass to the camera.

Comfort Women is an uninspired sleaze fest; it is a bottom-of-the-barrel WIP film and definitely isn't Brucesploitation. WIP fans will be disappointed by the lack of catfights; they'll prefer to stick with more notable examples of the genre such as *House of Bamboo Dolls* (1973) or *99 Women* (1969).

142 FIST OF FURY 1991 II — 1992
DIRECTED BY RICO CHU TAK-ON

This begins with dull flashbacks to the climax of *Fist of Fury 1991* (1991) as a means of swinging viewers into the story. Stephen Chow beats Corey Yuen in the ring, and then defeats his bad student—Vincent Wan Yeung-Ming—in the final of a mixed martial arts competition. Ming dies as a result of this fight and his brother Yuen Wah wants revenge. In the meantime Chow's kung fu trainers have gambled away all his prize money; he's being bugged by Nat Chan Pak-Cheung who wants to be his student.

The film takes a while to get going but manages to take off when Chow goes to live with Pak-Cheung and his aunt played by Josephine Siao Fong-Fong. At first Siao won't admit she knows kung fu, because she wants her nephew—who she's brought up—to get married and continue the family line; not to die young as a result of fight challenges like his father. Continuing another aspect of the storyline from part 1, Chow's relationship with Sharla Cheung Man remains complex and compromised. Cheung Man has duel roles as Chow's girlfriend and Pak-Chueng's cousin. There are a lot of gags about mistaken identity and some very lame gay 'jokes'. At first the cousin wants to get it on with Chow, but in the end she finds love with Pak-Chueng. This couple are kidnapped by Wah's gang and Chow is told they will be harmed unless he agrees to take part in a competitive fight with the brother of the man he beat at the climax of part 1. To ensure no harm comes to her nephew and his future wife, Siao teaches Chow the electric fist kung fu technique. Kenny Bee's main function in this sequel is to romance Siao, who rediscovers her femininity as a result. *Fist of Fury 1991 II* is an even more generic parody of kung fu and wuxia films than the first instalment, and there aren't too many Bruce Lee references beyond Chow donning a yellow jumpsuit with black stripes for the climatic fight in which he defeats Wah. It is worth watching for by Josephine Siao's excellent parody of a chivalrous wuxia heroine; she completely overshadows Chow and might even help some viewers overlook the reactionary clap-trap that passes for humour in parts of this movie.

143 RETURN OF THE FAT DRAGON — 1993

AKA *KING SWINDLER*

DIRECTED KEVIN CHU YEN-PING

Despite its alternative title this flick has no connection to *Enter the Fat Dragon* (1978) beyond the fact both feature Sammo Hung. This is a family film with a lot of toilet humour. Sammo plays a drunkard and gambler with a taste for fighting. He gets arrested and single mom undercover cop Sandra Ng ends up looking after his young son while he's in jail. Her two year old and Hung's eight year-old team up to create havoc. Cue twenty tiresome minutes of kids being cheeky and tweeny bopper adventures. The kids want their mom and pop to get together so they can be brothers but Hung likes being single. Under the influence of Ng, Sammo's kid persuades his dad to go straight so Hung takes up unlicensed boxing, his trade before he became a swindler. He'd switched to being a card sharp after his wife left him with a small baby to care for. With heaps of sentimentality about family life, a bundle of low-grade slapstick, and too many unfocussed plot elements, Hung and Ng get it together. The climax is a boxing match Sammo is being forced to throw because his and Ng's sons have been kidnapped. The kids free themselves and turn up ringside during the third round, just as Hung has taken a dive as instructed, so Sammo bounces up and hammers his opponent as the cops arrest the villains. The final pay off is Hung asking Ng to marry him and the two of them freeze-framed at the start of an argument. Hung spends more time imitating Simon Yuen's *Drunken Master* (1978) character than doing Bruce Lee knockoffs, although most of the fighting is just Sammo doing his own thing. Definitely one of Hung's weaker efforts.

144 FIST OF LEGEND — 1994

DIRECTED BY GORDON CHAN KA-SEUNG

A remake of Lo Wei's *Fist of Fury* (1972) with Jet Li taking Bruce Lee's role as Chen Zhen. This starts in Japan where Li is studying engineering. A bunch of karatekas break up a university lecture Li is attending and tell him to go back to China, he proceeds to beat them up. The karateka's sensei turns up and tells his students he hopes they've learnt their lesson. He also tells Li his master is dead after being beaten in a fight. Leaving his Japanese girlfriend Shinobu Nakayama behind, Li returns to the Ching Wu school to pay his respects to his sifu. The plot progresses through a series of confrontations between Ching Wu students and the Japanese. The master was poisoned by the Japanese before he fought an inferior karateka. Billy Chow's fascist Japanese character kills this karate 'champion' before attempting to frame Li for the murder. Nakayama turns up when Li is in court to (falsely) testify she was in a hotel with him on the night of the killing.

Most of the Ching Wu school are disgusted that their best fighter would do the shag nasty with a woman who isn't Chinese. Li ends up living outside town with Nakayama as she's ostracised at his school. Before this Li's friend and the new master of the school Chin Siu-Ho, forces Li to fight him. Li defeats his friend but refuses to take over the school. Siu-Ho retreats to a brothel because he's in love with a prostitute who works there. The Japanese sensei, Nakayama's uncle, is sent to battle Li but he's an honourable man and teaches his opponent how to beat the lead Japanese fascist played by Chow. The Ching Wu men have received another challenge from the Japanese, and they need Siu-Ho to fight the match but don't know where he is; fortunately his girlfriend turns up to tell them. They get Siu-Ho to leave the brothel with his true love, who the school buy out of sex slavery. The next day when Siu-Ho must fight Chow, Li turns up. He's just found a note from Nakayama saying she's going back to Japan to wait for him there until the war is over—because she wants him to do his own thing in China, which he can't with her by his side. Li goes with Siu-Ho to the confrontation with Chow. Siu-Ho is easily defeated, but Li then beats Chow. As the two Ching Wu men are leaving, Chow tries to run them through with a sword and is killed by Li. The Japanese ambassador insists someone must be executed for this murder to avert war, and Li volunteers. However the Chinese police substitute another body for Li's and he gets to leave Shanghai alive.

While this remake is more nuanced than the original *Fist of Fury* in terms of its treatment of the Japanese, it is still stuffed to the gills with absurd patriotic and nationalistic bullshit. It also sets about transforming Bruce Lee's hokey 1972 b-movie star vehicle into a 'quality' production with a more subtle story, and in the process loses all the charm of the original. Instead of Bruce Lee's hilarious overacting when emoting anger—which makes him look every bit as much like a fascist nutjob as the Japanese in the original film, and provides a very different kind of balance to that found in *Fist of Legend*—we have a restrained non-performance from Jet Li. The star of this movie has about as much charisma as a plank of wood. This isn't Brucesploitation, it's crap aimed at the type of person who judges movies by the so-called 'standards' set by Hollywood blockbusters.

145 DRAGON IN FURY   2004
DIRECTED BY MAU KIN-TAK

Gordon Lui hires Dragon Shek's rickshaw. Lui is attacked by ninjas and easily sees them off. Shek is impressed and asks Lui who he is, then begs to be his student and is accepted. After the credits Shek turns up at Liu's grave many years later, it seems the old master died during a challenge match with a Japanese fighter. Shek has been away from his wife and his school for several years and now regrets this. A bit later Japanese martial artists and their translator turn up at Liu's school with a sign that according to the English dub describes the Chinese as cowards; various online sources say this reads 'Sick Men of Asia'—just like the calligraphy presented to the Ching Wu school in *Fist of Fury* (1972). Shek takes the sign to the Japanese dojo and roughs up its members, including the fighter who beat his master in the challenge match that allegedly killed him.

The plot proceeds by copying and sometimes changing in small ways scenes from *Fist of Fury* and an earlier remake *Fist of Legend* (1994). Here Billy Chow reprises his role as a fascist Japanese general from *Fist of Legend*. It turns out Chow had Lui poisoned because his karateka wasn't good enough to beat the kung fu master in a fair fight. When the Japanese champion whinges about the methods used to secure his victory, Chow kills him and has the death blamed on the Lui's students. Joey Man at first appears to be Shek's spouse but it transpires she is actually the twin sister of his wife; she is spying for the Japanese because they bought her out of prostitution. By the time Shek discovers she's his sister-in-law, he loves her anyway because she's transformed herself into an ultra-nationalistic Chinese zealot. Karen Chueng plays a student of Lui but she is secretly an undercover Chinese detective investigating a link up between the British and the Japanese in the opium trade. Not much is made of this beyond Chow being named as a key-player; the British end of this operation isn't even depicted. Man —who occasionally appears as a black clad ninja type figure—saves Shek from a Japanese swordsman but is imprisoned and poisoned by Chow. Despite Chueng going to free the sick Man, the detective doesn't lead her to safety but instead tearfully carries out the dying woman's request for a mercy killing. Shek recovers from his wounds—inflicted by the swordsman Man saved him from—and goes to confront Chow in a challenge match. The local head of the Chinese patriots has already escaped with Chueng, and even Shek gets away after winning his fight with Chow.

Although some scenes are fairly closely modelled on Lo Wei's 1972 version of this story, others copy the 1994 remake, and Shek's performance is much closer to Jet Li's tedious turn as Chen Zhen than Bruce Lee's carpet chewing insanity in this role. As such this isn't so much Brucesploitation as Jetsploitation, and therefore belongs to the outer limits of the genre we're interested in. To damn with faint praise, I'd say I preferred *Dragon In Fury* to *Fist of Legend* because it looks so cheap I thought I was watching something made for TV; that said neither the Jet Li vehicle nor this are actually worth seeing.

146 FINISHING THE GAME: THE SEARCH FOR A NEW BRUCE LEE   2007
DIRECTED BY JUSTIN LIN

This is a mockumentary that mines the alternative history genre. It imagines that rather than Golden Harvest in Hong Kong having the rights to finish Bruce Lee's last film using doubles, a racist Hollywood studio made the casting call to find an actor to complete the official *Game of Death* (1978). The period look of the flick is less than convincing, and the segments of martial arts films attributed to a possible stand in called Breeze Loo (played by Roger Fan) are closer to eighties ninja productions than seventies chop and block. That said, there are hardly any fight scenes in the movie—it is a comedy not an action film. The flick basically follows the crew behind the alleged production and various wannabe actors in mock fly-on-the-wall style. Ultimately this doesn't have much to do with the Little Dragon, it is more about the desperation of those trying to make it in Hollywood, the problems actors face, and the predilections of Hollywood insiders. Bruce Lee is just a peg writer/director Lin hangs his real interests on. The first five minutes or so is just about watchable and a cameo appearance by an incredibly repulsive Ron Jeremy as a porn actor/director is almost worth seeing; this segment isn't a parody, it is exploitation. Given that Lin is now a relatively successful Hollywood director of entries in the *Fast and Furious* and *Star Trek* franchises, it isn't surprising that by the time you're ten minutes into this movie it becomes a total bore.

ENDMATTER

BRUCE LEE

'HIS' TRUE STORY EXPLODES ACROSS THE SCREEN!

ALL NEW ACTION!

HERMAN COHEN presents

THE DRAGON LIVES

Color By Deluxe ®
A FILM VENTURES INTERNATIONAL RELEASE

© FVI 1978

BRUCE LEE, BRUCESPLOITATION AND JOSEPH VELASCO
BUT NO FULL-BLOWN THEORETICAL SUMMING UP!

This discussion of Brucesploitation revolves around 146 films; 148 if you want to count the two incorporated into *The Real Bruce Lee 1 & 2* twice. In my preamble I explain why I exclude a number of titles. I might have upped the flicks discussed and ranked slightly if I'd been able to access movies I've seen cited online as Brucesploitation but was unable to source with an English dub or subtitles. Titles I looked for but didn't find include: *Revenge of Fist of Fury* (circa 1978, directed by Chang Ping Han), *Return of Dragon* (1998, directed by Artis Chow A-Chi) and *Looking for Bruce Lee* (2002, Directed by Kang Lone). Any overview of a film genre is necessarily incomplete, but as far as I can tell *Looking for Bruce Lee* is outer limits material, while *Revenge of Fist of Fury* and *Return of the Dragon* might make the periphery or even semi-periphery if I found myself able to view them.

I classify 41 of the films I looked at as belonging to the core of the genre, and another 23 as semi-periphery; which means I see Brucesploitation as currently and unambiguously consisting of about 64 films. My periphery contained another 22 flicks, whether or not these belong to the genre can be argued over. So I see Brucesploitation as currently consisting of a maximum of 86 movies, but in reality somewhat less that this. I placed 60 titles in my outer limits category, meaning that others have cited them as Brucesploitation but I do not accept this classification. I could have covered many more titles as outer limits but chose to restrict this category and mention in my introduction and elsewhere films I felt were very obviously not Brucesploitation, despite some people claiming they should be treated as such.

Whatever way you look at Brucesploitation it is a very small genre, since even those who are far slacker than I am about what fits within it would be hard pushed to find much more than a few hundred movies that could be given this label. Because Brucesploitation is relatively compact in comparison to say sci-fi or martial arts flicks in general, it provides a good model from which to discuss what genre is and how it functions. I'd be interested to know how Brucesploitation compares in size to other genres such as Chansploitation and cripsploitation (exploitation films with cripples as anti-heroes); I'd suspect that there are fewer of the former and more of the latter, but this is just a guess. Right now I'm not up for making a detailed examination of these other two genres.

English language Brucesploitation is padded with a relatively large outer limits due mainly to marketing gambits by North American film distributors. Stars such as Bruce Liang who could be sold on their own names in South East Asia are relatively unknown in the overdeveloped world, so vehicles featuring this actor and others had words such as Bruce placed in their English language titles and were sold on a Bruce Lee ticket despite their content having nothing to do with the Little Dragon. My exclusion of flicks from the genre that only enter it due to English language marketing considerations may help to close the gap between understandings of Brucesploitation in different parts of the world. It appears that Brucesploitation was more of a phenomenon for western than Asian audiences.

Allegedly the mainstream American film director Quentin Tarantino prefers watching Brucesploitation to actual Bruce Lee flicks, and if this is true then I find myself in agreement with him. That said, I was tempted to include all Bruce Lee's adult star vehicles as examples of Brucesploitation. I don't think it is difficult to argue that *Enter the Dragon* (1973) fits the genre, but Lee's earlier fu films could be seen as exploiting his local to Hong Kong success as Kato in *The Green Hornet* TV show. I still love *Fist of Fury* (1972) because Lee's overacting hilariously undermines the 'patriotic' content of the movie; I also view *Way of the Dragon* (1972) as a schlock classic. The climatic fight with Chuck Norris never fails to make me laugh because rather than taking place in the Colosseum, it was obviously mostly filmed on a movie stage with unconvincing painted backdrops. The low humour in the first part of the film also grooves me. The country bumpkin persona Lee adopts and his endlessly comparing Rome unfavourably to Hong Kong is a laugh riot, especially when this ridiculously narrow world view is completely undercut by Bruce's character insisting that when it comes to martial arts one should learn from all styles and not assume that Chinese boxing is inherently superior; which is how the ongoing small mindedness gag is undercut in the English dub. While less of a groove sensation than Lee's two follow up films, *The Big Boss* (1971) is nonetheless highly entertaining too.

Today I find it hard to believe I actually liked *Enter the Dragon* (1973) when I first saw it more than forty years ago at the age of 12. Now it just looks like tedious sub-James Bond Hollywood crapola to me. Of course, Bruce moves beautifully in his fight scenes and I can still appreciate that, but he also looks gravely ill since he'd reduced his body fat to a ridiculous degree; this is especially evident in his combat scene with the porky but incredibly agile Sammo Hung. Competitive bodybuilders do the same thing, and to me also look like they're sick; many die prematurely just as Bruce Lee did. Given that *Enter the Dragon* was the first X-rated film I managed to view at a cinema, I was going to be thrilled by whatever I saw after successfully blagging my way in. Looking at it now much of the flick is boring padding. The Jim Kelly and John Saxon flashbacks are a real waste of screen time, as is Saxon's presence throughout the movie. Likewise Lee is awful in his non-fight scenes, having adopted a stupidly subdued persona compared to his previous three movies; presumably in a bid to appeal to 'international'—that is mostly North American—audiences.

One way in which Bruce Lee's star vehicles resemble Brucesploitation is in their endless recycling of the same elements. Nunchucks first appear in Lee's mid-sixties *Green Hornet* series, and then reappear in his Hong Kong movies. Lee had a cameo in an episode of *Ironside* ("Tagged for Murder", first broadcast on 26 October 1967) and the Quincy Jones theme tune is referenced in the music cues for *Way of the Dragon* (1972) and *Enter the Dragon* (1973), although these are riffs on a groove and not straight rip-offs. Lee appeared in four episodes of the 1971/2 TV series *Longstreet* and the cod martial arts philosophy he develops there is tediously recycled in *Enter the Dragon*—and if Lee had lived to complete *Game of Death* himself it seems that would have featured even more of this jive talk. The natty tracksuit Lee wears in *Longstreet* is also revamped in the official *Game of Death* (1978), although the colours and cut are changed. *Way of the Dragon* revisits Lee having an uncomfortable encounter with a prostitute, which is also an element in *The Big Boss* (1971), and reuses Paul Wei Pin-Ao in his obnoxious but camp bad guy translator role from *Fist of Fury* (1972). In line with what Henri Bergson has to say in *Laughter* (1900), these repetitions are side-splittingly funny. Had Lee lived longer then we'd have had a lot more of this comic recycling; he was working from a rather limited template as an actor and director.

Reversing from the ridiculous into the sublime, one of the things that most disappoints me about Lee now is how in his fight scenes everything he does looks like a perfectly executed demonstration. I'd prefer some rougher edges, which is why I'd rather watch Bruce Le, at least when he's being directed by someone like Joseph Velasco. The scenes with the snake in *Enter the Dragon* look too controlled and safe compared to Bruce Le's interactions with serpents in *Enter the Game of Death* (1978) or *Bruce King of Kung Fu* (1980). Le training snake style with real snakes is to me a lot more thrilling than anything Bruce Lee committed to celluloid; even if according to some sources Bruce was bitten by the cobra used in *Enter the Dragon*, in the final edit he is shown as being in complete control when dealing with the snake.

But it isn't just the cream of Brucesploitation flicks that stand up better to repeated viewing than Bruce Lee's movies, there is a whole world of martial arts films that do this too. Bruce Lee provided me with a good entry point into a wider world of fight flicks, and Brucesploitation in many ways does the same thing. Which is another reason why I thought it worth covering films in the outer limits of the genre in some detail—beyond title and marketing they may have little to do with the Little Dragon, but many are martial arts anti-classics in their own right. And far more exploitative than anything in the Brucesploitation genre are some of the documentaries about Lee, which grossly overstate his influence and importance as regards martial arts films. *Path of the Dragon* (1998) is probably the very worse offender.

For me Brucesploitation deconstructs the mythology of Bruce Lee by emphasising mechanical and repetitive aspects within his performances. For those who decide to view Lee from a Chinese nationalist perspective, he can end up being conflated with the roles he played, and in particular Chen Zhen and Kato. Thus after 1997, Brucesploitation made within the People's Republic of China seems to act as a conduit for Chinese state propaganda, and for local bureaucrats Lee seems to function in a manner analogous to other local folk heroes with a martial bent such as Wong Fei Hung, Fong Sai Yuk and more recently Lee's Wing Chun teacher Ip Man. Neither Bruce Lee nor Ip Man endorsed Maoist politics— Lee in interviews claimed to be apolitical, despite his 'philosophy' blatantly betraying his bourgeois origins—one wouldn't know this from watching films such as *Hero Youngster* (2004), *Legend of the Fist* (2010) or *The Grandmaster* (2013). Folk heroes can be manipulated for all sorts of political ends, and this is Lee's fate for now too.

An extended look at any 'iconic' figure is likely to diminish most people's appreciation of them, unless they are predisposed to fan worship. Examining Brucesploitation entailed not only thinking about Bruce Lee, but also learning new things about him. He is not to blame for his privileged family background—which is particularly evident on his mother's side—but it does put his ability to achieve global fame in a different perspective than if he'd grown up as a 'son of the streets' as some hagiographies imply. What came as a real surprise to me when reading interviews with his siblings was that they claimed he'd never learned to swim or ride a bicycle. This makes Lee's impressive development as a martial artist appear very one-side. So while I can still enjoy Bruce Lee's adult Hong Kong movies, I'm definitely less impressed by him now than when I began my systematic exploration of Brucesploitation. But I think the same would be true of almost any figure I'd chosen to research.

In terms of genre theory my view of Brucesploitation would seem to contradict film 'theorist' Christian Metz's notion that there are four phases of genre in film: viz, experimental, classic, parody and deconstruction. Brucesploitation seems to start with parody in the form of Ramon Zamora vehicles like *The Pig Boss* (1972) and remain at the level of parody until it is hijacked by the state capitalists of the People's Republic of China to spread poisonous nationalist propaganda. Rather than Metz's theories, Isidore Isou's notion of there being amplic and chiselling phases in culture seems more appropriate to an understanding of Brucesploitation. Earlier flicks such as *The Black Dragon's Revenge* (1975) tend to be sleazier and more willing to play with the various rumours surrounding the death of Bruce Lee. This salaciousness factor—driven by producers—also accounts for why some of Bruce Li's Little Dragon bio-pics are almost enjoyable despite that actor being about as exciting to watch as paint dry. By the late-seventies the shock value of the myths circulating about Bruce Lee had been largely exhausted, and so film-makers concentrated more on the cinematic aspects of this kung fu icon and ignored his mythological biography. The resultant focus on come-on gestures, nose thumbing, freezing movement prior to and after punches, face pulling, shaking and stomping, had the happy effect of chiselling away at Bruce Lee's icon aura by demonstrating that rather than being anything natural, his screen image had been carefully constructed from a series of overdone and ultimately ridiculous signifiers. Brucesploitation as a vehicle for Chinese state propaganda might be seen as a new amplic phase.

When dealing with Brucesploitation one inevitably comes up against the worst product of the Little Dragon's celebrity, the Bruce Lee fanboy. Usually male, these saddos tend to think that Lee was superhuman and could do no wrong. They take any criticism of Lee as a personal affront and many of them are deeply offended by Brucesploitation films. My own view of Lee is rather different, I tend to approach him in the way that Otto Rühle portrayed Marx in his biography *Karl Marx: His Life and Works* (Viking Press, New York, 1929). While earlier writers had painted Marx either as a monster with terrible ideas or a communist saint, Rühle saw him as a deeply flawed man whose obvious personal shortcomings were necessary to enable him to produce the theory required by the proletariat. I'd see Bruce Lee as deeply flawed and obsessive too, but it was precisely those faults that enabled him perform so well in three hokey but extremely entertaining kung fu flicks.

Lee's so-called philosophy is very much a product of its time, and might be viewed as amusing hippie bollocks if fanboys weren't prone to taking it seriously. Lee's individualism and emphasis on 'self-expression' is very much an outgrowth of the sixties zeitgeist, and fits well with many forms of 'countercultural' capitalism since his 'theoretical' formulations are paradigmatically bourgeois. That said, given a cultural obsession with the figure of the scholar in parts of South East Asia, Lee's desire to project himself as both a 'warrior' and a 'philosopher' should also be seen as a ridiculous attempt to present himself as an ideal fusion of these archetypes to parts of his audience. This is not something that has much resonance with viewers like me, especially as I am not prone to giving philosophical bullshit—regardless of whether it comes from Martin Heidegger, Bruce Lee or some other bourgeois hack—any credence whatsoever. Lee is often reported to have studied philosophy at the University of Washington from 1961 to 1964, but that institution on the part of its website dedicated to famous alumni describes him a drama major. Presumably philosophy was a secondary subject for Lee, and since he didn't graduate he probably didn't take either this or acting too seriously at the time.

I'm not a martial artist and I'm not in a position to pass definitive judgements on Bruce Lee's contributions to unarmed combat. Nonetheless, while Lee was clearly a highly trained athlete and inspirational mixed martial arts coach and teacher for those who came into direct contact with him, that doesn't necessarily make him a great fighter. Lee's fighting abilities weren't tested in competition and my gut feeling is that Lee's contributions to martial arts have been overstated; celebrity contributions to anything are invariably hyped-up. It should go without saying his extreme exercise and dietary regime would have almost certainly resulted in an early death had he not died first from a swelling of the brain. Jacky Cheung's character Frankie Lone in the film *High Risk* (1995) AKA *Meltdown* is mainly intended to skewer Jackie Chan as a movie fake, but takes a few pops at Bruce Lee too. The not exactly subtle point is that the everyday lives—and actual street fighting abilities—of movie stars are nothing like what we see on screen. I don't cover *High Risk* above because it is a parody of many things including Hollywood action movies, but Bruce Lee satire is in there alongside much else including Jet Li as Frankie Lone's bodyguard and Billy Chow performing what might be taken as a piss-take of Jean-Claude Van Damme.

Another movie I viewed because some claim it is Brucesploitaiton was *Black Mask* (1996). It's basically a superhero film with Jet Li providing a typically dull performance in the lead role. The mask and hat Li wears to disguise himself look vaguely like those worn by Bruce Lee in his Kato role in the *Green Hornet* TV show (hence the claims this is Brucesploitation), but there the similarities end. While Li does a little wushu (less than in many of his flicks), *Black Mask* isn't really a martial arts movie but more a generic action film. So I didn't deal with it above because it wasn't worth including too many relatively well-known and well-covered films in my outer limits category, and especially not those that I'd see as falling outside the martial arts genre.

I also didn't address kung fu movie documentaries and trailer compilations that include elements of Brucesploitation such as *Cinema of Vengeance* (1994—the material of interest here is recycled in the same team's *Top Fighter* from the following year too) and *Kung Fu Trailers of Fury* (2016) because they are a mixed bag and clearly en bloc lie outside the genre I'm dealing with. However mention should be made of the spectacularly inept and inaccurate *Hong Kong Fury* (2004). This is basically a compilation of film trailers with voice-over introductions by someone called Rozar. The penultimate trailer is for *True Game of Death* (1979) which is wrongly described as starring Bruce Li, and this is followed by promotional material for *Goodbye Bruce Lee, His Last Game of Death* (1975), which is called rare—although it's actually one of the best known Brucesploitaiton titles—and the fact this flick really is a Bruce Li vehicle isn't mentioned. Also, of course, both these films were Taiwanese productions, as are other flicks included in this compilation such as *The Eight Masters* (1977). Presumably if the makers of this documentary/trailer compilation had known anything about martial arts movies they wouldn't have included Taiwanese product in *Hong Kong Fury*—which is billed on the front of the UK DVD cover as: "An in depth look at the classics of Hong Kong cinema". Unfortunately this is the level of misinformation one is faced with when researching not just Brucesploitation but also martial arts films in general.

To shift to a different issue entirely, Brucesploitation and old school kung fu flicks also reveal (if you know how to look) the way Taiwanese cinema completely obscures the real history of that island, due both to a desire to appeal to Chinese audiences around the world and government censorship. Likewise, it is a function of Bruce Lee himself becoming 'iconic' that these days one rarely hears mention of him looking like a member of the sixties boy band The Beatles. But with his moptop hair and collarless suit (in *Fist of Fury),* for many in England and elsewhere in the mid-seventies, he came across as a throwback to the first wave of the so-called British Invasion of the north American pop charts.

Much more work could go into researching the man I could call 'the king of Brucesploitation', director Joseph Velasco. Currently there is very little information about him readily available to English speakers, or as far as I can tell in any language whatsoever. In many ways Velasco's films speak for themselves. He started out on his Brucesploitation journey with *Bruce's Deadly Fingers* (1976) and is credited with being the director of the iconic *Clones of Bruce Lee* (1980), although how much of the latter movie he is actually responsible for is open to question. The means by which he came to be credited as director of an export version of the Indonesia movie *Cobra* (1977) when it is clearly the work of Rempo Urip is another mystery that has yet to be fully cleared up. Velasco appears to be the director of around eleven Brucesploitation anti-classics, even if the last two of these are simply cut-and-paste efforts that mix and match his—and other people's—earlier movies. Some other work to which Velasco's name has been attached was

203

marketed as Brucesploitation although the content of the films doesn't warrant such hype.

Velesco's first film *Tough Guy* (1972) AKA *Kung Fu the Head Crusher* was falsely sold as Brucesploitatin under the title *Kung Fu Master —Bruce Lee Style*. I deal with this title above but all of Velasco's pre-*Bruce's Deadly Fingers* movies are worth looking at since their casts and plots are reused throughout the director's Brucesploitation cycle. After giving Chan Sing the lead role in his first movie, Velasco deployed Cheung Lik (who has a supporting role in *Kung Fu the Head Crusher*) as his star in *A Tooth for a Tooth* (1973) AKA *Japanese Connection, Kung Fu's Hero* (1973), *Kung Fu King* (1973), *The Big Risk* (1974), and *Superior Youngster* AKA *Karado the Cat from Hong Kong* (1974). These are all very cheaply made old school bashers with the focus on action and martial arts. The plots concern struggles for possession of 'objects' (papers, a gold mine, women who are being sex trafficked) and these are basically an excuse for punch-ups.

The first five of the six films Velasco made before entering the Brucesploitation racket are insanely repetitious both within and between themselves; this combined with their fast and furious action lends them a dream-like quality. We see the same actors, playing more or less the same characters, often at the same locations. Several also feature topless women in sexual situations with voyeurism thrown in. Despite female nudity the titillation focus seems to be much more on the men. This is most obvious in a scene in *The Big Risk*, where a minion is watching his boss getting a blow job through a keyhole and while doing so eats a banana in a really gross way. One can only assume the underling wishes he was giving the boss a blow job. The banana skin is thrown on the floor and another hood slips on it and goes crashing through the bedroom door, ending up in bed with the boss and his lady. In *Kung Fu King* a flunky is naked in bed with the boss's woman when his master arrives home. The transgressor hides under the mattress and the boss proceeds to have sex with his sweetheart, with the minion peeking out to get a good look at the physical action. Eventually the bed collapses and the flunky's voyeurism is exposed. In *A Tooth for a Tooth* the boss is aware of his valet peering at him having sex, while simultaneously sticking a digit in his mouth, a signifier of gay desire like the banana in *The Big Risk*. In the same film a safe lock being picked with a piece of wire—more penetrative phallic symbolism—is juxtaposed with a sex scene. In Velasco's early movies the women seem to be ciphers through which the men can give sublimated expression to their more polymorphous perverse urges.

Tiger Force (1975), Velasco's last movie before he embarked on his Brucesploitation odyssey marks a major change in direction. While still very low budget it clearly had a lot more money spent on it than any of his previous films, and it also boasted a Filipino co-director in the form of Danny Ochoa. Here Chan Sing repeats his role from Velasco's *Kung Fu the Head Crusher*; he's an undercover cop infiltrating a dangerous criminal gang with support from Cheung Lik. Only this time because Velasco has risen from no budget to low budget, a helicopter, a light aircraft and speedboats are involved. While the Hong Kong talent in the form of the lead actors and choreographer Yuen Woo-ping is used to amp up the unarmed combat, there are also blazing gun battles. Chan Sing looks way cooler than Chow Yun Fat in later gun fu movies when he has a pistol in each hand. Velasco learnt a lot from this shoot, since it looks nothing like his earlier films but minus the gun scenes it resembles some of his later output. We also have the first shot of Manila airport in a Velasco movie, something that would become a recurring image in his work with Bruce Le. By the time he'd made this his sixth movie, Velasco had used many of the actors —Bolo Yeung, James Nam and Chiang Tao number among those I haven't yet listed—and scenarios that he'd repeat again and again with his Brucesploitation output. These early films also feature some classic Velasco WTF? moments: in *Kung Fu King* Cheung Lik leads a troop of lion dancers into a field where a beheading is about to take place, a diversion that enables him to save the life of a framed man. Lion dancers also appear in *Kung Fu's Hero,* presumably because Velasco had free or cheap access to them.

Velasco's locations seem to depend very much on his budget. So while the low budget *Bruce's Deadly Fingers* has the urban backdrop also seen in parts of *Tiger Force, The Treasure of Bruce Lee* (1979) is set in the countryside where it was apparently easier and cheaper to film, and this has the no budget vibe of Velasco's first five movies; alongside a load of cut-and-paste material from an earlier James Nam flick. Another Velasco film I haven't mentioned yet is *Thundering Ninja* (1987). This cuts new ninja footage into an old Jimmy Wang-Yu flick *The Criminal* (1977). The result is a generic Filmark International production that looks like it could have been directed by almost anyone, including Godfrey Ho and Al Adamson. *The Criminal* hardly shows Wang Yu at his best, while the new material is uninspired. This is easily Velasco's worst movie assuming he actually had a hand in making *Thundering Ninja.*

And so while my trek through the wilds of Brucesploitation lowered my opinion of Bruce Lee, it raised my estimation of Joseph Velasco! Had it not been for my desire to better understand this martial arts subgenre it's unlikely I'd have ever come to the realisation that as a director Velasco is every bit as significant as Jess Franco and Lucio Fulci!

A Note on the Title of this Book

Re-Enter the Dragon has been listed in various places as a Bruce Le feature. Wikipedia said: *"Re-Enter the Dragon* is a 1979 Martial Arts Brucesploitation film starring Bruce Le. Not much is known about the film and it is hard to find..." The flick's Internet Movie Database entry currently doesn't list a cast beyond Bruce Le and contains no plot synopsis – however it does claim the film was made in colour in Hong Kong in 1979 with a mono Cantonese language soundtrack and a 2.35 : 1 aspect ratio. An old Grindhouse Cinema Database entry provides extra data in the form of a Spanish language poster for the alleged film with the title *El Puño Del Dragón,* which translates as *The Fist of the Dragon*. This carries the strapline: 'feroz como un tigre... su violencia no conocio piedad!!!' or, "fierce as a tiger... his violence knew no pity!" The poster on the Grindhouse site bills *El Puño Del Dragón's* lead actors as Bruce Le, Ho Max Wai and Chan Man. Therefore this does not seem to be the 1979 Jackie Chan flick released in English as *Dragon Fist* and in Spanish as *El Puño Del Dragón*. Nor is it likely to be *The Eagle's Killer* (1979) with Hwang Jang Lee also released in Spanish as *El Puño Del Dragón*. I suspect the film *Re-Enter the Dragon* may not exist. Other elusive Brucesploitation titles include *The Young Dragon* (1979), which has an IMDB entry that currently boasts a poster and an unlikely plot synopsis - as well as actor credits including Michael Wai-Man Chan and Bruce Le, with Joseph Kong listed as director. It may be that both the titles I'm addressing here had promotional material made for pre-sales but were never actually shot, or else were ultimately issued under different names. That said, it remains possible these titles have been conjured up as a result of hoaxes or misunderstandings - and that one or more people are producing retro-looking posters for films that don't actually exist. Now that's Brucesploitation!

10

BRUCESPLOITATION FLICKS TO CHECK OUT IF YOU'RE NEW TO THE GENRE AND WANT AN OVERVIEW

1	*Black Dragon Vs Yellow Tiger* (1974)	2
2	*Black Dragon's Revenge* (1975)	5
3	*Bruce Lee, His Last Days, His Last Nights* (1976)	9
4	*Bruce and The Golden Chaku* (1977)	48
5	*Cobra* (1977)	13
6	*Dragon Lives Again* (1977)	14
7	*Enter Three Dragons* (1978)	56
8	*Bruce Against Iron Hand* (1979)	58
9	*True Game of Death* (1979)	25
10	*The Clones of Bruce Lee* (1980)	28

ANTI-ACKNOWLEDGEMENTS
AND FURTHER SOURCES OF CONFUSION

Any book dealing with a film genre will draw to some extent on what has already been covered by others, even if this is only to correct what has gone before. In terms of online resources I have looked repeatedly at the *Hong Kong Movie Database, Hong Kong Cinemagic, City on Fire,* and the defunct but still available Geocities site *Many Bruces*. The *Korean Movie Database* and *Film Indonesia* also proved useful on a smaller number of occasions. *The Clones of Bruce Lee* site might have been consulted more if much of it had not been taken offline before I really got stuck into the subject of Brucesploitation. Alongside Andrew Leavold's *Blogspot* posts mainly (but not exclusively) devoted to Weng Weng, the best resource I found for Filipino movies in English was *Video 48* at *Blogspot,* but I'm still hoping there is something better out there that I've somehow overlooked.

When it comes to books there isn't much that directly addresses my subject. I have mentioned *Here Come the Kung Fu Clones* by Carl Jones, which is a slim fan publication about Bruce Li, and therefore has a focus on the intertwined cinemas of Hong Kong and Taiwan. Many other readily available publications show a similar bias towards Hong Kong and often don't give much coverage to the flicks I'm looking at here: for example *The Essential Guide to Hong Kong Movies* by Rick Baker, Toby Russell, Lisa Tilston et al (Eastern Heroes Publications, London 1994); *Sex and Zen and a Bullet In the Head* by Stefan Hammond and Mike Wilkins (Titan Books, London 1997); *Hollywood East* by Stefan Hammond (Contemporary Books, Chicago 2000); *Hong Kong Action Cinema* by Bey Logan (Overlook Press, Woodstock 1995).

Chasing Dragons: An Introduction to Martial Arts Films (I.B. Tauris, London 2006) by David West devotes space to Japan, Hong Kong and the USA but ignores The Philippines, Korea and Indonesia; all of which produced Brucesploitation as well as other martial arts movies. That said, while West's views are far from a perfect match with mine, I like the simplicity and clarity of his writing; while I disagree with West on many points, his damning opinions about Robert Clouse as a director and Jean-Claude Van Damme's limited repertoire of onscreen moves are hilarious and accurate. I feel that if West had been less generous as a critic—but remained as moralistic—then his book could have been a total laugh-riot; although obviously he was aiming for and achieved something else! I tend to view West's dislike of the nihilism he sees as characterising much seventies Japanese martial arts cinema—especially when dovetailed with his appreciation for earlier humanistic samurai movies that critique feudalism—as an apology for and defence of capitalism. At least some of the nihilism West dislikes should be understood via theories of alienation as an attack on capitalist social relations.

Asian Cult Cinema by Thomas Weisser (Boulevard Books, New York 1997) devotes a couple of confused pages to Brucesploitation. To provide an example of its shortcomings, Weisser mistakenly thinks *Big Boss 2* (1978) AKA *Dragon Lee Fights Again* is the same flick as *Big Boss Part II* (1976), and that Dragon Lee who is only in the former, also appears in the later with Bruce Le (and others). Every bit as poor at covering Brucesploitation is *Intercepting Fist: The Films of Bruce Lee and the Golden Age of Kung-Fu Cinema* edited by Jack Hunter

(Creation Books, London 2005). Chapter 6 of *Intercepting Fist* consists of six skimpy pages (about fifty percent of which is pictures and blank space) entitled 'Biopix and Brucesploitation'. *Bruce Lee and I* (1976, the year of release is wrongly rendered as 1975 in this book) AKA *Bruce Lee His Last Days, His Last Nights,* is dismissed in two sentences, with the second running as follows: "Ting Pei goes topless and, naturally, is shown to be guiltless in the death of the kung-fu superstar." It is clear from the way the nude scenes in *Bruce Lee and I* are edited that it's actually a body double (and not Ting Pei) who 'goes topless'; Ric Meyers makes the same mistake in his book, dealt with below, and I suspect the error here may have been recycled from there. Likewise the term guiltless is misleading since Ting Pei was clearly grief stricken by Lee's death and grief often entails feelings of guilt.

Much of the text in *Intercepting Fist's* super-short chapter on Brucesploitation consists of lists of films, and Jack Hunter who compiled it was obviously confused not just about their dates of release but even their names and alternate titles! For example, in the list of Bruce Li flicks, *Bruce Against Iron Hand* (1979) is listed as two different films—rather than the one it is—under the alternative titles of *Bruce Lee Vs Iron Hand* and *Bruce Lee's Iron Finger*; in both instances the year of release is—as far as I can tell, and I'm sure I've done more checking on this than Hunter—incorrect. This woefully inadequate overview of Brucesploitation concludes with the following: "This avalanche of trash finally started to subside as the 1980s progressed…." Which left me wondering if the book's editor Jack Hunter (AKA James Williamson AKA Julian Hallett, who compiled/wrote this section) had ever actually seen a Brucesploitation movie, or if he'd just read about them in other people's film books and then grabbed further misinformation from online sources without checking it. Likewise, given that elsewhere Hunter exhibits a taste for the Eurosleaze film genre, it is peculiar that he should deploy 'trash' as a pejorative term here.

VideoHound's Dragon: Asian Action and Cult Flicks edited by Brian Thomas (Visible Ink, Detroit 2003) is a mixed bag when it comes to Brucesploitation. It reviews a reasonable number of films that relate to this genre, and the plot summaries are clearly based on recent viewings of the movies in question (rather than other people's reviews or hazy memories) and overall are well done. However, the two sections specifically dedicated to Brucesploitation are less than thrilling. The first, subtitled 'Too Many Fists of Fury' is largely a list of films that have titles that in some way resonate with English language releases of Bruce Lee's flicks. The list contains a seemingly random mix of Brucesploitation and movies that I've never seen discussed as belonging to the genre but that sound a bit like Bruce Lee titles. It includes *Asian Connection* (I assume the 1995 movie is being invoked, clearly it isn't the 2016 flick with this title) but not *Amsterdam Connection* (1978) or *Japanese Connection* (1973) which both also sound a bit like the US title of Lee's second adult star vehicle *The Chinese Connection* (1972). Likewise, titles such as *Enter the Ninja* (1981) and *Enter the 36th Chamber of Shaolin* (1985) seem to be included mainly because they begin with the same two words as *Enter the Dragon* (1973). The inclusion of only one 'serious' Bruce Lee documentary *Bruce Lee: A Warriors Journey* (2000) adds to the random feel of the list; while the fact that it consists of nothing but titles—without even the year of release—further amps up the sense of confusion.

The other Brucesploitation section in *VideoHound's Dragon* is subtitled 'The Clones of Bruce Lee' and proves equally useless. Bruce Li, Dragon Lee and Bruce Le are given as the chief clones; alongside a number of falsehoods including the claim Bruce Le starred in *Bruce Lee Fights Back from the Grave*—he doesn't even appear in this movie. The error I've just listed is repeated in the separate review, which also wrongly states this Korean production is a Hong Kong film and re-airs the fake rumour that the director was Italian exploitation legend Umberto Lenzi. While *VideoHound's*

Dragon is a wide-ranging overview of Asian cinema—it even includes some Indian horror films and anime—and works as an introduction to many genres, it is a long way from perfect when it comes to Brucesploitation. It's other shortcomings include too much focus on campy horror films such as the *Blood Island* series with regard to Filipino cinema, while much of this region's marvellous martial arts movie heritage—including of course its Brucesploitation—is ignored.

Chinese Martial Arts Cinema: The Wuxia Tradition by Stephen Teo (Edinburgh University Press, Second Edition 2016) and *Hong Kong Cinema: The Extra Dimension* by Stephen Teo (BFI, London 1997), provide some background information to Brucesploitation despite a focus on Hong Kong, and to a lesser extent Shanghai. Teo's EUP book partially corrects theoretical shortcomings as regards his frankly ridiculous exposition of Bruce Lee and nationalism in his 1997 work. While there is plenty of Chinese nationalism in the Little Dragon's films, reactions to it—not to mention who is responsible for it and Lee's take on it– are considerably more complex than Teo's writing suggests: "The case of Bruce Lee is of particular interest because his international appeal does not appear to contradict his forthright insistence on his Chineseness. Western admirers of Lee view him differently from his Eastern admirers, and the differences revolve around his nationalism. To many Western viewers Lee's nationalism is a non-starter... The English critic Tony Rayns has argued that Lee's narcissism is a trait which distinguishes him more than his nationalism. To the West Lee is a narcissistic hero who makes Asian culture more accessible. To the East he is a nationalistic hero who has internationalised some aspects of Asian culture." 'Newsflash' for Stephen Teo: not only is Bruce Lee not a hero to the overwhelming majority of people in the world (that is both 'east' and 'west'), billions all around the world have never even heard of him.

The jump Teo makes in conflating the views of Tony Rayns (which in any case he may not have accurately summarised) with those of a monolithic 'west' is patently absurd. Likewise it ought to be obvious that most of those in 'the west' who view Bruce Lee as a 'hero' couldn't give two shits about whether or not he is narcissistic—or indeed whether he makes Asian culture more accessible to them—and that those who view him as narcissistic are unlikely to see him as a hero. And again, the overwhelming majority of Bruce Lee fans from culturally non-Chinese communities in 'the east'— which consists of considerably more than China and the Chinese diaspora—are unlikely to see their idol as a 'nationalistic hero'. That said, since it would be equally stupid to assume that all those who are culturally Chinese are also nationalists, it would have been more prudent of Teo to say only that to parts (perhaps—at a stretch—even the bulk) of Bruce Lee's culturally Chinese audience he is 'a nationalistic hero'. Nonetheless, I wouldn't put Lee down by calling him that because to me saying someone is a nationalist is an insult that's only one step away from describing them as an unreconstructed fascist. Teo's Chinese nationalist rhetoric in *Hong Kong Cinema* is so overstated that it amounts to little more than unctuous bullshit. Of course all nationalism is bullshit regardless of whether it is British, German, Russian, Italian etc. And it should go without saying that nationalism isn't the only utterly repulsive ideology to have originated in Europe and then spread to China amongst other places; anarchism, which is the flip-side and mirror image of statist nationalism, is another really stupid European belief system taken up by some Chinese 'intellectuals'.

Teo's take on Bruce Lee's career trajectory had he lived seems to be based more on wish-fulfilment than a consideration of the facts. In *Hong Kong Cinema* Teo writes: "The first work to be directed and scripted by Bruce Lee, *The Way of the Dragon*, is sadly, a flawed and transitional work which must now remain as Lee's testament, a reminder of themes which could have developed further and with more assurance and confidence had he lived. Up to this production, Bruce Lee had not only espoused the art of Chinese kung fu, he had also dealt with the theme of the Chinese immigrant who must face discrimination and oppression: double blows to the pride and dignity of the Chinese character as they put roots in foreign lands...." Contra Teo, rather than simply focusing on Lee, I would see writer/director Lo Wei as an important source for the Chinese nationalism in the Little Dragon's first two movies for Golden Harvest. Evidence for this can be found some of Wei's other films.

I don't cover *None But the Brave* (1973) above but in it Wei explores the same historical period and anti-Japanese sentiments as he does in *Fist of Fury* (1972). *None But the Brave* is less successful than the director's earlier hit precisely because Cheng Pei-Pie doesn't overact in the lead role; whereas for this viewer, Lee's carpet chewing hamminess in *Fist* undermines Wei's political message by exposing—and at least for me satirising—political nationalism as an ideology that transforms those who adhere to it into absurd nutjobs. Obviously while the underdogs in conflicts configured along ethno-nationalist lines are rarely as obnoxious as the dominant players in the politics of bigotry, should the power dynamics be reversed then so too will outside perceptions of who is the more unpleasant party. One only has to think about recent conflicts between China and The Philippines with regards to territorial claims in the so-called 'South China Sea' to realise this has already occurred vis-à-vis Chinese nationalism.

Other films written and directed by Wei such as *New Fist of Fury* (1976) also show this film-maker as being addicted to a rabble rousing nationalism. Obviously Wei was never going to make a film depicting proletarian internationalism squaring up to imperialism, nor attempt to develop the 'abstract' Chinese cultural nationalism Teo hallucinates into the films he made with Bruce Lee—something that might have functioned in a manor akin to the black power movement in the USA. While the project Teo outlines may have interested Lee—let's not forget that on his mother's side he came from a very rich and politically extremely influential family, so given his bourgeois origins such inclinations would not be surprising—it is clear enough to me that the Little Dragon would not have sacrificed his desire for money and celebrity in order to promote such ideas. Likewise, despite Teo's insistence that he is talking about 'abstract nationalism', ultimately it isn't possible to separate this from state based political nationalism since it flows into it. Teo's championing of Chinese nationalism is necessarily as obnoxious to those who identify as say Tibetan or Uighur, as British nationalism is to those who see themselves as Scottish or Welsh; let alone those who refuse any and all national identities.

Curiously, according to a report about Bruce Lee entitled 'The man who was Mao's hero' by Raymond Zhou in the *China Daily* (updated 17/12/2010), the repressive and reactionary figurehead for state capitalism in China from the fifties to the seventies was a fan of the Little Dragon's films and liked what he saw as their political message. Of course, Lee is not responsible for the actions or views of his fans, and one assumes Wei would have been horrified by Mao's alleged reaction because he appears politically closer to the CPC's rival but less successful Chinese nationalists in Taiwan. According to Zhou's article: "While watching *Fist of Fury* for the first time, Mao dissolved in tears and said 'Bruce Lee is a hero!' Mao watched the movie three times, and this is thought to be more times than any other film that was screened for him. Obviously different people respond in different ways to the same movie; as someone who does not identify as Chinese and who despises all forms of nationalism—but especially British nationalism—I dissolved into laughter the first time I saw *Fist of Fury* at the age of twelve because Lee's performance in the film is so silly. It seemed to me back then in the mid-seventies—and still seems the same way to me today more than forty years later—that Lee's performance ultimately amounted to burlesque and buffoonery that undermined nationalist sentiment.

While I can see why Chinese nationalists might view *Fist of Fury* as propagating their beliefs, it appears that those caught in the thrall of this reactionary ideology are incapable of viewing things from my perspective. Zhou in the article cited above goes on to say: "As Mao correctly observed, Lee's movies portray the fight between good and evil and Lee invariably embodied the good. That's something everyone can relate to." Really? Whether or not Lee was in agreement with Wei's nationalism in *Fist of Fury* is a moot point. For me, Lee's over-the-top performance in the film undermines its message regardless of whether this was intentional on the Little Dragon's part or not. Contra Zhou I do not think *Fist of Fury* portrays a fight between good and evil, instead it demonstrates that each and every nationalist ideology is reactionary clap-trap. The idea that everyone will relate to Lee's movies in the same way is totalitarian. In regard to this Teo is somewhat more sophisticated than Zhou, because he sees Lee as having a split nationalistic and narcissistic reception; although this is also an enormous simplification of a far messier reality. And while nationalists might see incidents such as the smashing of the 'No Dogs and Chinese' sign by Lee in *Fist* as an act of patriotism, for those who aren't swayed by such ideologies the fact that the film's star choreographed his acrobatics here to resemble Korean—and perhaps even Japanese—martial arts board breaking displays, results in it looking to me as much like a party trick as a political act; although it can of course be both. The message Wei wanted to send his audience and the one Lee's performance evokes oppose to each other, and it is this tension that makes *Fist* work so well as a movie.

Returning to Teo's speculations about Lee, from what we know of the Little Dragon's ideas for the unfinished *Game of Death* (1978), this academic is wrong when he suggests Lee 'espoused the art of Chinese kung fu' (although Wei may have done so) since it is clear he wanted to break with all national styles in the martial arts. *Stoner* (1974) which Lee was slated to star in but due to his death it was made without him also seems to indicate Teo is mistaken in thinking that *Way of the Dragon* was a transitional piece from which Lee might have moved into a more sophisticated and 'abstract nationalism' than the atavistic patriotism Wei imposed on *Fist;* which Lee's histrionic performance kicks against.

Stoner began life with the working title of *The Shrine of Ultimate Bliss* and was conceived as another *Enter the Dragon*-style spy thriller/martial arts blockbuster aimed squarely at the international market. Originally it was going to be bankrolled by Warner Brothers and co-star ex-James Bond actor George Lazenby and Japanese martial arts movie sensation Sonny Chiba alongside Lee. Allegedly the original marketing tagline for the movie was: "It's Lee! It's Lazenby! It's Bruce Versus Bond!" This makes the flick sound like a piece of Brucesploitation even if the proposed budget was astronomical for a martial arts film at the time. *Stoner* was the film Lee was working on alongside *Game of Death* in the weeks before he died, and one of the reasons that Lazenby was in Hong Kong at the time of the Little Dragon's death. When Lee passed on both Warner Brothers and Chiba pulled out of the project, but the production went ahead with Lazenby and Angela Mao as the stars. The film we now have in the form of *Stoner* is probably better than what we'd have got if Hollywood had been involved with it. All of which suggests that had Lee lived he would have developed his career in directions that would have had little appeal to either Teo or people like me who aren't convinced by Teo's arguments about Lee and nationalism. And again, while I have seen odd references to both *Stoner* and *Yellow Faced Tiger* (1974, written for Lee but rejected by the Little Dragon before his death) as Brucesploitation, my feeling is that few fans take the assertion these flicks belong to the genre seriously since both movies were marketed on the basis of the stars they ultimately featured (Lazenby and Mao in *Stoner*, and Chuck Norris and Don Wong Tao in *Tiger*) rather than their 'what-might-have-been' connection to Lee; which is why I don't address them in the main body of this text.

Since I was born and live in London and I sometimes get paid to review films—and books, art and music—I presumably count as what Teo in *Hong Kong Cinema* configures as a 'western critic'. If so he really doesn't understand what I like about Bruce Lee—although I'm not claiming all those he lumps together as 'western critics' share my tastes. Teo claims: "Lee's indulgence in playing the bumpkin does not stand him in good stead with Western critics who will be put off by the grossness and crass naivety of his character, because it strikes so close to home. This bumpkin easily reminds Westerners of the infamously rude Chinese waiters in Chinese restaurants all over Europe. On top of this negative image is Tang Lung's buffoonery." Teo is supposedly an academic but in this passage he comes across as something more akin to a raving idiot! If I didn't like buffoonery there is no way I'd dig Rudy Ray Moore's movies, and I absolutely love them. Likewise it's ridiculously silly to suggest Bruce Lee reminds me, or indeed most 'Western critics', of Chinese waiters in European restaurants—he doesn't. The average Chinese waiter in Europe doesn't have the kind of cut muscle definition the Little Dragon displays in his adult movies. I should perhaps also add that in my experience Chinese waiters are generally as polite as non-Chinese waiters—and that European restaurants with rude staff tend to go out of business sooner rather than later.

I also disagree with many of Teo's other views, and see his emphasis on the emergence of postmodernism in the Hong Kong new wave as misleading; low-brow directors who appear to be of no interest Teo—including Joseph Velasco and Godfrey Ho—were making post-modern movies in the territory in the 1970s and 1980s. Other aspects of Teo's *Hong Kong Cinema* are frankly baffling, such as his repeated use of the term 'male bondage'—often in conjunction with the word loyalty—when he seems to mean male bonding. If some of the views Teo expresses in *Hong Kong Cinema* were presented as having come from a fictional idiot savant, they would be denounced as too far-fetched. Whoever edited Teo's book for the BFI was asleep on the job. The text should have been professionally re-written before being published to remove its many absurdities.

Looking elsewhere, *China Forever: The Shaw Brothers and Diasporic Cinema* by Poshek Fu (University of Illinois Press, 2008) is in parts broader in geographical scope than Teo's offerings, but isn't much help in getting to grips with Filipino or Korean cinema. Poshek's other books including *The Cinema of Hong Kong: History, Arts, Identity* (Cambridge University Press, 2000, co-edited with David Desser) and *Between Shanghai and Hong Kong: The Politics of Chinese Cinemas* (Stanford University Press, 2003) are narrower in their territorial coverage—although the former does give space to audience reception of Hong Kong films in the USA. Another academic called Paul Bowman devotes as much ink in his books *Theorizing Bruce Lee: Film-Fantasy-Fighting-Philosophy* (Rodopi, Amsterdam 2009) and *Beyond Bruce Lee: Chasing the Dragon Through Film, Philosophy, and Popular Culture* (Wallflower Press/Columbia University Press, New York 2013) to expositions of contemporary western academic celebrities such as Jacques Rancière as the Little Dragon; which may or may not interest cultural studies students but certainly doesn't groove me.

Kung Fu Cult Masters: From Bruce Lee to Crouching Tiger by Leon Hunt (Wallflower Press, London 2003), sits somewhere between academic and fan discourse. I found both the section on Brucesploitation and the book overall disappointingly narrow; once again the focus is very much Hong Kong. The following observation by Hunt is indicative of how he either misses the mark or is slyly misleading when writing about Brucesploitation: "...only one film in the Lee canon actually generated sequels (and, later re-makes and revisions). *Fist of Fury* is arguable the key Lee film for those eager to construct nationalist readings of his persona...." Actually Yang Yang made a sequel to *Way of the Dragon* (1972) in the form of *Black Dragon Vs the Yellow Tiger* (1974), and Chan

Chue made a sequel to *The Big Boss* (1971) with *The Big Boss 2* (1976) (neither is mentioned by Hunt in his text or filmography); the Lee films the stories in these two flicks continue did not generate multiple sequels (plural) or revisions like *Fist of Fury*. In terms of early remakes and revisions, Jun Gallardo's misleadingly named *Game of Death* (1974) was very quick to rip-off *Enter the Dragon* (1973). Likewise what Hunt means when he invokes the 'Lee canon' is never properly defined, although on the basis of his text it seems safe to conclude that he doesn't view the official *Game of Death* (1978) as belonging to it. But what, for example, is the status of the actor's childhood films in Hunt's 'Lee canon'? Is *Thunderstorm* (1957) a part of the 'Lee canon'? And if so (to raise a question that couldn't be asked until after Hunt's book was published), is *Curse of the Golden Flower* (2008)—which draws on the same play as Lee's adolescent film—a revision of *Thunderstorm*?

The book I most like that might be invoked here is *The Ultimate Guide to Martial Arts Movies of the 1970s: 500+ Films Loaded With Action, Weapons and Warriors* by Dr. Graig D Reid (Black Belt Books Valencia CA 2010). In terms of the historical period surveyed this cuts off too early for it to be comprehensive about Brucesploitation, but it does cover the start of the genre in terms of capsule overviews (Reid calls them martialologies) that focus on fighting techniques as much as plots. It also covers films from around the world. In his introduction Reid gives a brief outline of the kind of themes one should learn to recognise in Chinese (somewhat problematically defined as Hong Kong/Taiwan), Japanese and South Korean martial arts films—since according to Reid these geographical areas produced the most movies in the genre he's covering. The Philippines, which is an important production area for Brucesploitation, doesn't lag so far behind but isn't given such generous treatment. Still I like Reid's approach: "The one thing I have discovered over time is that every film has its moments. Even though a film may truly suck the royal bird or be at the low end of the spectrum, if there is one moment of martial glory, a great kick, a series of punches or a fighter against a group of baddies that for some reason just clicks, then that film is always worthy to be watched, even just for that moment." True indeed, especially if you want to comprehend a genre (which is why I sat through so many lousy Bruce Li films while writing this text).

Since nationalism frequently functions as a key narrative strand within Brucesploitation flicks, as background those interested in the genre may find it useful to familiarise themselves with perhaps the best known historical work on the subject, viz *Imagined Communities* by Benedict Anderson (Verso, London 1983); assuming, of course, they haven't already read it. Anderson's focus is the book as a pivot of nationalist conjuration and he devotes a good deal of his attention to South East Asia (since this was his area of academic speciality and he spoke a number of languages that are used in the region). What Anderson has to say about the book requires translating to film, including Brucesploitation movies, in as far as this has not been done to date. *Constructing Nationhood in Modern East Asia* edited by Kai-Wing Chow, Kevin M Doak and Poshek Fu (University of Michigan Press, Ann Arbor 2003) is also of interest here; although it doesn't touch base with The Philippines. This book is useful in reminding us that martial arts films tend to simplify Ming/Manchu dynastic conflict, and that the Han identity in which many of these flicks are grounded is a relatively recent creation; it emerged during the late-nineteenth/early twentieth-century, as dynastic organisation was replaced by what were initially imported ideas of nationalism grounded in European models. This book also serves to underline the complexity of the Taiwanese identity and its convoluted relationship to Japanese colonialism, which is often brutally simplified in kung fu films. The essays on Korea might also serve as a starting point for discussing why so many of the films from that peninsula dealt with above have historical settings.

Before finishing I should give a big shout out to Ric Meyers, a man whose books on martial arts movies and other subjects have contributed to making him a figure much hated by a broad cross-section of cult film fans. What amazes me about Meyers is just how many words of abuse have been heaped upon him by movie bloggers. Should you want to know what many fu fans dislike about Meyers, you can check out the seven long blogs the *Cool Ass Cinema* website devoted to him under the title *The Tao of Ric: True Lies and a Fistful of Meyerisms*. There is an eighth long blog in this series devoted to what Meyers doesn't know about western grindhouse cinema that riffs on his non-fu book *For One Week Only: The World of Exploitation Films* (Eirini Press, 2011, a 'revised' version of a 1983 publication): this final rant more or less concludes with a picture of infamous Spanish anti-auteur Jess Franco overlayed with the words: "To that twat Ric Meyers, I am SPANISH… not MEXICAN."

Since others have said more than enough about Meyers, I don't really need to add much. However, it is worth noting he hates Brucesploitation, having stated in his book *Great Martial Arts Movies* (Citadel Press, New York 2002): "Even the best of these films were dreadful. A western equivalent would be to have Hollywood make a bunch of Dirty Larry movies staring Clint Westwood…. The directors and writers of these travesties (Brucesploitation flicks) manage to sink anything their star can't…" Actually Clint Westwood movies sound like a great idea to me; although obviously they'd be way better if they were made in Italy and Spain rather than Hollywood. And contra the implication of Meyers' Dirty Larry aside, Brucesploitation wasn't a purely 'eastern' genre—Ric seems to have forgotten that one of the best Brucesploitation anti-classics *Fist of Fear, Touch of Death* (1980) was made in the USA; admittedly on the east coast and not in Hollywood.

Meyers devotes several paragraphs to the official *Game of Death* (1978), which he sees as the worst piece of Brucesploitation ever, but he apparently never cottons on that its director Robert Clouse and the supporting cast of b-list Hollywood actors make it as much American (western) as it is 'Chinese'. Golden Harvest wanted an international blockbuster and allowing a desire for profits to override any aesthetic judgements they may have had, bought in the USA film-making elements that ensured *Game of Death* sucked shit thru a straw. And when talking about the North American titles of Bruce Lee's movies, Meyers conflates the USA with English speaking audiences; as if there weren't native English speakers in other parts of the world—such as England—hello? Meyers more or less concludes his chapter on Chinese films by claiming: "…the bottom line is that the sun which shone brightly over the Hong Kong film industry now shines on American shores. Nearly all the greats of the martial arts movie are either working in Hollywood or looking for work there." Aside from being repulsive these manifestations of American patriotism are as stupid as Meyers' notion of the so-called greats of martial arts. Did Joseph Velasco seek to work in Hollywood? I doubt it. But then Meyers doesn't give Velasco proper consideration, he just captions a poster for this director's *Karado the Cat from Hong Kong* (1974) with the words: "In the wake of *Five Fingers of Death* came inferior works like this." But Meyers' 'inferior' is for me a superior anti-classic! Nonetheless, if the text I'm now concluding makes me as unpopular among fight flick fans as Ric Meyers, then this will be a major achievement! And if it doesn't, well that's just the way it goes…

Finally the one film fanatic I knew who was always happy to watch martial arts movies with me, and who shared my love for directors like Jess Franco and Lucio Fulci, died in the summer of 2014 before I really started work on what's here. What I've written would have greatly benefited from extended discussions with her about it—but very sadly that wasn't to be. Therefore this work is dedicated to the memory of Marga Tormo Moll (born Bolbaite 1968, died London 2014), who I know would have laughed a lot while reading my take on Brucesploitation—and who always made me laugh a lot too.

INDEX

10 Commandments of Lee (1978)
  AKA *Master and the Kid*
  AKA *Shaolin Master and the Kid*
  AKA *Fury of the Shaolin Master*
  AKA *One Man Army*
  111 ....23, 162
18 Bronzemen (1976) 64
1975 San Diego Comic-Con convention 66
5 Pattern Dragon Claws (1983)
  AKA *Fists of Lightning*
  AKA *Thunderfist*
  AKA *Thundering Fist*
  130 .... 23, 180-181
7 Doors of Death
  SEE *The Beyond* (1981)
99 Women (1969) 193
Abdul-Jabbar, Kareem ....
  37, 54, 55, 56, 60, 61, 72, 81, 82, 130, 134
Accattone (1961) 145
Adamson, Al 23, 165, 166, 205
Ali, Muhammad 8, 123
Allied Artists (video co) 118
Amazon.com (web site) 16
Amsterdam Connection (1978) 208
An Chu, Kim 69, 71
Anderson, Benedict 213
Angry Dragon, The
  SEE *Dragon Lee Vs the 5 Brothers* (1978)
Angry Tiger
  SEE *Spirits of Bruce Lee* (1973)
Angry Young Man
  SEE *Lee the Angry Man* (1983)
Ant, Adam 183
Apocalypse Now (1979) 56
Aquarius Releasing (distributor) ....
  65, 66, 67, 68, 150, 151
Arrate, David 118
Arrow (distributor) 38
Asian Connection (1995) 208
Asian Cult Cinema (magazine) 207
Asso Asia Films (film company) 69, 153
Atlas Films (film company) 37
Atom Ant Meets Karate Ant (tv episode) 8
Atom Ant Show, The (tv series) 8
Au-Yeung Jun, Ulysses 22, 23, 152, 154
Avenger, The
  SEE *Queen Boxer* (1972)
Avenging Fury
  SEE *Fist of Fury III* (1979)
Bad Bet on a 459-Silent (tv episode) 94
Bae Su-Cheon 95, 119, 120
Baker, Rick 207
Bamboo House of Dolls, The (1973) 169
Banks, Aaron 65, 66, 67, 68
Bar-Kays, The 107
Barnett, James 178
Baron, Bruce 177, 178, 185, 187
Barry Lyndon (1975) 56
Barry, John 56
Bates Alcantara Advertising Agency 63
Batman (tv series) 8

Batzella, Luigi 21, 107, 109
Bava, Mario 168
Bay of Blood (1971) 168
Beach, Mr 8
Beatles, The (group) 124, 203
Beaudine, William 20, 92, 94
Bee, Kenny 135, 1992
Belafonte, Harry 66
Benn, Jon T. 64, 71, 107
Bergson, Henri 200
Best Film & Video (distributor) 45, 156, 160, 177
Between Shanghai and Hong Kong: The Politics of Chinese Cinemas (Fu) 212
Beverly Wiltshire Filmworks (prod co) 49
Beyond Bruce Lee: Chasing the Dragon Through Film, Philosophy, and Popular Culture (Bowman) 212
Beyond, The
  AKA *7 Doors of Death* (1981) 66
Beze, Fabienne 78
Bialla, Ralf 66
Big Boss 2
  SEE *Bruce Against the Odds* (1977)
Big Boss 2 (1978)
  AKA *Dragon Lee Fights Again*
  AKA *Dragon Bruce Lee 2*
  18 ....12, 19, 22, 49-51, 153, 207
Big Boss 2, The (1976) 213
Big Boss of Shanghai, The (1979) 13
Big Boss Part II (1976) 12, 207, 213
Big Boss Untouchable (2002)
  AKA *Dragon the Master 2*
  1 .... 22, 85, 136
Big Boss, The (1971) 13, 16, 41, 46, 51, 64, 85, 86, 89, 100, 102, 105, 135, 200, 213
Big Risk, The (1974) 204
Billy Liar (1963) 165
Black Dragon Fever
  SEE *Kung Fu Fever* (1979)
Black Dragon Vs the Yellow Tiger (1974)
  AKA *The Growling Tiger*
  AKA *Tiger from China*
  2 ....19, 27-28, 115, 206, 212
Black Dragon's Revenge, The (1975)
  AKA *Death of Bruce Lee*
  5 .... 11, 19, 31-35, 40, 66, 201, 206
Black Mask (1996) 203
Black Spot (1991)
  AKA *Earth* and *Fire*
  AKA *Vicious Passageway*
  85 .... 22, 134-135
Blair, Linda 35
Blank, Marion 175
Blind Fist of Bruce
  SEE *Blind Fists of Bruce Lee* (1979)
Blind Fists of Bruce Lee (1979)
  AKA *Blind Fist of Bruce*
  119 168
Blood Island (film series) 209
Bloodsport (1988) 108
Blow Job (1964) 29

Bo-Cheung, Hon 22, 23, 149, 164
Bodyguard
  AKA *Karate Kiba, The* (1976) 68
Bodyguard, The (1974) 12
Bolo Yeung 41, 49, 54, 55, 56, 57, 61, 64, 70, 71, 79, 95, 98, 100, 103, 104, 108, 121, 125, 127, 132, 147, 163, 172, 173, 204
Bond, James (fictional character) .45, 172, 177
Bond, James (film series) ....
  46, 56, 79, 80, 107, 127, 166, 200, 211
Bonet, Charles 11, 31, 32, 33, 34
Bongo Rock (tune) 120
Bongolia (tune) 104
Boss, The (1973) 13
Bouchet, Barbara 41
Bowman, Paul 212
Boxer from Shantung (1972) 13, 140
Boxer's Omen (1983) 169, 192
Brick Lane Market, London 8
Bronson Lee, Champion (1975)
  94 .... 22, 145-146
Bronson, Charles 146, 147
Brown, James 33
Brown, Jim 66
Bruce Against Iron Finger
  SEE *Bruce Against Iron Hand* (1979)
Bruce Against Iron Hand (1979)
  AKA *Bruce Against Iron Finger*
  AKA *Iron Finger*
  58 ....21, 104-105, 206, 208
Bruce Against Snake in the Eagle's Shadow (1979)
  AKA *Bruce Vs Snake in the Eagle's Shadow*
  75 ....21, 124
Bruce Against Supermen (1975) 47, 67
Bruce Against the Odds (1977)
  AKA *Big Boss 2*
  AKA *The Mighty Four*
  AKA *Four Brave Dragons*
  AKA *Lone Shaolin Avenger*
  102 .... 12, 22, 153
Bruce and Shaolin Kung Fu (1977)
  AKA *Ching Wu and Shaolin Kung Fu*
  47 .... 20, 95, 119, 122, 127, 128
Bruce and Shaolin Kung Fu 2 (1978)
  AKA *Ching Wu and Shaolin Kung Fu 2*
  70 .... 21, 119-120, 122, 123, 152
Bruce and *The Dragon Fist* (1977)
  AKA *Furious Dragon's Rage*
  103 .... 22, 153-154
Bruce and the Golden Chaku (1977)
  AKA *Golden Chaku*
  48 .... 20 , 96-97, 206
Bruce and the Shaolin Bronzemen (1982)
  AKA *Enter the Game of Shaolin Bronzemen*
  AKA *King Boxer II*
  81 ...... 22, 48, 57, 127, 130-131, 133, 154
Bruce and the Shaolin Poles (1977)
  AKA *Secret of the Shaolin Poles*
  104 .... 23, 154-155
Bruce Fights Back
  SEE *Ninja Strikes Back* (1982)

215

Bruce Has Risen
  SEE *Deadly Strike* (1978)
Bruce Hong Kong Master (1975)
  AKA *Hong Kong Superman*
  96 ....22, 147
Bruce Is Loose (1977)
  AKA *The Green Dragon Inn*
  105 ....23, 155-156
Bruce King of Kung Fu (1980)
  AKA *Legend of Bruce Lee*
  26 ....19, 61-62, 201
Bruce Lee Against Superman (1975)
  AKA *Bruce Lee Vs the Supermen*
  AKA *Superdragon Vs Superman*
  6 ....19, 35-36, 125
Bruce Lee and I
  SEE *Bruce Lee: His Last Days, His Last Nights* (1976)
  SEE ALSO *Fist of Unicorn* (1973)
Bruce Lee Connection, The 12
Bruce Lee Fights Back from the Grave (1976)
  AKA *Visitors In America*
  99 ....18, 22, 65, 150-151, 208
Bruce Lee in GOD (2000)
  38 ....20, 81-82
Bruce Lee in New Guinea (1978)
  AKA *Bruce Li In New Guinea*
  AKA *Bruce Li in Snake Island*
  71 ....21, 120-121
Bruce Lee Story, The
  SEE *Bruce Lee: A Dragon Story* (1974)
Bruce Lee Strikes Back
  SEE *Kung Fu Fever* (1979)
Bruce Lee the Invincible (1978)
  AKA *The Invincible*
  AKA *Bruce Li the Invincible Chinatown Connection*
  113 ....23, 47, 159, 163
Bruce Lee True Story
  SEE *Bruce Lee: The Man, the Myth* (1976)
Bruce Lee Vs Chinese Frankenstein
  SEE *On the Verge of Death* (1973)
Bruce Lee Vs Gay Power (1975) 14
Bruce Lee Vs Iron Hand
  SEE *Bruce Against Iron Hand* (1979)
Bruce Lee Vs the Chinese Frankenstein (1978)
  114 ....23, 164
Bruce Lee Vs the Supermen
  SEE *Bruce Lee Against Superman* (1975)
Bruce Lee We Miss You
  SEE *The Dragon Dies Hard* (1975)
Bruce Lee, My Brother
  SEE *Young Bruce Lee* (2010)
Bruce Lee, the Man and the Legend (1973) ..15
Bruce Lee: A Dragon Story (1974)
  AKA *Super Dragon: The Bruce Lee Story*
  AKA *The Bruce Lee Story*
  1 ....19, 27, 149
Bruce Lee: A Warriors Journey (2000) 208
Bruce Lee: His Last Days, His Last Nights (1976)
  AKA *Bruce Lee and I*
  AKA *I Love You, Bruce Lee*
  9 ....19, 20, 38-40, 52, 89, 206, 208
Bruce Lee: The Man, the Myth (1976)
  AKA *Bruce Lee True Story*
  10 ....8, 15, 19, 40-41, 55, 117
Bruce Lee's Deadly Kung Fu
  SEE *Story of the Dragon* (1977)

Bruce Lee's Dual Flying Kicks (1978)
  AKA *Dual Flying Kicks*
  112 ....23, 162-163
Bruce Lee's Greatest Revenge (1978)
  AKA *Bruce Le's Greatest Revenge*
  AKA *Way of the Dragon 2*
  53 ....21, 100-101
Bruce Lee's Iron Finger SEE *Bruce Against Iron Hand* (1979)
Bruce Lee's Last Days 89
Bruce Lee's Secret
  SEE *Story of the Dragon* (1977)
Bruce Lee's Ways of Kung Fu (1977)
  AKA *Dragon Lee's Ways of Kung Fu*
  AKA *Ways of Kung Fu*
  106 ....23, 153, 156-158, 182
Bruce Le's Greatest Revenge
  SEE *Bruce Lee's Greatest Revenge* (1978)
Bruce Li In New Guinea
  SEE *Bruce Lee in New Guinea* (1978)
Bruce Li in Snake Island
  SEE *Bruce Lee in New Guinea* (1978)
Bruce Li the Invincible Chinatown Connection
  SEE *Bruce Lee the Invincible* (1978)
Bruce Li's Jeet Kune Do
  SEE *Story of the Dragon* (1977)
Bruce Li's Magnum Fist (1978)
  AKA *Magnum Fist*
  AKA *Great Hero*
  115 ....23, 164-165
Bruce Strikes Back
  SEE *Ninja Strikes Back* (1982)
Bruce Takes Dragon Town (1974)
  AKA *Bruce Takes the Dragon*
  AKA *Dare You Touch Me?*
  91 ....22, 142-143
Bruce Takes the Dragon
  SEE *Bruce Takes Dragon Town* (1974)
Bruce the Super Hero (1979)
  22 ....19, 56-57, 172
Bruce the Top Master
  SEE *Bruce's Ninja Secret* (1988)
Bruce Vs Bill (1981)
  122 ....23, 171-172
Bruce Vs Snake in the Eagle's Shadow
  SEE *Bruce Against Snake in the Eagle's Shadow* (1979)
Bruce, D-Day at Macao (1975)
  AKA *Little Superman*
  AKA *Little Hero*
  AKA *Fist of Vengeance*
  AKA *Kung Fu Superman*
  95 ....22, 146-147
Bruce, Kung Fu Girls (1975)
  AKA *Five Pretty Young Ladies*
  97 ....22, 27, 147-149, 165
Bruce, Lee 156
Bruce's Deadly Fingers (1976)
  AKA *Bruce's Fingers*
  11 ....19, 41, 57, 59, 133, 203, 204, 205
Bruce's Fingers
  SEE *Bruce's Deadly Fingers* (1976)
Bruce's Fists of Vengeance (1980)
  27 ....20, 59, 62-63
Bruce's Last Battle
  SEE *Bruce's Ninja Secret* (1988)

Bruce's Ninja Secret (1988)
  AKA *Bruce's Secret Kung Fu*
  AKA *Bruce's Last Battle*
  AKA *Bruce the Top Master*
  83 ....22, 131, 133
Bruce's Return
  SEE *Return of Bruce* (1977)
Bruce's Secret Kung Fu
  SEE *Bruce's Ninja Secret* (1988)
Buñuel, Luis 66
Caesar, Adolph 65, 66, 67
Caine, Kwai Chang (fictional character) .45, 47
Camacho, Art 191
Cameroon Connection (1985) 14, 15
Camp, Colleen 55
Can Dialectics Break Bricks? (1973) 67, 102
Canavarro, Bobby 45
Cao Yu 67
Carol, Linda 184, 185
Carradine, David 14, 35, 45
Carry, Julius 183
Castellari, Enzo G. 78
Castillo, Celso Ad. 23, 162
Chaku Master (1974)
  3 ....19, 28-30
Challenge of the Tiger (1980)
  AKA *Gymkata Killer*
  AKA *Seize the Formula*
  62 ....21, 80, 107-109, 166
Challenge the Dragon
  SEE *Way of the Tiger* (1973) 28
Champ Against Champ (1980)
  AKA *Champ Vs Champ*
  AKA *Twelve Gates of Hell*
  121 ....23, 169-170
Champ Vs Champ
  SEE *Champ Against Champ* (1980)
Chan Chue 12, 213
Chan Fei-Lung 141
Chan Ka-Seung, Gordon 24, 194
Chan Lau 31, 35, 42, 99, 100, 125, 126
Chan Man (appears to be Michael Chan Wai-Man) 205
Chan Ngai-Wai, Zackey 22, 153
Chan Pak-Cheung, Nat 193
Chan San-Yat 19, 59
Chan Sing
  ....120, 121, 139, 151, 152, 162, 163, 204
Chan Tung-Man 20, 98
Chan Wa 19, 49
Chan Wai-Man, Michael 12, 41, 90, 91, 116, 141, 152, 163, 172, 173, 175, 176, 205
Chan Yiu-Lam, Charlie 90
Chan, Jackie
  11, 68, 69, 76, 83, 151, 152, 161, 181, 202, 205
Chan, Johnny 68
Chan, Unicorn 47, 89
Chang Cheh 155
Chang Hu 96
Chang Kang 76
Chang Ping Han 199
Chang, Bruce 57
Chang, Chaplin 81
Chang, Jacky (AKA Cheung Lik AKA Chang Lic) 72
Chang, Johnny 12
Chang, Susan 56

216

INDEX

Chao, Emily 143
Chaplin, Deborah 150
Chase, The (1971) 118
Chasing Dragons: An Introduction to Martial Arts Films (West) 207
Chen Zhen (character) 11, 12, 83, 84, 95, 105, 110-111, 197, 201
Chen, Jacky 83
Cheng Kei-Ying 69
Cheng Pei-Pie 210
Cheng Siu-Siu 151, 152
Cheng, Olivia 177
Cheung Bo-Man, Karen 82, 85, 195
Cheung Kei, William 19, 49
Cheung Lik 50, 68, 69, 70, 71, 72, 103, 120, 127, 131, 139, 163, 204
Cheung Man, Sharla 135-136, 193
Cheung Mong, Bruce 153
Cheung Ning 133
Cheung, Jacky 202
Cheung, Roy 82
Chia Ling 140
   SEE ALSO Judy Lee
Chiang Sung AKA Joseph Velasco 14
Chiang Tao 41, 56, 57, 64, 68, 69, 75, 103, 108, 109, 119, 122, 123, 127, 132, 134, 135, 154, 171, 172, 173, 204
Chiba, Sonny 56, 68, 98, 107, 144, 146, 211
Chin Siu-Ho 194, 195
China Daily (newspaper) 210
China Forever: The Shaw Brothers and Diasporic Cinema (Fu) 212
Chinatown Connection (1990)
   139 . . . . 24, 30, 191
Chinese Connection III
   SEE *Fist of Fury III* (1979)
Chinese Connection, The (1972) 208
Chinese Ghost Story (1987) 192
Chinese Godfather, The (1974)
   AKA *Chivalrous Knight*
   43 . . . . 20, 89-91, 117
Chinese Gods (1976) 15
Chinese Iron Man (1974)
   AKA *Iron Man*
   AKA *Young Hero of Shaolin II*
   92 . . . . 22, 106, 143-144
Chinese Mack, The
   SEE *Martial Arts* (1974)
Chinese Martial Arts Cinema: The Wuxia Tradition 209
Chinese Stuntman, The (1982)
   AKA *Counter Attack*
   33 . . . . 20, 74-75
Ching Wu (martial arts school) 48, 76, 95, 101, 105, 123-124, 151-152, 194-195
Ching Wu and Shaolin Kung Fu
   SEE *Bruce and Shaolin Kung Fu* (1977)
Ching Wu and Shaolin Kung Fu 2
   SEE *Bruce and Shaolin Kung Fu 2* (1978)
Ching, Tin 171
Chiu Chow Kung Fu (1973) 15
Chivalrous Knight
   SEE *The Chinese Godfather* (1974)
Choe Dong-Joon 20, 76
Choe U-Hyeong 19, 54
Chong, Million 157
Chow A-Chi, Artis 199

Chow Kai-Wing 213
Chow Ming 117
Chow, Billy 82, 83, 84, 194, 195, 203
Chow, Raymond 38
Chow, Ruby 49, 135
Chow, Stephen 135, 136, 194, 1992
Christ, Jesus 67, 184
Chu Tak-On, Rico 22, 24, 135, 1992
Chu Yen-Ping, Kevin 24, 194
Chui Dai-Chuen 21, 91, 116
Chui Man-Kwai, Martin
   101, 105, 128, 173, 182, 183
Chum, Amy 57
Chung Gwok-Hang 22, 140
Chung, Lily 82
Cinema of Hong Kong: History, Arts, Identity, The (ed. Fu & Desser) 212
Cinema of Vengeance (1994) 203
Citizen Kane (1941) 130
City On Fire (web site) 9, 207
Clark, Jim 53
Clones of Bruce Lee, The (1980)
   28 . . . . 10, 15, 16, 20, 64-65, 69, 70, 71, 72, 103, 107, 176, 203, 206
Clones of Bruce Lee, The (web site) 11, 189, 207
Clouse, Robert 9, 19, 44, 55, 60, 61, 81, 207, 214
CMV (dvd label) 101
Cobra (1977)
   13 . . . . 19, 42-45, 100, 203, 206
Cocteau, Jean 82
Cohen, Rob 10
Cold Blooded Murder (1981)
   123 . . . . 23, 172-173
Comfort Women (1992)
   141 . . . . 24, 192-193
Communist Manifesto, The (Marx & Engels) .51
Communist Party of China 84
Concord of Bruce
   SEE *Ninja Vs Bruce Lee* (1982)
Conspiracy
   SEE *Enter the Panther* (1975)
Constructing Nationhood in Modern East Asia (ed. Chow, Doak, Fu) 213
Cool Ass Cinema (website) 214
Cooper, Henry 8
Corman, Roger 65
Corpse Mania (1981) 168
Coudrey, Jovy 177, 178
Counter Attack
   SEE *The Chinese Stuntman* (1982)
Criminal, The (1977) 205
Crush (1972) 102
Cultural Centre of The Philippines 62
Curse of the Golden Flower (2008) 213
Curtis, Sam 117
Dante, Count 53
Dare You Touch Me?
   SEE *Bruce Takes Dragon Town* (1974)
Deadly Hands of Kung Fu
   SEE *The Dragon Lives Again* (1977)
Deadly Silver Ninja, The
   SEE *The Dragon, the Young Master* (1978)
Deadly Strike (1978)
   AKA *Wanted! Bruce Li, Dead or Alive*
   AKA *Bruce Has Risen*
   72 . . . . 21, 85, 121-122, 143

Death Dimension (1978)
   116 . . . . 23, 165-166
Death of Bruce Lee
   SEE *The Black Dragon's Revenge* (1975)
Death Wish (1974) 147
Debord, Guy 37
Deep Throat (1972) 65
Desser, David 212
Diaz, Edna 158
Dik, Shut 19, 22, 27, 147, 149
Dirty Dozen, The (1967) 143
Doak, Kevin M. 213
Dolgen, L. 20, 85, 86
Dolgen, Lauren 86
Dolgin, Larry 20, 81, 85, 86
Dong-Ho, Kim 70, 72
Don't Cry for Me Argentina (tune) 60
Doo-Yong, Lee 22, 150
Dr. Mabuse (character) 92
Dr. Mabuse, der Spieler (Jacques) 92
Dracula (1931) 16
Dracula (fictional character) 45, 46
Dragon and the Cobra, The
   SEE *Fist of Fear, Touch of Death* (1980)
Dragon Bruce Lee 2
   SEE *Big Boss 2* (1978)
Dragon Dies Hard, The (1975)
   AKA *Bruce Lee We Miss You*
   7 . . . . 6, 19, 36-37, 55
Dragon DVD (dvd label) 90
Dragon Fist (1979) 205
Dragon Force (1982)
   AKA *Power Force*
   127 . . . . 23, **138**, 177-178
Dragon in Fury (2004)
   145 . . . . 24, 83, 195-196
Dragon Inn (1967) 155
Dragon Lee Does Dallas
   SEE *The Last Fist of Fury* (1977)
Dragon Lee Fights Again
   SEE *Big Boss 2* (1978)
Dragon Lee Fights Back
   SEE *Muscle of the Dragon* (1981)
Dragon Lee Vs the 5 Brothers (1978)
   AKA *The Five Brothers*
   AKA *The Angry Dragon*
   54 . . . . 21, 51, 101-102
Dragon Lee's Ways of Kung Fu
   SEE *Bruce Lee's Ways of Kung Fu* (1977)
Dragon Lives Again, The (1977)
   AKA *Deadly Hands of Kung Fu*
   14 . . . . 11, 19, 45-47, 159, 163, 172, 206
Dragon Lives, The (1976)
   AKA *He's a Legend, He's a Hero*
   67 . . . . 21, 117, 182, **198**
Dragon on Fire
   SEE *Enter Three Dragons* (1978)
   SEE ALSO *The Dragon, the Hero* (1979)
Dragon Returns
   SEE *Return of Bruce* (1977)
Dragon the Master (2001)
   39 . . . . 20, 82-83, 85, 167
   SEE ALSO *The Dragon, the Young Master* (1978)
Dragon the Master 2
   SEE *Big Boss Untouchable* (2002)
Dragon, the Hero, The (1979)
   AKA *Dragon on Fire*
   76 . . . . 21, 103, 125-126

217

Dragon, the Lizard, the Boxer, The (1977)
`107` 23, 47, 158-159
Dragon, the Young Master, The (1978)
  AKA *Dragon the Master*
  AKA *Dragoneer 8—The Unbeatable*
  AKA *The Deadly Silver Ninja*
`118` 23, 167
Dragon: The Bruce Lee Story (1993) 10, 12, 117
Dragoneer 13: The Significant
  SEE *Enter the Invincible Hero* (1981)
Dragoneer 5: The Indomitable
  SEE *Golden Dragon Silver Snake* (1980)
Dragoneer 8: The Unbeatable
  SEE *The Dragon, the Young Master* (1978)
Dragon's Infernal Showdown, The (1980)
  AKA *Dragon's Showdown*
`79` 21, 128-129
Dragon's Showdown
  SEE *The Dragon's Infernal Showdown* (1980)
Dragon's Snake Fist, The (1979)
`59` 21, 105
Driller Killer (1979) 68
Drunken Master (1978) . . 10, 68, 152, 168, 194
Dual Flying Kicks
  SEE *Bruce Lee's Dual Flying Kicks* (1978)
Duel Maut (Deadly Duel)
  SEE *Steel Fisted Dragon* (1977)
dvddrive-in.com (website) 181
Dynamo (1978)
`19` 19, 51-53, 107, 136
D'Amato, Joe 65
Eagle's Killer, The
  SEE *Puño Del Dragón, El* (1979)
Earth and Fire
  SEE *Black Spot* (1991)
Eastwood, Clint (actor) 45, 46
Eastwood, Clint (fictional character) 123
Edge of Fury (1978)
`117` 23, 166
Eight Masters, The (1977) 203
Emery, Linda 90
  SEE ALSO *Linda Lee*
Emmanuelle (fictional character) 45, 46
Emmanuelle 3 (1980) 109
Emmanuelle Goes to Cannes (1980) 109
Emperor of the Underworld (1994) 85
Engels, Friedrich 51
Enter the 36th Chamber of Shaolin (1985) . 208
Enter the Dragon (1973) . . . .
  8, 16, 28, 30, 31, 35, 41, 44, 46, 48, 49, 51, 54,
  57, 58, 59, 62, 64, 69, 71, 79, 81, 83, 85, 90,
  91, 95, 96, 98, 100, 101, 102, 103, 104, 105,
  108, 109, 115, 117, 121, 122, 125, 135, 147,
  166, 173, 182, 183, 200, 201, 208, 211, 213
Enter the Fat Dragon (1978)
`55` 21, 59, 102-103, 135, 194
Enter the Game of Death (1978)
  AKA *King of Kung Fu*
`20` 19, 54-55, 56, 77, 80, 82, 201
Enter the Game of Shaolin Bronzemen
  SEE *Bruce and the Shaolin Bronzemen* (1982)
Enter the Invincible Hero (1981)
  AKA *Dragoneer 13—The Significant*
`124` 23, 173-174, 178, 186

Enter the King of Kung Fu (1981)
  AKA *Zen Kwan Do Strikes Paris*
  AKA *Kung Fu Leung Strikes Emmanuelle*
  AKA *Kung Fu Emmanuelle*
`125` 23, 175
Enter the Ninja (1981) 208
Enter the Panther (1975)
  AKA *Conspiracy*
`98` 22, 149-150, 165
Enter Three Dragons (1978)
  AKA *Dragon on Fire*
`56` 4, 21, 68, 103, 126, 173, 206
Essential Guide to Hong Kong Movies, The (Baker, Russell, Tilston et al) 207
Eun, Lee 19, 49
Evita (musical) 60
Exit the Dragon, Enter the Tiger (1976)
  AKA *Star of Stars*
`12` 19, 41-42
Exorcist, The (1973) 35
Exorcist, The (fictional character) 45, 46
Eye of the Dragon
  SEE *Ninja Strikes Back* (1982)
Fails, J.W. 188
Fairchild, Morgan 108
Fan, Roger 196
Farewell to Cheyenne (tune) 139
Fast and Furious (film series) 196
Fei, Lung 142, 143, 152, 162
Fei, Meng 154, 155, 158
Ferrara, Abel 147
Feuillade, Louis 35
Fierce Boxer and Bruce, The (1977)
  AKA *The Fierce Boxer*
`108` 23, 159-160
Fierce Boxer, The
  SEE *The Fierce Boxer and Bruce* (1977)
Fierce One, The (1974)
  AKA *Jaws of the Dragon*
`93` 22, 144-145, 161
Fight At Hong Kong Ranch, A
  SEE *Golden Dragon Silver Snake* (1980)
Film 2000 (dvd label) 75, 78, 81
Film Indonesia (web site) 207
Filmark International (film company) 205
Finishing the Game: Search for a New Bruce Lee (2007)
`146` 24, 196
Fish and Fury (1972) 10
Fist of Death
  SEE *Jackie and Bruce to the Rescue* (1982)
Fist of Fear, Touch of Death (1980)
  AKA *The Dragon and the Cobra*
`29` 15, 20, 47, 65-68, 214
Fist of Fury (1972) 12, 16, 21, 41, 46, 47,
  51, 54, 55, 60, 62, 69, 74, 76, 77, 81, 83, 84, 89,
  90, 95, 96, 100, 104, 110, 120, 123, 124, 134,
  136, 139, 140, 143, 144, 152, 154, 172, 194,
  195, 200, 203, 210, 211, 212, 213, 1977, 1979
Fist of Fury (1979)
  SEE *Fist of Fury III* (1979)
Fist of Fury 1991 (1991)
`86` 22, 135, 136
Fist of Fury 1991 II (1992)
`142` 24, 193-194
Fist of Fury 3
  SEE *Fist of Fury III* (1979)

Fist of Fury II (1977)
`49` 20, 97, 100, 106, 144
Fist of Fury II (1979)
  SEE *Fist of Fury III* (1979)
Fist of Fury III (1979)
  AKA *Avenging Fury*
  AKA *Chinese Connection III*
  AKA *Fist of Fury*
  AKA *Fist of Fury II*
  AKA *Fist of Fury 3*
`60` 21, 105-106, 144
Fist of Fury: The Legend of Chen Zhen
  SEE *Legend of the Fist: The Return of Chen Zhen* (2010) 21, 110
Fist of Legend (1994)
`144` 12, 24, 83, 111, 194-195, 196
Fist of Unicorn (1973)
  AKA *Unicorn Palm*
  AKA *Bruce Lee and I*
`42` 10, 12, 20, 27, 47, 59, 89, 90
Fist of Vengeance
  SEE *Bruce, D-Day at Macao* (1975)
Fist, The (tv series) 11
Fistful of Dollars, A (1964) 123
Fistful of Dragons
  SEE *Steel Fisted Dragon* (1977)
Fists Like Lee
  SEE *Martial Arts* (1974)
Fists of Bruce Lee (1979)
  AKA *Interpol*
`77` 21, 126-177
Fists of Lightning
  SEE *5 Pattern Dragon Claws* (1983)
Fists to Fight
  SEE *New Fist of Fury* (1976)
Five Brothers, The
  SEE *Dragon Lee Vs the 5 Brothers* (1978)
Five Daughters Affair, The (tv episode) 8
Five Fingers of Death
  SEE *King Boxer* (1972) 127
Five Pretty Young Ladies
  SEE *Bruce, Kung Fu Girls* (1975)
Flannery, Susan 94
Flood, John "Cyclone" 67
Fong Sai-Yuk (character) 154, 155, 201
For One Week Only: The World of Exploitation Films (Meyers) 214
Forced to Fight
  AKA *Invincible Super Chan* (1971) 67
Foreman, T.E. 165
Foster, Norman 20, 92
Four Brave Dragons
  SEE *Bruce Against the Odds* (1977)
Franco, Jess 126, 158, 176, 205, 214
Frankenstein, Victor (fictional character) . 164
Friday the 13th (film series) 44
Friend, Robert L. 20, 94
Frightmare (1974) 68
From Russia With Love (1963) 180
Fu Sheng 155
Fu, Poshek 212, 213
Fulci, Lucio 61, 66, 205, 214
Fung Yun-Chuen 171
Furious Dragon's Rage
  SEE *Bruce and the Dragon Fist* (1977)
Furious Killer, The
  SEE *The Furious* (1981)

INDEX

Furious, The (1981)
   AKA *The Furious Killer*
   126 .... 23, 175-177
Fury of the Dragon (1976)
   46 .... 11, 15, 20, 94-95
Fury of the Shaolin Master
   SEE *10 Commandments of Lee* (1978)
Future Hunters (1986)
   AKA *Spear of Destiny*
   134 .... 24, 184-185
Gainsbourg, Serge 76
Gallardo, Jun 19, 20, 30, 93, 213
Gam Kei-Chu 105
Gam-Loi 33
Game of Death (1978)
   21 9,
   11, 19, 28, 37, 38, 40, 41, 44, 46, 52, 54, 55-56,
   57, 58, 59, 60, 61, 64, 69, 72, 74, 75, 76, 77,
   78, 81, 82, 83, 93, 98, 103, 107, 125, 126, 130,
   134, 175, 188, 191, 196, 200, 211, 213, 214
Game of Death II (1981) 20, 28, 61, 72, 151
   SEE ALSO *Tower of Death* (1981)
Game of Death, The (1974)
   4 .... 19, 30-31, 213
Garcia, Eddie 30, 31
Garica, Tito 108, 109
Ghost of the Fox (1990)
   AKA *Way of Fox*
   140 .... 14, 24, 107, 192
Gin, Lui 20, 89
Godard, Jean-Luc 69
Godfather, The (1972) 180
Godfather, The (fictional character) 45, 46
Gold Connection, The (1979)
   AKA *Iron Dragon Strikes Back*
   120 .... 23, 168-169
Golden Chaku
   SEE *Bruce and the Golden Chaku* (1977)
Golden Dragon Silver Snake (1980)
   AKA *Dragoneer 5: The Indomitable*
   AKA *A Fight At Hong Kong Ranch*
   30 .... 20, 68-69
Golden Harvest (prod co) 49, 61, 196, 210
Goldfinger (1964) 79
Good Times (dvd co) 143
Goodbye Bruce Lee, His Last Game of Death (1975)
   AKA *The New Game of Death*
   8 .... 17, 19, **26**, 37-38, 55, 163, 203
Grand, Alexander 45, 171, 172
Grandmaster, The (2013) 201
Great Hero
   SEE *Bruce Li's Magnum Fist* (1978)
Great Martial Arts Movies 214
Green Dragon Inn, The
   SEE *Bruce Is Loose* (1977)
Green Hornet, The (1974)
   44 .... 11, 15, 20, 35, **88**, 92-93, 94, 95
Green Hornet, The (film serial) 36
Green Hornet, The (tv series) ....
   61, 92, 94, 110, 117, 190, 200, 203
Green, Alan 65
Griffith, James 53
Grindhouse Cinema Database (web site) .. 205
Grindhouse Experience Presents Ultimate Dragon Collection 10 Film Set 16
Growling Tiger, The
   SEE *Black Dragon Vs the Yellow Tiger* (1974)

Guiding Light 85
Guy! The Guy!, The
   AKA *Kung Fu Revenger* (1974) 27
Gymkata Killer
   SEE *Challenge of the Tiger* (1980)
Hallenbeck, Darrell 20, 92
Hamilton, Guy 79
Hammond, Stefan 207
Han Kwok Choi 168, 169
Han Ying-Chieh 104
Harries, Steve 19, 59
Harris, Brad 108, 109
Harrison, Richard 107, 108, 109, 185
Harvey, Ron (aka Jasper Milktoast) 66
Hashim, Edmund 94
Hawkwind (group) 80, 122
Hayes, Isaac 139
Heidegger, Martin 202
Here Come the Kung Fu Clones (Jones) 10, 11, 207
Hero Youngster (2004)
   AKA *Juvenile Chen Zhen*
   40 .... 20, 83-85, 201
Heung Ling 22, 141
He's a Legend, He's a Hero
   SEE *The Dragon Lives* (1976)
Higgins, Tom 58
High Risk (1995)
   AKA *Meltdown* 202
Ho Chung Tao 47
Ho Kwong-Ming 146
Ho Max Wai 205
Ho Tsung-Tao 21
Ho, Godfrey ....
   11, 12, 16, 20, 21, 22, 23, 24, 67, 68, 69, 80,
   81, 85, 103, 105, 125, 128, 129, 157, 167,
   169, 173, 178, 180, 182, 183, 185, 205, 212
Ho, Linda 32, 33, 34
Hollywood East 207
Holmes, Lee 11, 189
Hon Gwok Choi 106, 1979
Hon Ma Lee, Mary 51
Hong Kong Action Cinema (Logan) 207
Hong Kong Cinema: The Extra Dimension (Teo) 209, 212
Hong Kong Cinemagic (web site) .15, 161, 207
Hong Kong Fury (2004) 203
Hong Kong Movie Database (web site) 15, 127, 161, 207
Hong Kong Superman
   SEE *Bruce Hong Kong Master* (1975)
Hong, Elliott 23, 180
Horan, Roy 73
Horst Wessel (tune) 164
Hot Stuff (tune) 56
House of Bamboo Dolls (1973) 193
Houston, Fitz 191
Hsiao Hu 117, 118
Hsiao Wang
   AKA *Little Wang* 124, 125
Hua Shan 19, 20, 51, 1977
Huang Chien-Lung AKA Bruce Le 14
Huang Kin-Lung AKA Bruce Le 14
Hung, Joseph AKA Joseph Velasco 14
Hung, Sammo (aka Hung Kam-bo) ....
   21, 56, 59, 102, 110, 135, 136, 147, 194, 200
Hunt, Leon 10, 212, 213

Hunter, Jack (aka James Williamson
   AKA Julian Hallett) 207, 208
Hunters and the Hunted, The (tv episode) ...92
Hutch, Willie 183
Hwang Jang Lee............. 72, 73, 74, 78, 79,
   80, 108, 109, 178, 180, 181, 182, 183, 184, 205
Hyeon Kim, Shi 19
I Am Curious Yellow (1967) 68
I Gotcha (tune) 148
I Heard It Through the Grapevine (tune) 27
I Love You, Bruce Lee
   SEE *Bruce Lee: His Last Days,*
   His Last Nights (1976)
I Spit on Your Grave (1978) 188
Idol, Billy 183
IFD Films & Arts Ltd (film company) 85
Iking Boxer (1973) 10
Ilsa (film series) 13
Ilsa Meets Bruce Lee In the Devils Triangle (n.d.) 13
Image of Bruce Lee (1978)
   AKA *Storming Attacks*
   57 .... 21, 103-104, **112**
Imagined Communities (Anderson) 213
In Search of Space (LP)
   SEE *X in Search of Space* (LP)
In the Realm of the Senses (1976) 46
Incredible Bongo Band, The (group) . 104, 120
Inosanto, Dan 44, 60, 75, 81, 93, 125
Intercepting Fist: The Films of Bruce Lee and the Golden Age of Kung-Fu Cinema (Hunter) 207, 208
Internet Movie Database (website) 14, 15, 205
Interpol
   SEE *Fists of Bruce Lee* (1979)
Invasion from Outer Space Parts 1 and 2 (tv episodes) 92
Invincible Super Chan
   SEE *Forced to Fight* (1971)
Invincible, The
   SEE *Bruce Lee The Invincible* (1978)
Ip Man 41, 111, 201
Iron Dragon Strikes Back
   SEE *The Gold Connection* (1979)
Iron Finger
   SEE *Bruce Against Iron Hand* (1979)
Iron Man
   SEE *Chinese Iron Man* (1974)
Ironside (tv series) 200
Isou, Isidore 104, 201
Iwamatsu, Mako 92, 93
Jackie and Bruce to the Rescue (1982)
   AKA *Jackie Vs Bruce to the Rescue*
   AKA *Fist of Death*
   34 .... 20, 76-78, 125
Jackie Vs Bruce to the Rescue
   SEE *Jackie and Bruce to the Rescue* (1982)
Jackson, Michael 188
James, Bill 20, 62, 63
Japanese Connection
   SEE *A Tooth for a Tooth* (1973)
Jaws of the Dragon
   SEE *The Fierce One* (1974)
Je t'aime (tune) 76
Jeong Jun 150
Jeong-Nan, Kim 95
Jeremy, Ron 196

219

Ji Han-Jae 60
Jigsaw (group) 58
Jones, Carl 10, 11, 207
Jones, Quincy 200
Jones, Randy 146
Jung-Yong, Kim 22, 23, 153, 156
Juvenile Chen Zhen
    SEE *Hero Youngster* (2004)
Ka Wa 45
Kam Bo...............................23, 168
Kang Lone 199
Kant Leung Wang-Fat 20, 22, 85, 136
Kao Kang Thompson 31, 35
Karado the Cat from Hong Kong
    SEE *Superior Youngster* (1974)
Karalexis, Serafim 67, 68, 86
Karate Bullfighter (1975) 56, 107
Karate Kid (1984) 188
Karate Killers, The (1967) 8
Karate Tiger
    SEE *No Retreat, No Surrender* (1986)
Karate: The Hand of Death (1961) 181
Karim, S.A. 23, 159, 160
Karl Marx: His Life and Works (Rühle) 202
Kato (character) 8, 11, 35,
    36, 61, 67, 92, 93, 94, 110, 190, 200, 201, 203
Kelly, Jim 66, 85, 165, 166, 200
Kentucky Fried Movie (1977) 15
Kerver, Robert 127
Kiat, See 158
Kim Tai-Jong AKA Tang Lung
    ....27, 28, 55, 72, 73, 74, 76, 77, 78, 115, 188
Kin, Sek 62, 85
King Boxer (1972) 10, 41, 126
King Boxer II
    SEE *Bruce and the Shaolin Bronzemen* (1982)
King of Kung Fu
    SEE *Enter the Game of Death* (1978)
King Plaster (1972) 10
King Swindler
    SEE *Return of the Fat Dragon* (1993)
King, Mark 157
Klugman, Jack 108
Ko, Philip
    SEE Ko, Phillip
Ko, Phillip ..31, 34, 35, 50, 103, 125, 126, 162
Kong Hung AKA Joseph Velasco.........14, 160
Kong Hung, Joseph AKA Joseph
    Velasco 12, 14, 20, 83, 85
Kong, Joseph AKA Joseph Velasco 205
Koob, André 20, 78, 79, 80
Korean Movie Database (web site)
    ....64, 69, 77, 102, 161, 170, 207
Kraftwerk (group) 186
Kristoff, Romano 62
Ku Feng 104, 176
Ku Wen-Chun 141
Kuei Chih Hung.................23, 168, 169
Kum-Hung Wong AKA Bruce Le 14
Kung Fu (tv series) 14, 35, 45
Kung Fu Avengers
    SEE *Soul Brothers of King Fu* (1977)
Kung Fu Contra as Bonecas [Kung Fu Against
    Dolls]
    SEE *Bruce Lee Vs Gay Power* (1975) 14

*Kung Fu Cult Masters: From Bruce Lee to
    Crouching Tiger* (Hunt) 212
Kung Fu Emmanuelle
    SEE *Enter the King of Kung Fu* (1981)
Kung Fu Express (mag) 156
Kung Fu Fever (1979)
    AKA *Black Dragon Fever*
    AKA *Bruce Lee Strikes Back*
    23.................................19, 57
Kung Fu Finger Book 41, 57, 133
Kung Fu King (1973) 204
Kung Fu Leung Strikes Emmanuelle
    SEE *Enter the King of Kung Fu* (1981)
*Kung Fu Masters: From Bruce Lee to Crouching
    Tiger* (Hunt) 10
Kung Fu Master—Bruce Lee Style (1972)
    AKA *Tough Guy*
    AKA *Kung Fu the Head Crusher*
    AKA *Revenge of the Dragon*
    87........................22, 139, 204
Kung Fu Monthly (mag) 8
Kung Fu Queen
    SEE *Queen Boxer* (1972)
Kung Fu Superman
    SEE *Bruce, D-Day at Macao* (1975)
Kung Fu the Head Crusher
    SEE *Kung Fu Master—Bruce Lee Style* (1972)
Kung Fu Theatre (dvd co) ....
    42, 43, 45, 145, 156, 160, 176, 177
Kung Fu Trailers of Fury (2016) 203
Kung Fu's Hero (1973) 204, 205
Kung Tien 156, 157
Kuo Nam Hung, Joseph 22, 64, 143
Kwak Mu Seong.......................... 122
Kwan Yung-Moon 131, 132
Kwok, Master 180, 181
La sorella di Bruce Lee [the sister of Bruce Lee]
    SEE *Chiu Chow Kung Fu* (1973)
Ladalski, John 74, 75
Lahardi, Iksan 20, 98, 100, 1977
Lai Ngai 23, 158, 159
Lai, Bruce 10, 64, 68, 69, 71, 103, 164
Lai, Joseph 67, 85
Lam Kwok-Cheung............. 19, 23, 54, 171
Lama Avenger, The
    SEE *Three Avengers* (1979)
Lang, Fritz 92
Lapid, Lito 56
Lasing Master (1980) 10
Last Dragon, The (1985)
    133........................23, 183-184
Last Fist of Fury, The (1977)
    AKA *The Ultimate Lee*
    AKA *Dragon Lee Does Dallas*
    AKA *The Last of the Ching Wu School: Righteous
    Martial Party*
    ■ 20, 47, 48, 85, 97
*Last of the Ching Wu School: Righteous Martial
    Party, The*
    SEE *The Last Fist of Fury* (1977) 20
Last Strike, The
    SEE *Soul Brothers of King Fu* (1977)
Last Year At Marienbad (1961) 141
Lau Dan 173
Lau Hok-Nin 32, 34
Lau Kar-Wing 21, 110, 154
Lau Wai-Keung, Andrew 21, 110

Lau, Danny 52
Laughter (Bergson) 200
Law Cheung-On AKA Alexander Lo Rei 28
Law Do-Bong, Albert 23, 172
Law Kar-Ying 84
Law Kei ...19, 20, 23, 45, 47, 83, 158, 159, 163
Law Ma, John 19, 38
Law Yui AKA Alexander Lo Rei 28
Lazenby, George 165, 166, 211
Le, Bruce 9, 10, 12, 14, 15, 19, 20,
    21, 22, 24, 41, 45, 48, 49, 54, 55, 56, 57, 61, 62,
    63, 64, 65, 69, 75, 78, 79, 80, 85, 95, 100, 101,
    107, 108, 109, 119, 120, 122, 123, 127, 130,
    131, 132, 133, 134, 143, 145, 154, 156, 160,
    161, 171, 172, 173, 176, 177, 184, 185, 188,
    189, 192, 193, 200, 201, 204, 205, 207, 208
Le, Jet 12
Lea, Bruce K.L. 150
Leavold, Andrew 207
Lee Fung-Lan 116
Lee Gam-Kwan, Larry 120
Lee Hoi-Gei 104, 105
Lee Hoi-Sang 73, 74, 173
Lee Hyeok-Su 23, 169, 170
Lee Kam, Miss 32
Lee Siu-Ming 76, 77
Lee the Angry Man (1983)
    AKA *Angry Young Man*
    131.............................181-182
Lee Ye-Min ..101, 105, 128, 173, 174, 178, 179
Lee Ye-Min, Susan 178, 179, 180
Lee Ying 139, 140
Lee Ying-Ying, Carrie 153
Lee, Bronson (character) 11, 145, 146
Lee, Danny 38, 52
Lee, Dragon ....
9, 10, 12, 47, 48, 49, 50, 51, 55, 57, 61, 64,
    68, 69, 70, 71, 72, 81, 85, 101, 102, 103, 105,
    126, 128, 129, 156, 157, 167, 169, 173, 178,
    179, 180, 181, 182, 183, 187, 207, 208
Lee, Jack 57, 58, 59, 62, 63
Lee, Judy 139, 140, 152
    SEE ALSO Chia Ling
Lee, Lily 192, 193
Lee, Linda 9
Lee, Myron Bruce 166
Lee, Shannon 163
Lee, Steve 42, 44, 45, 98, 99, 100
Lee-Lee Lau 146
Legend of Bruce Lee
    SEE *Bruce King of Kung Fu* (1980)
Legend of Chen Zhen, The
    SEE *Legend of the Fist: The Return
    of Chen Zhen* (2010)
Legend of the Fist: The Return of Chen Zhen
    (2010)
    AKA *Fist of Fury: The Legend of Chen Zhen*
    AKA *The Legend of Chen Zhen*
    64...................21, 201, 110-111
Legendary Fok, The (tv series) 11
Lei, Bruce 42, 45
Lenzi, Umberto 65, 151, 208
Leo, Fernando di 13, 41, 78, 168
Leung Kar-Yan........................... 162
Levene, Terry 65, 66, 68
Li Fai-Mon............................21, 115
Li Kuan-Chang 19, 36

INDEX

Li, Bruce AKA Ho Chung Tao 9, 10, 12, 20, 21, 27, 28, 35, 36, 37, 38, 40, 41, 47, 49, 51, 52, 53, 61, 67, 74, 75, 77, 81, 98, 103, 104, 105, 106, 117, 118, 119, 120, 121, 126, 127, 143, 144, 149, 150, 152, 163, 164, 165, 166, 168, 169, 177, 178, 184, 202, 203, 207, 208, 213
Li, Jet 12, 111, 155, 194, 195, 196, 203
Liang, Bruce .. 11, 45, 104, 105, 146, 147, 199
Lie, Bruce 143
Life of Brian (1979) 67
Lightning of Bruce Lee (1973)
  89 ....22, 140-141
Lim Ja-Ho 128, 178, 179, 180
Lim, K.Y. 59, 63
Lin Bing 19, 21, 23, 37, 117, 162, 163
Lin Fu-Ti 23, 162
Lin, Justin 24, 196
Lin, Pearl 122
Line of Death
  SEE *On the Verge of Death* (1973)
Little Hero
  SEE *Bruce, D-Day at Macao* (1975)
Little Superman
  SEE *Bruce, D-Day at Macao* (1975)
Liu Chun-Ku, Tony 19, 31
Liu Hung-Sheng.......................22, 142
Liu, John 23, 125, 126, 163, 175
Liu, Natasha 175
Lo Lieh 12, 41, 48, 49, 80, 126, 155, 176
Lo Meng 98
Lo Rei, Alexander
  AKA Alexander Lou 28
Lo Sing 93
Lo Wei 22, 64, 151, 152, 194, 196, 210, 211
Lo Yi AKA Alexander Lo Rei 28
Lo, Billy 55
Logan, Bey 207
Lone Shaolin Avenger
  SEE *Bruce Against the Odds* (1977)
Lone Wolf and Cub (film series) 162
Lone, Frankie 203
Longinus 184
Longstreet (tv show) .52, 65, 66, 105, 107, 200
Looking for Bruce Lee (2002) 199
Lou, Alexander
  SEE Alexander Lo Rei
Louie, Bill 66, 67, 68, 171, 172
Lui Siu-Lung AKA Bruce Le 14
Lui, Gordon 195
Lui, Jacky AKA Bruce Le 14
Lung Tien-Hsiang 59, 60, 61, 124
Lust, Caution (2007) 111
Ly, Bruce
  SEE Rey Malonzo
  SEE ALSO Henry Yu Yung
Mackenzie, Patch 165
Mad Max (film series) 184
Magic Fly (tune) 42
Magnificent Seven, The (1960) 143
Magnificent, The (1979) 174
Magnum Fist
  SEE *Bruce Li's Magnum Fist* (1978)
Magnum Muslim .357 (2014) 59
Maharaj, Anthony 24, 185, 188
Mai Ling 129
Majors, Lee II 191

Mak, Michael 23, 177, 178
Maka, Karl 110
Mallinson, Matthew 20, 65
Malonzo, Rey AKA Bruce Ly... 28, 29, 30, 96, 97
Man from Hong Kong, The (1975) 58
Man from UNCLE, The (tv series) 8
Man With No Name (character) 123
Man With the Golden Gun, The (1974) 145
Man, Joey 195
Mang Hoi 146
Manila International Airport 96
Manila Open City (1968) 30
Mann, Larry D. 92
Many Bruces (web site) 185, 189, 207
Mao, Angela 54, 118, 119, 211
Mao, Chairman 84, 210, 211
Markovic, Jim 19, 47
Marlowe (1969) 50
Martial Arts (1974)
  AKA *The Chinese Mack*
  66 .... 21, 91, 116-117
Martial Monks of Shaolin Temple (1983)
  132 ....23, 182-183
Marx, Karl 51, 202
Master and the Kid
  SEE *10 Commandments of Lee* (1978)
Master of the Flying Guillotine (1976) 82, 95, 122
Master of the Universe (tune) 80, 122
Mau Kin-Tak 24, 195
Mauro, Raf 180
Mayfield, Curtis 104
McKinney, Kurt 188
McQueen, Steve 37
Men from the Monastery, The (1974) 155
Meng Chui, Kitty 89, 158, 159
Meng, Cheryl 128
Metz, Christian 201
Meyer, Alice 59, 60
Meyers, Ric 208, 214
MIA (dvd label) 86
Miao, Nora 151, 152, 183
Mighty Four, The
  SEE *Bruce Against the Odds* (1977)
Milano Calibro 9 (1972) 11
Min Bok-KI, Peggy 128
Ming Chew 124, 125
Ming Patriots, The
  SEE *Revenge of the Ming Patriots* (1976)
Ming, Piggy 131, 132
Mishkin, Bill 156
Mishkin, Elaine 156
Mishkin, Lewis 156
Mission for the Dragon (1980)
  AKA *Rage of the Dragon*
  80 ....22, **114**, 129-130
Mission Terminate (1987)
  AKA *Return of the Kickfighter*
  137 .... 24, 185, 188-189
Moll, Marga Tormo 214, **225**
Montego Bay (tune) 107
Moore, Bobby 8
Moore, Mandy 177, 178
Moore, Rudy Ray 89, 212
Morricone, Ennio 126, 139
Most Dangerous Game, The (1932) 31

Motown (record co) 183
Mr Vampire (1985) 192
Ms. 45 (1981) 188
MTV (tv station) 183
Muscle of the Dragon (1981)
  AKA *Dragon Lee Fights Back*
  31 .... 15, 16, 20, 69-72
My Name Called Bruce (1978)
  73 ....21, 80, 122
Nadiuska 107, 108, 109
Nakayama, Shinobu 194
Nam Gi-Nam 20, 23, 64, 160, 161
Nam Seok-Hun 161
Nam, James 20, 21, 22, 23, 95, 119, 122, 124, 144, 146, 160, 161, 204, 205
Neglia, Louis 67
New Fist of Fury (1976)
  AKA *Fists to Fight*
  100 .... 22, 151-152, 210
New Game of Death, The
  SEE *Goodbye Bruce Lee, His Last Game of Death* (1975)
Ng Ka-Chun 20, 76, 77
Ng Ngai-Cheung, Ben 85
Ng See-Yuen 20, 22, 72, 146
Ng Sze-Yuen 19, 40
Ng, Sandra 194
Ninety-Nine and a Half (tune) 118
Ninja Champion (1986)
  135 ....24, 185-188
Ninja Over the Great Wall (1990)
  AKA *Shaolin Fist of Fury*
  84 ....22, 133-134, 192
Ninja Strikes Back (1982)
  AKA *Bruce Strikes Back*
  AKA *Bruce Fights Back*
  AKA *Eye of the Dragon*
  35 .... 20, 70, 78-80, 85, 166
Ninja Terminator (1985) 185
Ninja Vs Bruce Lee (1982)
  AKA *Concord of Bruce*
  36 ....20, 80-81, 122, 189
Ninjitsu Fighting Techniques (manual) 58
No Retreat, No Surrender (1986)
  AKA *Karate Tiger*
  136 .... 24, 37, 183, 188
None But the Brave (1973) 152, 210
Norris, Chick AKA Corliss Randall 78
Norris, Chuck 27, 28, 48, 66, 80, 109, 125, 134, 200, 211
Norton, Richard 184, 185, 189
Nottingham Forest FC 169
Novak, Mel 55
Nowhere to Run (tune) 118
Nude for Satan (1974) 109
Ob-La-Di,Ob-La-Da (tune) 124
Occupation Committee of the People's Free Sorbonne University (groupuscule) 84
Ocean Shores (vid co) 143
Ochoa, Danny 204
Odaejeja (*The Five Disciples*)
  SEE *Dragon Lee Vs the 5 Brothers* (1978)
Oddjob (fictional character) 79
Odysseus (king of Ithaca) 79
Ohgushi, Toshi
  SEE Toshikazu Ôgushi

On the Verge of Death (1973)
  AKA *Line of Death*
  AKA *Bruce Lee Vs Chinese Frankenstein*
  65 .... 21, 28, 115, 164
Once Upon a Time in the West (1968) 139
One Down, Two to Go (1982) 66
One Man Army
  SEE *10 Commandments of Lee* (1978)
Orphée (1950) 82
Orr, James 24, 189
Oshima, Nagisa 46
Ouellette, Jean-Paul 23, 191
Oyama, Masutatsu 56, 107
P.T. Insantra Film (prod co.) 45
Page, Teddy 130
Pai Lot Chai Sing 141
Pak, Bruce AKA Kwak Mu Seong . 122, 123, 124
Pallardy, Jean-Marie 20, 78, 80
Pascual, Evangeline 30
Path of the Dragon (1998) 201
Patrick, Robert 184, 185
Pegasus (dvd co.) 81
Philippine Racing Club 131
Pick Up the Pieces (tune) 126
Pig Boss, The (1972) 10, 27, 201
Pink Floyd (group) 109
Play That Funky Music (tune) 118
Pleasure Island (1980) 109
Po Su Pi 119, 123
Poisonous Rose Stripping the Night
  (1985) 187, 188
Poon, David 19, 57
Poonvivat, Pracha 20, 64
Popeye (fictional character) 45, 47
Posadas, Jun AKA Francis Posadas ... 19, 57, 59
Poundland (discount chain) 9
Power Force
  SEE *Dragon Force* (1982)
Prescott, Janet 94
Preying Mantis, The (tv episode) 92
Prince 183
Pukulan Bangau Putih
  SEE *The Fierce Boxer and Bruce* (1977)
Puño Del Dragón, El [fist of the dragon] (1979)
  AKA *The Eagle's Killer*
  AKA *Re-Enter the Dragon* 205
Pusherman (tune) 104
Qiu Yuen 167
Queen Boxer (1972)
  AKA *Kung Fu Queen*
  AKA *The Avenger*
  88 .... 22, 66, 103, 139-140
Queen Elizabeth Hospital, Hong Kong .. 64, 176
Rabanne, Paco 14
Radetzky March (tune) 109
Rage of the Dragon
  SEE *Mission for the Dragon* (1980)
Rancière, Jacques 212
Randall, Corliss 78
Randall, Dick 64,
  67, 70, 78, 79, 80, 81, 86, 108, 109, 118, 166
Randall, Richard 86
Ravenscroft, Trevor 184
Raw Force (1982) 15
Ray Is for Killing, The (tv episode) 94
Rayns, Tony 209

Re-Enter the Dragon
  SEE *Puño Del Dragón, El* (1979)
Real Bruce Lee 2, The (2004)
  41 .... 20, 22, 85-86, 136, 199
Real Bruce Lee, The (1977)
  15 .. 19, 20, 47-48, 67, 81, 85, 86, 199, 1977
Rebellious Reign (1980) 12
Reefer Madness (1936) 84
Reid, Graig D. 213
Return of Bruce (1977)
  AKA *Bruce's Return*
  AKA *The Dragon Returns*
  16 .... 19, 48, 57, 80
Return of Dragon (1998) 199
Return of Fist of Fury (1978)
  74 .... 21, 122-124
Return of Red Tiger (1977)
  109 .... 23, 145, 160-161
Return of the 18 Bronzemen (1976) 64
Return of the Dragon (1977)
  110 .... 23, 162
Return of the Fat Dragon (1993)
  AKA *King Swindler*
  143 .... 24, 194
Return of the Kickfighter
  SEE *Mission Terminate* (1987)
Return of the Tiger (1977)
  AKA *Silent Killer from Eternity*
  69 .... 21, 118-119
Revenge of Fist of Fury (c.1978) 199
Revenge of the Dragon
  SEE *Kung Fu Master—Bruce Lee Style* (1972)
Revenge of the Drunken Master (1984) 68
Revenge of the Ming Patriots (1976)
  AKA *The Ming Patriots*
  101 .... 22, 120, 152
Robbe-Grillet, Alain 8, 57, 186
Robbie, Seymour 20, 94
Robinson, Clint 28
Rocky (1976) 188
Rollin, Jean 157
Romero, Eddie 30
Rozar 203
Russell, Toby 207
Rühle, Otto 202
Sada, Abe 46
Sahyeongsamgeol [Death Penalty On Three
  Robots]
  SEE *The Clones of Bruce Lee* (1980)
Sakata, Harold 79, 80, 165, 166
Samson, Gary 145
San Juan, Luis 19, 28
San Juan, Ronaldo 20, 96
San Kuai 139
Sanders, Steve 53
Santiago, Cirio H. 24, 184
Saturday Night Fever (1977) 180
Saturn Productions Inc (prod co) 49
Saxon, John 85, 200
Schultz, Michael 23, 183
Schwartz, Dan 175
Scorpion Thunderbolt (1984) 126
Scott, Carl 98, 1977
Scott, Casey 181
Scott, Linda Gaye 92
Screams In Favour of De Sade (1952) 37
Seasonal Films (prod co) 188

Secret Ninja
  SEE *Secret Ninja, Roaring Tiger* (1982)
Secret Ninja, Roaring Tiger (1982)
  AKA *Secret Ninja*
  128 .... 23, 178-180, 186
Secret of the Sally Bell, The (tv episode) 94
Secret of the Shaolin Poles
  SEE *Bruce &The Shaolin Poles* (1977)
Seine tödliche Rache [his deadly revenge]
  SEE *Bruce Lee's Greatest Revenge* (1978)
Seize the Formula
  SEE *Challenge of the Tiger* (1980)
Sek, Dragon 82, 83, 86
Seo Jeong-Ah 173, 174, 178, 179, 182, 183
Sex and Zen (1991) 178
Sex and Zen and a Bullet in the Head (Hammond
  & Wilkins) 207
Sex dan Kriminal [sex and criminals](1996) .45
Seymour, Jane 108
Shadow Whip, The (1971) 121
Shaft (1971) 145
Shang-Kuan, Polly 148, 155, 164, 165
Shanghai Killers
  SEE *The Chase* (1971)
Shaolin Fist of Fury
  SEE *Ninja Over the Great Wall* (1990)
Shaolin Master and the Kid
  SEE *10 Commandments of Lee* (1978)
Shaolin Soccer (2001) 15
Shaw Brothers (film company) ... 38, 121, 155
Shaw, Jimmy 20, 21, 118, 1977
Shek, Dragon 195, 196
Shim Wu-Seob 22, 153
Shira, Sharon 108, 109
Shou Lung 47
Shrine of Ultimate Bliss, The
  SEE *Stoner* (1974)
Shu Qui 35, 110
Shum Shuk-Yee 121
Si Ming 177, 178
Si-Hyeon, Kim 19, 20, 21,
  22, 23, 24, 47, 57, 68, 69, 101, 105, 128, 129,
  167, 173, 178, 180, 183, 185, 186, 187, 188
Si-Hyun, Kim
  SEE Kim Si-Hyeon
Siao Fong-Fong, Josephine 193, 194
Silent Killer from Eternity
  SEE *Return of the Tiger* (1977)
Silliphant, Stirling 37, 38
Sim Sang-Hyeon 70, 71, 72
Simpson, O.J. 156
Sitsiritsit Alibangbang (tune) 29
Six Million Dollar Man, The (tv series) 191
Sixx, Nikki 183
Ske, Kwok Shek 23, 164
Skinny Tiger and Fatty Dragon (1990)
  63 .... 21, 110
Sky Dragon (aka Dragon Sek) 85
Sky High (tune) 58
Smith, Anthony 183
Smith, Paul L. 119
Snake Fist Vs the Dragon (1980) 12
Snake In the Eagle's Shadow (1978) 161
So, Edmond 82
Something Weird (dvd label) 181
Sorono, Sam 178

INDEX

Soul Brothers of King Fu (1977)
 AKA *The Tiger Strikes Again*
 AKA *The Last Strike*
 AKA *Kung Fu Avengers*
 50 . . . . 20, 97
Soul of Bruce Lee (1977)
 AKA *Soul of Chiba*
 51 . . . . 20, 98
Soul of Chiba
 SEE *Soul of Bruce Lee* (1977)
Space (group) 42
Spear of Destiny
 SEE *Future Hunters* (1986)
Spear of Destiny (Ravenscroft) 184
Spirit of Bruce Lee
 SEE *Spirits of Bruce Lee* (1973)
Spirits of Bruce Lee (1973)
 AKA *Spirit of Bruce Lee*
 AKA *Angry Tiger*
 90 . . . . 22, 141
Star of Stars
 SEE *Exit the Dragon, Enter the Tiger* (1976)
Star Trek (film/tv series) 196
Steel Fisted Dragon (1977)
 AKA *Fistful of Dragons*
 AKA *Duel Maut* [Deadly Duel]
 52 . . . . 20, 45, 98-100
Stein, Walter 184
Stoner (1974) 211
Storming Attacks
 SEE *Image of Bruce Lee* (1978)
Story of the Dragon (1977)
 AKA *Bruce Lee's Deadly Kung Fu*
 AKA *Bruce Lee's Secret*
 AKA *Bruce Li's Jeet Kune Do*
 17 . . . . 19, 49, 117
Strauss, Johann 109
Streetfighter, The (1974) 107
Substance (distributor) 177
Suen Ga-Lam 139, 141
Summer, Donna 56
Sung Gam-Loi, Addy 31
Super Dragon (1976)
 AKA *The Young Bruce Lee*
 68 . . . . 21, 117-118
Super Dragon: The Bruce Lee Story
 SEE *Bruce Lee: A Dragon Story* (1974)
Super Gang, The
 SEE *The Supergang* (1984)
Super Ninja (1984) 189
Superdragon Vs Superman
 SEE *Bruce Lee Against Superman* (1975)
Supergang, The (1984)
 AKA *The Super Gang*
 82 . . . . 22, 131-132
Superior Youngster
 AKA *Karado the Cat from Hong Kong*
 (1974) 204, 214
Swartz, Harold B. 19
Sweet Lady (n.d.) 85
Symbionese Liberation Army 43
Sze-Ma Lung 74
Tagged for Murder (tv episode) 200
Tai-Jong, Kim
 SEE Kim Tai-Jong
Taimak 183
Tan Tao 158, 159
Tan, Dorian 154, 163, 175

Tanaka, Noboru 46
Tang Lung (fictional character) 28, 212
Tang Lung (Korean actor)
 SEE Kim Tai-Jong
Tang Lung (Taiwanese actor) 28, 115
Tang Ti 20, 89
*Tao of Ric: True Lies and a Fistful of Meyerisms,
 The* (web pages) 214
Tarantino, Quentin 199
Teen Mom (tv show) 86
Telefilms International (prod co) 49
Temple, Shirley 81
Teo, Stephen 209, 210, 212
Tex, Joe 148
Thai, Bruce 10, 64, 103
Theme from Shaft (tune) 139, 140
*Theorizing Bruce Lee: Film-Fantasy-Fighting-
 Philosophy* (Bowman) 212
They Call Him Bruce Lee (1979)
 24 . . . . 19, 57-59, 62, 63
They Call Him Chop Suey (1975)
 45 . . . . 20, 59, 93-94, 102
They Call Me Bruce (1982)
 129 . . . . 23, 180, 190
They Still Call Me Bruce (1987)
 138 . . . . 24, 189-191
Thomas, Brian 208
Thorne, Dyanne 13
Three Avengers (1979)
 AKA *The Lama Avenger*
 61 . . . . 21, 106-107
Three the Hard Way (1974) 66
Thunderfist
 SEE *5 Pattern Dragon Claws* (1983)
Thundering Fist
 SEE *5 Pattern Dragon Claws* (1983)
Thundering Ninja (1987) 205
Thunderstorm (1957) 213
Thunderstorm, The (play) 67
Ti Tang 89
Tiger Force (1975) 204, 205
Tiger from China
 SEE *Black Dragon Vs the Yellow Tiger* (1974)
Tiger Strikes Again, The
 SEE *Soul Brothers of King Fu* (1977)
Tilston, Lisa 207
Tin-Lung 85
Ting Shan-Hsi 22, 147
Ting Pei, Betty 27, 31, 32, 33, 35, 36, 37,
 38, 39, 40, 41, 45, 59, 90, 91, 117, 130, 208
To Man-Bo
 19, 20, 21, 49, 69, 72, 100, 104, 1979
Toei Company (film company) 146
Tong Lung
 SEE Tang Lung
Tong Tin Hei 177
Tong Yim Chaan 106
Tooth for a Tooth, A
 AKA *Japanese Connection* (1973) 204
Top Fighter (1995) 203
Top Fighters: 10 Film Collection (2009 box
 set) 85
Toshikazu Ôgushi 20, 81
Tough Guy
 SEE *Kung Fu Master—Bruce Lee Style* (1972)

Tower of Death (1981)
 AKA *Game of Death II*
 32 . . . . 20, 61, 72-74
Trans-Europe Express (1966) 186
Trans-Europe Express (tune) 186
Treasure of Bruce Lee, The (1979)
 78 . . . . 11, 21, 127-128, 205
Tremblay, Pierre 186, 187
Trouble for Prince Charming (tv episode) . . .94
True Game of Death, The (1979)
 25 . . . . 8, 9, 19, 56, 59, 61, 124, 203, 206
Tsang Chi-Wai, Eric .45
Tsen, Dana 103, 104, 121, 166
Tso Nam Lee. 19, 20, 23, 41, 98, 100, 166, 1977
Twelve Gates of Hell
 SEE *Champ Against Champ* (1980)
Ultimate Dragon Collection, The (boxed
 set) 147
*Ultimate Guide to Martial Arts Movies of the
 1970s: 500+ Films Loaded With Action,
 Weapons and Warriors* (Reid) 213
Ultimate Lee, The
 SEE *The Last Fist of Fury* (1977)
Unicorn Palm
 SEE *Fist of Unicorn* (1973)
*Unnamable II: The Statement of Randolph
 Carter, The* (1992) 191
Unnamable, The (1988) 191
Urip, Rempo 19, 42, 45, 203
Vampires, Les (1915-16) 35
Van Clief, Ron 31-35, 40, 57, 66
Van Damme, Jean-Claude 188, 203, 207
Vanity 183
Vasquez, Lita 130
Velasco, Joseph . . 10, 11, 12, 14, 19, 20, 21, 22,
 23, 41, 42, 45, 48, 49, 54, 55, 57, 64, 68, 72,
 78, 79, 80, 85, 103, 120, 121, 122, 124, 127,
 130, 131, 133, 139, 150, 159, 160, 161, 175,
 176, 189, 199, 201, 203, 204, 205, 212, 214
Vengeance Video (distributor) 169
Vicious Passageway
 SEE *Black Spot* (1991)
Video 48 (web site) 207
VideoAsia (dvd co) 16, 78, 85, 86, 101, 147
*VideoHound's Dragon: Asian Action and Cult
 Flicks* (ed. Thomas) 208, 209
Village People, The (group) 118, 146
Visitors In America
 SEE *Bruce Lee Fights Back
 from the Grave* (1976)
Viénet, René 67, 102
Wagner, Wende 92
Walls, Samuel 68, 69, 103
Wan Yeung-Ming, Vincent 136, 1992
Wang Chien-Lung AKA Bruce Le 14
Wang Ping 12
Wang Yu, King of Boxers (1973) 118
Wang-Yu, Jimmy 82, 115, 205
Wanted! Bruce Li, Dead or Alive
 SEE *Deadly Strike* (1978)
Warhol, Andy 29
Warner Brothers (film company) 85, 211
Warriors, The (1979) 66
Watanabe, Ken 62
Watchmen (2009) 111
Waters, John 8
Watford FC 169

223

Way of Fox
  SEE *Ghost of the Fox* (1990)
Way of the Dragon (1972) 16, 27, 28, 41, 46, 48, 50, 59, 61, 69, 74, 80, 81, 89, 90, 102, 107, 109, 115, 125, 134, 135, 162, 200, 209, 211, 212
Way of the Dragon 2
  SEE *Bruce Lee's Greatest Revenge* (1978)
Way of the Tiger (1973) 28
Ways of Kung Fu
  SEE *Bruce Lee's Ways of Kung Fu* (1977)
Weekend (1967) 69
Wei Lang 124
Wei Pin-Ao, Paul 74, 75, 89, 90, 106, 200
Wei, Dick 188, 189
Weisser, Thomas 207
Wen Chiang-Long 143, 144
Weng Weng 207
West, David 207
Whang In-Shik 89
When a Child Is Born (tune) 154
When Taekwondo Strikes (1973) 95
Whitecross Street 8
Whitfield, Norman 183
Wikipedia (web site) 10, 205
Wild Cherry (group) 118
Wilkins, Mike 207
William Mishkin Motion Pictures (distributor) 156
Williams, Kenneth 131
Williams, Van 36, 92, 94
Williamson, Fred 'The Hammer' 65, 66
Wise Guys Fool Around (n.d.) 85
Wiz, The (1978) 183
Woman Called Sada Abe, A (1975) 46
Won, Bruce 190
Wonder Woman (character) 149
Wong Chi-Yeung, Karel 85
Wong Fei Hung 201
Wong Kei-Lung AKA Bruce Le 14, 21, 121
Wong Kin-Lung AKA Bruce Le 14
Wong Kwok-Leung 42
Wong Ping...............................32
Wong Shum Leung 41
Wong Sing-Loy 21, 23, 117, 181, 182
Wong Siu-Jun 22, 131
Wong Tao, Don 211
Wong Wa-Kei 21, 106
Wong Yan 158
Wong Yuen-San 146, 147
Wong, Carter 129, 152, 172, 173, 176
Wong, Casanova 74, 153, 173, 174, 178
Wong, Tino 125
Wong, William 185
Woo Gam 90, 116, 146, 162
Woo, John 9, 147
Wu Chia-Chun 19, 21, 35, 124, 125
Wu Feng 52
Wu Min-Hsiung.....................23, 155
Wu Tang Clan (dvd co) 152
Wu Wai-Shing, Ray 20, 82
X In Search of Space (LP) 122
Xu Xiao-Long 83, 84
Yamashita, Tadashi 11, 98, 145, 146
Yang Cheng-Wu, Tiger 73
Yang Kwan, Peter 102, 139, 140
Yang Yang 19, 27, 212
Yasuaki Kurata 166
Yasuaki, Kurata 89, 154
Yellow Faced Tiger (1974) 211
Yen Nan-See, Nancy 143, 144
Yen, Donnie 84, 110, 111
Yeo So-Ryong AKA Bruce Le 14
Yeung Gat-Aau 21, 120, 121
Yeung Kuen, Richard 21, 103
Yeung Wai 153
Yi Ming............................... 151
Yi, Bruce 164
Yim Leung 22
Yim, Michelle 166
Yip, Master 61
Yojimbo (1961) 123
Young Bruce Lee (2010) 15
Young Bruce Lee, The (1987)
  37 .... 20, 48, 81
  SEE ALSO *Super Dragon* (1976)
Young Dragon, The (1979) 205
Young Hero of Shaolin II
  SEE *Chinese Iron Man* (1974)
Young, Gig 55
YouTube (web site) 9, 16
Yu Chien, Angela 171
Yu Feng 76, 77
Yu Fung-Chi, Florence 22, 103, 139
Yu Yung, Henry AKA Bruce Ly..........30, 191
Yueh Hua 155, 162
Yuen Biao 55, 83, 84
Yuen Chi-Wai, Marsha 83
Yuen Qiu 31, 101
Yuen Si-Wo 142
Yuen Wah 81
Yuen Woo-ping 139, 204
Yuen, Corey 24, 135, 136, 188, 1992
Yuen, Simon 45, 168, 194
Yukio, Noda 20, 22, 98, 145
Yun Fat 204
Yune, Johnny 24, 180, 189
Yung Chen, Ma 139, 140
Yung, Suzy 41
Zamora, Ramon
  10, 11, 30, 59, 93, 96, 102, 158, 159, 162, 201
Zatoichi, The Blind Swordsman (fictional character) 45, 46, 47
Zen Kwan Do Strikes Paris
  SEE *Enter the King of Kung Fu* (1981)
Zhong Kui (mythological character) 46
Zhou, Raymond 210, 211
Zombie Flesh Eaters (1979) 61

For Marga Tormo Moll
1968-2014

SOME OTHER BOOKS OF
THE LEDATAPE ORGANISATION

ONE HUNDRED YEARS OF SOVIET CINEMA. A SENSES OF CINEMA BOOK EDITED by **DANIEL FAIRFAX.** Originally prepared in October 2017 by online journal **Senses of Cinema** to mark the 100th anniversary of the Russian Revolution, this volume includes more than fifty articles surveying the vast landscape of Soviet, and post-Soviet, filmmaking. Many of the canonical works of film history are covered but so are films and genres that have received less interest from international critics and scholars even if they were popular successes domestically. **Full colour** throughout. 2018, 7½ x 9¼ in., 240pp, PBK or HBK

SONIC ANTIQUARIAN by **THEE ROCKHUNTER.** From the back alleys of pub rock to the heady myths of classical Hauntiquarianism, The Rockhunter accompanies you on a journey without a destination in a land with so many names the map's worn through by over-printing. Thee Rockhunter produces surprisingly intimate narratives using music criticism as his template – overall, he appears more interested in long-term, universal signs and meanings than in addressing an audience and celebrating the 'progression' of cultural typologies. Rock history's never made more, or less, sense. Profusely illustrated and featuring a comprehensive bibliography and index. 7½ x 9¼ in., 122pp, PBK

SIGN WARS: THE CULTURE JAMMERS STRIKE BACK by **DAVID COX.** A whole new generation of media activists and culture jammers have taken on the government and corporate advertising worlds. New technologies have helped artists, writers, film-makers and activists to challenge and reverse the one-way flow of mind-numbing mainstream media. Camcorders, ham radio, mobile phones, the Internet and various other inexpensive means of exchanging signals have empowered this new generation. David Cox takes us on a fascinating journey as he traverses the west coast of the United States and the east coast of Australia with descriptions of successful jamming and innovative campaigns. 5½ x 8½ in., 266pp, PBK

TOP FELLAS: THE STORY OF MELBOURNE'S SHARPIE CULT by **TADHG TAYLOR.** Gang Wars! Rock n' Roll! Fine Knits! Top Fellas is the story of Melbourne's 1960's/70's sharpie cult told in a lively, borderline amoral, style. Packed with first hand accounts from ex-sharps and rock n' rollers like Lobby Loyde, Angry Anderson and Skyhooks Greg Macainsh, illustrated with over fifty photos of teenagers in cardigans, Top Fellas is the most thorough account of an Australian mass-pop movement ever put into print! Originally published with great success in 2004 it inspired a revival of interest in the sharpie phenomenon. 5½ x 8½ in., 122pp, PBK

ASK YOUR BOOKSELLER FOR LEDATAPE BOOKS
AVAILABLE VIA INGRAM, GARDNERS AND OTHER WHOLESALERS

OUR SHIT BEATS THEIR GOLD

FATAL VISIONS: THE WONDER YEARS 1988-1989 by **MICHAEL HELMS**. At freaking last! A collection of the ultra-scarce first six issues of Melbourne's own infamous trash film zine, devoted to bottom of the package video titles, late late night TV movies, films that played announced as drive-in supports and in hard tops where they were lucky to play for one week only. **7½ x 9¼ in., 248pp, PBK or HBK**

FATAL VISIONS: THE GOLDEN AGE 1990-1998 by **MICHAEL HELMS**. The second volume in the **Fatal Visions** series is a personal selection from the final fifteen issues A showcase for some of the most exciting writers working in the field: a trashfilm tour of Europe by Jack Stevenson; Mexploitation Explained; Bruce Milne's seminal article on The Cramps; Interviews include Abel Ferrara, Alejandro Jodorowsky, Lance Henriksen, Peter Jackson, Charles Napier and John Woo. Plus hundreds of cinema & video reviews. **Foreword by Jack Sargeant. 7½ x 9¼ in., 296pp, PBK or HBK**

UNQUIET DREAMS: THE BESTIARY OF WALERIAN BOROWCZYK by **SIMON STRONG**. Borowczyk started off as an animator and moved into graphic erotica and subsequent exploitation tropes before creatively imploding spectacularly with his bizarre contribution to the Emmanuelle series. Inspired by seventies filth like **Continental Film Review** and **Sex Stars System**, this study examines contexts and connections, obscure minutiae, corny jokes and blurry screen grabs of topless women from seventies softcore flicks. **Full colour throughout. 7½ x 9¼ in., 134pp, PBK or HBK**

THE SEARCH FOR WENG WENG by **ANDREW LEAVOLD**. This book is the definitive search for Weng Weng, an even wilder and woollier tale told by the film-makerhimself, as he travels from Imelda Marcos' birthday party to the poorest slums of Manila, on the trail of one the Philippines' most unlikeliest heroes – and most heartbreaking stories. Part detective story and midget bio, part gonzo travelogue, part Filipino B Film history lesson, and part magical Quest for the Holy Grail – if the Grail is a two foot nine James Bond of the Philippines. **7½ x 9¼ in., 240pp, PBK or HBK**

EVEN THE OLD DUDE IS COOL! WILLIAM BURROUGHS ON THE SILVER SCREEN AND THE WHEELS OF STEEL by **SIMON STRONG**. It's a searing indictment of contemporary publishing that the first full-length survey of WSB's influential intrusions into the fields of film and music must come from the pen of the world's most obscure and frustrating experimental novelist. Boasting more than 323 items, this uh idiosyncratic survey is as comprehensive and insightful as it is undisciplined and incoherent. Nevertheless, even the most ardent Burroughs scholar will find something new here, even if it's just been made up for funty laff value. Nice try pal. **Full colour throughout. 7½ x 9¼ in., 120pp, PBK**

but wait ... there's more!
ledatape.net

Lightning Source UK Ltd.
Milton Keynes UK
UKHW03f1521091018
330261UK00004B/57/P